THE
ANALYSIS
OF
LITERARY
TEXTS
CURRENT
TRENDS
IN
METHODOLOGY

Bilingual Press/Editorial Bilingüe

Studies in Literary Analysis

THE
ANALYSIS
OF
LITERARY
TEXTS
CURRENT
TRENDS
IN
METHODOLOGY

THIRD AND FOURTH
YORK COLLEGE COLLOQUIA

EDITED BY
RANDOLPH D. POPE

Bilingual Press/Editorial Bilingüe
YPSILANTI, MI

ISBN: 0-916950-14-X
Printed simultaneously in a softcover edition. ISBN: 0-916950-13-1

Library of Congress Catalog Card Number: 79-54144

Printed in the United States of America

Cover design by Richard S. Haymes

809
A532

Permission to reprint Marcelle Thiébaux's "A Mythology for Women: Monique Wittig's *Les Guérillères*," which first appeared in *13th Moon* (summer 1978), is gratefully acknowledged.

81- 4729

Oral versions of the papers contained in this volume were presented at: Contemporary Methods of Literary Analysis: Third Colloquium on Hispanic, French and Italian Literature, held on April 29, 1977 at York College of CUNY, and Contemporary Methods of Literary Analysis: Fourth Colloquium on English, French, Italian and Spanish Literature, held on April 28, 1978 at the Graduate Center of CUNY.

Table of Contents

VI. Linguistics

VII. Psychoanalysis

VIII. Rhetoric

IX. Semiotics

X. Sociology

XI. Structuralism

I. The Criticism of Criticism

ON THE ARROGANCE OF CRITICISM

Henri Peyre

These pages will perhaps be judged as an arrogant plea for modesty. If so, the author is the first to proclaim his own share of guilt. He in no way professes to be endowed with more humility than any of his American colleagues or than his French compatriots, whose primary virtue has seldom been humility. Simply, at the end of a long career which he once entered because he found in literature a source of delight as well as an outlet for abstract speculations on how to interpret it, having steadily endeavored to impart to an ever growing audience of students and cultured readers the enjoyment and the insights afforded by literature, he feels dismayed at the sorry plight of imaginative letters today in Western Europe and in America. He well knows that aging men have always lamented that creative vigor, originality, wisdom and style were disappearing as they themselves were declining. He has written whole books to deplore the age-old breach between writers and their critics who proved incapable or unwilling to feel and to understand the new talent arising among them. The law of generations reacting against one another inevitably decrees that the ascending one begin by rejecting what the previous one has achieved, so that it may deliver its own message and create its own and perhaps fresh technique. In that task of destruction followed by reconstruction, it often was assisted in the past by a group of critics, assembled around some young reviews, which strove to find, or to train, a public for the new sensibilities or the iconoclastic doctrines.

Something has snapped in that process of rejuvenation. The primacy of science and of technology in our culture, the competition of mass media, the strident claims of psychology, psychiatry, and sociology to delve into our inmost beings more relentlessly than imaginative writing may in part account for the relative poverty of our fiction, drama, and poetry today. Whatever the causes, with a population five or six times greater than this country had at the time of Emerson, Poe, Thoreau, Melville, Hawthorne and others, we dare not boast of a proportionately richer galaxy of talents than during that "American Renaissance" of over a century ago. The number of our literary reviews reaching a wide general public has dwindled; the share allotted to arts and letters in the few remaining ones has shrunk even more markedly, and it has not been taken over by reasonably informed literary discussion over the media.

In contrast, the number of specialized academic reviews, often inaccessible except to other professors and to a small band of graduate students, has multiplied. New ones are burgeoning at universities in every state of the union. Few reach more than a few hundred readers and we dare not even hope that those readers will be afflicted with lengthy insomnia so as to find the time to absorb the learned contents and not drop into somnolence. James Russell Lowell is quoted as declaring a hundred years ago or more, "Before we have an American literature, we must have an American criticism." America in the nineteen-seventies has, on its campuses at any rate, become a paradise of critics. Around 1950-60, in the surge of pride which followed the American achievement in World War II, scientists used to boast that, of all the scientists who ever existed on this planet, ninety percent were then living. For critics, linguists, and "hermeneuts," the proportion may well be ninety-eight percent. They address each other in dead seriousness at learned colloquia, with not even the gift of humor once possessed by Roman augurs who, Cicero tells us, could not look at each other without discreetly laughing. They seem to take it for granted that works of imaginative literature are composed for the sole purpose of being taken to pieces by engineers of criticism and that, the more relentlessly a poem can thus be analyzed, the more profound or the more pleasure-giving it must be. In truth, the word "pleasure" is seldom encountered in today's critical volumes. When Roland Barthes, in 1973, came out with a slim volume entitled *Le Plaisir du Texte*, a shudder of panic shook his devotees. Were critics descending so low as to indulge Epicureanism and actually finding delight in their pursuits, forsaking that gravity which a renowned magistrate of another age, Montesquieu, had called "le bonheur des sots"?

We live in an age in which science and technology are primary. Disciplines which once seemed to lie outside the pale of science (psychology, anthropology, sociology, linguistics) have attempted to become scientific— that is, to define their standards, to resort to objective criteria, to adopt sets of rules and to formulate methods universally applicable, to substitute the quantitative, the measurable and the statistical for the qualitative and the subjective, and finally to predict, if not to influence, the future. Among the consequences entailed by the adoption of scientific methods were a growing specialization and the adoption of new, and often forbidding, terminology. The gains achieved by those disciplines, whose ambition was to climb on the bandwagon of the empirical, statistical, and even economic sciences, have been enormous in some cases. Team work accomplished by anthropologists and sociologists "on the terrain" has yielded valuable information. Few of the practitioners of those sciences, however, would venture to claim rigorous accuracy for them. They have been disappointed by the reductionism to which imitators or mechanically-minded disciples have, in many cases, brought down their methods. Recent examples have shown us, in the realms of economics and military science, the frailty of the predictions rashly made about the amount of destruction necessary to bring to their knees Asiatic peoples fighting against all odds and unafraid of the prospect of death. Criticism, every twenty years or so, seems to feel discontented with the impressionism to which its appraisal of literary works often resorts. Its practitioners are embarrassed when their colleagues in the sciences and in social studies ask them to define their standards. Theirs cannot very well be uniform, inflexible and infallible. None of the terms used in aesthetic judgments—greatness, forcefulness, beauty, intensity, ugliness—is subject to a satisfactory definition. There are too many diverse ways of creating a new type of beauty and of characterizing greatness or genius. The least unsure prophecy which can be ventured in the realm of literary criticism is that the talent of today which stands the strongest chance of surviving tomorrow is the one which refuses to abide by the standards evolved from the study of past creators. The critic of the last century who put up the strongest plea for standards on aesthetic judgment was, in France, Hippolyte Taine. He argued for his famous triad—race, "milieu" and moment—not very clearly defined by him, at least where the third term was concerned. He was, in fact, much less rigid in the application of his dogmatic views. His deeper aim was to reach what we like nowadays to call a structure, that is to say, the interdependency of the different elements, through subordinating the secondary features to the "faculté maîtresse." His mistake was not to leave enough room for chance. He could not account for the unpredictability of genius. But he conceded readily that it was not possible to devise, for history, sociology, and criticism, theorems similar to those of geometry and that the relations one could establish among the groups of facts which make up social and aesthetic life are not liable to numerical evaluation.[1]

The fundamental weakness of literary criticism is a consequence of its privilege. That privilege is not to allow a scientific approach and not to dispose of criteria which any insensitive or blunt mind could then attempt to apply mechanically. The share of the rational is almost as limited in criticism as it is in imaginative creation. "How irrational criticism has to be in order to keep up with creation!" Jacques Barzun exclaimed somewhere. A long time ago, the most lucid of all poetical geniuses and one who stood close to science, Goethe, had remarked to Eckermann on May 27, 1827, "Do not always believe that everything must be vain if it is not some abstract thought or idea ....A poetic creation is all the better for being incommensurable and rationally incomprehensible." If the greatness, or even the charm, of Virgil or Dante or Velásquez had been defined in a final manner and we knew precisely why they deserve our admiration, we could merely refer new readers to the critics who first analyzed their works and refrain from composing those treatises and articles through which we earn our academic promotions.

The weakness of our pursuit lies in the awareness by critics of their lack of self-sufficiency. They are tempted to look up to other disciplines for their standards and for their methods. With some it was psychology, then sociology, or semantics, then lately linguistics adorned with the adjective "structural." A language may consist of a systematic ordering of parts and a society, as Lévi-Strauss contended, enjoy a culture in which every element is related to the whole and receives from the whole its meaningfulness. The conclusion was drawn that a text, likewise, constitutes a systematic ordering of parts. Those parts are articulated into ingenious arrangements such as engineers may conceive in their wildest dreams. A sprinkling of terms revived from the old rhetoric adds an air of mysterious pedantry to those disquisitions which are sedulously calculated so as to baffle the naive reader. Every science seems to need a terminology of its own, which gives it a minimum of precision. Since no two critics ever can agree on the exact meaning to be read into words like "classicism," "romanticism," "symbol," "expressionism," they resort to learned terms which keep the common reader at a safe distance: "syntagma," "catachresis," "paradigm," "oxymoron," "metonymy," "synechdoche," *et al.* Literature is taken to be an activity primarily concerned with language. Language, in its turn, is concerned solely with itself. The "signifying" is everything. The "signified" is treated contemptuously as something which should not intrude. The science from which criticism appears to take its cue is cryptography. The practitioners of that "science" assume the manners of magicians encoding and then decoding a mysterious message. They impress the naïve tyro with their dropping on every page words and phrases which seem to refer to secrets that they alone have the skill to decipher—"actant," "mutant," "locuteur," "intertextuality," "dialectical relationships." Here and there, so as to hint that they have not abdicated all sense of humor, those practitioners of hermeneutics read in the texts which they claim to elucidate puns worthy of Balzac's Gaudissart, the commercial traveller entertaining the provincial "tables d'hôtes." To the traditional signs of punctuation, they have added the lavish use of transversal bars, a sign of recognition among the conoscenti. We end up with the notion that literary works are written primarily for engineers, who take them to pieces. Let no uninitiate enter the sanctum and look for delight, or wonder, or even for a meaning. Language is the beginning and the end. The critic's demonstration, banishing the signified and the diachronic, all intrusion of unpredictable life, recalls the impeccable reasonings of economists, specialists of psychological warfare and generals who claimed to foresee every contingency which might have upset their well-oiled machine in Southeast Asia. The trouble is that in Vietnam it all went wrong. Humanists of the old school, distrusting the stress on the quantitative and the measurable, would have foreseen it, and they did; they were not heeded.

The assumption that a work of art must have a structure in which the parts and the whole fit in as in a sophisticated mechanism is itself challengeable. Dissymetry is, in human faces and bodies, in architecture, in landscapes, an element which appeals to many. The supreme quality of the greatest works of fiction is often their ability to allow the unforseen, the altogether illogical, the disorderly, to irrupt into the flexible structure of the novel. Of course, treasures of ingenious sophistry may be expended on contending that superfluous sections of a much admired work were in reality essential to its symbolic structure. This has been repeatedly attempted for the first cantos of the *Odyssey* dealing with Telemachus; Horace knew better, who avowed that Homer occasionally slumbers. Shakespeare cared little about a structured unity when he composed what is perhaps his most disorderly and his greatest tragedy, *Anthony and Cleopatra.* Nor did Molière when he dashed off *Don Juan*, with scenes which appear to have been pulled from the bottom of a drawer, as the French say, and yet contribute to the fascination of that classico-romantic drama. Goethe did not proceed differently in the second part of his *Faust.* Laborious justifications for the four extraneous episodes in *La Princesse de Clèves* have been attempted; if anything, they detract from the beauty of the novel, hardly better structured than any others of the so-called classical age.

There is a technique of the digression which the Latin story teller of the *Golden Ass* well knew how to use to good effect. Montaigne likewise was the master of it; naive and misguided (and unconvincing) are the painstaking efforts of critics to discover a hidden continuity or a harmonious arrangement of parts in the "Apologie de Raymond Sebond" or in the baffling, purposely nonchalant and fanciful essay "Sur des Vers de Virgile." Diderot was a master of the digression in his novels, his dialogues and even in his essays of historical appearance (on the reigns of Claudius and Nero). Balzac's *Béatrix* and his *Illusions perdues* lose nothing for having been made up of disjointed sections, written at intervals of several years. *War and Peace* is the least structured of fictional masterpieces: Tolstoi lavished didactic digressions almost as much as did Proust in his long work. Lucienne Julien-Cain, in her book on Valéry (1958), relates how, when the editor-in-chief of *La Nouvelle Revue Française* visited Valéry in order to take away from him the text of "Le Cimetière marin," the poet was most uncertain as to the order in which the stanzas should or might be placed. He felt like just drawing by lot which should come where, and it probably was not all in jest. T. S. Eliot did not, any more than Valéry, yield to inspiration. Yet the structure of *The Waste Land* is no more impeccable than that of *La Jeune Parque*. The section "Death by Water" was not originally part of the poem. Ezra Pound is the one who advised borrowing it from the last part of "Dans le Restaurant." And the striking poem "Gerontion," originally to be part of *The Waste Land*, was later omitted. We might well be admiring its harmonious disposition in the poem, had it been left there.

The arrogant engineers who, in France, have attempted to take over fiction, the short story, and criticism, have probably wished to react against their immediate predecessors, the Existentialists. The latter professed an unbounded faith in the over arching value of freedom in all activities. They were intoxicated with it. So had been their own predecessors toward whom they seldom proved grateful and who, nurtured in Bergsonism, had broken with the earlier determinism and had rejuvenated the Heraclitean flux. In contrast, the fanatics of systematic correlations, brandishing in one hand their new Bible, the *Grammaire de Port-Royal*, in the other their Gospel, the notes on the once ignored lectures of Saussure, spurn the much maligned diachrony and any succession in time. They only consent to analyze simultaneities and find no rest until they decipher the secret code which allegedly underlies and supports all human activities.

In truth, they have not applied their rigid doctrine to poetry with conspicuous success, or to any long, meandering novels. They have hardly considered it worthwhile to discover the new in literature. Yet no critic in our opinion is worthy of the name if he refuses to meet the challenge of the new, as yet unclassified and apparently unstructured works which give a jolt to our analytical mental habits. Their favorite hunting ground has been the "récit" and the short story, probably the most mechanical of all literary genres and one which too often is lacking in mystery. One of the high priests of the structuralist religion, who can talk with his tongue in his cheek, Roland Barthes, gravely pronounced in a solemn "Introduction à l'analyse structurale du récit" (*Communications*, Paris, Seuil, 1970, p. 30).

> Is everything functional in a récit?. . .No doubt, there exist several types of functions, for there are several types of correlations. Nevertheless a récit is always made up of functions: everything in it, to a greater or lesser extent, signifies. . . .It is a pure system. There is not, there never is a wasted unit.

The most spontaneous of activities, artistic creation, is thus reduced to a neat piece of machinery. Authors protest. Little do those overweening dissectors of their work care. An American poet who was also a storyteller, Randall Jarrell, once made fun of those pedantic colloquia where critics assemble and, for the fiftieth time and vying with each other in subtlety, gape at the impeccable organization of a certain book in Wordsworth's *Prelude* or in the "Ode on Intimations of Immortality." If the poet came back to life and dared raise his voice to uphold the rights of inspiration, they would contemptuously retort to him, "Go back to your stye, pig. What do you know about bacon?" Authors have lately raised their voices—most recently, Saul Bellow. He offered a moving plea for the "signified" in literature, and even for what would have, in Victorian times been called a moral message: "The individual struggles with dehumanization for the possession of his soul. If writers do not come again into the center, it will not be because the center is preempted. It is not. They are free to enter, if they so wish."[2] But too many writers have been intimidated by the dogmatism and the display of esoteric knowledge on the part of critics. They dare not write for the public, for the naive reader with an eager, but "unstructured" mind any more. They stand in awe of the terrorizing critics, spreading what the French call "la terreur dans les lettres."

Meanwhile the literature of the nineteen-seventies haughtily goes its way. It escapes into science fiction, erotic fantasies, experiments with language, the slicing of words and the concoction of pseudo-Freudian puns. It has turned into an elaborate private game almost as loaded with arcana as criticism itself. Where can one find in today's fiction, American or French, that social criticism which constituted such a valuable part of literature in the last century? Or love affairs where the heart, the imagination, the intellect, and not just the sense would be involved? Where the underprivileged, the unemployed, the veterans of Vietnam, the youth bewildered by their newly won sexual freedom, the thousands among us who are haunted by the threat of nuclear slaughter, might find a magnified portrayal of their anguish? With not a little sophistry, the leaders of recent criticism, joining their voices with those of some little read but boastful novelists, have tried to contend that, by challenging language, they are questioning, or even destroying, the very sources of power of the ruling classes, since language is the most potent force which insidiously recuperates the youth and turns it into a rampart for the establishment. Those who thus assert the revolutionary nature of their writing activity not only live as bourgeois, sedulously aloof from the working classes (which could not understand their jargon), but receive from the establishment secure and ample salaries as professors at the Collège de France, the Ecole des Hautes Etudes, and as exchange professors in American universities. Meanwhile the hated bourgeoisie laughs secretly at those fake revolutionaries, safely ensconced in their studies, signing a resounding petition every six months for some cause or other, indifferent to the plight of the poorer mortals and leaving the levers of power to financiers, newspaper magnates, and arms manufacturers.

This abdication on the part of critics, displaying an arrogance which ill conceals their awareness of being the uninfluentials of the modern world, strikes a French professor teaching in America as doubly regrettable. First, because the captive audiences that we address in this country in the colleges are made up almost solely of undergraduates. One or two percent of them may end up writing literary, artistic, cinematographic, or musical criticism. The others yearn for an intelligent enjoyment of the arts. There should be ways for an able teacher to train sensibility and even imagination, as well as analytical gifts. Through a perverse imbalance, we insist upon treating those eager and fresh minds as if they were all graduate students being conditioned to boredom. Moreover, American professors of French seem to have made a very special point of jumping on the bandwagon of all the latest, most ephemeral vogues prevailing in the advanced circles in Paris. Yet we in America constitute, through our remoteness in space and through the autonomy of American universities, an advance posterity which should retain a wise perspective when looking at Western Europeans. We have the right and the duty to sift what Europe is offering to us, and to retain only what promises to be substantial and lasting. We have scant reason for siding with cliques, coteries, and schools, to argue for or against *Tel Quel, Change*, or *La Voix du Peuple*, to espouse one or another form of structuralist criticism or of new, newer, newest fiction.[3]

"Un grand critique doit être un peu bête," Pushkin is supposed to have once declared; or, if he is not, we would add, he might well "faire le bête" and discard his arrogant affectation of superiority. A number of wise men, revolutionary in their day, have uttered warnings which we might heed. Jowett, the famous translator and commentator of Plato, wisely submitted, "The true use of interpretation is to get rid of interpretation and leave us alone in the company of the author." T. S. Eliot wrote in *The Sacred Wood*, and then oft repeated, that the aim of the study of literature is to help us return to the work itself "with improved perception and intensified, because more conscious, enjoyment." Do many of us, so called scholarly critics, fulfill that noble, yet modest, requirement? Maurice Blanchot, in 1971, quoted the philosopher Hoelderlin who declared that whatever the commentary of a difficult poem may propose, it should always end by considering itself as superfluous, "de trop." "The last stage of interpretation is also the most demanding: to know how and when to disappear, in the face of the pure and mere assertion of the poem." Indeed, any exegesis of a work of art has the primary duty, once it has duly done its task, to obliterate itself and take refuge in silence.

THE GRADUATE CENTER OF THE
CITY UNIVERSITY OF NEW YORK

Notes

[1] Taine clarified his position, far more modest and sensitive that it is often taken to be, in a letter to Ernest Havet of April 29, 1864 and in another to Sainte-Beuve on May 30, 1864.

[2] It was no other voice than that of Ezra Pound who proclaimed blandly, "The function of the teaching profession is to maintain the health of the national mind." *Literary Essays*, 1954, p. 59.

[3] The English have adopted, as a rule, a more detached attitude toward the newfangled critical vogues of Paris, if one may judge from a few lines by Francis Scarfe (himself a specialist of modern French literature and for fourteen years a resident in Paris) in the *Times Literary Supplement* of March 30, 1973, ". . . To consider, for example, the review *Poétic* (or for that matter *Tel Quel* with its frequent boudoir revolutions), it would be impossible to find such a dung-heap of pearls and tripe anywhere in Britain, though I would not say the same about America. . . . In no European country is such a concentrated effort being made to discredit the very idea of criticism. . . Far removed from the common reader, as from the average intellectual, the slanted impressionistic essays that are pouring out are largely the work of gangs of exalted exhibitionists."

METHODOLOGY AND EXEGESIS: THE ITALIAN SIDE

Dante Della Terza

I have just been asked by my students, as if in an unforseen anticipation of your present invitation, to explain in the informal atmosphere of the classroom what I learned about literary criticism during the years of my intellectual training in Italy. The students' inquiry, though expressed in a dispassionate, rather neutral tone, hides, I believe, their deeply-rooted desire to establish a relevant kind of relationship with their teachers, a more humane approach to the instruments of knowledge, and also their understandable craving for guidance in the labyrinth of contrasting methods and irreversible precepts. If I feel ready, here and now, to overcome a persistent skepticism about the possibility of translating one system of ideas into another without risk of equivocation, it is because of the acquired confidence that even the less common intellectual experiences, however mysterious and undecipherable or out of touch with our present reality they may seem, strike a sudden note of familiarity when they happen to coincide with thoughts we are shaping or formulating on our own.[1] Perhaps my students and the many students I see in this room, while building up their personal experience of literature, will find in their feelings a spark of understanding for my works and will detect one day in their thoughts the presence of remote seeds which appeared to them at the time without a future and destined to be fruitless. After all, any dialogue involving both sides of the Atlantic can only start with an act of faith that to some extent, somewhere, a common ground exists for the expansion of the students' eagerness to acquire meaningful knowledge and the teachers' avocation to overcome the generation gap and the language barrier.

In order to qualify the issue of the mediating function which I am taking on my shoulders for the sake of the argument and without special merits, I shall try to explain how I see retrospectively the position of those who taught me literature and the problems they had to face. During the years of my apprenticeship—the mid-nineteen-forties and early fifties, the Italian cultural scene was still rather selective and cautious toward the external world of thoughts and literary hypothesis. Let me introduce you to this now remote Italian stage through a few significant examples. Exactly a decade separates

10   METHODOLOGY AND EXEGESIS

the appearance in Switzerland of Erich Auerbach's seminal book, *Mimesis*, and its highly successful Italian translation.[2] The very year of its publication, the book, however, was reviewed by one of my most prestigious teachers, the historian Delio Cantimori, a highly qualified interpreter on Italian soil of German contemporary culture.[3] Cantimori's attitude appears at first non-committal since he merely indicates the existence of the book without advising a translation into Italian. The book, he says, filled with erudite arabesques and sociological subtleties suffers from its length and the slowness of the analyses ("la lenta lunghezza delle analisi"). By carefully rereading Cantimori's discussion now, I find, however, precious elements of a mood which I would like to qualify as the Italian way of feeling about culture and cultural achievements.

Auerbach's book has, according to my understanding of it, a dimension which is horizontal and involves a painstaking analysis of extremely individualized features through which the authorial realism comes to light, and another which is vertical and points toward a reality that, being problematic, is everywhere and nowhere. We have, on the one hand, a realism called figural which finds its fulfillment in the drama of the Christian mind, on the other, a kaleidoscopic and acentric reality which has in itself the seed of its dissolution and is self-propelled toward future achievements.[4] The slow rhythm mentioned by Cantimori involves, I trust, only the horizontal dimension of the book, the over-careful and very subtle textual analyses, while, in my opinion, the vertical dimension of a longed-for and never reached "total" reality inserts in the structure of each chapter of *Mimesis* an added and contradictory quality of dissatisfied commitment to the degree of truth not represented in the work of the writer under scrutiny, and therefore a spiral of acceleration not to be overlooked, and with it a teleological gravitation of the reader's attention toward the conclusive statements of the book.

Despite my basic disagreement with Cantimori's view of *Mimesis*, I must acknowledge that the words he uses to emphasize the limits of Auerbach's work are to me most interesting and fully intelligible. By speaking of skepticism, radical relativism, and positivism, he introduces a vocabulary with heavily negative implications in the Italian philosophical language of the first half of the century. But what do skepticism, relativism, and positivism have in common, according to the reviewer? Auerbach's study of his authors' stylistic tools implies a positivistic knowledge of their sources, a precise and equally positivistic evaluation of their theory of history, of their poetics, of their ethical convictions, as well as of those of their contemporaries. But the overcoming of the barrier separating us from the authors at stake appears to the critic as a task which only seldom can be achieved. Here the name of Heidegger comes to the fore, the German philosopher being at once mesmerized, as the Auerbach seen through Cantimori's eyes appears to be, by ancient formulations of philosophical problems, and repelled by the impossibility of reaching through them any truth able to satisfy us. For the influential Italian reader of the forties, positivism and irrationalism à la Heidegger become indeed the two hostile concepts to exorcise.

I have, of course, no overwhelming proof that it is indeed Cantimori's review that slows down possible Italian interest in Auerbach's work. It is, however, true that one of the historian's remarks on the thickness of the book and the slowness of the analysis ("la mole e certa lentezza di analisi") is repeated, word for word, by Cantimori's friend, Cesare Pavese in a letter of May 5, 1950, to the future translator of *Mimesis*, Sergio Romagnoli.[5] But Pavese, who read the book for the publisher Giulio Einaudi, was inclined to sponsor its translation for a reason which seemed to have escaped Cantimori's perception: By following the trend to realism throughout the centuries, the book strikes a syntonic note with Italian cultural interests of the moment ("è di grande interesse, è tempestivo" Pavese writes). Pavese's approval is, however, still very cautious ("qualcun altro dica di si").[6] He is at peace with himself only when a reader equally as authoritative as Cantimore, the philosopher and cultural historian Norberto Bobbio, gives the book the needed blessing. Pavese's tragic death delays the publication of *Mimesis* by six more years which I am unable to account for. The book reaches the Italian public at the twilight of Neorealism. In a period of turning inward for Italian letters and of increased allegiance to the polymorphic aspects of reality, Auerbach furnishes the militant critic with the right tools for understanding the intricacies of the Italian literary moment. A critic of great instinct, Pier Paolo Pasolini, with a solid grasp on the situation, starts discussing trends in the contemporary Italian novel, taking into account the rejuvenated, though very ancient, stylistic terminology used by Auerbach.[7]

The second and third examples are deduced from pages written by Benedetto Croce in the very last years of his life. They involve Ernest Robert Curtius' *Europäische Literatur und Lateinisches Mittelalter* published in Bern two years after Auerbach's *Mimesis* and never translated into Italian,[8] and the very influential book by Vladimir Propp on the historical roots of fairy tales, published by Giulio Einaudi in 1949 with a preface written by the ethnologist Giuseppe Cocchiara.[9] Croce, among other things, takes issue with Curtius on a broad methodological point—the theory of genres, genres being considered by the German scholar "the most beautiful gardens of literature," by the Italian, abstractions deduced from the individual works of art which are the only realities to be taken into account in a critical judgment.

As far as Propp is concerned, Croce is reminded of Andrew Lang's theory according to which fairy tales are the stratification of ancestral memories of a primitive and savage life. The Italian philosopher is brought by his own aesthetics, which he has coherently defined as "Science of expression and general linguistics," to consider fairy tales as the ever-renewed proof of the poetic—hence inventive and individual—roots of human language. They are poetic stories which are reinvented each time by the voice of a new ingenious narrator. Every time we try to extrapolate from the tale an historical truth, we are defeating, according to Croce, our purpose, since we travel the road of unartistic assumptions which brings us toward the world of abstraction, out of touch with the reality of the very fairy tales, unless we identify them with the endless ocean of being ("con l'infinito mare dell'essere") can never be really traced. Here again while it would be difficult to state without doubt that it was Croce's authoritative criticism which delayed for seventeen years a renewal of interest in Propp's thesis in Italy,[10] it is, however, more than possible that the influential rigor of Croce's point of view together with the political overtones assumed by the heated debate in the late forties about art, folklore, and society created a climate of partisanship and distrust around the name of the author which could be only slowly dissipated.[11]

The first impression one receives in studying the above-mentioned examples, which come to the brink of a rather drastic condemnation of positivism and irrationalism and of what appeared to the impatient critic to be disorganized erudition or theoretical misconceptions of some sort or other, is that we are confronted with an exigent body of doctrines operating within well-defined cultural boundaries.[12] Mine is, of course, a simple appraisal of a situation and does not imply either condemnation of or pride in the Italian state of affairs. The dithyrambic attitude of a scholar of the early fifties according to whom "Italian literary criticism inspired by the theoretical awareness coming from Croce's aesthetics" had reached such a degree of "maturity and penetrating refinement that foreign criticism could hardly have dared to compete with it"[13] strikes a note of ill-conceived pride as bewildering to my mind as the complaint of a critic of the seventies deprecating the "Neapolitan dictatorship" and the "philosophical sclerosis" of its critical method.[14] Italian culture of the years I am describing, well-organized around the demiurgic personality of Benedetto Croce who furnished it with a rather extraordinary methodological awareness, being what it is, nothing we can say or do will change the basic assumptions upon which it is based. Croce with his encyclopedic curiosity and his vigorously logical mind, with his first-hand knowledge of foreign cultures, acts for more than half a century as a screen and as a filter, as an incentive to and an example of meaningful scholarly work, and as a barrier toward the outside world. His influence on Italian editorial policy deserves in my opinion to be carefully studied.

The consequences of this very peculiar situation in Italian letters in the first half of our century should be observed in the pattern of behavior of the major critics who are usually labeled as followers of Croce, as "Crociani." I am fully aware that in his excellent book, *The literary analysis in Italy. Formalism, Structuralism, Semiology*, D'Arco Silvio Avalle stresses primarily the dichotomy between formalists who are subtle disclosers of the poets' most secret achievements such as Giuseppe De Robertis, and critics like Croce basically interested in defining the all-encompassing sentiment dominating the work of art.[15] But this is not, unfortunately, the way I was brought up to understand things during the years of my apprenticeship in Pisa. The critics who paid allegiance to Croce were also the same who, with methodological clairvoyance, showed the inclination to separate form from content in their practical approach to literature, resolving what came to be called the rigid monism of Croce's aesthetics into a discourse where a significant role was given to the analysis of the poets' tools. The reader would become accustomed to a kind of ritual where the most intransigent Croce, a radical foe of rhetorical categories and the theoretician of poetry as "pure or lyric intuition," was called to task by a Croce who in his volume of 1936, *La Poesia*, had given considerable weight to the same categories whose theoretical importance he had elsewhere understated or denied altogether. The justifying role attributed to Croce by his followers and the inborn structures of accommodation cautiously detected by them in his work are the rhetorical setting within which the Italian critics I was aware of, Luigi Russo and Mario Fubini, used to operate during my college years. Fubini, a scholar who could discern with the penetrating eye of the critic of style the expressive function of the enjambement in Tasso's epic poetry, was the same who would reserve his well-rationalized enthusiasm for one of his most plausible intellectual ancestors, Francesco De Sanctis, finding in some authoritative though rare statements on style by the Neapolitan critic, a justification for his methodological procedures.[16] Luigi Russo, who liked to cite a Romanist, Cesare de Lollis, as the most appealing of the Italian "Stilkritikern," would also reassuringly bring him back to the Crocean way of thinking by reminding his student that de Lollis himself used to consistently redirect specific formal features toward "the intimate spirit" of poetry.[17] Russo was my mentor in Pisa and his overwhelming personality and impressive style have left a lasting trace in my memory. He know how to bring to the focus of a critical definition an eloquent background of thought and a literary perspective elaborated with fervor through the years, in which the writers brought to our attention and the tradition to which they belonged became mirrored. After all these years, however, I can see more clearly what kind of problems he had to face. It is indeed his relationship with Croce which appears to me, today, most problematic, and objectively speaking a hinderance to his independence as a critic. Sensitive as he was to the historical setting in which the literary work ought to be placed, he would strongly emphasize above and beyond the challenging task of defining it in its poetic relevance, the world of aesthetic theories, impassioned myths and political moralities that are the soil in which poetry is born. But torn between the metahistorical values of the poetic experience along the line of the aesthetic autonomy stressed by Croce and the theory of the historicity of the work of art, Russo seemed occasionally to be tempted by a purely verbal unification of the two exigencies while leaving untouched the philosophical difficulties he had, at the beginning, so courageously faced.

When Croce, answering Russo's objections, stresses the point that historical and speculative structures are never born together with the poem but either before or after it, since, if it were not so, they would be identical with the poem itself, he says something that, within his system of truths, which is Russo's as well, can hardly be challenged.[18] Russo is called upon to overcome an analogous difficulty when discussing the task of the critic vis-à-vis the object of the literary work. In this domain his intervention is of importance and deserves not to be overlooked, since no Italian critic I know of has contributed as much to the exploration of what Georges Poulet has defined as the "phenomenologie de la conscience critique."[19] Here the comparison with Poulet's essay I have in mind can be relevant and for many aspects illuminating. When writing on French critics and criticism, Poulet is confronted with a loose body of doctrines which could better be defined as a series of mental attitudes pertinent to a plurisemantic critical civilization. The cases at stake are in fact very different one from the other, as is the interpretive commitment of each critic. The common point of departure is only one—the astonished awareness critics acquire in reading a text that an alien existence is taking hold of them, an experience that although belonging to someone else, to the author, feels as if it were their own, as if it belonged to them, the readers. The personal reaction toward the alien object called text changes drastically, however, if the critic's name is, say, Jacques Rivière, Jean Pierre Richard, or Maurice Blanchot. One can have the case of an overwhelming subjectivity that confines the "conscience d'autrui," that is the unattainable and distant object of the critic's inquiry to an opaque Limbo, as in Jacques Rivière. The critic can sponsor in competition with the artist the reproduction and recreation of the existing text through a living web of images which stand to signify the literary language as J. P. Richard does, or have the transposed reality represented by the work of art successfully deprived of the reality of its being through a critical language that intellectualizes its results to the extreme, as in Maurice Blanchot. *Tot capita, tot sententiae.* Russo's attitude, compared to Poulet's, shows an orientation toward the phenomenology of criticism which is strongly hierarchical and therefore much more embryonic. The critic, Russo says, should not be an "artifex additus artifici," an artist in competition with another artist (as Richard is according to the opinion of Poulet), but he is equally not the "philosophus additus artifici," who according to Croce's stern admonishment must resist the temptation to sing along with the poet ("das Mitsingen ist verboten").[20] The formula Russo accepts as the only truthful one which stresses the function of the critic as a "philosophus additus sibi ipsi" speaks of a work of art uplifted (*aufgehoben*, as Hegel would put it) in the mind of the critic who has absorbed in his thoughts the deepest and most secret aspirations of the artist.[21] But having once entered the blind ally of a solioquy barely camouflaged under the pretenses of a dialogue with the text, isn't the critic returning to the competitive formula a la Richard, dear in Italy to D'Annunzio's friend Angelo Conti, according to which the reader takes upon himself the impossible task of replacing the song of the artist with his own? In a sense, while in the pluralistic approach to criticism stressed by Poulet several ways of dealing with the literary work, in spite of personal shortcomings or failures, appear to be possible, in the Crocean universe one formula alone makes good "philosophical" sense and it is the one sponsored by Croce. As for Russo, one should however note that what he keeps of Croce's formula is the equivalence between the critic and the philosopher. This fact is not without interest. Russo, an original essayist and, in a broad sense, a gifted writer, had learned the hard way how to keep his own temperament under control and at the service of the authors he was called upon to judge. Toward this constant effort of self-containment he found, I trust, in his Crocean, hence "philosophical" education, a firm and, without any doubt, helpful support.

The above-mentioned reservations toward critical formulas and statements of truths which were the core of Luigi Russo's methodology do not intend to be a desecrating and gratuitous denial of his inspiring role in my intellectual life. By breaking the chain of verbal allegiances which crystallized my loyalty toward the past in solid but static principles, I would like to show objectively, more than to exorcise, the hypertrophic function of the model in the Italian culture of the last decades. To put the problem in another way and to give a more appealing ring to my words, I would say that after all the line Croce-Russo-Fubini represents a frontier of knowledge neither more nor less convincing than the one far less integrated and organic, more dichotomic and antagonistic built on the opposition between the "formalist" De Robertis and the content-oriented Croce. A history of Italian criticism and critical methodology based on dichotomy or integration is in both cases the product of a subjective fallacy, of an Erlebnis. Whether we insist on the convergence or on the divergence of the critical ideals operating in Italy, what is really at stake is the noetic concept of self-sufficiency of the so-called Italian way of thinking. To me De Robertis is no more the herald of the future, a structuralist avant la lettre, than Russo and Fubini are the sentries of the past. The "interjectio admirandi" dear to De Robertis is as remote from a phenomenological understanding of the work of art, from the acknowledgment of its objectivity as Russo's striving for a self-fulfilling verbal pathos reached through the operation of uplifting one level of truths—the poet's level—to the schemes of the critic's mental discourse.

Of course, another way out would be that of denying any truth to a possible recognition of shortcomings in the Italian methodological experience and considering Croce not as a filter, a barrier, or even the security wall upon which our own pride or self-assurance relies, but rather as the outpost of Italian intellectual achievements, the mentor of a generation of critics operating in Europe or on the American continent. There is, certainly, much truth in such a statement of pride, but here again caution is necessary in order to fully understand the meaning of the expansion of Crocean thought. I can only regret that an outstanding scholar, the late G. N. G. Orsini is not here, is not with us any longer to accept or dispute the truthfulness of my statement, but according to me, while Croce's influence as a philosopher of aesthetics and literary critic is considerable, the map along which the absorption of his principles outside of Italy takes place is far from clear. The French translation of Croce's *Breviary* by the historian Georges Bourgin says very little about the way French critics felt about aesthetic principles before or after the translation. Since Bourgin is an historian of the Italian Risorgimento and not necessarily in touch with the French literary situation, his translation only indicates the presence of a cultural inter-relation between the leading Italian intellectual group around Croce and the French intellectuals who were Italianophiles. As for the Anglo-Saxon world, Orsini's book on Croce is an indispensible tool for penetrating the ways Croce was read and quickly mis-understood, or at least, understood as one of the many options open to literary criticism and aesthetic methodology and no more than that. We have reached now a zone inhabited by a type Gianfranco Contini has appropriately called "postcrociano."[22] The "postcrociano" is more than his predecessor a citizen of the world; he knows how to cope with experiences that are not easily dismissable with the definition of *déjà vu*. The mentors he cherishes have prestigious names. Besides the Marxologists and the critics of Utopia, Lukács and Walter Benjamin, who came to fortify the intellectual revival of the Italian left based upon the work of Antonio Gramsci,[23] one finds Leo Spitzer who made of Italy the "patria" of his last years, Roman Jakobson very much at ease in Rome as in Milan or Pavia, in Florence and Pisa as in Bari, keeping company with the semiologist Umberto Eco and the structuralists and philologists of "Strumenti critici," Maria Corti, Cesare Segre, and d'Arco Silvio Avalle. Italy has become a microcosm where Poly-lalia is the most courted lady. The Italian landscape, until the early fifties a splendid "chasse gardée," no longer shows any concern about being over-run. As the Italian mentor of a new generation, Gianfranco Contini stands tall in a very original position. A specialist of early texts and an accomplished Romance philologist, he has assumed a mediating role between the historicists whose critical language he has helped to explore and the formalists whose studies of the poetic variants he has brilliantly pursued, applying his subtle and penetrating techniques of inquiry to Petrarch as well as to Leopardi. Very much at ease when following the constructive steps taken by the poet toward the shaping of his world of feelings and thoughts, he shows an extra-ordinary skill in dissecting the work of art in its manifold semantic possibili-ties. But he can as well take on the habits of the cultural historian and explore the links between Croce's thought and non-Crocean trends operating in Italy and elsewhere. The sentence with which Roman Jakobson concludes his *Essais de linguistique générale*, "Linguista sum, linguistici nihil a me alienum puto," could very well apply to Contini's activity if we replace the word "linguista" with the more comprehensive and not less respectable word "criticus."[24]

The textual critics who are well aware of the philological lesson of Giorgio Pasquali and Michele Barbi continue to play a special role in the world of Italian letters. A recent book written by the well-known Boccaccio scholar, Vittore Branca, in collaboration with Jean Starobinski brings to the atten-tion of the reader the itinerary of diffusion of the ancient texts such as the *Regula Sancti Benedicti* and the *Cantico of Frate Sole* or the intricate paths of success travelled by Boccaccio's Decameron handled with interested, unpredicted idiosyncrasies and sudden exclusions by its most natural read-ers, the members of the mercantile companies.[25] It is worth noting that the interest à la Lachmann for the construction of a "stemma codicum" is accom-panied in the modern interpreter by a deep curiosity for the horizontal diffu-sion of the text, for the sociological and historical characterization of the public to whom the book is addressed. The intelligent reader becomes receptive to the lesson of his teachers, to the legacy that is, left by Michele Barbi, but also to the suggestions which stem from Auerbach's seminal research on *Literary Language and its Public in Late Latin Antiquity and in the Middle Ages*.[26] Therefore while the Boccaccio interpreter rooted in Branca's methodology would discard as being too abstract the tendency expressed by Todorov's *Grammaire du Décaméron*[27] to bring the individualized features of Boccaccio's stories to archetypal models, he would strongly agree that the so-called "polymorphic diffraction" of the text—that is, the erosion of its compactness through the manipulation of interested readers—is extremely important for an understanding of the history of the social group to which Boccaccio's reader belongs.

But what about the text per se? Whether we want to consider it in its making (Contini), as a "product productif" (Starobinski), or as an organism ready to be enjoyed or simply dissected for better detection of its functions, we must abandon, according to the "new" Italian critic, the search for metatextual implications unrelated to a knowledge of its underlying structures. The decoding of a work of art, to use the language of the semiologist, not only implies the description and the evaluation of the linguistic signs by which it is to be identified, but also the making and the unmaking of a tradition. To study the variations of a work of poetry, Cesare Segre says, means to relate them horizontally to the system of structures within which they become significant. Any extrapolation of the variant implies a destruction of the work of art qua organic structure.[28] We are confronted here, I believe, with a smart use of the concept of "pertinence" derived in Segre directly from the Danish linguist Louis Hjelmslev and, in its most radical formulation, from the co-founder of the school of Prague, Nikolaj Sergeevic Trubeckoj. But while such a concept is used by the two great linguists proscriptively to isolate phonetics and semantics from their field of scientific inquiry,[29] the literary critic grasps its positive and prescriptive import for studying the strata of the work of art and their inter-relation, for a more "historical" formulation of its making. Recent books by Segre such as *I segni e la critica* and *Le strutture e il tempo*,[30] explorations in the labyrinth of the linguistic codes such as the one promoted by Maria Corti in *Metodi e fantasmi*,[31] and Avalle's deconstruction and reconstruction of Montale's subliminal poetic memory[32] all show the skill reached by the generation of critics we have called "post-crociani." The denunciation of the autobiographical fallacy bravely advanced by Leo Spitzer in the last year of his life, even in its mildest form of leading the attention of the reader from the formal textures to the spiritual "etymon" to which they are connected, paves the way for the study of the work of art per se as if detached from the authorial responsibility. Thus the secrets of the poetic mood can be hopefully explored according to the rules of the grammar of poetry sponsored by the great champion of Russian formalism, Roman Jakobson. By reading, however, the pages of Segre, what strikes me is the innate equilibrium which allows him to explore the applicability of the theory of the models or the "analyse du recit" to medieval or late medieval texts without ever forgetting the philological caution he has learned as editor of the *Chanson de Roland* and of Ariosto's *Orlando furioso*, as the heir of learned linguists and Romance philologists such as Santorre Debenedetti and Benvenuto Terracini. In the innovating trend he represents, inspired not by destructive, iconoclastic radicalism, but rather to be understood as a rejuvenation of what is lasting ("ringiovanimento del duraturo") there is hope and a guarantee of the survival of the Italian critical tradition.

HARVARD UNIVERSITY

Notes

[1] I am reminded of a convincing thought beautifully expressed by Benedetto Croce in his intellectual autobiography. "Books," Croce says, "remain inert and mysterious when they are read before we have elaborated on our own their content. They become efficient and operative only when they are able to establish a dialogue with us in order to help us to clarify thoughts we have barely sketched, to fulfill in well formulated concepts our foreboding of concepts, to fortify us and reassure us that the road we are travelling is the right one." B. Croce, "Contributo alla critica di me stesso," in G. Contini, *Letteratura dell'Italia unita 1861-1968* (Florence: 1968), p. 450.

[2] Erich Auerbach, *Mimesis. Dargestellte Wirklichkeit in der Abendländischen Literatur* (Bern: 1946). *Mimesis. Il realismo nella letteratura occidentale* (Turin: 1956).

[3] Delio Cantimori, book review of E. Auerbach's *Mimesis etc.*, in *Annali della Scuola Normale Superiore*, 1946, s.II, XV, pp. 222-23.

[4] See my article, "Erich Auerbach," in *Belfagor*, May 1963, pp. 306-22.

[5] Cesare Pavese, *Lettere 1945-1950*, a cura di Italo Calvino (Turin: 1966), p. 518.

[6] Cesare Pavese, *Lettere*, cit., p. 529.

[7] Cf. especially Pasolini's intervention in the special issue of the periodical *Ulisse* dedicated to "Le sorti del romanzo." The issue appeared during the winter 1956-57.

[8] Benedetto Croce, "Dei filologi 'che hanno idee'," in *Terze pagine sparse* (Bari: 1955), pp. 180-85.

[9] B. Croce, *Terze pagine sparse*, cit., pp. 21-27. Propp's *Le radici storiche dei racconti di fate* appeared in Turin in 1949.

[10] Cf. V. J. Propp, *Morfologia della fiaba* (Turin: 1966). The reappearance of Propp in Italian should be considered within the framework of the massive effort by the Italian literary establishment to cope with Russian formalism and the school of Prague; the years between 1965 and 1970 (especially 1966) are from this point of view extremely crucial. Cf. V. Erlich, *Il formalismo russo* (Milan: 1966). V. Sklovskij, *Una teoria della prosa* (Bari: 1966). *Il circolo linguistico di Praga. Le tesi del '29*, int. by E. Garroni (Milan: 1966). R. Jakobson, *Saggi di linguistica general* (Milan: 1966). B. M. Eichenbaum, *Il giovane Tolstoi; la teoria del metodo formale* (Bari: 1968). J. Tynjanov, *Il problema del linguaggio poetico* (Milan: 1968). In 1968 also appears in Turin the anthology *I Formalisti russi* edited by Tzvetan Todorov and prefaced by Roman Jakobson, and in Rome, the book *Formalismo e avanguardia in Russia* by Ignazio Ambrogio.

[11] A sign of this bitterness appears documented in a letter by Cesare Pavese to

Giuseppe Cocchiara from Turin, Nov. 15, 1949, in C. Pavese, *Lettere,* cit., p. 435. Croce's view on Propp appeared first in a daily paper of broad diffusion, the *Corriere della Sera*, on Nov. 3, 1949.

¹²I do not intend to put on the same level Cantimori's and Croce's reaction toward irrationalism, aware as I am of Cantimori's complex attitude toward a writer and philosopher like Nietzsche. It is, however, true that in this article he has Croce clearly in mind and reacts according to the Crocean doctrine. On Cantimori we have a very good book by Giovanni Miccoli, *Delio Cantimori. La ricerca di una nuova critica storiografica* (Turin: 1970).

¹³The passage deserves to be quoted in Italian. "E se nella nostra rassegna la parte del leone sarà presa dalla critica italiana, spero non ci si vorrà accusare di faziosità nazionale, ma si preferirà ammettere lealmente che la critica italiana forte della consapevolezza teorica datale dell'estetica del Croce, è giunta oggi a un tale grado di maturità e di penetrante affinamento, che quella straniera non può assolutamente competere con essa, o, peggio, porlesi accanto in un assurdo agone di rivalità." Cf. Bruno Maier, *Profilo della critica su Italo Svevo* (Trieste: 1951), p. 40.

¹⁴Cf. Marcello Pagnini, "La critica formalistica," in *I Metodi attuali della critica in Italia*, edited by Maria Corti and Cesare Segre, ERI (Turin: 1970), p. 288.

¹⁵D'Arco Silvio Avalle, *L'analisi letteraria in Italia. Formalismo, Strutturalismo, Semiologia* (Milan-Naples: 1970).

¹⁶M. Fubini, "Ragioni storiche e ragioni teoriche della critica stilistica," in *Critica e poesia* (Bari: 1966), pp. 106-26.

¹⁷L. Russo, "Carducci critico," in *La critica letteraria contemporanea* (Florence: 1967), p. 5. On L. Russo cf. Giovanni Da Pozzo, *La prosa di Luigi Russo* (Florence: 1975), and, in English, my article "Luigi Russo (1892-1961): An Outline of a Critical Biography," *Italian Quarterly*, Summer 1962, VI, 22, pp. 26-51.

¹⁸B. Croce, "Due schiarimenti," in *Terze pagine sparse*, cit., p. 180. The name of Giovanni Gentile's "young student" about whom Croce reminisces is without any doubt Luigi Russo. Croce has more specifically in mind Russo's "Il problema della genesi e dell'unità della Commedia," now in *Problemi di metodo critico* (Bari: 1929), pp. 39-79.

¹⁹Georges Poulet, "Phénoménologie de la conscience critique," in "Quatre conferences sur la 'Nouvelle critique'," *Studi Francesi* (Turin: Jan-April 1968), pp. 17-32.

²⁰René Wellek, in his "Benedetto Croce: literary critic and historian," *Comparative Literature*, V, 1 (winter 1953), pp. 75-82, rightly assumes that around 1899 in discussing Gustav Gröber's rhetorical categories Croce "came for a time to defend a view of creative criticism, of criticism as creation, as art" (p. 81), but later more appropriately linked criticism with reason and thought.

²¹Cf. Luigi Russo, "Ritorni ed esaurimento di vecchie ideologie romantiche," in *La critica letteraria contemporanea*, cit, p. 398, and especially "La critica letteraria del Croce e il nostro storicismo," in *La critica letteraria contemporanea*, cit., p. 129.

²²Cf. G. Contini, *L'influenza culturale di Benedetto Croce* (Milan-Naples: 1967), especially pp. 54-57 where some points dear to the new generation of critics are vigorously stressed.

²³The diffusion of Lukács in Italy starts in 1949 with the translation of his book on Goethe. By now almost everything he has written has been translated. The interest for Benjamin started much later in 1962 when Renato Solmi published a book of essays, *Angelus Novus*, in Turin. Benjamin's *L'opera d'arte nell'epoca della sua riproducibilità tecnica*, another book of essays, appeared in Turin in 1966. Cf. Cesare Cases, "La

critica sociologica" in *I metodi attuali della critica in Italia,* cit., pp. 23-40.

²⁴For Contini cf. his two recent books of essays: *Varianti e altra linguistica. Una raccolta di saggi (1938-1968)* (Turin: 1970), and *Altri esercizi. (1942-1971),* (Turin: 1972).

²⁵Vittore Branca, Jean Starobinski, *La filologia e la critica letteraria* (Milan: 1977).

²⁶E. Auerbach, *Literary Language and its Public in Late Latin Antiquity and in the Middle Ages* (New York: 1965).

²⁷Tzvetan Todorov, *Grammaire du Décaméron* (The Hague-Paris: 1969).

²⁸Cf. especially C. Segre, "Sistema e strutture nelle *Soledades* di A. Machado," in *I segni e la critica* (Turin: 1969) pp. 95-134.

²⁹An intelligent exposition and sharp criticism of the proscriptive use of "pertinence" by the linguists Hjelmslev and Trubeckoi is in Sebastiano Timpanaro Jr., "Lo strutturalismo e i suoi successori," in *Sul materialism* (Pisa: 1970). Cf. especially pp. 151-54.

³⁰C. Segre, *Le strutture e il tempo, Narrazione, poesia, modelli* (Turin: 1974).

³¹Maria Corti, *Metodi e fantasmi* (Milan: 1969).

³²D. S. Avalle, *"Gli orecchini" di Montale* (Milan: 1965).

II. Archetypal Criticism

GARCIA MARQUEZ' *MECEDOR*
AS LINK BETWEEN PASSAGE
OF TIME AND PRESENCE OF MIND

M. Audrey Aaron

> I had three chairs in my house; one for
> solitude, two for friendship, three for
> society.
>
> Thoreau, *Walden*

A continued relationship with *Cien años de soledad*[1] serves to deepen the conviction that at its heart this novel is poetic. It is poetry not only in those moments of true magic such as the levitation of Remedios, *la bella*, who one March afternoon was assumed up into the clouds, or the constant rain of miniscule yellow flowers which marked the death of the founder José Arcadio Buendía, but more precisely in the sense that it has signal recourse to figurative language in the attempt to both widen and bring into sharp focus the thematic edifice of the entire work. Considering the dense and complicated structure of this novel, such an assertion places a heavy burden on any one or group of symbols, but it is my thesis that GM has used one that occupies a strikingly prominent role; it is the almost unnoticed and humble *mecedor*, the rocking chair. Its varieties (the term is mentioned some twenty-five times) range from the wooden *mecedorcito* of little orphaned Rebeca, through the Viennese rockers which witnessed the tempestuous love of Amaranta Ursula and Gastón, to the strong, throne-like *bejuco* rocker of Pilar Ternera.

The concept of poetic symbol as used with reference to GM needs the following qualification. Rather than suppose that he employed it with conscious intent from the beginning to the end of the creative process, I would prefer to believe that it was used initially without conscious intent, that it emanated from his deepest, probably unconscious self. Although the *mecedor* as symbol makes an early arrival when Rebeca comes to join the Buendía household, the full scope of its symbolic implications is not made fully apparent until the later portions of the novel. The image of the rocking chair was certainly an element in the body of childhood memories GM confesses to be both matter and cause of his writing up to and including the present novel.

At some point in the period of composition (probably toward the end) the image of the rocking chair together with its possibilities as symbol may have been lifted from its simple and pristine existence in the unconscious and thenceforth used advertently by the novelist as a correlative of what may be the dominating and organizing theme of the novel, that of memory. This simple and spontaneous origin may also account for the fact that such a figure, on one level, can go unnoticed.[2] During the final days of his existence the patriarch José Arcadio Buendía was consoled by a recurring dream of an infinite series of rooms: "Soñaba que se levantaba de la cama, abría la puerta y pasaba a otro cuarto igual, con la misma cama de cabecera de hierro forjado, *el mismo sillón de mimbre* y el mismo cuadrito de la Virgen de los Remedios en la pared del fondo" (124; my emphasis). If the infinite series of rooms exactly alike may refer (as do the mirrors elsewhere in the novel) to the repetitive nature of history, of the past, the presence of the same wicker chair may safely be said to suggest the act of remembering, and will become the wicker rocker so consistently used in the same context.

The *mecedor* is an appropriate and natural symbol to concretize the dual concept of solitude and memory, the complex *soledad-memoria*. Although I find the novel's bi-partite theme of solitude and remembrance inextricably linked, nevertheless, time demands that this study concentrate insofar as possible on the relationship between the rocker and memory.

As in the dramas of García Lorca, repeated reference to common objects tends to point to a more profound, hidden purpose. Other essential pieces of furniture are mentioned, in particular the bed (or hammock) but none so insistently as the rocking chair. Whereas other furniture forms (excepting the bed) are designed to support objects, the chair supports man, is designed to match his age and physical condition, and "is best seen and evaluated with a person sitting in it, for chair and sitter complement one another."[3] An authority in the field declares that the innovative rocking chair "preserves much more vividly than straight chairs the impression of personality."[4] Moreover, it is usually a family possession, associated with grandparents and passed on to descendants, thus becoming a symbol in itself of family continuity and repetition. I think we may rest assured that the "relatos fantásticos" (13) which GM heard from the grandmother with whom he spent his first eight years, doña Tranquilina Iguarán Cotes, were told from a wicker rocking chair. During her last days, her reason having fled, Ursula held frequent chats with her ancestors whom she encountered in her bedchamber, among them, "Tranquilina María Miniata Alacoque Buendía, su abuela, abanicándose con una pluma de pavorreal en su mecedor de tullida" (289).

Whereas the bed is associated with sleep and dreams, the rocking chair suggests memory, especially for those whose life cycle is drawing to a close, or for whom a catastrophic event has limited all time to the past. In mental time the present is constantly consumed, used up in an expectation of the future or a remembrance of the past. As chronological age advances memory takes on greater awareness that the future is being foreshortened, causing an elongation of that portion of consciousness we call memory; and remembering is primarily a solitary and crepuscular activity. One can sing, dance, play cards or tennis with others, but one does not remember in concert; that may be why rocking chairs come in singles. During the seemingly interminable deluge of Macondo "Aureliano Segundo no se dio cuenta de que se estaba volviendo viejo, hasta una tarde que se encontró contemplando el atardecer prematuro desde un mecedor. . ." (268). Thus it is that the "curved time" of the novel is reflected in the physical construction of the rocking chair; both it and the cradle rest on curved wooden pieces, and together they symbolize birth (the opening) and death (the close) of the human life cycle.

The innovative nature of GM's concept of time in CAS is not due primarily to its cyclical nature, as such a theory of time has been universally that of primitive man, and in the modern novel was adopted by Joyce from Giambattista Vico's influential cyclical theory of history. It lies rather in combining cyclical time with a return to a traditional or lineal narrative technique. In consequence, the reader, seemingly anchored to a straightforward story line, is periodically jolted by the sensation of being "out of time," of moving in an orbit which collides or combines, even repeats the path of other cycles. This is totally free time, paying debt to neither clock nor calendar and arranged according to fancy, and producing moments outside of time, a kind of "super time." The conflation of the two theories of natural time (lineal and cyclical) guides all syntactic and semantic units of the novel, and, more importantly for this study, allows natural time to obey the laws of memory— that is to say, that objective, external time follows paths parallel to subjective, psychological time in its dynamic capacity to anticipate the future at any moment or to protract the past into one immeasurable moment of crucial awareness.[5] It is here that memory as one of the dominant, if not the predominant, structural themes of the novel has its origin.

The novel opens with a wheel-like sentence which typifies this intimacy between the two orders of time. (Please pardon the repetition of a masterly but now overworked sentence.) "Muchos años después, frente al pelotón de fusilamiento, el coronel Aureliano Buendía había de recordar aquella tarde remota en que su padre le llevó a ver el hielo" (9). A diagram will show how the *present* (Muchos años. . .fusilamiento") anticipates the *future* ("El coronel. . .de recordar") at which time the *past* ("Aquella tarde. . .el hielo") will become *present* again, and the wheel has come full circle.[6] Action which originated in chronological *order* has been displaced by the dynamic *disorder* of memory: Beginning at a point in the present (the *después*) from which the inexorable future (most commonly the structure *haber de* + inf.) is anticipated, it is the power of memory which turns the wheel back to the past, the *antes*; in other words, when Colonel Aureliano, facing death before a firing squad, remembers an exciting day at a gypsy circus when he was eight, this memory effectively blotted out the present, the row of guns pointed at his heart. Throughout the novel time can be distinguished as a regressive spiral, a continuous flow of the present toward the past, as for some characters the past is the only time of meaning and significance.[7] Anita Arenas remarks that "El tiempo no gira en redondo, es la conciencia del hombre quien por medio del recuerdo, actualiza momentos que quiere recordar o que desea olvidar."[8] This continued play upon the use of memory to keep the past alive constitutes the most significant kind of cyclical time; it is via this syntactico-semantic device that GM exploits the transcendental role of memory in the novel. The importance of memory in the thematics of the novel is first emphasized by the curious nature of the first Biblical plague to attack Macondo. It began with a seemingly harmless insomnia but evolved inexorably toward a far more critical result, forgetfulness. Memory processes were lost and Macondonians were threatened with the loss of self-identity, "hasta hundirse en una especie de idiotez sin pasado" (44). It was Ernest Völkening who first pointed out that the phrase "idiotez sin pasado" contains a key which allows us to decipher one of the fundamental designs of the author.[9] In a last attempt to rescue an imperiled past José Arcadio Buendía decided to construct "una máquina de la memoria" (48). But memory machines do not have to resemble revolving dictionaries as did his contraption. Many pages later Aureliano Babilonia, waiting for the elderly Fernanda in the kitchen, was startled to see her arrive dressed in the queenly finery she had worn at the carnival when she first appeared in Macondo. Anyone might think she was insane, but the author declares that "no lo estaba. Simplemente, había convertido los atuendos reales en una máquina de recordar" (308). GM's use of these two phrases, "una máquina de la memoria" and "una máquina de recordar" has a significance not initially perceived, as the reader's attention is deflected by the nonsubstantial, even frivolous, nature of such expressions. But the preoccupation with memory is evident, and I suggest that in many instances the rocker functions similarly, as an apparatus for remembering, which often in real life it is.

The rocker as symbol is associated predominantly with feminine characters. The memories consequent upon solitude are common to both the men and women of the Buendía family, but its effects follow a more complex line of development in GM's women. Their intensity of recollection in the isolation which destiny has assigned them often proceeds from a single source, the loss of love or the inability to meet its demands. Furthermore, the *mecedor* recurs most frequently with Rebeca and Pilar, possibly because these two figures, overflowing the stream of lineal time, move synchronically in cyclical, mythical time. Rebeca, overtly portrayed as an archetype of man's hidden, mythical past, has roots in time which seem to go back even further than those of Macondo's founders, while Pilar lives long enough to meet and reconstruct for its last scion the grandeur and misfortunes of the Buendía line.

Rebeca

The symbol of the *mecedor* embraces her entire life cycle. From the moment of her arrival until the last occasion she is seen alive, it is a symbol correlative with her existence. So constant is the *mecedor* in her characterization that it takes on, to a degree, the function of an attribute in traditional Christian iconography, such as the lamb for St. Agnes and the dog for St.

Roche. Rebeca's propensity for solitude manifested itself from the beginning by her refusal to be incorporated into the family, preferring to sit in a remote corner of the house in the "pequeño mecedor de madera con florecitas de colores pintadas a mano" (42-43) which she had brought along, perhaps a reminder of a familiar past, a refuge in the present period of alienation. This child's rocker will grow as symbol and undergo physical changes as it accompanies Rebeca to an adolescence of solitary character and impenetrable heart, because "[ella se] empecinaba en seguir usando el mecedorcito de madera con que llegó a la casa, muchas veces reforzado y ya desprovisto de brazos" (61).

Three factors in Rebeca's story indicate that GM sees her in terms of the earliest ages of human development, a period man may not forget with impunity—the insomnia plague, her passion for eating earth, and the bag containing her parents' bones. One evening the Indian Visitación awakened to find Rebeca "en el mecedor, chupándose el dedo y con los ojos alumbrados como los de un gato en la oscuridad. . . Era la peste del insomnia" (44) which Rebeca had brought with her. The pages describing this phenomenon are among the most original, profound and humorous in the novel. In the course of the sickness, people dreamed while awake and could see the dream-images of others as well as their own. "Sentada en su mecedor en un rincón de la cocina. . ." (45) Rebeca dreamed of her parents, and though Ursula earnestly examined and tried to identify them, they were unknown; even Ursula's sharp eyes could not pierce through so much time.

Along with the rocker Rebeca brought to Macondo a "talego de lona que hacía un permanente ruido de cloc, cloc, cloc, donde llevaba los huesos de sus padres" (42). Müller[10] suggests that the bag of bones was nothing more than that same increasing burden of the past which Ursula felt in her declining years, and which overwhelmed the last Buendía as he sank into the rocking chair, his soul crushed by the weight of so much past. Years later, desperate over the uncertainty of her engagement to Pietro Crespi, Rebeca had recourse to Pilar's cards which told her that she would not be happy while her parents remained unburied. She shuddered but remembered herself entering the house, "con el baúl y el mecedorcito de madera y un talego cuyo contenido no conoció jamás (70). Thus, as she envisions her earliest experiences in Macondo, she remembers the rocker.

You'll recall the subsequent course of her volcanic life: the agony of her impatient heart during the courtship of Crespi which occasioned the bitter competition with Amaranta, the torrential love affair with the "protomacho," José Arcadio, *hijo*, and her brief happiness before his strange assassination. After his funeral she turned her back on the future, enclosed herself as within a tomb in their house, was never again seen abroad; at the moment the shots rang out, interest in the present and concern for the future died, her life was reduced to memory. During the long years of seclusion that remained to her she found peace in that house where remembrances were materialized by force of implacable evocation. Our last glimpse of her is through the eyes of the Colonel who visits her on business and finds her, the classic image of alienation and introversion, "Estirada en su mecedor de mimbre, mirando al coronel Aureliano Buendía como si fuera él quien pareciera un espectro del pasado" (139).

Amaranta

Amaranta, whose name from the Greek pastoral tradition means "love lies bleeding" is the complementary opposite of Rebeca. She is like Rebeca in that her unquenchable hatred of her adopted sister makes of her a possible protagonist in one of Unamuno's *nívolas*, a woman whose entire life is nourished by one all-enveloping passion. But what Rebeca, with a valor admired by Ursula, reached out and fought for, Amaranta, equally passionate, lacked the courage even to accept, as her timidity watered by hatred refused entry to a possible healing love. After the suicide of the rejected Pietro Crespi, a nephew was her next temptation to abandon the solitude of her tormented heart, an attraction which climaxed at Aureliano José's maturity: "Sentada en el mecedor de mimbre, con la labor interrumpida en el regazo, Amaranta contemplaba a Aureliano José con el mentón embadurnado de espuma . . ." (126). And from her rocking chair she set up an impregnable barrier against another more formidable attempt to break down her closely guarded solitude, that of a patient suitor who carried within an amaranthine bleeding love: this rocker was the same one in which "Amaranta jugaba damas chinas con el coronel Gerineldo Márquez" (349). After Gerineldo's pretentions were sharply terminated Amaranta "se encerró en el dormitorio a llorar su soledad hasta la muerte" (143). Unlike Rebeca, who in her calamitous solitude banished all life to preserve the memory of a unique love, Amaranta banished all love to preserve the life of a unique hatred, because "la soledad le había seleccionado los recuerdos" (190); solitude banished the trivial as it isolated and aggrandized the most bitter of memories, those of Rebeca.

Amaranta Ursula

Were it not for what her mother called an invincible cowardice, Amaranta might have conceived the child with the pig's tail. But it took the courage of an Ursula and the passion of an Amaranta, brought together in the person of Amaranta Ursula, to do so, and thus bring about the destruction of the Buendía lineage. It is a part of the irony of the tone and structure of the novel that Amaranta Ursula, having acquired the custom of taking a kind of wakeful and thoughtful siesta in the gallery, knitted the clothes for her expected child seated in the very wicker rocker wherein her great-great aunt Amaranta had knotted her own shroud.

Pilar Ternera

Because of its unique structure, CAS does not have one central personage or event to unify the whole, but it does have two characters whose orbits are wider and more ample than the others, and act as *hilos conductores* to lead the reader through the century-long maze. These two are Melquíades and Pilar, in particular the latter. She is the only personage who is present at the beginning and at the end of the story, where she reappears to perform an act of consolation for the last Buendía of Macondo.

The climactic appearance of Pilar at the novel's end has been forecast in two "rocking chair vignettes" which serve to illustrate the parallelism of opposites. Prior to his flight to her bed, the first Aureliano made a hesitant, exploratory visit to Catarino's tavern where he witnessed the arrival of "una mujer tan gorda que cuatro indios tenían que llevarla cargada en un mecedor" (50); later he noted that in front of a back tavern door "estaba sentada y se abanicaba en silencio la matrona del mecedor" (51). This stout woman guarded her "one woman bordello" (in reality her frail mulata granddaughter) in miserly exploitation of lust, whereas generous Pilar, despite the countless numbers who approached her, "Nunca cobraba el servicio" (135). A similar but opposite contrast is this incident from Pietro Crespi's courtship of Rebeca: suspicious that the Italian's daily visit might not always conform to proper behavioral standards, Ursula "se sentó en un mecedor a vigilar la visita de los novios" (79).

As the one hundred years approached their end the last Buendía, Aureliano Babilonia, encountered Pilar. The youth had just emerged from the seclusion of the *cuartito* which had been his world since childhood, when in the company of his four friends he visited a bizarre bordello, one whose design and appointments imitated the tropical world, and where an "espléndida y taciturna anciana vigilaba el ingreso en un mecedor de bejuco" (333). It was Pilar, who long ago "had given up the pernicious custom of keeping track of her age and she went on living in the static and marginal time of memories" (333). On recognizing in Aureliano a Buendía she felt time returning to its origins. Thenceforth the young man took refuge in the compassionate understanding of his own unrecognized great-great grandmother. In her bed the first son of José Arcadio Buendía has prostituted himself; as the depository of all knowledge of the Buendías, from her rocking chair she now bestowed on the last Aureliano the priceless gift of memory: "Sentada en el mecedor de bejuco, ella evocaba el pasado, reconstruía la grandeza y el infortunio de la familia. . ." (333).

In this key moment a significant variation in the *mecedor* must not be overlooked. Three of the four times Pilar's rocker is mentioned in these last several pages (333-36) it is specified for the first time, not of wood, not of wicker, but of *bejuco*. *Bejuco* is a climbing tropical plant with strong, flexible root-like stems, a kind of bindweed, used for all manner of ligatures, even for making furniture.[11] The choice is a most careful one on the author's part, as not only does such a rocker blend in appropriately with the tropical ambient of the bordello's decor; it allows the two powerful maternal figures of the novel, Ursula and Pilar, to move back into time, to converge, and to encounter their common source, their true-to-life origin in Doña Tranquilina Márquez. It was from the lips of this grandmother, "sentada en un *mecedor de bejuco*"[12] that the eight-year-old Gabriel listened to the fables and legends wherein popular fancy had kept alive the ancient and splendid past of Colombia, of the Aracataca region; it was from the imagination of this white-haired and blue-eyed old lady that the fascinated and sensitive boy received the burden of the primitive past from which he would not be freed until he was able to write the book which now lays dying. The moment is dramatic, for the reader knows the curtains are beginning to close, as the circle is closing; it is moving because such an insight into the unusual and intimate relationship between creator and creation is rarely glimpsed in literary history. And it is the simple rocker which effects this truly "real maravilloso."

In these final scenes the two dominating elements in Pilar's human character (she is magician and prostitute) will coalesce into one mythical character, that of the Earth Goddess. Conjointly, the *mecedor* gains in metaphorical value as chair, it is now a throne-chair. Its beginning now having been found, the proper order of things in time closes her circle as

> Pilar Ternera murió en el mecedor de bejuco, una noche de fiesta, vigilando la entrada de su paraíso. De acuerdo con su última voluntad, la enterraron sin ataúd, sentada en el mecedor que ocho hombres bajaron con cabuyas en un hueco enorme, excavado en el centro de la pista de baile (336).

Macondo's cycle at an end, Pilar, here a clear figure of the Earth as Mother[13] (or the Earth Goddess) returns to her own first principle under the earth. She appears majestic, like a pre-Columbian carving of an archaic priestess, as the rocking chair-coffin is lowered into the axis-womb of the earth, dug in the center of the world (the dance floor of the bordello) and whose parallel was the *castaño* in the center of the Buendía patio. Reminiscent of ancient telluric ceremonies, her "vestal virgins" throw into the opening their offering to assure continued fertility, or to the end that perhaps once more a family and a village not-Macondo, in the course of countless centuries, may break through the barriers of time and solitude to discover and painfully acquire the self-knowledge to be safe-guarded by memory.

There remains for consideration only the magnificent sentence in the penultimate paragraph of the saga, the culmination of the *mecedor* as symbol of the *soledad-memoria* theme. Crushed by Amaranta Ursula's death in childbirth, having wandered in desperation through the familiar parts of Macondo, seeking consolation from friends no longer about, "buscando un desfiladero de regreso al pasado" (347), Aureliano Babilonia returns at dawn to the white house and

> Se derrumbó en el mecedor, el mismo en que se sentó Rebeca en los tiempos originales de la casa para dictar lecciones de bordado, y *en el que* Amaranta jugaba damas chinas con el coronel Gerineldo Márquez, y *en el que* Amaranta Ursula cosía la ropita del niño, y en aquel relámpago de lucidez tuvo conciencia de que era incapaz de resistir sobre su alma *el peso de tanto pasado* (349; emphases mine).

The structure of this sentence merits attention. The first clause exemplifies the quaternary structure so favored by GM wherein four prepositional phrases all refer to three now-dead users of the rocker and to Aureliano Babilonia himself, linking him via this modest piece of wicker furniture with all the past generations of Macondo; this is the same family rocker that had stood in the shaded gallery surrounding the patio of the white house since the time of its enlargement by Ursula.

The three women named are those described previously as most closely associated metaphorically with the *mecedor*, all engaged in some characteristic activity while seated in this chair which had weathered all the years of the Buendías. It must be noted that the earlier reference to each activity (pp. 66, 123, 343, 345) records the event but does not mention the rocker; it is named now, as person and event are history and linked together at this moment of tragic climax as the last of their line, whose sole activity now is to *remember*, Aureliano sinks into the rocker.

The lightning flash of lucidity which reveals the burden of memory, of the past, is the same that will allow him to see the entire one hundred years as a single moment of time; this one moment in which the six generations are freed from time finds its spatial counterpart in the rocker, for it is from the rocker that he saw the dead infant being dragged away by all the ants in the world; from that place and in that moment he remembered the epigraph of the mysterious parchments, now perfectly clear, and then understood his own destiny, that he would never leave the little room of Melquíades alive. The cyclonic gusts of wind destined to destroy Macondo were also voices from the past, a destructive hurricane from the long ago that would exile the "city of mirrors" from the memory of men. And even as he read

. . .empezó el viento, tibio, incipiente, lleno de voces del pasado, de murmullos de geranios antiguos, de suspiros de desengaños anteriores a las nostalgias más tenaces (350).

UNIVERSITY OF IDAHO

Notes

[1] Gabriel García Márquez, *Cien años de soledad* (Buenos Aires: Sudamericana, 1967). All citations are from this edition; the name of the novelist and the title will be abbreviated "GM" and "CAS" respectively.

[2] The validity of the debatable psychoanalytic interpretation of the novels of García Márquez finds plausible support in Walter Lauffer's feature review of the work on GM by three Mexican doctors (Camacho, Vives and Solís) presented at a symposium of the Asociación Sicoanalítica Mexicana, "García Márquez en el diván de sicoanalista," "Diorama," *Excelsior* (México), 9 enero 1977, pp. 10-11.

[3] *Encyclopedia Britannica* (Chicago: H.H. Benton, 1943-73), Macropaedia 7, 786a.

[4] Walter A. Dyer and Ester A. Fraser, *The Rocking Chair, an American Institution* (New York: The Century Company, 1928). The authors find the rocking chair an American idea beyond doubt, its use attested as early as 1774, and have evidence that Franklin invented the rocking chair sometime in the vicinity of 1760.

[5] For some of the ideas relative to time in this section see Hans Meyerhoff, *Time in Literature* (Berkeley: University of California Press, 1955).

[6]This sentence opens the "protochapter" of the novel and the reader must wait until its end for the "present" (the sight of ice at the circus) to be narrated in an order only partially lineal. Examples of this stylistic device (I have counted twenty-six such sentences with but slight variations in pattern) are found to be more numerous in approximately the first half of the book; as the novel's own cycle draws to its end this recourse naturally is less frequent as less effective.

[7]In this context GM's first published work, *La hojarasca*, has special significance. In a formal dialogue with Mario Vargas Llosa he has stated that because *La hojarasca* was what he was able to compose when it was still impossible to write the total novel he had envisioned for so many years, it is the true antecedent of CAS. For the personages of this short novel (the *niño* excepted) the past is the time filled with meaning and content, the present being merely the point of reference for the past. This concept of time is stated acutely by Isabel as she describes Meme, an Indian servant: "Se tenía la impresión de que consideraba el transcurso del tiempo una pérdida personal, como si advirtiera con el corazón lacerado por los recuerdos que si el tiempo no hubiera transcurrido. . ." that past and better life would still be hers. GM, *La hojarasca* (Buenos Aires: Sudamericana, 1972), p. 40.

[8]Anita Arenas, "El tiempo: engranaje de una generación ausente en *Cien años de soledad,*" *Revista de literatura hispanoamericana* (Zulia), Jul.-Dec. 1972, 3, pp. 67-79.

[9]Ernesto Völkening, "Anotado al margen de CAS," *Nueva Novela Latinoamericana,* ed. Jorge Laforque (Buenos Aires: Paidos, 1969), I, p. 144.

[10]Leopold Müller and Carlos Martínez Moreno, *Psicoanálisis y literatura en CAS* (Montevideo: Paysandú, 1969), 2da edición, pp. 33-34.

[11]It is regrettable that the English edition was satisfied to translate *bejuco* as "wicker," as botanically the two are far apart. Bartolomé de las Casas in his *Apologética Historia de las Indias* was one of the first sixteenth-century Spaniards to describe this novelty. Cf. ed. Serrano y Sanz (Madrid: Bailly-Baillière e Hijos, 1909), NBAE, XIII, pp. 33-34.

[12]Osvaldo Robles Catano, one of the last friends of the family to see Doña Tranquila alive, describes his visit to Aracataca where he found her alone in the decrepit old house, now blind, and "sentada en un mecedor de bejuco." His interview was published in *El Informador* of Santa Marta, Colombia during 1968. Cf. Mario Vargas Llosa, *García Márquez: historia de un deicidio* (Barcelona: Monte Avila, 1971), p. 24, n. 15.

[13]For a general survey of this topic see J. A. MacCulloch in *Encyclopedia of Religion and Ethics* (New York: Chas. Scribners' Sons, 1955), V, pp. 129-31. Of great interest relative to the figure of Pilar Ternera is Flavio L. Chaves, "O bordel de Macondo." *Ficçã Latino-americana* (Porto Alegre, Brazil: Da Urgs, 1973), pp. 97-107.

FORBIDDEN PLACES:
BECQUER'S SCENE OF WRITING

Gari Laguardia

There is a scene in Bécquer's fiction which is repeated over and over again. It is a circumscribed space which contains a temptation. The boundaries of this place are not to be crossed. Describing one such area the poet exclaims, "¡El umbral de esta puerta/sólo Dios lo traspasa!"[1] In Bécquer's fiction, however, boundaries are invariably invaded by his protagonists. The results of this crossing-over into the proscribed area are just as invariably disastrous. For example, in "La ajorca de oro" Pedro enters the cathedral of Toledo to steal a gold band from the Virgin's statue and goes mad; in "Los ojos verdes" Fernando insists on frequenting a supernatural well and is drowned by the ghostly nymph who dwells there; and in "El monte de las ánimas" Alonso braves a haunted mountain to retrieve the blue kerchief of his beloved and is devoured by wolves. Enough examples could be adduced to claim that there is not a single case in Bécquer's prose fiction where this structure is not represented in one form or another. Here I will examine several representations of that scene from an explicitly psychoanalytical perspective. The results of this inquiry will lead to the identification of a central representational structure in Bécquer.

Any discussion of "forbidden places" within a psychoanalytical context imposes certain limitations on the interpretation of these places. In classical psychoanalytical theory the locus of forbidden desire ultimately reduces itself to the place where incest is formalized—the body of the parent. Should desire remain tied to that area, its fate is to suffer unending frustration due to the "law"[2] which enforces the ban on that place. The idea of "castration"— that is, the deprivation of what is instrumental to the achievement of desire—is the inevitable corollary to any infraction of that "law." Viewed through psychoanalytical spectacles, the information summarily adduced in the first paragraph above would invite equally summary conclusions. I mention this to forestall hasty and ultimately banal interpretations (i.e. Bécquer struggled with an Oedipus complex). On the one hand, an analysis of this type is, in fact, obliged to identify those structures that are equivalent to psychoanalytical constructs. But on the other hand, given the fact that the object of analysis, a text or a series of texts, has its own particular aims and processes, the attempt should be made to integrate such constructs into these.

The first portion of this analysis can begin with an examination of "El caudillo de las manos rojas." This *leyenda* is Bécquer's first mature essay in this genre. The theme and style by which Bécquer has come to be known find the first fully realized expression in this text. There is some justice then in viewing this story as a prototype of Bécquer's literary preoccupations. For my purposes this text is a useful place to begin since here "forbidden places" appear repeatedly, and as each is in turn violated each in turn is more precisely defined.

The story begins with the violation of proscribed territory. Pulo-Dehli illicitly returns from exile to rendezvous with Siannah, the betrothed of his older brother, the King of Ossira. While making love to Siannah he is discovered by Tippot, his brother. There is a fight and the king is killed. Pulo becomes king and marries Siannah but is overcome by a sense of guilt which inexorably destroys his peace of mind. He can never forget his crime because his hands have been indelibly marked with blood which despite his every effort cannot be washed away. The oedipal connotations which accrue to killing a king and taking his woman are relatively undisguised here. Indeed they are re-emphasized later on in the narrative when another regicide is described. Pulo's own father, whose place he now occupies through fratricide, was himself murdered by his own men. In the context of the story, regicide is therefore metonymically related not only to fratricide but to parricide and can be interpreted as representing the latter condensation. What bears underlining, however, is that the obstacle to the protagonist's desire remains alive symbolically through his conscience. Consummation of desire is still beyond his grasp: "...en balde han...invocado al genio de los sueños de nácar...El remordimiento, sentado a la cabecera del lecho, los ahuyenta con un grito lúgubre y prolongado, grito que resuena incesante al escucharlo" (p. 50). We might say that the "father" represented here by personified guilt is still the master of his domain—the matrimonial bed. That area is still out of bounds.

Pulo must consequently exorcise this figure by removing the figurative mark of castration, the blood on his hands. As long as this mark remains operative he will be unable to achieve the desired relations with his wife. Therefore, he consults an oracle in the hope that he will be allowed to expiate his crime and remove the blood. The instructions he receives are concise. With Siannah he is to travel to the source of the Ganges and once there wash his hands. In order to be absolved he must at all costs obey one injunction— he is to refrain from having sexual relations with his wife.

Midway through the journey Pulo violates the injunction. The violation takes place in the shadow of a tree which is described as "corpulento y magnífico" (p. 59). This setting provokes two pertinent associations in the minds of the protagonists. Siannah inquires, "¿Es cierto que existe un árbol cuya sombra causa la muerte?" (p. 61). Shortly after she asks a parallel question, "¿Es verdad que existe un árbol cuya sombra agita la sangre en las venas y enciende el amor?" (p. 62). These binary contrasts are expanded throughout the scene. Pulo describes his love for Siannah as "casto y puro otras veces, ahora...un crimen" (p. 62). He then asks her to sing him to sleep: "arrulla mi sueño como una madre, ya que no como una esposa" (p. 62). Siannah sings two songs. The first is a bloody epic: "Las espadas de la tribu tienen sed, y la sed de las espadas se templa con sangre" (p. 63). This song disturbs Pulo and he asks for a change of venue. Siannah then sings a love song: "La sangre se agolpa a mi corazón, rebosa en él y enciende mis mejillas" (p. 65).

Simplifying a bit, we observe that these oppositions adduce signifiers, each of which can symbolize binary concepts. Thus a tree can symbolize love or death, love can symbolize purity or criminality, Siannah can symbolize mother or wife, and song can symbolize strife or eros. The question that now arises is whether this articulation of dual signifieds is merely a rhetorical exposition of traditional pairings or whether it constitutes a coherent pattern of thought which codifies an implicit set of moral rules. If we take the general context of this scene into account we must conclude that the latter analysis is the correct one. Moreover, the parallel dyads in representing thought, or more precisely the image of thought, also define the situation being narrated. The structure they formalize is one which presents Pulo with a set of alternatives in his attempt to resolve a situation clouded by illicit *blood relations.* (Indeed, the shared referent which ties these sets of binary oppositions into a structure is the relation they bear to blood which is represented metonymically as part of the body or metaphorically as defining kinship.) Given the predicate that relations between Siannah and Pulo are under a temporary ban, the operative alternative should be read as follows: The tree symbolizes the death that results from sexual relations which are, at the moment, criminal because Siannah is occupying the conceptual space of "mother." This fact ensures that communication between them (the "song") cannot convey anything but strife and discord. Once the negative blood relations are removed from the scheme (when Pulo washes his hands at the source of the Ganges) the alternative option described above will no longer obtain. The tree will then symbolize the love which arises from the pure relations between a man and his wife, and as a result communication between them will be marked by erotic harmony. When Pulo engages in sexual intercourse with Siannah he chooses the first alternative, ensuring, on the one hand, the unpleasant consequences derived thereby and confirming, on the other hand, the situation described by it. He also forecloses the possibility of the second ever coming to pass. The place of desire then is not to be a *locus amoenus.* We are now entitled to ask why, given the pleasant alternatives to such a dire situation, the protagonist should willfully ensure that "happiness" will forever be beyond his reach. The answer to this is brought to light in the narration which follows the violation of the prohibition. There it is made clear that what may have appeared to be the articulation of an oedipal drama in the manner commonly known is merely the pretext which lays the ground for a definitive regrouping of the signifiers of desire.

After the consummation of the proscribed act of intercourse, Siva, the God of death and destruction, visits Pulo with a dream. The dream is a symbolic recapitulation of the events of "waking life" which preceded it. The setting of the dream is a forest where a severe storm is in progress. An extended simile compares the storm's thunder to "la profecía de los blancos fantasmas de. . .antepasados" (p. 68). The prophesy concerns "el camino de la muerte" (p. 68). Pulo is characterized as the only warrior brave enough to "arriesgarse en sus agrestes y enmarañados senderos" (p 68). This is, of course, the repetition of a familiar pattern of action: the defiant penetration of a dangerous area. In this place Pulo and Siannah are attacked by a tiger which Pulo kills. This is an obvious reminiscence of Pulo's slaying of his brother. The tiger's body, however, metamorphoses into a snake. Just as the slaying of his brother merely obtained a transferral of anxiety for Pulo, the slaying of the tiger gives birth to another danger. Pulo is no match for the snake which is described as a fearsome reptile growing "con rapidez prodigiosa" (p. 71). Pulo's dagger is of no use against this formidably phallic figure. He is soon prostrated: "el puñal se ha escapado de sus manos desfallecidas y el velo de muerte se extiende ante sus ojos" (p. 62). As Pulo is about to expire a diamond arrow shoots out of the snake's eyes, killing it. Pulo has been saved by Vishnu. Standing over the fallen warrior Vishnu is described in detail. He is a giant and resplendent figure. His forehead touches the clouds and his massive frame casts an "immense shadow" (p. 72). Lying in this shadow Pulo receives a sharp reprimand from the god for breaking the injunction. Pulo's response to this chastisement is significant: "El rubor de su falta colora sus bronceadas mejillas. . ." (p. 73). What the reader is witnessing here is a reformulation of the seduction scene where under the shadow of a "corpulent and magnificent" tree Pulo and Siannah enjoyed illicit sexual relations. There, one of the attributes of the tree was to provoke love by agitating "la sangre en las venas" (p. 62). We might remember too that immediately preceding the act of intercourse, Siannah via her song exclaims, "La sangre se agolpa a mi corazón, rebosa en él y enciende mis mejillas" (p. 65). In this light Pulo's blushing acquires a particular meaning. (Blushing, after all, is produced by a rush of blood to the cheeks.)

We can now begin to understand the deep motivation behind Pulo's willfull violations: they have enabled him to actualize a masochistic fantasy. In Freudian terms Pulo's encounter with Vishnu would be a classic representation of the objectives of "moral masochism."[3] Such people are constantly in the position of being victims of fate. Through no apparent fault of their own they encounter an endless series of situations where it is impossible to resist the temptation to commit "sinful" acts. These situations, in Freud's view, are in fact not innocently arrived at; on the contrary, they are avidly sought out in order to "enjoy" the concommitant "chastisement" dealt to them by real figures or "the great parental power of Fate."[4] For these persons suffering "chastisement" could be traced back through a regressive series of fantasy metaphors. The wish to be reprimanded is a thinly veiled transformation of a wish to be beaten by the father which in turn represents a deeply repressed desire "to have some passive sexual relations with him."[5] This in turn, in a male subject, is related to the vicissitudes of the Oedipus complex in its "negative" form, where the parent of the same sex is taken as the model for an erotic object. (Siannah, we might mention, disappears from the narrative at the conclusion of Pulo's dream.) The conclusion of the *leyenda* amply attests to this unexpected twist.

There we will observe Pulo act like the masochist who as Freud states "must do something inexpedient, act against his own interests, ruin the prospects which the real world offers him, and possibly destroy his own existence in the world of reality."[6] He is given the opportunity to do so by Vishnu (who, it should be remembered is only a "fiction" in a dream concocted by Siva). Pulo is offered one more opportunity to expiate his "crime." He is to return to Kattak and search out a crow with a white head who will lead him to the place of restitution. This place is the ruins of a temple which was built at the behest of Pulo's father before his murder. Pulo is to restore the temple.

Following the crow towards his destination Pulo figuratively retreads the road of the "repressed." At one point during his journey he is seized by an attack of anxiety. The crow is able to account for Pulo's anxiety. The area they are about to traverse was the scene, the crow says, of "la derrota de tu padre" (p. 79). The crow then insists on retelling the story of the regicide as a way to "salir con bien de este peligro" (p. 79). All the while "Pulo escucha, sobrecogido de un religioso pavor, la historia del sangriento combate en que su padre perdió la vida. . .cuya terrible sencillez nunca había arrancado una lágrima tan ardiente a sus ojos cual la que entonces rodó abrasadora sobre su mejilla" (p. 83). Pulo's intense reaction is, of course, overdetermined. The scene which is unfolding before his mind's eye in vivid detail replicates the other regicide which gave birth to the tragic series of events that constitute the narrative. The remorse and pain which these produce in Pulo once again "burn" the protagonist's cheeks.

The stage is now set for the return of the father. The crow tells Pulo to kneel because "tu padre va a dejar el seno de la tumba" (p. 83). The old king appears in the form of a red flame. It is he who will lead Pulo to the spot where restitution and expiation are to be accomplished. The flame, "lanzándose al vacío, comienza a caminar con dirección al ocaso" (p. 83). Finally it settles "sobre la cumbre de la colina en cuya falda duerme el viento de la noche" (p. 84). As the burning tip of an object rising from a "lap," the "father" asserts his presence in a manner that underlines the symbol of his authority— the phallus. Towards this symbol Pulo "maravillado y absorto, sube la suave pendiente que conduce al término de su peregrinación" (p. 84).

In the heart of his father's ruined temple Pulo receives the instructions that will enable him to "put his conscience to rest and wash away the bloodstains on his hands" (p. 85) (my translation). He is to rebuild the temple and on the altar where the flame now flickers he is to place a monumental statue of Vishnu. The statue is to be carved from the "gigantesco tronque de un árbol desconocido" (p. 85) which will wash ashore once the rest of the temple is completed. At that time a pilgrim will arrive at Pulo's palace. He is to carve Vishnu's image out of the massive trunk. Pulo must, however, beware from looking at the work in progress. Should he glance at the statue before it is completed all will have been in vain; Pulo will continue to suffer the blows of "el amor y la conciencia cuyos golpes matan sin que se vea la mano que los dirige" (p. 76). Since in a very basic sense this precisely defines Pulo's objectives it is not surprising that he fails to observe the injunction. "Impatient" because he does not hear the sculptor at work Pulo steps into the forbidden workshop separating "las colgaduras de seda y oro que cubren la puerta de la habitación" (p. 91). There, horror-stricken, he beholds "el informe busto de un horroroso ídolo" (p. 91). The statue is not of Vishnu but of Siva whose eyes "parecen prontos a brotar el rayo y la muerte" (p. 91).

Realizing that the time for his apotheosis has arrived, Pulo orders the idol set up on the altar of his father's temple. There, after delivering a harangue to his subjects in which he portrays himself as a victim of cruel fate, he plunges a sword into his chest. The description of his suicide underlines the sensual dividend derived from the act: "el caliente borbotón de sangre que brotó de su herida saltó humeando al rostro del genio" (p. 94). This scene is merely the repetition of Pulo's blushing as a result of Vishnu's reprimands. The tree that provokes love (inflaming the blood) and death receives its extreme formulation at this point. The inflamed blood can no longer be contained and gushes out orgasmically leading to death. The drama of blood relations thus comes to an end with the triumph of masochistic sensuality; the subject literally explodes before the transfigured parental phallus. Some years later, addressing himself specifically to the art of poetry, Bécquer described his imagination as an overflow of moral activity that without an object to expend itself upon creates "ensueños y fantasías en los cuales buscaba en vano la expansión. . ." (Cartas literarias a una mujer, p. 632). He then expands on this idea by comparing the poet to a sealed jar filled with liquid over a flame. The steam eventually causes the jar to explode. "Este es el secreto," he adds, "de la muerte prematura y misteriosa de algunas mujeres y de algunos poetas. . ." (p. 632). Juxtaposing the image from "El caudillo. . ." to the one from the "Cartas literarias. . ." may appear perverse but is not beside the point, as we will observe presently.

For the moment, the "forbidden" place can now be formulated with concision. My reading of "El caudillo. . ." shows that these places are junctures in the text where the narrative telescopes significant events within the boundaries of a particular scene. This scene is articulated as a literally delimited space. On this stage the protagonists enact the drama of desire. The resolution of the drama consists of the defeat of the subject. This victimization is itself the metaphor of a desire which turns out to be something other than what would have been expected. The metaphor allows the subject to play an integral role in the "forbidden place," a place which in essence is the place of the Father. There the subject's victimization serves as a sign that actualizes his desire, indicating at the same time that the desire has been requited.

This structure is not unique to "El caudillo. . ." It is central to all of Bécquer's mature productions.[7] To be sure, there are variations in apparent theme and outcome. What is invariably consistent is that the woman, so prominently alluded to, is ultimately expelled from the intimate center of Bécquer's scene of writing. The woman is never a fully distinct "other" upon whom the subject's desires come to fruition. In the drama articulated in the place of the Father, she is either done away with or identified with, becoming the subject's double. In short, she either disappears or becomes a man. All of the essential features of this situation are present even in the earliest of Bécquer's writings. One example is of particular interest. In that case the protagonist is Bécquer himself. I am referring to a diary written over a period of four days in February of 1852 when the poet was seventeen. The notebook in which the entries appeared had at one time belonged to Bécquer's father, who had died eleven years before. In that notebook his father, who was an artist, had kept the records of the sales of his paintings. Bécquer and his brother Valeriano, who was to continue their father's profession, used the notebook to draw and jot down verse.[8] The diary itself is devoted entirely to a chance encounter on the streets of Seville and its consequences. On February 23 Bécquer writes that he had seen a young woman whom he had been courting the previous summer. As we find out immediately, the poet never actually saw *her*: "Yo al pronto no la conocí...a tiempo de pasar junto a ella, cerré los ojos por motivo del polvo y el aire que aquel día combatía con mucha fuerza y cuando los abrí estaba perfectamente delante de su padre, *al cual reconocí*..." (p. 639). The woman, then, is recognized by means of her father. Indeed, the only glimpse Bécquer catches of his putative beloved is tenuous: "Volví la cara para verla, y ya no le ví la cara, porque iba de espaldas, lejos, y confundida entre la multitud" (p. 640). By the end of the day Bécquer is lamenting that he cannot get the girl out of his mind: "A mi ya casi olvidado amor bastó su vista, una nueva mirada, para hacerlo resucitar con más fuerza" (p. 640). The two entries that follow relate Bécquer's fruitless wanderings in the vicinity of the house where his girlfriend lives. The house is shuttered and there is no sign that anyone lives there. Then on the evening of the twenty-sixth the poet notices a movement at a window. A curtain is raised "como si alguna persona estuviera mirando" (p. 641). However, since it is dark the poet cannot distinguish the identity of the figure at the window. He continues his vigil and shortly the curtain is lowered. This does not discourage him and he stubbornly maintains his watch. Soon the curtain rises again, is drawn again, and the poet hears what he takes to be the sound of closing shutters. He finally leaves, mulling over the identity of the figure at the window. Was it the girl? Was it the father? In the closing sentence of this entry Bécquer expresses the intention of returning to that spot on the following day: "En fin, volveremos mañana; levantaremos otro pliegue a la misteriosa cortina que encubre este asunto" (p. 641). The curtain was not to be raised the next day; the entry of the twenty-seventh is blank. However, in the years to come the curtain would be lifted periodically. Literally, in "El caudillo..." when Pulo draws the curtain to the room where he is to discover the true nature of his quest, he realizes at last what fate has in store for him.

The blank entry of the twenty-seventh is, then, the scene of writing: the page to be filled. Here it is particularly significant because it is literally the place of the father; the space where the dead father inserted the signifiers of his productivity: the commissions accrued for his art. According to Freud the male subject is faced with two apparently contradictory injunctions: 1) You shall be like your father; 2) You shall not do what your father does.[9] The first can only be accomplished provided the second is observed by the breaking of the oedipal circuit. If that is accomplished the first can proceed uneventfully. The examples we have been examining compel the observation that the second injunction remains tied to oedipal constructions. Consequently, like an anchor, it limits the movement of the imagination obliging it to cover the same ground over and over. The father is perennially the rival and obstacle. But the desire to be like him bespeaks admiration, and if the subject wishes to partake of his power, finding his replacement impossible, he must accede to him in a passive position. He thus allows himself to generate, to produce, much as a woman gives birth to a child. When Bécquer sets out to mark the scene of writing with his pen he enters a locale fraught with background. But if he enters the scene of writing as a rival, the mark left there reduplicates another scene. The message delivered by this communication, this accumulation of marks, betrays, as we have observed, that the initial act of rivalry, of penetration, is but the first step of a seduction that will see the tables turned.

We might remember that in "El caudillo. . ." the initial incursion into hostile territory resulted in a fratricide. In the notebook where Bécquer wrote the four entries of his diary, there was also another surrogate presence— Bécquer's brother, Valeriano. Indeed Valeriano, as Bécquer himself would indirectly acknowledge eighteen years later, would appropriate the role of the father. Both Gustavo and Valeriano had originally wanted to be painters like their father. It was Valeriano, however, who became a painter. Gustavo, although apprenticed to his uncle's studio, soon found out that his talents were not sufficient for that profession. Years later Valeriano had a hand in provoking Gustavo's separation from his wife. After this they often shared a household until Valeriano's death. When Valeriano died in 1870 Gustavo wrote a short "semblanza" in memory of his brother. In that short essay the curtain was once again raised. The first thing Bécquer remarks upon are life and death: "nuestro padre era pintor, y murió siendo nosotros muy pequeños, también a los treinta y cinco años" (p. 1211). Then, almost inconspicuously, amidst the obligatory biographical data he introduces a childhood memory: "Es una puerilidad, pero yo recuerdo que siendo muy chico nos quitaban la luz después de acostados, y Valeriano, las noches de luna, abría el balcón y dibujaba a aquella claridad dudosa" (p. 1211). In a sense, this screen memory recuperates the prototype of the locus of desire and its structure. It is a place with three figures: subject, wish, and obstacle. The wish of course is the acquisition of instrumentality in the activity practiced by the obstacle. The wish, invariably frustrated on a primary level, gave rise to a resentment against the obstacle which through its by-product, guilt, enabled the creation of a metaphorical scene where the subject could participate in generation. This involved, as we have seen, a number of significant reversals, but for Bécquer instrumentality in the manner of the paternal figure was not possible. In his art this impossibility becomes the root of the basic structure which generates the process and content of his poetry, reflecting, to modify Coleridge's phrase on imagination, "on its own reflections." As Bécquer himself tells us on one occasion: "Yo no sé porque los poetas y las mujeres no se entienden mejor entre sí. Su manera de sentir tiene tantos puntos de contacto . . ." (*Cartas literarias*. . . I, p. 620). Some years later describing his work as the children of his dreams he gives us a glimpse of his mind's sanctuary where his muse "fecunda como el lecho de amor de la miseria. . .concibe y pare. . ." ("Introducción Sinfónica," p. 39).

Recalling the screen memory of Valeriano in this light, the description of habits by his friend F. Moreno Godino is suggestive:

> La postura horizontal era en él una enunciación, y siempre la adoptaba cuando estaba solo y no escribía o dibujaba. Gustábale la luz tenue filtrándose entre persianas o cortinas, porque la penumbra de la muerte debilitaba ya sus ojos, que no podían soportar grandes claridades.

Valeriano's death, which drew out of Bécquer's memory the scene described in the *semblanza*, a scene fraught with ambivalence and anxiety, figuratively constituted one such burst of clarity. At this point the present met the past in a particularly jarring way. The loss of this central referent and support of Bécquer's fictional world overcharged his weakened mental circuits, circuits which he once significantly compared to swollen veins in need of draining ("Introducción Sinfónica," p. 40). To him Valeriano's death was like a lance poised on an abcess. Three months later Bécquer himself died, a death which was due, in part at least, to the hand of "the great parental power of fate." The same "hand" described in the passage from "El caudillo. . ." already quoted, where it is described as an amalgamation of love and guilt whose killing blows work unseen; the same hand, no doubt, which is also unseen is responsible for snapping the strings of the harp, an image which Bécquer used to compare the "muertes prematuras" of women to those of poets.

STATE UNIVERSITY OF NEW YORK
AT PURCHASE

Notes

[1]"Rima LXXIV" in *Obras Completas* (Madrid: Aguilar, 1969), p. 453. Edition referred to hereafter in the text by page number in parenthesis after quote.

[2]The incest prohibition enforced by the threat of "castration." Cf. "The symbolic value of castration—in which the agent is the symbolic father who incorporates the law: the interdiction of incest—is in fact that of breaking this incestuous circuit, thus opening up object choices outside of it." A. Wilden, *The Language of the Self* (Baltimore: Johns Hopkins Press, 1968), p. 188.

[3]See S. Freud, "The Economic Problem in Masochism" in *General Psychological Theory*, P. Rieff ed. (New York: Collier, 1963), pp. 190-201.

⁴Ibid., p. 200.

⁵Ibid., p. 199.

⁶Ibid., p. 200.

⁷As demonstrated in my study *The Dialectic of Desire in Gustavo Adolfo Bécquer.* *DAI* 36: 5337A-38A.

⁸See Dámaso Alonso, *Del Siglo de Oro a este siglo de siglas* (Madrid: Gredos, 1962), pp. 107 ff.

⁹S. Freud, *The Ego and the Id* (New York: Norton, 1962), p. 24.

¹⁰Quoted by Rica Brown in *Bécquer* (Barcelona: Aedos, 1963), p. 368.

RITES WITHOUT PASSAGE:
THE ADOLESCENT WORLD OF
ANA MARIA MOIX'S *JULIA*

Sara E. Schyfter

Leslie Fiedler has noted in *Love and Death in the American Novel* that one of the most interesting developments in contemporary literature is the frequency and importance of youth as a symbol of innocence and instrument of true insight.[1] This myth of adolescence, established in Western culture since Rousseau introduced his Romantic notion of Original Innocence, has has a long and fruitful history. In British and American letters, for example, the works of Mark Twain, Samuel Butler, Somerset Maugham, D. H. Lawrence, James Joyce, D. H. Salinger, and F. Scott Fitzgerald attest to the recurrence and significance of this theme.[2] In Spanish literature, however, relatively few novels of adolescence have appeared, and those that have were written within the last thirty years. Why has the adolescent, as subject and symbol, not attracted the imagination of Spanish novelists until so recently? Furthermore, why is it that so many of the adolescent heroes of contemporary Hispanic letters have women writers as their creators? Several possible explanations may be found for this phenomenon, but perhaps the fundamental reason resides in the fact that the adolescent is a symbol of modern man and woman in a period of doubt and confusion. Thus, the more traditional Hispanic culture was not ready, until very recently, to adopt the adolescent as its prototype and as a voice for the confusion of our age. Though the Spanish adolescent novel can find its origins in the *Lazarillo de Tormes* and Valera's *Pepita Jiménez*,[3] the contemporary image of the Spanish adolescent essentially comes into being in the works of Carmen Laforet, Dolores Medio, Ana María Matute, and Teresa Barbero and reaches a unique treatment in *Julia*, a recent and fascinating novel by Ana María Moix [4]

It was not by accident that the first significant novel written by a woman after the Spanish Civil War should have been *Nada* (1944) by Carmen Laforet. This novel represents the birth of the adolescent female character as a prominent literary archetype, a symbol of a generation of women seeking to define for themselves a place in the war-torn, tradition-obsessed Spain. The search for identity that is typified by the adolescent in American and European literature is doubly intensified when that character is born female and Spanish. As female and adolescent her role is that of a stranger and an outsider, a figure of vitality and determination projected against a society that demands passivity and subservience from its members, particularly its women. The adolescent, however, represents that new generation of women who, rebellious, alone, and frightened, can receive neither guidance nor courage from their mothers or grandmothers. The fathers, either absent or dead, are missing from the world of these young women, and are unable to offer them any assistance; while their brothers, though present, serve no meaningful role. Thus, the young female adolescent is cast in a world devoid of adult models.

In *Nada* the female protagonist is essentially triumphant for she leaves the nightmarish world of her family for the possibility of a new beginning in Madrid. Likewise, in *Nosotros los Rivero* (1953) by Dolores Medio the young woman has overcome the limitations of a restricting and difficult childhood and returns to her hometown a famous writer. The heroine of this novel, however, has not been completely successful in her search for identity. The novel ends ambiguously in that the secret "leyenda" of the Rivero family, an artistic and unorthodox clan, is still basically unresolved. The optimism evidenced in these two novels will no longer be shared by the characters of Ana María Matute, particularly in her trilogy *Los mercaderes* (1959-1969). Here the adolescent is trapped and alienated in a world that is dominated by either the corruption of the adults, symbolized in *Primera memoria* and *La trampa* by the grandmother, representative of the established order of the Church and the upper classes, or by the violence of a war-obsessed society as in *Los soldados lloran de noche*. In the latter novel, the characters search for meaning in one final and reckless commitment to an idealistic cause, a commitment that proves fatal to them. In *La trampa*, the last novel of the *Mercaderes* trilogy, the search for purposefulness is also fraught with frustration. Matia, the heroine of *Primera memoria*, is now a grown woman who turns towards her son's best friend for sexual and psychological companionship, an unnatural incestuous resolution to an empty life. Thus, the trajectory of the female adolescent in search of identity serves only to intensify her pessimism and alienation.

Another interesting novel dealing with the adolescent female is *El último verano en el espejo* (1967) by Teresa Barbero whose heroine relives her adolescence as she awaits the birth of an unwanted child. In this novel, Marta is totally estranged from herself and her husband. Trapped in a no-longer-fulfilling marriage, she is unable to break with her past and begin life again with Pablo, the husband of Elena, of whom she is enamoured. As she reflects on her childhood memories Marta remembers her loves, including an erotic incident with one of her girlfriends. In addition, she is told that Elena, her lifelong friend, has always loved her. The revelation of a homosexual feeling on the part of Elena is traumatic and frightening to the heroine, who then decides to stay with her husband. At the end, Marta, whose child died two days after birth, is pregnant again. No possibility of fulfillment, either sexually or emotionally, seems now open to her.

This pessimistic perception of woman's entrapment and alienation is dramatically explored by Ana María Moix in *Julia*, where the adolescent turns from heterosexuality and activity to an essentially lesbian and passive relationship in a desperate attempt at human contact. *Julia* is the portrait of a young girl's love for her mother, of her feelings of rejection by that mother and of her latent homosexual love towards Eva, her teacher. The extraordinary innovation of the novel is that it dares to touch on the theme of the homosexual female, a theme that has generally been avoided in literature until very recently, particularly in Spain where such topics have until now scarcely been broached.

Any interpretation of *Julia* can be greatly aided by contemporary theories on the nature of the psychosexual development that leads to a lesbian orientation in the female child. Charlotte Wolff in her authoritative book, *Love Between Women*,[5] states that emotional incest with the mother is the very essence of lesbianism, for the mother-daughter relationship is that area that can create the greatest conflict for the growing girl. Because the mother is the girl's first and most important love, any form of rejection by that mother assumes traumatic dimensions in the world of the girl-child. Thus, while the father may perhaps be the girl's first flirtation, he can only be her secondary love. Mothers are believed to prefer their male children, both because of some biological magnetism that attracts them to the male, as well as because of the greater admiration that the boy enjoys in the man-made opportunity of being her mother's first love is lost to her brother or her father. When the little girl realizes that the male is the winner and that she is relegated to second place in her mother's affections, feelings of deep nostalgia and frustration are aroused within her which serve to further increase the desire of the girl for the mother. These feelings produce intense distress and often invoke rebellion. It is a tragic twist of fate that in childhood when the girl most needs her mother's love, she feels that she is rejected and abandoned by her. Thus, the girl's psychosexual destiny begins with doubts and uncertainty. The effect of this insecurity forces her to ingratiate herself with her mother. Sometimes she tries to be a very good and clever girl. Often, however, she attempts to identify with the male and do things that the mother admires, becoming what is generally labeled a tomboy. At other times, the girl imitates her mother, long before she is ready to, and tries to undermine the mother's position by playing an exaggerated feminine role. The girl who opts for the latter resolution rarely becomes a lesbian. These children perpetuate the traditional feminine values not only as a means of escape from their insecurity but also in order to gain the admiration of their father or any other male. The child who feels that she is put second by the mother is not only insecure but lonely. This loneliness creates the need to recapture the lost paradise of the past, forcing the young girl to turn to other women in her search for the unattained union with the mother.

The emotional development that Ana María Moix describes in her novel is precisely that of a child rejected by the mother who prefers her male children to the clingy and unhappy little girl who follows her, whimpering and crying for attention. It is the story of Julia's search for a substitute mother and of a traumatic sexual violation at the hands of her brother's friend.

The novel begins with Julia, now a twenty-seven-year-old girl, unable to sleep and having the same nightmares that she had as a child of five. She awakens, terrified by gigantic monsters who have destroyed everything in their path and have now invaded her room. Julia is unable to push these figures away. In desperation she screams for Eva, her teacher, in the same manner as she had screamed for her mother during her childhood. Julia knows, however, that Eva is too far away to hear and that she cannot come to comfort her. Nevertheless, she fantasizes that Eva will come and that she is able to hug her and hide her head in the security of her embrace. At the same time Julia knows that she is too old to be tormented by such fears, too old to need Eva and that, indeed, it is high time for her to habituate herself "a vivir sin pensar en nadie, sin esperar a nadie, sin necesitar a nadie" (p. 13). The transition from childhood to adulthood which Julia must of necessity undergo seems, therefore, from the very start to be a transition from one state of loneliness into a more intense state of loneliness in which all hope for communion with another human being must be given up. Adulthood is an intensification of the torments of the child's threatened and confusing world.

The rejection of Julia by her mother is depicted most dramatically and represents the fundamental theme of the novel. Julia remembers her mother speaking to her and yet looking at herself in the mirror, or getting bored and calling a friend on the telephone. Often the mother sends the child away with Aurelia, the maid, for she cannot long bear the insistent demands for attention and love from her daughter. It is obvious that the mother prefers the two male children, Ernesto and Rafael. Julia remembers that she felt intense jealousy and hatred toward her male siblings and that she was frightened by her feelings, particularly since Rafael, her favorite brother, subsequently dies. Often she asked herself if Rafael "murió precisamente a causa de ese odio" (p. 16).

Julia's father also plays a significant role in the emotional development of Julia. He is seen as a weak and indecisive man rejected by the mother and controlled by the grandmother's wealth. The humiliation that he experiences in the household is intensified when he finds out that his wife is unfaithful to him. He then leaves the home for a period of nine years. In spite of his ineffectuality, he had attempted to become involved with the children (when Julia was a small child), particularly in their artistic endeavors, such as their paintings. He had indeed tried to develop some kind of creative sensibility within them and often read them poetry. Julia, however, was basically indifferent to her father. She had neither the time nor the love to give him. Her whole life was taken up with the absence of her mother. When the father leaves, Julia is able to establish a deeper relationship with him. This relationship, however, is marred by the inconsistency of her father's attentions and visits. After a prolonged absence, the father is forced to return to the mother's home because of financial problems. He begins to work in the grandmother's business establishment once more and thereafter he is a completely defeated human being. He is usually seen reading the newspaper, sleeping, or watching television. His only wish now is to be left alone: "Déjenme en paz, no quiero preocupaciones" (p. 33). Julia's feelings on the return of her father are described as follows:

> Tuvo que reprimirse para no echarse a llorar. Para no insultarle, y escupirle a la cara, para no reprocharle en su enorme debilidad su cobardía, su pobreza de espíritu y la falta de amor hacia ella. La había desahuciado (p. 36).

The father's return is seen by the young girl as a final triumph for the grandmother, the mother, and Ernesto, her only surviving brother. For Julia, it represents the end of a secret fantasied pact with her father, the realization that the belief in such a union had only been a dream: "la alianza con papá nunca existió" (p. 36). The father's return is one more step toward disillusionment and maturity on that journey toward adulthood that demands a continuous disengagement from others.

Throughout her life Julia is plagued by a sense of betrayal, aloneness and rejection. One significant episode that marks the psychosexual development of Julia and her emotional estrangement is the violation that she undergoes at the age of five on the beach near her summer home. The incident is told in very broad outlines. The actual sexual behavior of the assaulting young boy is not described. What remains indelibly marked on the young girl's memory is the complete sense of helplessness to which she was reduced by the violence of the assault. The incident is, of course, never confessed to anyone. It remains repressed in the young girl's psyche only to emerge at the end of the novel as the arresting trauma forever imprinted in Julia, the woman. A sense of aversion and fear is thus always associated with any kind of physical or emotional contact with a male. Even Andrés, the young professor who obviously loves Julia and who attempts to communicate a sense of concern and affection towards her, elicits her annoyance and boredom. It is only Eva who can offer the excitement and the intensity of emotion that Julia seeks.

In an attempt to describe or understand the great sense of emptiness and confusion that Julia experiences as a young woman, she sees her psyche divided into the Julita of her childhood and the Julia of the present. Of the two, it is Julita whose unfading presence continuously remains, forcing the grown Julia to remember the disconnected and painful images of her childhood. Thus, it is Julita who drives Julia back to that "Mundo inalterable e inmóvil, sin tiempo" (p. 63) in which her childhood was lived. From that world Julita rules the twenty-year-old woman, becoming "un dios martirizador para Julia, un dios que reclamaba continuos sacrificios para calmar su antiguo dolor" (p. 63). The pain that dominates Julia is the guilt instilled in her by the little Julita, that savage demigod, who demands atonement and suicide as the price for having violated society's taboos and having wanted to kill the mother, the father, and the two brothers.[6] In her anger and confusion, the child seeks to destroy the adult. Julia thus becomes the victim not only of a fundamental rejection, but also of a self-destructive guilt that frustrates any attempt at creative self-fulfillment. In this, Julia is a symbol of contemporary woman searching for liberation from her past and yet imprisoned within it by guilt and despair. The novel, thus, is more than a clinical study of a young girl's psychosexual development. It is a parable for the anguish of a generation confronted by the normless and meaningless isolation of a post-Civil-War Spain, a society in which everyone, particularly the young adolescent woman, experiences a deep sense of disorientation, confusion, and fear.

During part of the period that her father had absented himself from the home, Julia had been sent to the grandfather's estate. There she is taught as if she were a boy. She is expected, by the grandfather, to be a liberated intelligent woman. She is taught Latin, she is challenged intellectually, and most importantly, she is seen as someone with the potential to be free. This grandfather, however, was the dying hope of a liberation that did not come. He represents the liberals that were defeated by the traditional regime. Thus, when the grandfather dies and Julia must forever remain with her mother and her grandmother, all hope of that lifestyle is gone. Her return to her home is traumatic, because the faculties that her grandfather had nurtured in her are now rejected and criticized. She is to become a lady, less forceful, less cutting and critical; she no longer fits the traditional role assigned to the female. Her mother tries to encourage her to dress and take care of her appearance: "Una chica debe ser coqueta y presumida, de lo contrario parece un hombre" (p. 145); while her grandmother, more upset that she is no longer a believer, comments, "Una mujer que no va a misa y no reza, no es una mujer decente, y eso, naturalmente, se nota en la apariencia" (p. 161). Julia's struggle against these values estranges her from her family and her peers. Only Ernesto, when Julia is already a university student, offers her some sort of support. He, however, is too guilt-ridden by his inadequacy as an artist and by his homosexual affairs to be strong and affirmative. His weakness, cowardice, and total dependence on the family, particularly the mother, make him ineffectual and servile. After the death of Rafael, the only truly sensitive member of the family, the family is left with very few possibilities for the future. Neither Julia nor Ernesto are destined for self-fulfilling lives.

After her return from her grandfather's estate, Julia is academically and intellectually ahead of her classmates. Though this gives her an edge over the other students, she is isolated and alienated from her companions because of it. Those who befriend her exploit her knowledge while they reject her. A close friendship with the director of the school serves as an additional factor in estranging Julia from her fellow students. She is victimized by her peers, who, jealous of her favorite position with "la señorita Mabel," hide her books and her homework and accuse her of the mischief that they themselves commit. The director of the school tries to protect Julia by allowing her to help in the office during her recess. One girl, Lydia, however, does not desist from tyrannizing and manipulating Julia, forcing her to do the homework for her. She and her friends plant an obscene piece of paper on the priest's desk and Julia is the one who is accused. In desperation Julia flees to the office where the señorita Mabel embraces her and tries to comfort her. Lydia is watching from behind and Julia knows that this moment of communion will be dearly paid for

...Lydia espiaba a través de la puerta entreabierta y sonreía burlonamente para luego desaparecer. El miedo se apoderó de Julia, presintió una extraña y misteriosa venganza. Alguien intentaba quitarle algo que ni siquiera había llegado a poseer, algo que sólo había deseado (pp. 172-73).

Julia then leaves this school to attend the same school as her brothers.

Julia's independence, intelligence, and strength become almost an overwhelming cross of loneliness that she must bear. As a university student, older now, and less intensely in need of her mother, she nevertheless feels alone, isolated, with a deep sense of self-estrangement. As such she becomes a voice not only for the female adolescent in a society that is changing and whose norms have collapsed, but also for the female who must attempt to establish some sort of meaningful identity for herself in that culture. It is not surprising that she sees in Eva, her literature teacher, a model that she would like to emulate. Eva had been her father's first love, but he had chosen to marry instead the wealthy woman that is now Julia's mother. Because of this tragic choice, the lives of Julia and her father are essentially destroyed, both enclosed in an arid wasteland that parallels Spain's own political destiny. Eva is for Julia, as she could have been for Julia's father, the symbol of intelligence, action, liberation, and aliveness. Julia achieves an identity and a sense of uniqueness as she becomes Eva's research assistant, and within this relationship her life finally receives some meaning. Julia experiences her days with Eva as the most peaceful period of her life. Indeed, it is during the afternoons in Eva's study that Julia is able to recover in part the lost paradise of her youth. In Eva's presence Julia finds herself alive, "se sentía existir" (p. 204), and feels that finally someone notices her presence. Eva also obligates Julia to think, to form her own opinions, to engage herself in the creating and ordering of her existence

Hasta entonces, vivir significaba permanecer aislada de los demás, al margen, en otro mundo. Elaborar pensamientos, opiniones, resultaba absurdo. Habitaba en sí misma, y allí nadie le preguntaba nada (p. 205).

Through Eva, Julia receives a new birth, a new dimension, a new existence. The enchanted interlude in Eva's presence, a suspended space between childhood and adulthood is imbued with the pathos of a short-lived love affair. It represents Julia's attempt to finally achieve the denied union with her mother. When the relationship with Eva is discovered by the mother and destroyed by her, Julia feels that she has been permanently exiled from her Garden of Eden. Eva's name, therefore, is completely appropriate in the context of the mythic structure, the search for a lost paradise, that underlies the novel. In her Fall and in her expulsion from Eden, Julia reexperiences man's primal alienation. Her reaction, however, is to seek vengeance against those who have exiled her, against those who have made her incompetent to assert herself positively and constructively:

Se vengaría, necesitaba hacerles sufrir. Odiaba a Mamá, a la abuela Lucía, a Papá, a Ernesto, a Eva, y se odiaba a sí misma por no tener valor para. ..abofetearlos a todos, decirles: haré lo que me dé la gana. ..Corría desesperada hacia un muro insalvable que retrocedía a medida que ella avanzaba. Nunca lograría derribarlo, ni correr hacia otra dirección (pp. 212-13).

Unable to confront her family and express her hostility, Julia internalizes her anger and takes an overdose of sleeping pills, her only possible act of revenge against them and herself.

After taking the overdose of sleeping pills, Julia no longer fears the dark or the strange monsters that accost her in her nightmares. Neither does she fear solitude for she has come to terms with it. When she awakens in the hospital, "un resplandor insultante" (p. 218) of daylight greets her as she returns to consciousness. Julia has reached enlightenment. She has moved from the initial nightmare of the novel to the revelation of the Fall. Her rebellion, as in man's primordial defiance in Genesis, is recorded in the front page of the newspapers. Her grandmother accuses her of committing what, in effect, is Original Sin: "Qué desvergüenza, has cometido el pecado más grave contra Dios, te has condenado para siempre" (p. 214). Julia is herein initiated into the condition of mankind. The mother gives her the autonomy she sought, but it is now couched as another rejection: "De ahora en adelante puedes hacer cuanto te dé la gana, dijo Mamá. Pero si te metes en algún lío o tienes problemas no cuentes con nosotros" (p. 214). Julia's coming of age links her to the existential alienation of modern man and woman. She has been exiled from her family, and her past, and left in the social and spiritual desolation of contemporary Spanish society.

When Julia reawakens, her mother, now less hostile, reminds her daughter of her past love: "Julita de pequeña me querías, sólo deseabas estar conmigo, me seguías a todas partes como un perrito y cuando te dejaba esperabas mi regreso en el balcón" (p. 215). Julia wishes that she could return to her mother, to be again that "perrito faldero" that followed her everywhere. It is now too late for such sentiments and Julia, falling asleep again, remains silent. Thus, the possibility of communion with the mother is now lost forever; as is also lost the desire to struggle and reaffirm life outside the home: "podían transcurrir horas, meses, años a partir de aquel momento sin que ella se rebelara. Ni siquiera notaría el paso del tiempo. Algo, esencial en ella, había huido" (p. 215). Julia's feeling of emptiness represents the rite of passage into adulthood, where only the consciousness of defeat and alienation exist: "la habían desterrado a un lugar sin nombre, desconocido, fuera del tiempo y del espacio de los demás" (p. 216); at the same time her life has catapulted back to its beginnings. The little Julita of long ago, with her shorts and middy blouse, is the Ego that now emerges to confront and destroy her: "Había permanecido allí desde siempre, agazapada en los misteriosos rincones de su ser, en las ignoradas sombras de su mente, aguardando el momento oportuno de asaltarla para vencerla" (p. 216).

Thus, the self that had been so long denied arises triumphant at the end, seeking its revenge. The suicide attempt had been an effort to destroy the past, the painful memories of rejection, guilt, and violation that had been buried and forgotten. Julita, however, will no longer allow Julia to neglect her. The possibility of establishing any meaningful relationship of maturity and integration with the world outside is to be denied to Julia.[7] Julita will forever demand the attention of the adult. Escape into a positive and relevant universe is futile:

> Sólo deseaba dormir, dormir diez, doce, cuantas horas le fuera posible. Todos sus días eran iguales, monótonos. El mundo que la rodeaba un espacio irreal en donde los demás parecían vivir una existencia por completo diferente a la suya (p. 219).

Thanatos is victorious, sleep, death and passivity now rule.

The Julita that is triumphant at the end is the Double or *Doppelganger*, who represents the self that has been left behind, overlooked and unrealized. It is the self that must be come to terms with and that can never be taken for granted. It is the self that appears when the first self is in a state of great vulnerability. Often the two selves can only exist for each other. In the vast majority of cases the second self helps to strip away all the masks of self-deception and compels the Ego towards self-awareness and self-fulfillment. It is this second self that the child Julita embodies. In Ana María Moix's novel the resolution of the long quest for acceptance of the second self ends in failure. Having become acquainted with the strange projection of her emotional structure, Julia does not achieve an expanded vision of who or what she is. In knowing the other, Julia has become a victim rather than a beneficiary of the hidden insight that her unknown self could offer. If the other is also the I, as in this particular story, then the I in *Julia* is overwhelmed and engulfed by the other.[9]

The primary purpose of a *Bildungsroman* is to trace the development and the integration of the personality. *Julia* represents the modern female adolescent who fails to achieve an integrated sense of identity and who thus becomes a symbol of her culture and her generation. The adult is subordinated to the child, the forces of creative self-fulfillment are not unleashed and death triumphs over life. Such are the rites, rites without passage, of the female adolescent.

STATE UNIVERSITY OF NEW YORK AT ALBANY

Notes

[1]Leslie A. Fiedler, *Love and Death in the American Novel* (New York: Stein and Day, 1975), pp. 23-38.

[2]See W. Tasker Witham, *The Adolescent in the American Novel* (New York: 1964), for a comprehensive treatment of the adolescent in American letters between the years 1920 and 1960.

³For a study of Luis Vargas as adolescent hero see Robert Lott, *Language and Psychology in Pepita Jiménez* (Urbana: 1970).

⁴The novel, published in 1970 by Seix Barral in Barcelona, is now already in its second edition due to its immense popularity among the young people in Spain. The edition used in the present study is the second edition dated 1972. All citations from the text are taken from this edition.

⁵Charlotte Wolff, *Love Between Women* (New York: 1971).

⁶Alvarez, in *The Savage God* (New York: 1973), speaks of suicide as a result of a melancholia that is produced when guilt and hostility are too much to bear for the sufferer: "It is as though the melancholic believed that whatever was lost, by death or separation or rejection, had somehow been murdered by him. It therefore returns as an internal persecutor, punishing, seeking revenge, and expiation" (p. 101). In speaking of Sylvia Plath's death, Alvarez comments that, for her, suicide was also "an initiation act qualifying her for a *life* of her own. . . .for her, death was a debt to be met once every decade: in order to stay alive as a grown woman, a mother, and a poet, she had to pay—in some partial magical way—with her life" (p. 18). Suicide can, thus, be an initiation rite into selfhood, an act to be explored not only as rebellion and anger, but as a struggle towards freedom—the freedom to die—in a life that has been only long series of failures. It is significant to observe, however, that women *attempt* to kill themselves physically, and fail, far more often than men do. Phyllis Chesler, in *Women and Madness* (New York: 1973), explains this phenomenon: "Female suicide attempts are not so much realistic 'calls for help' or hostile inconveniencing of others as they are the assigned baring of the powerless throat, signals of ritual readiness for self-sacrifice. Like female tears, female suicide attempts constitute an essential act or resignation and helplessness" (p. 68).

⁷Eric H. Erikson, in *Childhood and Society* (New York: 1950), states that maturity begins when identity has been established and an integrated, independent individual has emerged who can stand on his own feet. Thus, self-sufficiency begins when the adolescent no longer continuously questions his own identity. However, when the Ego fails to integrate itself into a socially accepted form of Ego identity, neurosis results

. . .whenever integrity yields to despair and disgust, wherever generativity yields to stagnation, intimacy to isolation and identity to diffusion, an array of associated infantile fears are apt to become mobilized: For the superego is the internalization of the external inequality of parent and child; and only an ego identity safely anchored in the 'patrimony' of a cultural identity can balance the superego in order to produce a workable equilibrium" (pp. 367-68).

Julia obviously has not achieved the integration described by Erikson and exhibits many of the neurotic symptoms associated with such a lack.

⁸See C. F. Keppler, *The Literature of the Second Self* (Tucson: 1972), for a brilliant study of the double in literature.

⁹Rolf. E. Muuss, in *Theories of Adolescence* (New York: 1967), discusses Edward Spranger's theory of adolescence and maturity in *Psychologie des Jugendalters* (1955). According to Muuss, "Spranger suggests as a criterion for the achievement of maturity a relative degree of stability, harmony, self-acceptance and ego unity. One interesting characteristic of adolescence (adolescents have this characteristic in common with delinquents and schizophrenics, though to a milder degree) is that it has many egos which are in a constant fight for supremacy; the unification of the several fighting egos into a single stable psychic structure is considered the attainment of maturity" (p. 50). Julia's engulfment by the Julita ego represents her failure to achieve the stable psychic structure of maturity.

III. Feminism

WOMEN AND LOVE:
SOME DYING MYTHS

Elaine Hoffman Baruch

"Love is disappearing. . . .Only some stupid fools will still make it the chief theme of the world. Romeo and Juliet bore me prodigiously. We have at last learned now to make the sauce without those deplorable fish."[1] Verlaine was here speaking about poets. But what he said holds true in some measure for the rest of us as well. Romantic love is dying. And with it is dying the typology of women that nourished it.

From ancient times, dual and polar conceptions of women have fed the literary and cultural imagination (not always a romantic one, to be sure). They have been those of goddess and witch, virgin and whore, wife and mistress, all of them often having a paradigmatic and even mythical significance. But as Lionel Trilling recognized in his essay "The Fate of Pleasure," Joyce's Molly and Yeats' Maude are perhaps the last women in literature to carry mythical meaning.[2] This is a cultural change of profound significance whose consequences we have yet to realize.

Yeats both lived and wrote without resolving the sexual dualisms. In many of his major poems, he expressed an antithesis between beauty, passion, and the dream at one pole, and domestic serenity and order at the other. Maude Gonne, the beautiful Irish revolutionary, was linked in his mind with his love for Ireland, nature, and the great myths of the past, namely those of ancient Greece. But of Georgie Hyde-Lees, he wrote, "My wife is a perfect wife, kind, wise, and unselfish. . . .She has made my life serene and full of order."[3] Like some of the turbulent romantics of the nineteenth century, Yeats ultimately sought peace, not passion, in women, at least in marriage. But the Maudes of the world do not emigrate easily from the imagination. They settle in, however uncomfortable they may make the other tenants. It is the thought of Maude's Ledean body that drives the poet's heart wild, even in old age.

Joyce, the other great Irish writer of the century, also saw women in mythical terms. But Molly represents not so much one side of a duality as a paradoxical unity, embodying the antithetical mythical archetypes: virgin, whore, and wife.

Whether collective or essential, Molly as a voice of nature seems one of those residues of racial experience that haunts the darkness of our minds to emerge in dream or literature with hints of all but unspeakable significance.[4]

So wrote a male critic, W. Y. Tindall. I'm not sure, however, that women would view her in quite this way nowadays. And whatever one may think of it, feminism has taught us all to be interested in the feminine character rather than in the imaginative male response alone. From this point of view, one might question whether it is truly a woman's consciousness that comes through in that final affirmative soliloquy with its rush of flowers and sexual generosity. Despite the enormous power of Molly's characterization, one feels that Joyce's treatment of women and sex is sometimes infantile. As one of his critics and countrymen, Darch O'Brien, put it, "Irishmen continue to have it in for women, even when they have it out for them."

Nonetheless, Joyce as well as Yeats could still think of women as leading one upwards and onwards, as well as downwards and backwards. Such power is no longer granted them.

Eliot also reworks the ancient myths. However, he does so only in ironic counterpoint to the present, which is so impoverished, it cannot sustain them. In "The Love Song of J. Alfred Prufrock," mermaids and sirens no longer sing to men, but "each to each." I do not think that Eliot would like being the bedfellow of certain contemporary women poets, such as Anne Sexton and Margaret Atwood, but the fact is that they reinterpret the myths in similar ways. In all three, mythical figures no longer reach out to men as they once did but rather have an autonomous existence. However, the meaning of this transformation is quite different in Eliot and the women writers. Feminist poets want to destroy the traditional myths as shapers of consciousness, for they feel that it is a false consciousness that has been created, one that reifies women and deprives them of humanity. For these writers, civilization has always been a matter of discontents. Eliot is also discontented with modern civilation, not because it is like the past, however, but rather because it is unlike it. For him, traditional culture had a positive, one might even say, a transcendent function. The myths in their most powerful form released energy and gave form to human life.

In "The Wasteland," that vast burial ground for Western civilization, mythical types appear but only as ghosts or cripples. Cleopatra in the twentieth century is a neurasthenic. The great lovers of the past are reduced to an anaesthetized typist and her "young man carbuncular," bored and unfeeling on her divan, that combination sofa, bed, and clothes repository. The anomie of Eliot's scene points ahead to the new sexual morality and maps out the dark side of its landscape. His is one of the most devastating surveys of the death of love.

Yet, even with such a barren terrain before them, it was hard for many to let go of the idea of romantic love. In 1929, Joseph Wood Krutch made the observation that only when such love has fully disappeared will we know how bleak the world can be.[5] I'm not sure that I agree; other ages got along quite well without such love, but perhaps we have now arrived at the point where it is no longer with us.

Some authors, to be sure, have hung on gallantly to love, earlier in the century, for the most part, when it was somewhat easier to do so. For Lawrence, sexual love is itself the new religion—perhaps not so new when one considers that in the thirteenth century Gottfried von Strassburg had offered a love religion in his *Tristan and Isolde* as an alternative to Christianity. But for Lawrence, sexual salvation requires the putting to sleep of consciousness and rationality, a process that even his strongest devotees are unlikely to follow except in fantasy, where it poses no threat to the self, and his is perhaps less a myth of love than a myth of sex, as Malraux recognized years ago.[6]

As for the typology, much about Lawrence's women seems new, at first. He tried to incorporate within the wife those elements that had formerly existed only in the mistress, and sought to replace the old Tolstoyan morality with something more life affirming. But one doesn't have to be a feminist to take offense at his concept of "phallic marriage," in which each man rules a small kingdom. It is surely of some significance that those authors who have the most democratic view of men, such as Rousseau and Lawrence, also speak much about love within marriage, but in doing so, they adhere to a most undemocratic view of women. Lawrence's heroines, Lady Chatterley, for example, are mere satellite soul-mates for their men. As such their type reaches back to the medieval Heloise, to Plutarch's description of the wife in "Advice to Bride and Groom," and finally to St. Paul himself.

If the polar types are disappearing, not much of this disappearance is due to Lawrence or to any of the few other romantic writers of the century, for they hold on fiercely to a traditional polarization of women and of the sexes in general. Hemingway is a case in point. But it is a lost cause. Most women can only shudder at the utterances of his María and Catherine Barkley today.

The disappearance of the types is due, at least in part, to increasing interiorization. More and more we are retreating from the institutional expressions of our myths into a private sphere where we seek self-validation. This interiorization has much to do with women's influence. I don't mean by this simply the current outcry of feminists against the old typology, although assuredly they have been vocal in this matter. I am talking, rather, about women as creators of a new cultural view. At least until recently, it was generally fashionable, even among women, to speak of women as the mere conservers of culture. But when we look at certain writers, such as Djuna Barnes, Virginia Woolf, and even Doris Lessing, we must give credence to Madame de Stael's statement, made almost two centuries ago, that women have been discoverers of the interior self. They have been pioneers of the inner frontier. The more literature retreats from the interpretation of an external world, the less it rests on the rational processes of the mind, the more women both as writers and characters become important.

This is not to say that men have not been great experimenters—one need merely think of Proust, Joyce, and Eliot. However, it may well be that the twentieth-century concept of "spatial form," for example, with its rejection of linear plot progression as in Djuna Barnes' *Nightwood,* or the presentation of multiple consciousness, i.e., the more or less direct rendering of the interior life of different characters, as in Woolf's *To the Lighthouse,* or the representation of a single fragmented consciousness as in Lessing's *Golden Notebook* have been forms particularly influenced by and congenial to women.

The reasons for this interiorization are rooted in biology as well as culture. Childbearing and childrearing, preparing food and organizing domestic life are cyclical activities. The reality they represent is circular and repetitive rather than linear and progressive as are the activities of most men. Traditionally, the circumstances of their lives gave women a greater interest in the texture of experience rather than in its range. Even when individual women writers did not experience conventional women's lives, they no doubt were influenced by the norms for their sex, as all of us, even the rebels among us, inevitably are.

It is this tradition of interiorizing that informs the technique in *To the Lighthouse,* where Woolf dismisses World War I in one bracketed sentence. It is the death of her heroine, Mrs. Ramsay, that is by far the greater cataclysm. In her similarities to the great mythical figures of the past—Eve, Mary, Helen, Penelope—Mrs. Ramsay, the classically beautiful mother of eight, might seem to be grounded in typology. If one were so inclined, one might accuse Woolf of falling back on the usual stereotypes of women as the mere conservers of culture, for her woman artist, Lily Briscoe, is old maidish in Woolf's own terms; she isn't very good besides, for her work will hang in attics only. One wonders just what psychic or social conspiracy has kept women writers of both the nineteenth and twentieth centuries from offering as types their own image, that of the female artist who is successful. What deficiency in ego or desire to dwell on the fictive? Yet such questions turn out to be unjust to Woolf's intent, for if the artist teaches us to see, to unite disparate fragments into an integrated vision, it is the mother, according to Woolf, who teaches us to fuse the smells, sights, and tastes of the moment into the act of living itself, perhaps the greatest artistic achievement. In Mrs. Ramsay's feminine force and energy (presented in traditionally masculine terms), her power over self and others (it is she who imposes form and order on the life and lives surrounding her), Woolf provides a foil to Lawrence's phallic glorification. Woolf's concept of androgyny—that is, the fusion of those aspects of consciousness that have traditionally been assigned to one or the other of the sexes—is one modern answer to sexual polarization and the dualism of types.

While women's consciousness has influenced twentieth-century literary types and the general movement towards interiorization in the culture, vast social and intellectual changes, all of them affecting interiorization in some way also, have enabled women to turn from the traditional social virutes of self-sacrifice and chastity to the individual aims of self-development and sexual satisfaction.

In the past, society's primary need was to reproduce, a need that both fostered and was supported by the sexual typology of virgin, wife, and mother. The antithetical figures of prostitute, sorceress, and witch dealt with women's latent rebellion against their sexual restrictions (as well as men's attraction to and fear of female sexuality). All of these types were institutionalized within the social structure as a means of achieving social ends. However, now that reproduction is no longer a primary aim, the necessity for these dualistic types has largely disappeared. Moreover, the contraceptive revolution of medical technology has eliminated that chasm between reproduction and sexual pleasure that gave typological structure to our mythology for centuries.

Yet the dualistic types are still with us, dying but not gone. And that is because they are rooted not simply in the social structure but in the unconscious as well. To put it another way, one might say that the social structure represents the particular historic manifestation of a "timeless" psychological reality. Some non-Freudians feel that it is possible that the "reality" may itself be changed by a social structure whose revisions are far reaching enough. This has yet to be determined. But there is some evidence, for example, that technological changes are already affecting our unconscious symbolism. Perhaps other innovations will produce even more extreme modifications in the psyche.

By making conscious what was formerly unconscious, Freud himself has contributed to the dying of the myths. Freud posits the origin of polar myths, for example, the goddess/witch dualism, in the child's earliest experiences. When the mother brings food and warmth, comfort and nurturance, the child perceives her as the magical goddess figure. But when she deprives and frustrates as she inevitably must, the mother becomes the witch in the infant's limited world. In his "Contributions to the Psychology of Love," Freud examines the polarity of the wife/mistress and madonna/prostitute also, seeing in the unconscious fantasies of childhood and the prohibitions of adolescence the reasons for the dissociation in some men's erotic life, "divided between two channels, the same two that are personified in art as heavenly and earthly (or animal) love."[7]

While Freud saw the dualisms as originating in earliest experience, as the result of infantile perception and misperception of biological difference, he believed that the work of reason would depolarize the unconscious and moderate its ambivalences and contradictions—that is, he thought that we could free ourselves from the tyranny of the unconscious. Jung, on the contrary, felt that the mind had a predisposition towards dualism, much the way that animals have innate releasing mechanisms. For him, the types are archetypes existing from all eternity. If Jung is right, then no change in social structure or child rearing would seriously affect the typology of women; one would have to change the structure of the mind itself to do so. One wonders why Jung is so popular among feminists, considering that they want to eliminate the types. Despite his pessimism, Freud offers more hope to those who want change.

Yet most feminists, with the notable and praiseworthy exception of Juliet Mitchell, reject Freud, deploring that he was "culture bound." The irony is that they themselves grant culture total power over personality, ignoring those biological and psychological forces that might stand as bulwarks against the onslaughts of culture (a point that Trilling made in another context). Many women theorists are happy with the Marxist interpretation of the dualities simply as an artificially constructed system of rewards and punishments designed to keep woman marginal within the economy. They are happy with it because an economic system is seemingly easier to change than either biology or psychology. According to the Marxist view, ending the economic oppression of women would produce the death rattle of the typology. To a certain extent this has happened. Changing the work people do can change the ways in which they are viewed; sometimes, however, it merely changes the status that is awarded the work, and this has to do with reasons other than economic.

Furthermore, some of the consequences of increased economic freedom for women had not been forseen by socialists. Engles felt that only with economic equality could there be true romantic love, or "individual sex love" as he terms it. But what has happened is that increased equality has caused not only the disappearance of the typology but that of romantic love as well, a former source of power for women, whatever its detractors may say today.

If it is true as Freud said that "some obstacle is necessary to swell the tide of the libido to its height,"[8] it may be that romantic love can only thrive in an atmosphere of tension and difference, either that supplied by the prohibitions of the social order, as in adulterous love, or that provided by a polarization of the sexes as in traditional marriage. It is conceivable that the combination of romantic passion and equality cannot exist. Perhaps it would deny some deep needs of the psyche that we do not as yet entirely understand. It is also conceivable that an entirely different concept of love is possible—and necessary. In the meantime, however, we seem to be in limbo. The charismatic and powerful figures of the past, the Tristans and Isoldes, no longer express our consciousness. The best we can hope for are pseudo relationships of "anonymous selves floating around and occasionally bumping into each other, causing mild annoyance," as critic Ferdinand Mount said about the couples in Updike's *Marry Me*.[9]

This is because the cult of extreme individualism—the backside of romanticism at which we have now arrived—precludes the necessary self-surrender to another that romantic love entails, unless we wish to count surrender to ourselves as fulfilling the conditions. Romantic love also implies the exaltation of one person over all others. In this respect, too, we are perhaps more romantic than we might have guessed. There is one type we still hold up for admiration—ourselves. Whether this leads to fewer or more problems than our past idealization of others, I leave to the psychiatrists to determine.

So afraid are we, women as well as men, of losing our autonomy we concentrate on sensations only. The strongest orgasms are those which are self-induced, say Masters and Johnson. What greater testimony to heightened individualism could we hope to find. Many feminists deplore the vaginal orgasm as a mere myth propagated by men to keep women in subjection to them. It is therefore of some interest that one of feminism's sacrosanct literary texts (not that it was written with polemical intent), *The Golden Notebook*, takes a different stand.

In the past literature had often been subversive. The great romances of medieval literature, for example, were anti-social in their treatment of women and sex. They approved of biologically unproductive types, e.g., Isolde, and placed individual love above social duty.

Today, however, it is the norm itself which is rebellious. Culture no longer internalizes restraints. For the first time in history, society itself is condoning immediate sexual gratification. Despite the emphasis on sensations more or less violent in such authors as Roth and Mailer, it may be left to literature to resist the triumph of instant and uncommitted sexuality. This may be its new "subversive" position. Whatever one may think of Lessing as a writer, she does represent this phenomenon.

Despite her creation of a seemingly new type, that of "free woman," women who are free of marriage and conventional moral systems, women who are free to work and to engage in the political and creative process, Lessing's women are very much tied to men, so much so that one begins to wonder if the author isn't using the term "free woman" ironically.

Contrary to Elizabeth Hardwick's pronouncements on the matter, what Lessing shows is that the old seduced and abandoned heroine is not dead at all as a theme for fiction.[10] Precisely because Anna Wulf is free of the biological consequences of sex in ways that Tess of the d'Urbervilles wasn't, Lessing can more readily examine her heroine's existential vulnerabilities. One sees that the possibilities of being victimized do not disappear with the arrival of economic and sexual liberation. For that reminder alone, Lessing is important.

At the beginning of the century, Rilke wrote that women hold the Diploma of Proficiency in Love while men carry in their pockets only an elementary grammar.[11] Lessing would probably agree. It will take us a long time if ever to discover whether this difference in aptitude of the sexes lies in our genes or in social expectations. Perhaps the women in *The Golden Notebook* are emotionally atavistic, but romantic love is still something they desperately want for their own validation. It is something they never get. As far as a new typology of women is concerned, what we may have here is a case of old wine in new bottles or new wine in old.

For all her complaints about men—in some ways women writers are creating a typology of men that is as negative as any misogynistic church father's on women—Lessing does not envisage a world free of them, and she still holds on in some way to a vision of romantic love.

Though writing considerably earlier in the century, without any conscious polemical intent, Colette in many ways portrays more feminine power than do most contemporary writers, notwithstanding her emphasis on love and passion. Certainly with regard to dependencies, she provides some interesting reversals of sexual stereotypes. For this reason, she will probably be turned to more and more by those women who seek role models in literature. The younger man and the older woman, one of her major themes, is as new as the latest proposals for relationships in *Cosmopolitan* and *Ms.*—to name two disparate but sexually liberated publications—and as old as the mother goddesses and their consorts.

Colette's *Chéri*, set in the world of the demimondaine, presents a beautiful gigolo, Chéri, and his much older mistress, Léa. Though Chéri has his own fortune, his unwillingness to spend it puts him into a position of economic subservience, and much of the characterization of the coquettish lover—even his name sounds feminine—seems to overturn traditional concepts (at least within the Anglo-Saxon world) of male/female behavior. It is the woman here who is the teacher and guide, the man who is the naughty child.

In *The Last of Chéri*, which takes place in the lassitude of post-war Paris, Chéri no longer sees Léa, for with the passage of time, the obstacle of age has become an insurmountable barrier. He is married to a young and lovely wife, but he pays her little attention. His emphasis on chastity, his attempt to preserve himself inviolate, is an attempt to arrest the moment. His fear of time marring his beauty—he feels old at thirty—contrasts forcibly with Léa's acceptance of age, the passing of physical attractiveness, and even of desire itself.

In the Chéri novels, Colette has transformed the child heroine into the child hero who cannot transcend his own adolescence. One might say of Chéri as has been said of Madame Bovary, that he is totally lacking in insight into the self. But whereas Emma only wanted to give love, Chéri only wants to receive it. It is the lover here who commits suicide when he realizes that no one can take the place of the mistress who can no longer be his, disguised as she is in grey hair and fat. But it is not despair at losing *her* that causes the suicide. Rather it is *his* perfection as mirrored by a former beautiful Léa that he cannot bear losing. It is the women in the book who emerge victorious, for they are realists in love as in everything else.

Many works prominent in the feminist canon today are much more fearful of men and love and even culture, men's domain, and therefore seek to do without them altogether. Among the most popular ones are Kate Chopin's *The Awakening*, in which the heroine's ostensible route to freedom is suicide; Charlotte Perkins Gilman's *The Yellow Wallpaper*, in which it is madness; Sylvia Plath's work and life itself, in which it is a combination of both, and Margaret Atwood's *Surfacing*, in which it is a return to a pretechnological wilderness.

In Kate Chopin's *Awakening*, published in 1899, the heroine has a sensuous, sexual, and even artistic awakening of sorts. In her sexual awakening, Edna Pontellier is an American Bovary, but unlike her ancestor she is unwilling to live through men alone. She has thus been hearalded as a new type and well she might have been, if not for her suicide. Some positive minded readers today see her drowning as yet another aspect of her awakening, as a form of spiritual transcendence over a benighted social order. Actually, however, the main reason for the heroine's suicide stemmed not from any demands of vision or even character or plot, but rather from Chopin's desire to pacify the moralists in her audience for her heroine's adultery, a plan which failed, by the way. What we have in *The Awakening* is a thwarted *bildungsroman* built on the old myth of the coming of age of the hero, except that this time it's a hero manqué.

In Margaret Atwood's recent novel *Surfacing,* the unnamed heroine (Everywoman?) goes through a symbolic death by water but emerges in a reverse of Edna's "awakening" with the resolve never to be a victim again. Francine du Plessix Grey recently lauded the book for creating a new mythology for women. I'm not sure whether a new mythology can ever be created consciously, particularly when so much of it involves the reapplication of male myths to women, as this one does, with its allusions to birth of the hero myths and leatherstocking tales of self-sufficiency in the wilderness. More important, however, one might take issue with Atwood's conception of freedom since her heroine's devictimization consists of rejecting all forms of "male" technology. One wonders if there is any more extreme way of making oneself a victim. As Jacob Bronowski said with irony a few years ago, now that technology has helped to give us "a brain two or three times larger than the chimpanzee's we are free [of course] to use that brain to prefer the life— or even the brain—of the chimpanzee."[12] But when one sees so many feminists combatting the cultural deprivation of women by trying to insure that they become even more deprived, one wonders whose side they are on.

In Gilman's *The Yellow Wallpaper,* a slight but now extremely popular turn-of-the-century work by the author who also wrote the brilliant *Women and Economics,* it is madness that provides the escape from the male world. Current readings now seize on the heroine's doctor/husband as the arch symbol of patriarchal oppression and see the heroine as evincing laudable spiritual freedom. Incidently, like her heroine, Gilman suffered from depression, but for her, freedom took the route of divorce, not madness. In some instances, women's lives offer more evidence of a new typology than do their works.

More recently, Plath took the path of madness in life as well as writing to combat the primordial parental betrayal and the presence of disquieting muses. She didn't stop there. Suicide became the writer's *raison d'etre,* the culmination of her passion for excellence. "Dying/Is an art, like everything else./ I do it exceptionally well" is a statement she wrote in "Lady Lazarus" that proved to be prophetic.

Suicide, the murder displaced onto the self, is perhaps the ultimate vengeance on others, but it is hardly an act of spiritual transcendence. Plath's heroine was not a Roman matriarch, although one would scarcely guess this when reading some of the criticism. Rather she was a romantic with culture lag.

It is partly the pain of that disproportion between the awareness of freedom and the inability to achieve it that has given birth to the mad woman and the suicide as prominent types in women writers. They are not new types. They go back to antiquity. What is seemingly new is the attempt of feminist criticism to hold them up as types worthy of emulation. I say "seemingly," for actually such a view was common enough in romanticism, but common only to a small group.

The triumph of the irrational that we are now witnessing is occurring not solely within women's studies. The affirmation of the bizarre and the deviant, the glorification of impulse over reason is found in the culture at large. We are witnessing an upsurge of what in more religious ages would have been called the demonic. It is therefore not surprising to find that a major way of dealing with sexual polarization, the typology of women, and the problems of love and freedom is by obscurring sexual identity altogether. *Unisexual, homosexual, bisexual, androgynous,* these are all catchwords of the culture, which may point to a future time when the individual alone rather than any social unit such as the couple or the family is paramount. We have lost our traditional metaphysical and religious model of value, another reason for the death of the dualistic types and for our concentration on figures that once were marginal.

From Plato down through the Renaissance, the major paradigm of the world was that of a great chain of being, in which all of the creation from dumb stones to eloquent intelligences (angels in the Christian version) was arranged in a series of interconnecting links, hierarchically ordered. Even the individual psyche was conceived on a hierarchical principle, with reason on top, will underneath, and desire or emotion at the bottom rung. In a modified form, this attitude remains with us even in our pluralistic universe. When we speak of someone acting like a superman or a beast, or of letting one's feelings get the upper hand, it is generally this invisible ladder that is in the back of our heads, as metaphor if nothing else. But whereas Pascal could see man as "ni ange ni brute," but somehow holding together in a unity the extremes of existence, the possibilities available to us in the modern world are smaller in number. We have not only dispensed with angels, we have rejected devils as well, incorporating into the psyche those elements which were formerly projected onto the world. Now that the old dualisms of sacred and demonic no longer have meaning, we are turning to marginal types, those types that were once forbidden or at least peripheral in the culture.

One of the most fascinating literary treatments of the marginal types appears in a book published more than forty years ago: Djuna Barnes' *Nightwood*, which uses the great chain of being as a structural principle, much the way that Eliot uses myth, as a system of allusion to a civilization that is dying. Magnificent in its spectacle and fantasy, with a language and vision at once Elizabethan and dreamlike, the work, once one gets through the complexities of its form, seems to treat less the surreal than the real in our time. It is compelling in its treatment of both love and typology.

One last outpost of romantic love—indeed it may have been its earliest settlement, if one takes the works of Sappho and Plato as evidence—is homosexual love, and Barnes provides a provocative survey of its territory. Unlike that great romantic Stendhal, who believed that love was a process of crystallization, whereby more and more perfections are attributed to the beloved, Barnes sees it as one of fossilization—an example of the difference between nineteenth- and twentieth-century love. But fossilization may in fact be the ultimate romanticism, for it reveals a love which finds not only its resolution in death but its very being there. "Love becomes the deposit of the heart, analogous in all degrees to the findings in a tomb."[13]

Barnes shows that narcissism plays an even greater role in lesbian object choice than in the heterosexual one. "A man is another person—a woman is yourself, caught as you turn in panic; on her mouth you kiss your own."[14]

Contrary to certain radical feminists today, the author feels that lesbian love provides no way out of that conflict between love and freedom that they see as central, for love, of necessity, entails suffering and limitation on the freedom of the self. Yet Barnes is perhaps less interested in homosexual love than she is in the metaphysical implications of all love. Homosexuality may simply be her metaphor for our condition in nightwood, her "wasteland."

In her use of the concept of the great chain of being, Barnes sees our transcendence occurring downwards instead of upwards. One of her most interesting figures, Robin, is a descendant of Baudelaire's animal/child women. Unlike them, however, she seeks to be human. Insofar as she is the heroine of the book, she is no longer the other, in de Beauvoir's terms. Rather, she presents the aspirations of all of us. But through her seeming metamorphosis into a dog at the end of the work, Barnes may be saying that the link of the human is no longer available to us on the chain. Our state can only be bestial.

Although Barnes found enough vigor in the concept of the great chain to use it as the framework of her book, most people today, if they thought of this "chain" at all, would consider it an old fashioned and elitist metaphor, part of the scrap heap of culture. The predominant model of the world right now is not that of a vertical chain but rather one of a horizontal continuum. Hierarchies no longer seem natural to us. Since everybody is potentially equal, all differences in roles are viewed as superimposed by the culture.

Even the workings of the inner self are structured on egalitarian principles, for equality in the psyche is desired as much as equality in the social order. No longer are different values assigned to reason, will, and desire. Rather, all of these are to co-exist as equal citizens. It is instructive to compare our present model with Freud's construct of superego, ego, and id. If our concept of the self is analogous to our concept of the external world and there is every evidence that this is so, it is obvious that the power of fathers is declining, both externally and internally. No longer do we have to do battle with a fearsome superego. Having grown up in a permissive age, all the elements in the psyche can play nicely together—or at least ought to—and here's the rub, for not everybody can achieve the desired synthesis between reason and feeling, spirituality and sexuality, or, in Jungean terminology, masculinity and femininity, and this inequality becomes the source of a new means of differentiation. In our new view of consciousness, if not of worldly goods and performances, we are inexorably aristocratic. What we now have is a hierarchy of the self.

There is another problematic aspect to our concept of "equality." In our attempt to correct the wrongs of earlier periods, we twist ourselves into pretzels to insure the rights of all those formerly deprived, often to the extent of favoring the minority, the deviant, the idiosyncratic. Yet again we are left with hierarchy.

When we say that the main quest today is for the human, this quest seems to involve not so much the transcendence of cultural and historic boundaries (as it once did), as those of sex and class. It involves the granting of full voting rights to all those groups or impulses that were formerly classified as suspect and therefore subject to control.

In such a scheme, the old typology with its rigidly defined role differentiation is untenable. It is the reason that so often feminists label the types *images*, that is, merely reflections, illusions, fantasms, or *stereotypes*, drawing on all that term's overtones of artifice and reification. These examples of name calling ignore the vitality of the myths as models of consciousness for earlier periods, whatever they may be for our own—once again an illustration of many feminists' inability or unwillingness to make historical distinctions. But however dubious may be their means of presenting it, the resentment of these critics is understandable, considering their position, for the types do have great power, particularly in their mythical embodiments. "Myth has the task of giving an historical intention a natural justification, and making contingency appear eternal," writes Roland Barthes in his *Mythologies*,[15] who also suggests a counteraction to this power that many women writers are now practicing. "The best weapon against myth is perhaps to demythify it in its turn, and to produce an *artificial myth*: and this reconstituted myth will in fact be a mythology."[16] I have already stated that I do not think that one can consciously create new myths; nonetheless, reconstituted myths do have some importance, if not as literature, then as sociology, for they force us to examine the power of the old myth. Thus Adrienne Rich writes

> A man is asleep in the next room
> We are his dreams
> We have the heads and breasts of women
> the bodies of birds of prey
> Sometimes we turn into silver serpents[17]

What we are also seeing today is the transvaluation and reinterpretation of old myths. Monique Wittig's *Les Guérillères* is perhaps the most striking and powerful example of this tendency. Traditional symbols and myths are restructured with such compelling intensity that old meanings are swept away like so much dust. Suns here are female symbols, serpents are orphic symbols of knowledge, Eve is a seeker of wisdom, the golden fleece, and the holy grail represent the male search for the female.

Wittig's women are epic and glorious creatures, keenly aware of their own sexuality, the splendor of the vulva. Possessed of bacchantic fury and

amazonian gifts, they take arms against men who have robbed them of
their passion for knowledge, enslaved them through trickery, treated them
like goddesses or witches or drudges, invented their history, and appropriated all language for their own. Wishing to "break the last bond that binds
them to a dead culture, [the women] say that any symbol that exalts the
fragmented body is transient, must disappear."[18] They wish to destroy polari-
ties, a product of mechanistic reasoning, that binary system in which woman
is earth, sea, tears, humidity, darkness (in contrast to the opposites for man).
theirs is a violent rejection of a male-centered universe. If anatomy is destiny,
then their anatomy destines them triumphant in war, with their straight
backs, their lissome loins, their aggressive breasts. "When they have a prisoner they strip him and make him run through the streets crying, it is your rod/
cane/staff/wand/peg skewer/staff of lead."[19] In a litany, "They say, hell, let
the earth become a vast hell destroying killing and setting fire to the buildings
of men," and all their institutions.[20] Everything must be razed before a new
culture can rise.

   After this longest, most murderous war, the last possible war in history,
women and men will be reconciled. Spring will return, the summer grow
green again, lips find their way to lips, but it will be in a different world. In
the interim, the romantic, the erotic will be held in abeyance.

   Such is the case in Margaret Atwood's reworking of the Circe myth. In
her "Circe/Mud poems," the author reveals Circe from her own point of view
and absolves her from blame of centuries.

> It was not my fault, these animals
> who once were lovers
> it was not my fault, the snouts
> and hooves, the tongues
> thickening and rough, the mouths grown over
> with teeth and fur
> I did not add the shaggy rugs, the tusked masks,
> they happened[21]

But Atwood's transvaluation also deprives Circe of any erotic power. One
consequence of remythifying myth today is that sorceresses tend to look less
alluring than invaded. I'm not sure, however, that leaving Circe alone on her
island would mean increasing her dominion.

   Robert Lowell, one of the last of our romantics, had his own reinterpretation of the Circe myth. In one of his final poems, "Ulysses and Circe," he
wrote:

> Why am I my own fugitive,
> because her beauty made me feel as other men?[22]

These lines may grant Circe a magic which is in fact more real, more "human"
than Atwood's denial of it.

   We have yet to see whether women's power will increase when romantic
love and the old typology have disappeared completely, for political and
economic power may not be forthcoming in place of other forms. The polarization of the sexes that existed in romantic marriage was seemingly a sign of

great inequity. In some ways, however, romantic love was an equalizer in an age of hierarchy. By exalting a chosen individual over others, it was able to transcend differences of class and sex. It was even able to validate the forbidden, particularly outside marriage. But it could only exist with types, with barriers. Those are what fueled it. Now that everybody is theoretically equal, now that all impulses are respectable, there is no longer any need for it, nor could it exist.

But what do we have it its place? Self-love and the marginal types? Amazons and warriors? Are these our new mythology? We do not know, for if we knew with certainty what our myths were, they would no longer be myths. What we do know is that the old myths are dying. The allegorization of them is proof of this, for one only allegorizes to save a tradition or to criticize it, not to give birth to it.

It is possible, of course, that all of our present interiorization, all the isolation of the self from those around it, is a necessary precondition for a new mythology of love and wholeness that is yet to come. But it may equally be, in the words of Yeats, that last great mythologizer of the century, that some rough beast is slouching towards Bethlehem waiting to be born.

YORK COLLEGE OF THE
CITY UNIVERSITY OF NEW YORK

Notes

[1]This quotation of Verlaine is cited in translation by Henri Peyre in his essay "Baudelaire as a Love Poet," in *Baudelaire as a Love Poet and other Essays*, ed. Lois Boe Hyslop (University Park: Pennsylvania State University, 1969), p. 7.

[2]In *Beyond Culture* (New York: Viking, 1968), p. 72, n. (First published in *Partisan Review*, Summer 1963, pp. 167-91.)

[3]The statement, cited in A. Norman Jeffares, *W. B. Yeats: Man and Poet* (New Haven: Yale University Press, 1949), p. 192, is from a letter to Lady Gregory, quoted by J. Hone, *W. B. Yeats, 1865-1939*.

[4]William York Tindall, *A Reader's Guide to James Joyce* (New York: Noonday Press, 1959), p. 233.

[5]*The Modern Temper* (New York: Harcourt, Brace and World, 1929), p. 78.

[6]André Malraux, "D. H. Lawrence and Eroticism: Concerning Lady Chatterley's Lover," *Yale French Studies: Eros, Variations on an Old Theme*, XI, n.d., pp. 55-58.

[7]The statement appears in "The Most Prevalent Form of Degradation in Erotic Life," *Collected Papers*, IV, trans. Joan Riviere (New York: Basic Books, 1959), p. 209.

[8]*Ibid.*, p. 213.

[9]"The Novel of the Narcissus: New Fiction," *Encounter*, XLVIII (June 1977), 54.

[10]Cf. the chapter "Seduction and Betrayal," in *Seduction and Betrayal: Women and Literature* (New York: Vintage, 1975), pp. 185-218.

[11]He makes the point in a letter dated January, 1912, cited in Appendix I to the *Duino Elegies,* trans., intro., and commentary by J. B. Leishman and Stephen Spender (New York: W. W. Norton, 1939), p. 120.

[12]"Science and the New Reformation," *The Columbia Forum,* III (Summer 1974), 4.

[13]Djuna Barnes, *Nightwood,* with intro. by T. S. Eliot (New York: Harcourt Brace, 1937), p. 56.

[14]Barnes, p. 143.

[15]Roland Barthes, *Mythologies,* selected and trans. by Annette Lavers (New York: Hill and Wang, 1972), p. 142.

[16]Barthes, p. 135.

[17]The passage is from "Incipience," in *Diving into the Wreck: Poems 1971-1972* (New York: W. W. Norton, 1973), p. 11.

[18]Monique Wittig, *Les Guérillères,* trans. David Le Vay (New York: Avon, 1971), p. 72.

[19]Wittig, p. 106.

[20]Wittig, p. 130.

[21]The excerpt is from the collection entitled *You Are Happy* (New York: Harper and Row, 1974), p. 48.

[22]The poem is in *Day by Day* (New York: Farrar, Straus, and Giroux, 1977), p. 4.

EL MITO DEGRADADO DE LA FAMILIA
EN *EL LIBRO DE MIS PRIMOS*
DE CRISTINA PERI ROSSI

Gabriela Mora

"¿Qué vendrá después?" se preguntaba Mario Benedetti, luego de comentar la continuidad de la extendida metáfora contra "un orden ya carcomido" que veía entre *Viviendo* y *Los museos abandonados*, los primeros relatos de Cristina Peri Rossi.[1] Probablemente, se respondía él mismo, vendrá el "estallido renovador y la destrucción para construir" (327); y el devastador retrato familiar de *El libro de mis primos*, o la sobrecogedora presentación de una dictadura en *Indicios pánicos*, que siguieron de inmediato a la reflexión, se ajustan al vaticinio.[2] Ambas obras continuaron indagando con angustia mordiente en ese orden calificado por el crítico, que ha producido el hambre, la muerte y el exilio, no sólo en el Uruguay sino en el resto del continente.[3] Esos libros, y los que fueron apareciendo después,[4] han ido mostrando la imperativa necesidad de radicales transformaciones en la estructura socioeconómica latinoamericana, en una tenaz voluntad de creación de expresiones nuevas que busca convertir, al decir de Benedetti, un cataclismo social en "estremecimiento estético" (327).

Situada en la línea contemporánea señalada principalmente por Julio Cortázar,[5] los experimentos de Peri Rossi, apoyados por la pericia de su lengua poética, abren brechas en los diseños tradicionales de los géneros narrativos. Sin considerar sus invenciones en el específico campo de lo retórico, en la composición de sus relatos se observan, además de las rupturas temporales y los súbitos cambios de puntos de vista, el uso del verso en obras en prosa, la inserción de nombres o citas de personas históricas en medio de la ficción—que también es punzada a través de interpolaciones directas al lector o notas explicativas al pie de la página— y el empleo imaginativo de la tipografía como vehículo expresivo (bastardillas, mayúsculas en uso deshabitual, espacios en blanco, paréntesis, puntuación inusitada o eliminada, dibujos obtenidos por colocación especial de las letras), entre los más frecuentes.

Estos recursos que no agotan, ni mucho menos, la gama usada por la autora, se mencionan aquí porque se hallan entre los utilizados para crear la demoledora visión de la familia tradicional que proyecta *El libro de mis primos* que este trabajo se propone examinar. La modalidad predominantemente satírica que se adoptó para explorar viejos mitos adscritos al núcleo familiar, compone en él un cuadro cómico y patético que de incisiva manera descubre la debilidad original de algunos de los vínculos más íntimos. Las relaciones entre los sexos, los lazos maternales, los paternales, los filiales, muestran en la novela la endeblez de su base cuando se han establecido sobre el poder abusivo de un ser sobre otro más vulnerable. Aunque el libro se centra específicamente en una familia de la alta burguesía, sus observaciones—en especial aquellas concernientes a la mujer, que destacaremos— son válidas para otras clases del sistema socioeconómico que la obra impugna.

Una enorme y elegante casona remplazó en *El libro de mis primos* (*ELDMP* en adelante) los museos vacíos que antes había utilizado Cristina Peri Rossi (CRP para este trabajo) para simbolizar el mundo burgués a punto de ser destruido. Los hábitos, funciones y prejuicios de la enorme parentela que la ocupa,[6] le sirven a la autora menos para elaborar personajes literarios de redondeada individualidad, que para esbozar un retrato de la clase social que representan. Como en los relatos de *Los museos abandonados*, no hay en la novela especificidad geográfica, y en cuanto a la cronológica, la fecha junio de 1966, inserta en el título de un capítulo, pudiera indicar un año en que la actividad guerrillera se intensificó en el Uruguay. Pero fuera de este dato ambiguo, ya que los acontecimientos no singularizan en especial este mes,[7] no hay en el libro alusiones más directas al referente histórico. Tanto la ubicuidad como la imprecisión temporal de la narración son elementos que, junto con otros recursos, contribuyen a elaborar una visión altamente alegórica, pero no menos transparente de la realidad.

En su primera edición, la novela está dividida en 19 fragmentos de los cuales el primero es un poema paródico de la familia.[8] De los restantes, once tienen como narrador a Oliverio, que habla en primera persona como un niño desde un presente cercano a la narración, o como un adulto que recuerda su infancia cronológicamente ubicada en un pasado indeterminado.[9] Cuatro secciones, de acuerdo a la pauta dada por sus títulos, están presentadas a través del *yo* de Federico, primo guerrillero de Oliverio, desde sus escritos (VIII, XI), su Diario (XIV) y como directo narrador (XIX). Siguiendo la misma pauta, la primera persona enunciante de los otros capítulos correspondería a Oscar, hermano de Oliverio (XVIII), Alfredo, primo de Oliverio (VII), y tal vez a Alina, guerrillera.[10] La estructura del narrador, sin embargo, ofrece varios problemas necesitados de específica atención que no podemos dedicar aquí.[11]

Importa, no obstante, conocer algunos rasgos del narrador principal, Oliverio niño, porque su edad le confiere una calidad especial a su testimonio. La autora—que ha usado la perspectiva infantil en otras obras—ha dicho que los niños tienen una mirada sabia, no dañada por las renunciaciones y frustraciones del adulto, que los hace excelentes testigos del mundo que los rodea.[12] La imaginación y una extremada sensibilidad caracterizan a Oliverio, cualidad esta última traducida en irrefrenable tendencia al llanto. Oliverio llora por los motivos que hacen llorar a los niños, pero también por otros menos aparentes: un color bello, un recuerdo triste, la suavidad de un contorno. Una mezcla de lírico humor y ternura distingue los pasajes en que se alude a la "angustia", enfermedad que según los médicos,[13] provoca las lágrimas incontenibles:

> Entre las plantas, lloro despacito. Mi primo menor, Horacio, que es inocente... y suele andar detrás mío, siguiéndome los pasos ... me mira llorar finito entre las plantas y piensa que las estoy regando. "Echale un poco a ésta, que está tristecita" me dice, señalándome unos tallos flacos, que parecen agobiados por el peso de sus hojas. Yo voy hasta allí, me siento encima de una piedra que sobresale, y lloro un poco sobre la planta, que absorbe ávidamente mis lágrimas (43-44).

La hipersensibilidad de Oliverio otorga, naturalmente, particular significación a sus juicios, en especial a aquellos relacionados con sus inclinaciones y desafectos hacia los miembros de la familia. Por otro lado, la invención del ojo y de la lengua de Oliverio niño, proporciona una excelente motivación para el frecuente uso de elementos lúdicos que caracteriza no sólo el nivel lingüístico, sino también otras estructuras de la novela.

Un rígido código, respetado y conservado por generaciones, divide en forma estricta a los individuos del clan familiar de acuerdo a edades y a sexos. Los ojos masculinos de Oliverio son los encargados de dibujar los rasgos que definen a las hembras de la casa, todas perfectas cumplidoras de los oficios de parir y de limpiar, los esenciales del sexo:

> La limpieza ha sido la ocupación principal de las mujeres de nuestra casa, y casi la exclusiva, si descontamos la otra, la tarea de prolongar la especie y propagar la familia, empresa ésta que asumen con total dignidad y conciencia (14).

La extensa enumeración de actividades relacionadas con la acción de limpiar que sigue a este irónico comentario, satiriza sin piedad una labor tan absorbente que llega a ser—y aquí el trágico vuelco—"manera de sobrevivir y alcanzar la perfección" para las moradoras de la mansión (15). La madre de Oliverio, sombra distraída que vaga por la casa cumpliendo esta función, epitomiza el exagerado afán obligando a los niños a andar en patines afelpados y a tomar los objetos con manos enguantadas para protegerlos de la suciedad (18). De más está decir que esta abrumadora faena en mujeres que tienen criados, es metafórico modo de poner en evidencia la trivialización de las vidas cuyo exclusivo ámbito es la casa y su solo oficio el doméstico.

No hay que olvidar, sin embargo, que el dardo satírico tiene como blanco la alta burguesía. Sólo el ocio que permite la riqueza puede explicar las superfluas diligencias con que estas mujeres llenan sus horas, y que la única que parece rebelde a las normas, Alejandra, se pierda en ensueños provocados por las drogas o los libros de arte (171). Por esto, no sorprende que los varones se quejen de que "las mujeres no sirven para nada" (154), de que "con las mujeres no se puede contar porque se pasan el día peleando y discutiendo entre ellas" (170), y de que tanto Oliverio como su primo Alfredo vean a las tías como a un ruidoso hervidero de gallinas (71, 121-126).[14] La consideración de la otra función fundamental, la de reproducir, da ocasión para indagar corrosivamente en las instituciones del matrimonio y de la maternidad dentro del esquema burgués tradicional. Aparte del insólito desenfado para aludir a la hasta hoy 'sagrada misión', nótese en el párrafo que sigue la afilada referencia a la virtual inexistencia de la mujer antes de ser madre:

> Desde el momento que esa inversión de semen se realizaba, la *extraña* portadora de él, la *extranjera* que había abierto sus piernas ante uno de los nuestros, vaya a saber llevada por qué azar, se volvía un *objeto* venerable, ... *pasaba a integrar la familia* ... Desde ese momento ... sus contactos con el exterior se disolvían, pasaba a estar bajo nuestra protección, ya nadie ni nada podía restituirla al tránsito, a las calles ... como bajo la protección de un ejército de alabarderos, sus días se deslizarían ya prendidos para siempre a los nuestros (15, subrayado mío).

Fuera del desconocimiento mutuo de los cónyuges y de la calidad de objeto que el subrayado destaca, el énfasis puesto en el forzado aislamiento de la mujer, es complemento explicativo de la vacía existencia comentada anteriormente. Las numerosas referencias esparcidas en la novela a los motivos económicos y sociales como razón de ser del matrimonio, no dejan lugar a dudas sobre el origen de la degradada situación de la institución en el sistema en que se instala la ficción.

Muy pertinente a la posición de los sexos en la familia, es el capítulo X, "El velorio de la muñeca de mi prima Alicia", ejemplo de la pericia de la autora para crear aquella literatura preconizada por Cortázar, necesitada de un lector activo dispuesto a descubrir las numerosas inferencias propuestas en el texto. De la rica red de niveles y correspondencias tejidas en el escrito, nos interesa señalar con alguna detención, las que vemos apuntando a los fenómenos de la virginidad, de la violación sexual y la pasividad femenina, porque su alcance significativo se derrama a otros trozos de la novela.

Situado en la mitad del libro,[15] el capítulo está narrado por Oliverio niño en un presente correlativo con la acción contada. En un primer nivel de significación obvia está el hecho de que los primos, una vez que han decidido jugar a los doctores, aparten a las niñas, excepto a Alicia, porque es "boba", y es dueña de la muñeca que necesitan para el juego (91). El relato de las operaciones simuladas, una para agrandar los senos, y otra para abrir una cavidad en la sección púbica de la muñeca, resulta en un cuadro de rica polisemia en que el contrapunto entre el encendido erotismo de los primos, la progresiva violencia de sus acciones, los diferentes llantos de Alicia, y la inmovilidad de la muñeca, alude simultáneamente a diversos aspectos de la realidad adulta imitada a través del juego infantil.

El llanto de Alicia, segregada de la importante operación confiable sólo a manos masculinas, pasa por diversas etapas sugerentes del dolor/placer del desvirgamiento:

Yo empiezo a desnudarla. Estoy nervioso y todos me miran. Escucho cerca de la puerta, el llanto bajito de Alicia, que ahora llora monótonamente ... A medida que la tela se desliza y le va pasando por la cabeza, asoman sus dos piernas enceradas ... los muslos se abren, como dos puertas que cedieran ... todos los primos están alrededor, observando con avidez, y muy lejano, se oye el sollozo de Alicia, que ya no parece un llanto, sino un canto (94-95).

Más tarde el llanto se transforma en "lamento suavísimo" que al narrador le parece haber oído en una "iglesia", señal de llamada, en una serie, alusiva al matrimonio que va a tener significativa representación al final del capítulo.

Las fingidas intervenciones quirúrgicas son diestras imitaciones no sólo del bisturí y el escalpelo reales, sino de la feroz arremetida de la violación sexual, motivo presente en toda la sección. Pasaremos por alto la primera, la de los pechos, que abunda en esperpénticos toques, para observar por un momento la segunda, que los primos consideran la operación más "complicada" y "fundamental":

Las piernas bien abiertas, sujetas por nuestros primos, Gastón introduce hábilmente el bisturí en el centro del triángulo donde ella termina (donde termina su cuerpo su figura su *pasividad*), y lo hunde con fuerza, entrándole por abajo. Cuando la punta del instrumento ha penetrado con todo su peso, comienza un lento y trabajoso movimiento circular ... A su lado, Sergio ha comenzado a jadear ... Con un punzón, le ha pedido a Norberto que la cave, que la socave, que la barrene ... Ahora Gastón emplea también un largo y grueso clavo ... El clavo se entierra, rompe, raja, abrecha, destroza ... (102-103, subrayado mío).

La intensificación de la violencia del acto, lograda especialmente por las extensas enumeraciones de vocablos sinónimos de romper y destrozar (que tuvimos que abreviar), pone de relieve, por contraste, el fenómeno connotado por la palabra que subrayamos. La muñeca—claro símbolo de la mujer—es imagen exagerada de la pasividad que por siglos se ha institucionalizado como parte esencial de lo femenino. En manos de CPR, el objeto de cartón, en expresiva paradoja, cobra vida precisamente para reforzar la idea de cosa inane que se puede manipular a antojo representada por la muñeca:

Piernabierta con los ojos muy claros fijos en el techo, como si aquello que le está sucediendo más abajo del vientre le fuera ajeno, fuera de otra, *que no le perteneciera*, no le estuviera sucediendo a ella. Queda piernabierta, los ojos fijos en el techo, indiferente (96, subrayado mío).

La noción de la mujer enajenada, despojada aún de su propio cuerpo que destaca este párrafo, se hace más acerba al oponerla a esos alabarderos citados antes. La pasividad, la indiferencia se ve entonces como el resultado de una milenaria coacción destinada a mantener a la mujer principalmente como máquina reproductora, como se refuerza en la continuación del trozo.

La penúltima cita dejó entrever también la progresiva excitación erótica de los primos, paralela a la pasividad de la muñeca y a la acción de cavarla. Algunas comparaciones con animales: "perro que husmea desesperado", "monstruo de ocho patas que se mueven descompasadamente", le sirven a la autora para transponer la gradación ascendente del deseo que culmina con los primos "silabeando, babeándose, balando" (104). De esta manera el espejo imitador del juego infantil, refleja la pura violencia en que queda reducido el acto sexual cuando uno de los miembros de la cópula es únicamente objeto incitador. Para concluir la operación, se utiliza un procedimiento semejante al comentado más arriba. La dilatada faena de abrir el cuerpo cerrado de la muñeca—prolongada en varias páginas—acrecienta la expectativa de los niños ante el espacio desconocido, a la vez que, por oposición, magnifica el menguado resultado de la apertura. En paródica degradación del mito de la virginidad, así describe Oliverio el esperado momento del descubrimiento:

> Diego mira todo con azor asombrado. Él también quiere conocer el hueco la oquedad la magnífica cueva ... se inclina hacia la profundidad y mira ... Imagina un pozo enorme, que no termina nunca, cuyo valiosísimo misterio es, precisamente, estar vacío, no contener nada. La hemos ahuecado para eso. Para comprobar su ausencia (104-5).

Una primera lectura puede ver, de inmediato en este trozo, un parto de los montes que se mofa de la extraordinaria importancia que la preservación del himen ha tenido en el código social. Pero habrá que detenerse dos veces en la última palabra. ¿A qué ausencia alude el texto? El clásico hurgar infantil para ver qué existe más adentro de las cosas, es el mismo deseo que llevará al adulto a buscar la razón de ser, la esencia de lo que lo rodea. El hallazgo de la nada apuntaría entonces, al absurdo de buscar a la mujer por esa vía, es decir a definir la esencia de lo femenino por el sexo. Por otro lado, es natural que la ausencia pueda referirse a la del hijo, como los primos parecen indicar al sentirse impelidos a depositar dádivas en el hueco abierto, la primera de las cuales es—claro símbolo—la llave de una puerta (106). La ceremonia en que los jóvenes parodian el rito matrimonial ("celebrantes de un oficio sagrado", "cortejantes o sacerdotes" (105), termina, sin embargo, con la muerte de la "doncella desflorada", expresiva metáfora del destino específico de la violada y embarazada, y general, de la mujer cosificada que expone la sección. El entierro de la muñeca—ahora descolorida y llena de estrías alusivas a la preñez—reforzaría la idea del extrañamiento femenino aún en proceso tan imbricado a la propia carnalidad como es la concepción de una criatura. La maternidad, de acuerdo a esta muerte, no sólo no llenaría la ausencia, sino que signaría la desaparición de la mujer como lo había sugerido para la soltería la cita de la página 69. Así, la ausente sería la mujer misma, (en el sentido más profundo de lo que significa ausencia de identidad), cuya no-presencia, aún en las cuestiones que están en el meollo de la estructura social, traería funestas consecuencias, como repetidamente va exponiendo la ficción. No se nos escapa, sin embargo, que hay otras posibilidades de interpretación en la provocativa ambigüedad de toda la sección.

El mito de la virginidad, tan simbólico de la calidad de la mujer como posesión privada, y su degradación, mostrada recién, añade especial significación al capítulo XVII, en que figura prominentemente la abuela de Oliverio. El narrador niño había dibujado ya la silueta de la vieja Clara, de irónico nombre, cuya altivez y crueldad provoca en él el deseo de su desaparición (53). La obsesión de la anciana por mantener intactas las formas sociales, la subraya ahora Oscar, el práctico hermano de Oliverio, que presiente el peligro que se cierne sobre la familia. Así reflexiona el nieto sobre la irreductible voluntad de no cambiar de la abuela:

> Lo tenía todo dispuesto, todo previsto; afrontaría el Juicio Final con entera dignidad,... dentro de la casa como había vivido; de su casa, que fuera la casa de sus padres y de sus abuelos, la casa de sus hijos y de sus nietos; la casa que guardó, como una virgen consagrada al culto, el himen de los nuestros, jamás hollado, la rosa de los vientos aparcelada, pero intacta (170).

Este oficio de sacerdotisa del templo doméstico, resulta doblemente irónico cuando se yuxtapone a la violencia que el juego infantil, en imitación del mundo adulto, puso en evidencia. En la yuxtaposición, los cotejos casa/cuerpo/virginidad hacen inevitable la conclusión de que esta vieja vestal cuida y protege un lugar degradado. La abuela, el mejor ejemplo en la familia del triunfo de una educación destinada a mantener el sistema, es la guardiana ciega de la propiedad que se hereda por generaciones, y de las convenciones que han esclavizado y cosificado a la mujer. El símil casa/himen—evocador de fortalezas inviolables, excepto claro está para sus legítimos dueños—es indicio innegable de la connotación política que la autora le atribuye al código sexual. La utilización de la mujer para mantener una estructura socioeconómica que ha convertido a los seres humanos en vendibles mercaderías, está aquí señalada claramente. Por si quedaran dudas, esta preocupación de CPR se explicita mejor aún cuando pone en boca de Federico, el guerrillero, el cargo de que la mujer puede ser rémora que impida los cambios sociales. La acusación tiene peso porque Federico es el único de la familia que no sólo rechaza el *status quo*, sino que está luchando para destruirlo:

> porque grandes cosas se esperaban de nosotros ... hazañas monumentos, revoluciones ... para eso habíamos abandonado los palacios desertado las residencias asoleadas, para eso habíamos deshabitado los castillos las estancias los museos los pesebres donde *dulces Marías nos acechaban dispuestas* a protegernos siempre y *a someternos a un orden inalterado* (115, subrayado mío).[16]

Las mujeres de la novela, ricas, miedosas, ignorantes, justificarían el aguijón crítico dirigido menos a ellas que al sistema social que las deforma. Que la escritora está exponiendo con esto un problema candente, se prueba con recordar el uso insidioso que los regímenes represivos de Brasil y Chile—para nombrar sólo dos ejemplos recientes—hicieron de la mujer para convertirlas en aliadas de aquellos que se oponen a las radicales transformaciones que con urgencia necesita el continente.[17]

Antes de iniciar nuestra consideración sobre el dibujo del sector masculino en la obra, es necesario aclarar que esta división por sexos es mera herramienta facilitadora de este trabajo porque la novela, con ingenioso arte digresivo, mezcla constantemente a los diversos miembros de la familia. Tampoco nuestro más reducido comentario que sigue, refleja menor atención en *ELDMP* al sexo fuerte.

CPR se sirve igualmente del pincel caricaturesco para esbozar las siluetas de algunos hombres de familia, pintados como las mujeres, más como especímenes de una clase que como individuos. De manera general, la misión de perpetuar el apellido es también tarea fundamental para los varones del clan, pero a diferencia del sexo opuesto, existe para ellos una amplia gama de actividades que "está bien visto" que ejerzan. El ganar dinero, "adquirir bienes ... acciones de companías extranjeras, invertir dólares en bancos privados, construir casas en balnearios", se enumeran entre las muchas posibilidades, todas destinadas a acrecentar la riqueza y el poder de la familia (14).

En cuanto a funciones específicas, el padre y el abuelo de Oliverio son centros del proceso desmitificador del *pater familias*, llevado a cabo con la misma inusitada e incisiva irreverencia que vimos aplicada a los oficios femeninos. Recordado por Oliverio como un árbol gigante cuyo rostro perdido en las "celestes" alturas de niño no se atrevía a mirar (23), el padre se presenta en el momento de su agonía como un montón de huesos y pellejos, entusiastamente limpiado por la madre, y usado como campo de experimentación científica o pelota de jugar por los primos:

> En la tarea de sostenerlo y sacudirlo, mientras sus labios azules permanecían abiertos, colgándole como porciones de piel arrancadas del hueso, dos de mis primos llegaron a tal grado de entrenamiento y agilidad ... que solían entretenerse lanzándole de uno a otro lado de la cama ... o jugaban a contarle los dientes que le quedaban, las tiritas de piel que iba perdiendo (20).

La caduca fragilidad del ser humano, obviamente señalada en ese trozo, es sólo una de las claves que se nos propone descifrar en un cuadro en que se destacan los goznes desarticulados de las relaciones filiales. Reaccionando en contra del hombre indiferente que, perdido en sus cuentas, no acertaba a reconocer a cual hijo tenía por delante, y cuyo poder le inspiró sólo terror, el sensible Oliverio reflexiona así ante su moribundo progenitor:

> En la silla, babeante y tembloroso como un rollito de tela azul mojado por la lluvia, mi padre parecía otra cosa ... estaba a mis expensas, podía tenerlo en el hueco de una mano, sacudirlo ... hacerlo rodar como un balón ... dejar que los pájaros lo picotearan ... abrirle y cerrarle los ojos como a un muñeco de cuerda (23).

Fuera del deseo de venganza que la inversión de poderes provoca en el joven, importa indicar la frecuencia del uso del símil del muñeco para la clase a que pertenece la familia. La comparación se repite para el padre ("maniquí ni vivo ni muerto", 22), para la abuela ("muñeca de cera muy antigua a punto de derretirse", 53), y para los invitados de la casa ("multitud de muñecos", 64; "muñecos de cristal", 67), apuntando con ella a la deshumanización de la alta burguesía, y a su condición de marionetas a merced de sus convenciones, sus voraces ambiciones y sus temores.

El vindicativo anhelo de Oliverio va acompañado además por profundo rencor y desprecio hacia su padre, como se ve en la siguiente transcripción que golpea con violencia la supuesta fuerza de los lazos sanguíneos:

> Con un solo movimiento de mis manos, podía hacerlo estallar contra el suelo, como una fruta que se ha caído del árbol por el propio peso de su madurez, y ya en el suelo, su jugo *ensucia* la hilera de lozas ... O lanzarlo hacia el techo, contra el cual se ablandaría como un *gusano* aplastado (23, subrayado mío).[18]

En esta desmitificación de la fuerza de la sangre, se agregan en otras páginas, el deseo de Oliverio de que su padre no hubiera sido en realidad su padre (31), y el irónico descubrimiento de que la semejanza de un gesto y el color de los ojos es el único vínculo entre el hijo y el extraño que lo procreó (27).

Símbolo, como su hijo, de un sistema gastado que se resiste a morir, se presenta al abuelo en igual condición de cosa vieja que vegeta, "sin morir, solamente vivo" (83). Oliverio ha oído decir que el abuelo fue hombre que antaño sometió a la gente a gritos, castigó a los peones, maltrató a hijos y animales, sedujo a las criadas y quemó la tierra de sus vecinos (83). En el relato, a través de los ojos del niño, lo vemos como a un caricaturesco anciano silencioso, absorto en comer, su única preocupación. Por medio de extensas enumeraciones de hilarante efecto—que tuvimos que abreviar en nuestra ilustración—la escritora creó la imagen del pantagruélico apetito del anciano:

> Desde que soy chico, no oigo hablar a mi abuelo. En cambio, lo he visto muchas veces comer. Abre las compuertas de su boca y por el canal azul se hunde la comida; desaparecen las fuentes de arroz, las hileras de uvas, los tomates ... las lechugas ... frutillas, las jarras de vino, las pechugas de pollo; todo desaparece, se sumerje ... por la vía de su pico abierto, succionante como un hoyo lleno de viento (83).

La larga lista de alimentos consumidos caracteriza, creemos, no sólo el apetito del abuelo sino también la voracidad de su clase. El acopio de vocablos reproduce metafóricamente la acumulación de riquezas en que se ha empeñado la familia, fenómeno evidenciado en varios lugares del libro, en que se usa el mismo recurso. Véanse, por ejemplo, la infinidad de objetos suntuarios que llena la casa (estatuas, tapices, cristales, muebles finos, autos) que menciona el capítulo XIII. O, mejor aún, el cáustico fragmento que enumera las posesiones y prerrogativas que como "Caballeros del Orden Constituído", gozaron tanto el padre como el abuelo (116).

La lujuria desbocada de los primos Alfredo y Gastón, las iras irrefrenables del tío Alberto, la crueldad de las bromas del tío Andrés completan la visión del sector masculino cuyas acciones ponen de relieve la violencia de las pasiones encerradas en la mansión, y el ocio opulento en que vive la familia. En cuanto a Federico, la excepción a los rasgos marcados para el clan, deja de pertenecer a él en cuanto tiene la osadía de unirse a los enemigos de su clase. El unánime deseo de sus parientes de que el guerrillero desaparezca sin dejar huellas (140), muestra la quiebra definitiva de los lazos familiares cuando se trata de proteger los intereses.

El optimista final de la novela, narrado por Federico anunciando la llegada de los rebeldes a la ciudad, va precedido por un fragmento que es clara indicación de la imperativa necesidad de destruir la presente estructura familiar que propone el libro. Parece adecuado referirse brevemente a él no sólo porque confirma la idea central del desmoronamiento inevitable del sistema burgués, sino porque CPR eligió otra vez el juego para expresarla. Los niños imitan ahora a "soldados y guerrilleros", ocasión que se aprovecha para señalar algunos aspectos del referente uruguayo simulado en el juego. Oliverio, a quien siempre le toca hacer de guerrillero muerto (perspicaz reparto de papeles de los niños), cuenta así la preparación del combate:

> Sergio me da el revólver más chiquito, el que tiene el gatillo de mica y no dispara nada y se queda con los fusiles, las metralletas ... los cascos ... y a Norberto, que es guerrillero junto conmigo, sólo le da un machete ...
> —La misma cantidad de armas para cada uno—reclama ...
> —Así no es—protesta Sergio. Hay que jugar de verdad: nosotros nos quedamos con casi todo, los fusiles, las ametralladoras, los aviones y el cañón. Ustedes con las granadas y los palos. Así el juego es de veras. A ver quién gana. ¿Quién va a ganar así? (154).

La disparidad de fuerzas no obsta para que Oliverio, el fingido guerrillero provisto de una maravillosa piedra—reminiscente del hilo de sangre de *Cien años de soledad*—provoque la devastación deseada para la casa y la familia. La apocalíptica destrucción esta vez evocadora del final de la obra colombiana, arrasa con todo: desde la mansión, símbolo material del poder del clan, hasta la abuela, representante de la tradición más arraigada con la que apropiadamente termina el capítulo:

> ya no se oía nada
> más que el lento mecerse de la hamaca de la abuela
> solitaria y vacía (sic, 165).

La novela, se habrá entrevisto, ofrece estimulantes ambigüedades para posibles diferentes lecturas. Al problema de los narradores, que señalamos, se pueden añadir la figura de Federico y sus relaciones amorosas y poéticas, los atisbos de lazos incestuosos entre los miembros de la familia, el yo masculino preferido para contar toda la ficción, entre muchos puntos que invitan al estudioso. La intención desmitificadora de la institución burguesa familiar, por otro lado, es muy clara. El ambiente único, aislado que la autora creó magnifica la visión de un mundo que encierra sádicas crueldades, sexualidades desatadas, existencias que vegetan sin objeto; pero sobre todo, el deshumanizante efecto del poder. El libro descubre el imperio abusivo de viejos sobre jóvenes, de padres sobre hijos, de hombres sobre mujeres, de niños sobre niñas; golpeando a su través los nudos sanguíneos que enmascaran relaciones de posesión y de dominio.

La corrupción familiar, sin embargo, no significa según la obra que vaya a ser la fuerza que derribe la institución. La presencia de la guerrilla, y el final victorioso para las fuerzas rebeldes que se propone, muestran sin ambigüedades la posición de CPR respecto a los cambios sociales.

La escritora creó estructuras adecuadas para expresar su crítica visión. En el nivel retórico, las imágenes inusitadas, las originales onomatopeyas, hipérboles, repeticiones, neologismos son, entre otros recursos, claves esenciales de los rasgos paródicos que prevalecen. El inventado mundo caricaturesco participa del humor y del estremecimiento que se dice propio del grotesco,[19] tal vez el modo más adecuado para pintar la decadencia de la familia, reveladora a su vez de la profunda crisis del sistema de que es parte esencial.[20] La presencia de lo lúdico y de lo erótico, agregadas a la vertiente de lo político, se suman a la habilidad en el manejo de la lengua para colocar a la autora y a su obra entre los nombres notables de la literatura hispanoamericana actual.

COLUMBIA UNIVERSITY

Notas

[1]Mario Benedetti, *Literatura uruguaya siglo XX* (Montevideo: Editorial Alfa, 1969), pp. 327 y 324. *Viviendo* (Montevideo: Alfa) apareció en 1963; *Los museos abandonados* (Montevideo: Arca), salió en 1969, después de obtener el Premio de los Jóvenes el año anterior. Esta obra ha sido reeditada en España (Barcelona: Lumen), en 1974.

[2]*El libro de mis primos,* Premio Novela Concurso Treinta Años de *Marcha,* 1969, fue publicada el mismo año por la Biblioteca de Marcha, y es la edición que usaremos en este trabajo. *Indicios pánicos* (Montevideo: Nuestra América) apareció en 1970.

[3]La escritora misma vive en el exilio desde 1972, en España.

[4]Los volúmenes de poesía publicados incluyen *Evohé* (Montevideo: Girón, 1971), *Descripción de un naufragio* (Barcelona: Lumen, 1975), y *Diáspora* (Barcelona: Lumen, 1976). En el género narrativo: *La tarde del dinosaurio* (Barcelona: Planeta, 1976).

[5]A juzgar por una interesante entrevista hecha a la escritora por John F. Deredita, próxima a aparecer en *Texto crítico* (Jalapa, Veracruz), Cortázar se cuenta entre sus autores preferidos. En *El libro de mis primos,* los nombres de Oliverio y Horacio, parecieran un implícito homenaje al argentino que, por lo demás, escribió el prólogo de *La tarde del dinosaurio* de la uruguaya. Fuera de la intención de subvertir el lenguaje y los diseños literarios que, al igual que en Cortázar, se encuentran en Peri Rossi, hay compartidas preferencias entre ellos que sería interesante explorar: Por ejemplo, el "edecán" invisible de Oliverio, evocador del "paredro" cortaziano, y el motivo de la muñeca, tan importante en *El libro de mis primos* como en *62 modelo para armar.* Sobre la muñeca, no hay que olvidar el cuento "Las Hortensias" de Felisberto Hernández, escritor a su vez admirado por Cortázar, y "afín" a la obra de la uruguaya como lo indica la entrevista citada.

[6]Además de los padres, un abuelo y un hermano del narrador principal, Oliverio, contamos 9 tíos, 9 tías, 8 primos y 6 primas.

[7]Ni los reportajes hechos por María Esther Gilio en *La guerrilla tupamara* (La Habana: Casa de las Américas, 1970), ni los recuentos de Alain Labrousse en *Les Tupamaros* (Editions du Seuil, 1970, traduc. de Dinah Livingstone, Penguin Books, 1973) mencionan sucesos guerrilleros para el mes de junio 1966. En carta posterior a esta nota (mayo 20, 1978), la autora nos aclara que los acontecimientos que la inspiraron ocurrieron en 1969, fecha en que escribió la novela.

[8]La segunda edición (Barcelona: Plaza y Janés, 1976), suprimió el poema que abre la primera. En la carta citada a fin de la nota 7, la escritora nos dice que su intención fue remplazar el poema de la edición uruguaya con el titulado "Ellos los

biennacidos", escrito en 1968 y premiado en Uruguay. Los editores españoles no sólo no lo incluyeron, sino además de perderlo, hicieron otros errores en esta descuidada segunda edición. Por ejemplo, se omitieron las notas al pie de las páginas 78, 79 y 118 (correspondientes a 100, 102 y 154 de la segunda) que identifican a los autores cuyos textos se incorporaron a la novela.

[9]El tiempo en que se ubica la narración es impreciso; no sólo no hay claves cronológicas, sino además ocurren constantes mudanzas temporales. Generalmente los narradores comienzan en tiempo presente y pronto, un recuerdo o una asociación les coloca en el pasado. La abundancia del pretérito imperfecto sobre el indefinido, aumenta la imprecisión. Para Oliverio, entre los innumerables ejemplos de vaguedad temporal, compárese su lenguaje de niño en el presente del capítulo X (p.86), con la del adulto del IV, en que frases como "cierta repugnancia que he tenido desde la infancia" (20), sugieren un pasado lejano.

[10]El capítulo XVI se titula "Alina, junio, 1966", que haría suponer que Alina es la que narra. Sin embargo, no hay en ésta o en las otras secciones que tienen que ver con el mismo asunto (el grupo guerrillero de Federico), ninguna referencia a un miembro femenino en el pelotón insurgente. La lengua del narrador en el capítulo, no da ningún indicio sobre su sexo.

[11]Algunos problemas: La semejanza de la lengua de los diversos narradores, por ejemplo Alfredo y Oliverio, o Alfredo y Oscar. La posibilidad de que toda la ficción esté contada por Oliverio y que el libro sea la "obra" que sueña (29). O, de que el narrador único sea Federico, que es poeta, y pasa sus horas escribiendo, según el testimonio de Oliverio y Alina.

[12]Entrevista citada en nota cinco. Varios de los cuentos de *La tarde del dinosaurio* están protagonizados por niños, como también cinco de los ocho relatos que componen *Ulva Lactuca* (próxima a aparecer), según declara la autora en dicha entrevista.

[13]El trozo se burla de los conocimientos científicos, a la vez que pone de relieve la enorme incomprensión que separa al niño del adulto.

[14]El dibujo de las tías en estas páginas es altamente grotesco, pero la comparación con las aves se usa también para los varones: el abuelo (83), y tío Alberto (138), entre otros.

[15]En la primera edición, es el capítulo X de los 19, que incluye el poema inicial. En la segunda es el IX de las 18 secciones.

[16]La autora hace aquí una alusión a su propio quehacer literario. En *Los museos abandonados*, había usado palacios desiertos y castillos abandonados para metaforizar un mundo en desaparición. Por otro lado, la factura diferente de *El libro de mis primos* e *Indicios pánicos* indica también un intento de abandonar sus antiguos modos, buscando aquellos más 'revolucionarios'.

[17]Sobre esto véase *La cultura de la opresión femenina* de Michèle Mattelart (Mexico: Ed. Era, 1977) especialmente el capítulo III, "Cuando las mujeres de la burguesía salen a la calle".

[18]La imagen de la fruta podrida a punto de caer, se usa también para la abuela. En su caso, la anciana/fruta madura resiste tenazmente los embates de un metafórico viento "verde" que Oliverio imagina terminará derribándola (53), temprana señal en el libro hacia la destrucción final.

[19]Wolfgang Kayser, *Lo grotesco, su configuración en pintura y literatura* (Buenos Aires: Nova, 1964; trad. de Ilse M. de Brugger), pp. 167-68.

[20]Hernán Vidal reflexiona sobre este problema en "Narrativa de mitificación satírica: equivalencias socio-literarias", en Anejo Literatura latinoamericana e ideología de la dependencia, *Hispamérica*, año IV, anejo 1, 1975, pp. 57-72.

JULIAN DEL CASAL'S
PORTRAITS OF WOMEN

Priscilla Pearsall

Julián del Casal's portraits of women in prose and poetry were central to the development of his aesthetic world. There is a need to examine the way in which Casal's deeply ambiguous and fragmented attitude toward women evolved through his poetry and how it continued to develop in his prose.[1] It was in large part through the portraits of women that Casal developed the powerful, independent imagery that represents one of the culminations of his poetic vision.

Casal portrayed creative women like the French actress Jeanne Samary, the Cuban novelist Aurelia Castillo de González, and the young Cuban painter Juana Borrero. Cultivated intellectual women living in Havana interested him, women who seem the heiresses of the eighteenth century and who were a catalyst for others' creativity. Casal drew from a variety of subjects outside middle-class life, including, often, the courtesan and the prostitute. From the beginning we find a tendency to see the female as an aesthetic object rather than in terms of a more direct experience of her. It was easier for him to relate to a portrait—whether it was created through oils, photography, poetry, or prose—than to a *mujer de carne y hueso.*

The works to be examined in this paper are from 1890-91, the period in which Casal was publishing the poems of *Nieve,* his second book of poetry. These were years in which the aesthetic and confessional strands of Casal's poetry were developing rapidly; he wrote about portraiture at this time. One of the most revealing statements appeared in an article published March 3, 1890, in which he explains that the portrait exists not only at an aesthetic level, but on a psychological plane as well:

> Para hacer un buen retrato el artista digno de este nombre debe reproducir, no sólo la figura que tiene ante los ojos, sino el espíritu que la anima. . .Hay que mirar el modelo, decía el gran David y leer en él.[2]

Casal initially sought in his ethereal, idealized image of the woman the child's highly fantasized vision of the mother. Casal's own mother died when he was four years old, and this trauma left him obsessed with an unrealistic idea of her. In "A mi madre" in *Nieve* he writes that her image rises from the depths of his remote past;[3] he tended to project this vision on the women he portrayed. Accordingly, like much of his art world, Casal's *retratos de mujeres* must be understood in terms of the creation and destruction of illusion. They belong to a group of poems and articles in which Casal deals with the theme of the impossibility of love. In the early poem "La urna" he had written about his loss of enchantment with women. In *Nieve* the process is complete; in "A la castidad" Casal states flatly, "Yo no amo la mujer..." (*Poesías*, 120), for he feels that she is incapable of enduring love. Yet Casal sought in poem after poem to recapture the illusory vision of the woman that belonged to a lost infantile dream.

The ambiguity of the portraits is paralleled by a simultaneous loss of artistic idealism. In one of his earliest poems, "El poeta y la sirena," published when he was seventeen, Casal had assigned a transcendent role to the poet; he represented "la luz de la verdad," as his voice resounded in eternity (*Poesías*, 205). By the time Casal wrote *Rimas*, his artistic aspirations had run aground within the mist of his own mind:

> Como encalla entre rocas un navío
> que se lanza del oro a la conquista,
> así ha encallado el Ideal de artista
> entre las nieblas del cerebro mío... (*Poesías*, 188).

The portraits of women reflect the gradual disintegration of Casal's artistic and affective idealism, his increasing inability to believe that either love or art has any meaning. They are characterized, moreover, by his attempt to recreate, through aesthetic vision, the fantasies about both women and art which in truth he knew were lost forever.

We see how strong the element of illusion is in an early poem, "Ante el retrato de Juana Samary,"[4] published October 18, 1890. The poem represents the contemplation of a painting of Jeanne Samary,[5] the celebrated actress of the Comédie Française. Robert Jay Glickman, in his article "Letters to Gustave Moreau," has studied the way in which Casal's love was most intense when it was directed to someone far away.[6] In an article on Samary, published October 18, 1890, Casal discussed the way in which illusive, inaccessible women like the Samary of the painting stimulated his fantasies and were more desirable than any *amada existente* could ever be:

> Todo hombre, por muy poco desarrollada que tenga la facultad de soñar, tiene sus amadas ideales, por las que suspira, en horas de abatimiento, con todo su corazón. Esas mujeres, ya estén en el mundo, ya reposen en brazos de la muerte, llegan a adquirir mayor importancia que las amadas existentes, porque nunca se han conocido y la fantasía se complace en revistirlas de atributos inmortales.[7]

Casal writes that among the women he has loved without ever meeting, Jeanne Samary "figura en primera línea" (*Prosas,* III, 13). This is evident in the line with which he begins the poem, "Nunca te conocí, mas yo te he amado..." (*Poesías*, 127). Casal wrote the poem in front of the painting after receiving news of her death; the element of death and the remoteness of the woman link her with Casal's infantile image of the mother. Casal idealizes the painting calling it an "imagen ideal" (*Poesías*, 127), and he emphasizes Samary's ethereal, transcendent role when he calls her flight in death "el raudo vuelo hacia el bello país desconocido" (*Poesías*, 127). In addition, he underlines the dream-like quality of the entire collection, of which this is the first poem, by entitling it *La gruta del ensueño*. The desire to assign a transcendent role to woman in his art, yet its impossibility, was a conflict Casal never resolved. In his last poem, "Cuerpo y alma," published posthumously, Casal still desires this vision of woman, as he captures it for the last time in Poe's incorporeal heroines who inhabit the golden mists of dream and show the way to the elusive "palacio de la Dicha."[8]

Casal emphasizes first the surface happiness and beauty of the portrait, and then the contradictory emotional reality which it hides. Underneath the image he senses the woman's sadness and terror of death. Casal's poem is revealing not for what we learn about the French actress, but because of what it reveals about both Casal's aesthetic world and his psychology. The Poet can identify with his subject; he writes, "en ti hallaba un alma hermana,/ alegre en lo exterior y dentro triste" (*Poesías*, 127). The tension between the apparent gaiety and the interior sadness are characteristic of Casal's whole art world in *Nieve* at that time, for there is a constant contradiction between the beauty and luxuriance of his aestheticism and the developing melancholy of his confessional poetry.

Ultimately the vision of the woman is so ephemeral that it hardly exists; the poetry is shifted into an affective plane as he muses

> si tú nunca sabrás que yo te he amado
> tal vez yo ignore siempre quién me ama (*Poesías*, 128).

At the end of the poem Casal destroys the image he has created; the compelling reality is the poet's underlying sense of the inevitable failure of love.

In another poem from *Nieve*, "Blanco y negro,"[9] published November 1, 1890, two weeks after "Ante el retrato de Juana Samary," the attempt to seek a vision of transcendence through plasticity is more evident than in the previous poem. In "Blanco y negro" the woman is approached as a source of sculptural values through which the illusion of the infinite can be created. Ethereal images are heaped one upon the other; they emerge from the depths of the poet's unconscious into his awareness, associated through a stream of consciousness:

> Sonrisas de las vírgenes difuntas
> en ataúd de blanco terciopelo
> recamado de oro; manos juntas
> que os eleváis hacia el azul del cielo
> como lirios de carne; tocas blancas
> de pálidas novicias absorbidas
> por ensueños celestiales. . . (*Poesías*, 129).

The female images of "Blanco y negro" are surrounded by an ambience created through a series of related images which are ethereal and at the same

time extremely sensuous. Some of them evoke delicate tactile qualities:
". . .los finos celajes errabundos/por las ondas de éter. . ." (*Poesías*, 129).
There are joyous auditory values: ". . .francas/risas de niños rubios. . ."
(*Poesías*, 129); and, especially, shimmering visual qualities: "tornasoles/ que
ostentan en sus alas las palomas/ al volar hacia el Sol. . ." (*Poesías*, 129). This
world of sensation heaped upon sensation is the means of seeking a metaphysical realm.[10] Casal beseeches the profusion of imagery, which spirals
upward with accelerating speed, to carry him to transcendent heights; he
writes mysteriously that that which he has loved will probably be in this
infinite region.

In the second part of the poem there is another series of three-dimensional values, each more violently destructive than the other. They represent
an opposing downward spiral; the images here, too, are female

> hidra de Lerna armada de cabezas. . .
>
> . . .hachas
> que segasteis los cuellos sonrosados
> de las princesas inocentes. . . (*Poesías*, 130).

The plasticity of the second part exists in a world as filled with sensation as
that of the previous one. Now there are violently wracking impressions,
including visual, ". . .relámpago del cielo/que amenaza la vida del pro-
scrito/en medio de la mar. . ." (*Poesías*, 130); tactile, ". . .rachas/de vientos
tempestuosos. . ." (*Poesías*, 130); and entirely interiorized emotion, ". . .pesa-
dillas/que pobláis el espíritu de espanto. . ." (*Poesías*, 130). The downward
spiral, just as the ascending thrust, carries the poet to a nihilistic region
where he searches for an elusive *lo que yo he amado.*

The world of sensation of the first part of the poem is destroyed by the
second; it bore the seeds of its own destruction, for Casal's world of female
imagery is as filled with the pathologically destructive as it is with the
sublimely ethereal. They both lead only to "el seno de la nada."[11] As the
illusion created through female imagery collapses, its extreme luxuriance
contrasts with the nihilism which underlies it, for it represents a vain
attempt to pursue something elusive, beyond, which even Casal does not
understand, cannot define. The underlying preoccupation of the poem, just
as in "Ante el retrato de Juana Samary," is the frustration of love, here of
love lost and not clearly remembered. As in the earlier poem, an artistic realm
that had been created as a means of seeking transcendence is in the end the
way to a vision of nihilism and pathology.

There are other female images in *Nieve* in which we see the same
combination of ethereal and destructive values that we find in "Ante el
retrato de Juana Samary" and "Blanco y negro." One of them is the portrait
of Casal's muse whom he describes in the poem "La reina de la sombra,"[12]
published May 10, 1891. He portrays her as an incorporeal being existing in a
voluptuously supernal ambiance:

> Tras el velo de gasa azulada
> en que un astro de plata se abre

> y con fúlgidos rayos alumbra
> el camino del triste viandante,
> en su hamaca de nubes se mece
> una diosa de formas fugaces
> que dirige a la tierra sombría
> su mirada de brillos astrales (*Poesías*, 138).

Yet she also has a bizarre aspect; Casal shows in her *retrato* the juxtaposition of the sublime and the pathological so characteristic of his art[13]

> Ora muestra su rostro de virgen
> o su torso de extraña bacante. . .(*Poesías*, 140).

She is above all the muse of his confessional poetry:

> Esa diosa es mi musa adorada,
> la que inspira mis cantos fugaces,
> donde sangran mis viejas heridas
> y sollozan mis nuevos pesares (*Poesías*, 140).

It is this pathological element—not the ethereal—that Casal will increasingly emphasize in the portraits of women.

The failure to sustain the illusion of the ethereal qualities associated with woman takes its final toll in the poem "Kakemono,"[14] published March 22, 1891, three weeks before "La reina de la sombra." The poem can be related to the earlier "Ante el retrato de Juana Samary," for Casal also wrote "Kakemono" before a portrait of a woman. In this poem, however, the poet reproduces the Oscar Held photograph of María Cay so that the poem, instead of being the contemplation of a painting, represents the transposition of a photograph into poetry. María, the sister of a friend of Casal, had dressed for the photographer in the Japanese costume she had worn to a masked ball given a short time earlier.[15]

The title "Kakemono" means Japanese hanging scroll, and the poem is in fact envisioned as an Oriental screen. Casal uses the same technique of heaping imagery upon imagery that we saw in "Blanco y negro." We are drawn into his art world; sensation is heaped upon sensation in the creation of an extraordinarily sensually-charged poetic vision. The auditory, the olfactory, the visual, and the tactile all come into play as we become lost in Casal's artifice. Esperanza Figueroa Amaral has studied the way in which art form is piled upon art form as was never done in Europe.[16] The poem's rhythm, too, is typical of Casal. He breaks his hendecasyllables irregularly; this contributes auditorially to a sense of incantation to dazzle us further with his aestheticism. Yet the portrait is haunting for its absence of human emotion. Casal is interested in its artistic properties only; the woman he portrays interests him little as a person. In fact, her identity is changed as she is transformed into a Japanese woman.

In the poem we see the collapse of Casal's attempt to create illusion through the sensuous portrait of a woman; the ethereal, idealized vision glimpsed in "Ante el retrato de Juana Samary" is no longer accessible to Casal. The portrait is paradoxical because, although it is made as light and diaphanous as an Oriental screen by such technical elements as the use of light and the airy landscape images on the gown, it becomes entrapped in its own delirium of aestheticism. Its extreme sensuousness leads nowhere beyond itself.

In recreating the portrait of María as she looked on the night of the masked ball, Casal attempts to evoke, in an almost Proustian sense, the youthful illusions which he had felt then. Yet he reveals that his experience has been the opposite; although he can recreate the image of María, he is incapable of recapturing the memories and emotions of that night. The woman's image remains at the end of the poem as a hollow shell, weighed down by its own dazzling artistry, and stripped of the emotions of joy which originally gave it meaning. The theme of the poem becomes the failure of all illusion because plasticity has become incapable of reaching beyond itself to glimpse a metaphysical realm, and joyous, youthful illusion is revealed to be as evanescent as aesthetic vision. The emptiness of the image is all that remains; it evokes the artist's *glacial tristeza*, the feeling of interior coldness which was to become a hallmark of Casal's poetry.

The vision of the woman as image or aesthetic object and a sense of the failure of illusion pervade Casal's prose articles on women. On June 3, 1890, he published two portraits which are important to the development of the imagery of his later poetry. In one of these, entitled "La derrochadora,"[17] Casal portrays a Parisian *demi-mondaine*, a high-class prostitute; the figure of the courtesan was one that intrigued Casal, and he wrote numerous articles about her. She became for him a symbol of his aesthetic world, for her artificial beauty and elegance were as transitory yet compelling as those of his own artistic vision.

In this article we find that with the failure to create transcendent illusion through his aesthetic world, Casal's portraiture of women has lost its ethereally diaphanous quality. Now it is becoming increasingly hard and jewel-like. The *demi-mondaine* lives surrounded by objects; she reminds one of Manet's *Olympia* as we see her at her morning ritual of bathing and being perfumed by her maid among glitteringly polished mirrors, jewels, and jasper. Their hard surfaces are accentuated by the contrast with the soft texture of the courtesan's robe and skin. The maid transforms her into an aesthetic object and a sex object. In this world of *cosas*, in which she is herself another one, the woman spends her days buying art objects

> . . .en cada tienda, halla algo nuevo que comprar. Ya es un brazalete de oro, cuajado de pedrería digno de una Leonor de Este; ya un abanico ínfimo, con paisaje grotesco, todo hecho con tintas de relumbrón; ya una estatua de mármol, obra maestra de un artista desconocido, pero que firmaría un Falgiere; ya un cromo americano... (*Prosas*, I, 238).

The aestheticism, in spite of its hard, object quality, is now very evanescent; her search for these art objects is frenzied and compulsive. What she buys one day is discarded almost immediately to make room for the next day's purchases—as the prostitute herself is interchangeable with many others who are objects bought and used for a short time.[18]

The one emotional quality which Casal emphasizes in this woman is her lack of attachment to any other person; the *demi-mondaine* by definition has an ambivalent relationship to the bourgeois society which exploits her and off which she lives. The prose portrait is related to the *retratos* in poetry in their conflictual attitude toward love. Here the woman's attitude is entirely cynical; Casal writes that when anyone mentions love to her, her response is an ironic, "¡Desdichados! ¿Todavía créeis en eso?" (*Prosas*, I, 238).

Ultimately the portrait reveals much about Casal's aesthetic world for he was becoming as detached from reality as the woman he portrays.[19] He would write two years later in the *busto* of the young Cuban artist Juana Borrero that artists construct in their fantasy an ideal quarantine where they live "con sus ensueños."[20] Casal's portraits of women seem increasingly to belong to this family of imaginary beings created within his own fantasy.

As Casal felt that aesthetic illusion and reality were slipping from his grasp, he attempted to concretize that illusion—and eventually all experience—in compensation for its extreme tenuousness. In *Nieve* his art became one where, at times, everything was seen in sculptural terms. Although the concrete, dazzling aestheticism of the portraits of women becomes increasingly frentic, its coldness only reflects the underlying emotional sterility of the writer who created it.[21] Three days after he published this portrait of the French courtesan, Casal would write in a review of Aurelia Castillo de González's *Pompeya* that modern art is essentially the expression of ennui and pathology: "el malestar permanente, el escepticismo profundo, la amargura intensa, las aspiraciones indefinidas y el pesimismo sombrío. . ."[22] There is no better metaphor for Casal's own *glacial tristeza*, his sadness expressed in icily sculptural form, than the Parisian *demi-mondaine* as she is seen dwelling in a nightmare vision of life experienced entirely in terms of objects by a psyche devoid of emotion.

The vision of pathology with which Casal's portraits of women are so closely associated is given deeper expression in another prose portrait, "Croquis femenino,"[23] published the same day as "La derrochadora." The woman of this sketch, like the prostitute, remains unnamed, but she represents another type of woman Casal admired. She is one of the wealthy, cultivated Cuban women who lived apart from the *haute-bourgeoisie* of Havana, and whose houses were meeting places for writers and artists. Like the French courtesan, she lives in an environment dominated by objects. Casal gives an exhaustive inventory of her *salón*:

> Espejos venecianos, con marcos de bronce, ornados con ligeros amorcillos; pieles de tigres arrojados al pie de olorosos divanes; tibores japoneses, guarnecidos de dragones y quimeras; mesas de laca incrustadas de nácar, cubiertas de un pueblo de estatuitas; óleos admirables, firmados por reputados pintores, todo se encuentra en aquel salón. . . (*Prosas*, II, 141).

Just one month earlier, on April 26, 1890, Casal had writtren an article "Verdad y poesía"[24] rejecting Zola. Yet in these sketches Casal evidences a Zola-like preoccupation with exterior reality.

It is not, however, only exterior reality that is seen in terms of plasticity in this article; the objects which fill the world of the prose portraits are becoming interiorized. When Casal expresses the woman's psychology, he turns to the plastic qualities of the fairy tale to create an interior vision. He writes that this nameless woman is one of the people of his time who

> . . .viven siempre inclinados sobre sí mismos, mirándose por dentro, como si llevaran allí, a semejanza de la heroína de los cuentos de hadas, una gruta formada de piedras preciosas, donde ven una ninfa encantadora que se adormece entre los cantos de pájaros maravillosos y los aromas de flores desconocidas (*Prosas*, II, 140).

We see that even the woman's introversion is expressed in terms of glittering, gem-like preciosity, for the grotto, where she dwells within this fantastically sculptured psychological world, is formed of jewels.

Casal emphasizes that she, like the prostitute of "La derrochadora," is detached from reality and incapable of feeling emotion for the people around her. Her writes ironically that she is so pathologically linked with the objects in her environment that she has fallen in love with one of them, a portrait of Murat which hangs in a corner of her living room:

> En uno de los ángulos de su salón, hay un cuadro al óleo, puesto sobre un caballete de madera negra incrustada de bronce, que representa a Murat, con su traje de seda color de rosa, guarnecido de encajes; con su casco de terciopelo negro, coronado de plumas blancas; y con su espada brillante, de puño de oro, esmaltado de pedrerías, suspendida en el aire, en actitud de marchar al frente de invisibles granaderos (*Prosas*, II, 141).

The art object is now so interiorized that it is becoming the imagery of the woman's mind. She fills the void of her soul with three-dimensional values in an attempt to give form to the nihilism within. Casal writes that as she drives through the streets of Havana she resembles a legendary queen in exile, trying to forget her lost kingdom,

> . . .una Semíramis moderna derribada de su trono. . .que ha venido a olvidar entre los esplendores naturales del nuevo mundo, la imagen torturadora de su Asiria perdida (*Prosas*, II, 140).

The woman is herself an image tormented by an image in this *Through-the-Looking-Glass* delirium of highly fantasized plasticity.

In this *croquis femenino* the future development of Casal's aesthetic vision can be perceived, for Casal was becoming as haunted by imagery as the woman he portrays. At the end of another prose portrait written two and one-half years later, Casal would confess that the image of the person depicted has become an obsession that tortured him, and that its expression was a pathological necessity:

> . . .su imagen me obsede de tal manera que, cansado de tenerla conmigo, ya en mis días risueños, ya en mis noches de insomnio, yo he decidido arrojarla hoy de mi cerebro al papel, del mismo modo que un árbol arroja, en vigoroso estremecimiento, sobre el polvo del camino, al pájaro errante que, posado en su copa, entona allí una canción vaga, extraña, dolorosa y cruel.[25]

Casal's attitude toward the image is as ambiguous as his view of other aspects of his art world. The poet's desire to free himself of the pain and cruelty with which it haunts him constitutes in part a rejection of the image; yet it is something he sought incessantly.

As the plasticity of his artistic vision evolved, Casal became less and less dependent upon pictorial devices like portraiture and landscape for its development. At the same time that he was writing about his portraiture in the passage quoted above, Casal was publishing the poem "Dolorosa,"[26] in which we see the emergence of the powerful, independent image of the dagger. It emerges from the depths of the poet's psyche and evokes the conflict between the forces of life and death within. In "Dolorosa" the imagery, which evokes sexual mystery and violence, exists in a much more abstract, psychological world than that of the portraits. The retratos de mujeres, however, had already begun to evoke the artist's inner conflicts—his anguished attitude toward love, and the meaning of aestheticism—for Casal in the early portraits, especially, seems undecided about whether his artistic world is the means of searching for transcendence or a route to a vision of pathology. It is only in the later portraits that it becomes understood as the means to a vision of nihilism and pathology.

Three months after he published "La derrochadora" and "Croquis femenino," Casal published, on September 3, 1890, an article in which he dealt with the problem which was central to Baudelaire's essays on the Salon of 1859, that of the distinction between historical and photographic reality and the deeper interior reality of the novel.[27] Baudelaire had dealt with the question of reality specifically in relation to the portrait; he had said that portraiture meant capturing the drama of a life.[28] When we study the images of women created at the time Casal wrote on Baudelaire's theories and made his own earlier statements concerning portraiture, we see that the retratos de mujeres evoke not so much the lives of the women he portrays, as they reveal the unfolding drama of Casal's own aesthetic and emotional development. They are central to his poetic world, beginning with a gradual sense of the failure of aesthetic and psychological illusion, through the increasing plasticizing of experience, to the eventual interiorization of the art object until it becomes the imagery of a landscape of the mind. Casal's portraits of women necessarily fail as portraits for they are essentially narcissistic—highly polished mirrors of the evolution of an art world. Although their subject is other human beings, they remain as Casal's statement of the impossibility of communication and love. In their final pathological vision of hard, cold aestheticism in an emotional void, they evoke above all Casal's own glacial tristeza, the coldness at the center of the artist's soul.

NORTHERN ILLINOIS UNIVERSITY

Notes

[1]There have been several studies dealing with Casal's attitude toward women. Carmen Poncet sees Casal's dualistic vision of women as one more aspect of polarity in a work where everything tends to be seen in dualistic terms, the fragmented vision of an author hopelessly divided against himself. See Carmen Poncet, "Dualidad de Casal," *Revista Bimestre Cubana,* 53 (1944), 193-212. In the same year Gustavo Duplessis studied the ambiguity of Casal's attitude toward women. Gustavo Duplessis, "Julián del Casal," *Revista Bimestre Cubana,* 54 (1944), 31-75, 140-70, 243-86. Monner Sans discusses the mystery that surrounds Casal's relationships with women both in his life and in his art. José María Monner Sans, *Julián del Casal y el modernismo hispano-americano* (México: Colegio de México, 1952). More recently Robert Jay Glickman has noted Casal's compulsive need to give and receive affection, yet his inability to establish relationships with women. Robert Jay Glickman, "Letters to Gustave Moreau," *Revista Hispánica Moderna,* 37 (1972-73), 101-35. Carlos Blanco Aguinaga has studied Casal's poem "Neurosis" in which the woman is one more meaningless object in a decadent turn-of-the-century society. Carlos Blanco Aguinaga, "Crítica marxista y poesía: Lectura de un poema de Julián del Casal," in *Analysis of Hispanic Texts: Current Trends in Methodology,* ed. Mary Ann Beck and others (New York: Bilingual Press, 1976), pp. 191-205.

[2]Julián del Casal, "Armando Menocal: Nuevos retratos," in *Prosas* (La Habana: Consejo Nacional de Cultura, 1963), II, 63. Further notes in the text of this paper refer to Casal, *Prosas* (La Habana: Consejo Nacional de Cultura, 1963-64), I, II, III and Casal, *Poesías* (La Habana: Consejo Nacional de Cultura, 1963). All dates of publication for Casal's poetry and prose are from Esperanza Figueroa Amaral's chronological bibliography. Esperanza Figueroa Amaral, "Bibliografía cronológica de la obra de Julián del Casal," *Revista Iberoamericana,* 35 (1969), 385-99.

[3]Casal, *Poesías,* p. 117.

[4]Casal, "Ante el retrato de Juana Samary," in *Poesías,* p. 127.

[5]The portrait which is the subject of Casal's poem is generally identified as the Renoir painting of the actress. In the "Crónica semanal" published the day after the poem, however, Casal himself identifies the artist as the French portrait painter Jacques-Fernand Humbert. See Casal, "Crónica semanal," in *Prosas,* III, 13.

[6]Glickman, p. 106.

[7]Casal, "Crónica semanal," in *Prosas,* III, 12.

[8]Casal, "Cuerpo y alma," *Poesías,* p. 196. In "Cuerpo y alma," Casal's fragmented vision of women is especially apparent. Although he exalts Poe's incorporeal women and relates them to what he perceives to be the spiritual side of his nature, he equates the physical aspect of his being with frenetic, emotionless sex with a prostitute.

[10]The previous spring, Casal had translated an excerpt from Maupassant's *La Vie errante* which deals with one of the ideas most central to nineteenth-century thought, that the senses are the means to transcending the limits of the material. See "Casal's Translations of Baudelaire and Maupassant: The Failure of Transcendent Vision," in *Essays in Honor of Jorge Guillén on the Occasion of his Eighty-Fifth Year* (Cambridge, Mass.: Abedul Press, 1977), pp. 64-73.

[11]Casal had written only slightly more than one month earlier, on September 27, 1890, in his portrait of the Cuban poet José Fornaris, that the modern poet is a nihilist like Leconte de Lisle or Leopardi who want only to "disolverse en el seno de la nada." Casal, "José Fornaris," in *Prosas,* I, 278.

[12]Casal, "La reina de la sombra," *Poesías,* p. 138.

* [13]In the same year, on December 30, 1891, Casal would publish his poem "Sueño de gloria: Apotesois de Gustavo Moreau" (*Poesías*, 104); there a woman, Helen of Troy, symbolizes the decadent beauty Casal sought through his art. The image of Helen fuses the ethereal and the pathological, values which were becoming central to Casal's aesthetic. Casal admired Gustave Moreau's paintings of Helen and Salomé and transposed both of them into the poetry of *Mi museo ideal*, of which "Sueño de gloria" is the final poem. Moreau and Huysmans, both of whom had a decisive influence upon the poetry of *Mi museo ideal*, combined aesthetic and pathological elements in their portraits of women. See Mario Praz, *The Romantic Agony*, trans. Angus Davidson, 2nd ed (1933; rpt London: Oxford University Press, 1970); Frank Kermode, *Romantic Image* (New York: Macmillan, 1957), p. 70; and Lee Fontanella, "Parnassian Precept and a New Way of Seeing Casal's *Museo ideal*," *Comparative Literature Studies*, 7 (1970), 466.

[14]Casal, "Kakemono," *Poesías*, p. 132.

[15]Casal had discussed the Oscar Held photograph of María in "Album de la ciudad: Retratos femeninos" (*Prosas*, II, 95), published April 1, 1890, one year before "Kakemono" appeared. María Cay is the "cubana japonesa" of Darío's poetry. See Esperanza Figueroa Amaral, "El cisne modernista," in *Estudios críticos sobre el modernismo*, ed. Homero Castillo (Madrid: Editorial Gredos, 1968), p. 313. María Cay's family had lived in the Orient because her father had been the Cuban consul in Japan.

[16]Figueroa, "El cisne modernista," p. 313.

[17]Casal, "Croquis femenino: Derrochadora," in *Prosas*, II, 147.

[18]In this productive period during the final three years of his life, Casal would turn increasingly to Huysmans in the development of his aesthetic. In an article he wrote in 1892, Casal discussed the manner in which, for Huysmans, art was an unending search for sensuous stimulation; this sense of the artistic is apparent in these two prose portraits of women. See Casal, "Jorís Karl Huysmans," *Prosas*, I, 173.

[19]In the following year, on March 19, 1891, Casal wrote a letter to his friend Esteban Borrero Echeverría that he believed that the ideal life for him was now to live alone, in obscurity, "solo, arrinconado e invisible a todos, exceptos para usted y dos o tres personas." Casal, "Cartas a Esteban Borrero Echeverría," in *Prosas*, III, 85. Frank Kermode sees the isolation of the artist as essential to the pursuit of imagery. See Kermode, *Romantic Image*, p. 2.

[20]Casal, "Juan Borrero," in *Prosas*, I, 267.

[21]In an article of art criticism published July 11, 1890, one month after this portrait appeared, Casal wrote that in the final period of an artist's development his work reflects the coldness of his soul. Casal, "Academia de Pintura: Dos cuadros," in *Prosas*, II, 177,

[22]Casal, "Libros nuevos: I *Pompeya* por Aurelia Castillo de Gonzáles," ibid., p. 145.

[23]Casal, "Croquis femenino," ibid., p. 140.

[24]Casal, "Verdad y poesía," ibid., p. 115.

[25]Casal, "El hombre de las muletas de níquel," in *Prosas*, I, 233.

[26]Casal, "Dolorosa," *Poesías*, p. 178.

[27]Casal, "En el cafetal," in *Prosas*, I, 222.

[28]Charles Baudelaire, "Le Portrait," in *Salon de 1859*, in *Oeuvres complètes*, ed. Y.-G Le Dantec (Paris: Editions Gallimard, 1961), p. 1072. Casal's portraits of men are more perceptively written in that they capture the conflicts central to the lives of their subjects—as his portraits of women never do.

A MYTHOLOGY FOR WOMEN:
MONIQUE WITTIG'S *LES GUERILLERES*

Marcelle Thiébaux

Those of us who have experienced bewilderment, however admiring, over some of the rich obscurities in Monique Wittig's *Les Guérillères* (Paris, 1969),[1] may have turned with a sigh of comprehension to the final third of that work. There, indeed, are plain statements. Man is declared the enemy: "The male besiegers are near the walls." These bearded besiegers are saying familiar things—that the war of the women is "slave revolt, a revolt against nature." The men wonder at the women's bellicosity, arguing that after all, "they have supported you, they have put you on a pedestal...adored you like a goddess," and a few breaths later, that they have "burned you at their stakes...possessed violated taken subdued humiliated you to their hearts' content." The men press for their own indispensability, for without them there would be no one to make and pilot airplanes, no one to write books or to govern. Coldly enraged, the women accuse (some pages later): "He has robbed you of that passion for knowledge.... He has stolen your wisdom.... He has invented your history" (pp. 100-02, 110-11).

Ah, so that is what it is all about. No reader would have the slightest difficulty with any of this, explicitly stated as it is. And yet, that is not the only thing it is about. The whole meaning of *Les Guérillères* is not exhausted once the male/female war has been identified as the old desperate struggle for ascendancy. For *Les Guérillères* is very much about literature and how it is put together, about the necessary rending and rebuilding of traditional structures and of the recreating of language itself. Out of ruined fragments new mythologies, fictions, and syntaxes may by formulated. Certainly the toppling of traditional mythologies is a usual technique for innovative poets and forgers. Readers of Joyce's *Ulysses*, and of the poetry of Yeats and Eliot, may observe the conversion of ancient myths to the uses of the present, as well as a fresher, intenser use of language. The old connotations of words render them stale, inexpressive, worn smooth as coins through handling and familiarity; their meanings alter subtly through usage ("words slip and slide," wrote Eliot). So language—words and syntax—as well as the traditional literary structures were to be broken up and torn apart, in order to be renewed. Out of destruction, new unity. To appropriate a line of Yeats, "Nothing can be sole or whole that has not first been rent."

But there is, of course, a difference for the feminist writer like Wittig. Contemporary male writers remodeled the myths they inherited while maintaining a certain affection for holy Dionysus, Homer, Dante, or Red Hanrahan of old. On the contrary, the feminist writer feels compelled, "against our will," to rely on the received masculine language, at the risk of not communicating at all. Even the very technique of adopting and converting a mythology is well established among masculine writers and so cannot be considered a feminist innovation. But the feminist motivation for overturning and rebuilding the familiar literary structures is political as well as literary, a necessary gesture of denial of the authority of masculine culture.

Wittig is everywhere at pains to indicate this gesture. In her first novel, *The Opoponax*, she simply ignores the "true" definition of opoponax an herb used in perfumery. Instead she constructs fantastic meanings:

> The opoponax is indescribable because he never has the same form, and belongs neither to the animal, vegetable, or mineral kingdom. . . . His nature is unstable. . . . He prevents pupils from being able to close their desks, causes the faucet in the lavatory to drip, and floats over your face in the dawn on the windowsill, makes it hard for you to comb your hair in the morning.

In *Les Guérillères*, Wittig meets the matter of conventional meaning head-on: "The language you speak poisons your glottis tongue palate lips." Her women say to one another: "The language you speak is made up of words that are killing you. They say, the language you speak is made up of signs that rightly speaking designate what men have appropriated" (p. 114). The new reality will have to be given shape with new words. Later the women point out that "in what concerns them everything has to be remade starting from basic principles. They say that in the first place the vocabulary of every language is to be examined, modified, turned upside down, that every word must be screened" (p. 135). In *The Lesbian Body* (1975), Wittig's most recent novel, she describes the need to reflect a new action, to create new symbols and fresh fictional forms:

> The Amazons are women who live among themselves, by themselves and for themselves at all the generally accepted levels: fictional, symbolic, actual. . . . [O]ur symbols deny the traditional symbols. . . . [W]e possess an entire fiction into which we project ourselves. . . . It is our fiction that validates us.

Creating new forms means necessarily doing violence to received structures, both of language and genre. In *The Lesbian Body*, Wittig slashes the personal pronouns, for example, writing "J/e" (for "I"), thereby assailing the male writer's traditional usage of "je" to refer principally to himself. She fulfills her "desire to bring the real body violently to life in the words of the book." She "enters the language by force."

When Wittig writes about her literary purpose she uses words conveying force, violence, cutting, obliteration. The imagery of smashing and tearing in *The Lesbian Body* is evident in her celebrations of dismembered bodies, arranged in rich catalogues of blood, lymph, sinew, ganglia, plasma, blisters, nerves, excrement, buttocks, breast, and fur. These reiterated catalogues, it can be recognized, recreate the emotion of physical love of the fiercest intensity. Perhaps even more significantly, however, they are an imitation of the splintering of language, and serve as a trope for the vehemence of the creative act itself. The writer's workshop, Willa Cather once commented, is necessarily strewn with broken useless pieces, once the work of art—like a splendid machine—has been completed and wheeled out. Wittig chooses in *The Lesbian Body* to weld the broken pieces, *and* the business of breaking them too, into her completed structure.

Wittig's method and her declarations in the novels referred to make it clear that she breaks in order to rebuild. In a perceptive essay, to be recommended for an understanding of similar method in *Les Guérillères*, Erica Ostrovsky calls attention to the novel's cyclic pattern of destruction and recreation: "Wittig's affirmation that overthrow is necessary for new creation, is carried out in her destruction of existing myths and their re-creation into new forms."[2] From the syntactically fragmented poems that open and close *Les Guérillères*, Ostrovsky isolates the statement: *Tout geste est renversement.* This may be translated "ALL ACTION IS OVER-THROW," as David Le Vay has done; but it can also mean, perhaps more importantly, since we are talking about literature, that "every literary gesture (or invention) can be *reversed*" to yield new literary structures.[3]

The "literary gestures" I am interested in are the myths and poems that Wittig invokes and reverses. I would like to examine some of the mythologies that unfold in the novel quite apart from the language of explicit statement. For Wittig is a deeply literate and literary writer. What Laura Durand has called "the ghost of the academy" is discernible in the novel, though far more appealingly than Durand's expression would imply. Nor is Wittig steeped exclusively in classical myth. Mary Pringle Spraggins, in an essay containing excellent insights, reminds us of Wittig's use of one overarching modern myth, "crucial to an understanding of *Les Guérillères*, the Freudian myth of male physiological and psychological supremacy."[4]

The word "myth" comes from a Greek word that means *word*. Myths are things said. Myths acquire force and permanence because they are pronounced, spoken repeatedly. Wittig emphasizes this repetitive, incanta-tory power of myth by indicating "The women are saying," or "They say." Normally, French renders "they say," "people say," or "it is said," simply as the impersonal "on dit." Wittig uses this locution in *The Opoponax*. But significantly in *Les Guérillères*, Wittig insists on the feminine pronoun: "They say" is "Elles disent." Myths, then are things being said by women. women make and remake the myths. Myths both ancient and medieval keep recurring and acquiring accretions of meaning throughout the special history of women that unrolls in *Les Guérillères*.

A word about this history may be useful. Although the time scheme of *Les Guérillères*, isn't at all conventional, time takes on a discernible shape as the novel progresses. Four historical stages may be observed: (a) a primitive innocent 'golden age,' paradisal, abundant with fruits, spices, colors. Gradually there is an accumulation of allusions to (b) progress, architecture, technology. Already a sense of the past is developing. Archaeologists dig up pictures. Women look at the old photos. Some of the old ways are revaluated or abandoned. The third stage is heralded by (c) preparations for war. Choreographed battle formations in this phase replace the earlier more innocent dance formations. Dance and military configurations fuse in the form of the "carmagnole," the maddened blood-inspired dance said to be popular in the French Revolution. War in fact is waged. And finally (d) a reconciliation occurs between men and women with calm rejoicing, dance, and song. There is something like a recovery of the original innocence—with a difference of course. Men and women are together: the pronoun "we" is used for the first time. At each phase of this history, the women formulate some version of the principle of "O," the divine and earthly vulval circle, and their variety of responses to it. This "O" is the novel's unifying principle of order and structure in the universe, as well as in art, civilization, and culture.

At each stage of the women's history, myths, folktales, and fictions are incorporated and retold, "overthrown," and "reversed." My purpose will be to examine three related schemes or clusters, whether of myths or literary tradition, and to clarify their sources and identify their transformed meanings. First I'll introduce a cluster of interconnected myths concerning the creation and other religious narratives, indicating how Wittig reinterprets feminine experience in terms of traditionally masculine operations. Secondly, I will show how she revises the roles of female divinities, drawing upon the imagery of sun/fire/mirrors. And third, I will discuss the poems at the beginning and the end of *Les Guérillères*, disclosing the underlying bird symbolism, drawn from myth and poetry.

I

The opening scene of *Les Guérillères* depicts a group of women observing one of their number urinating while rain streams down all about them. The scene represents a fusion of two types of ancient myth: one of creation, one of destruction. The woman who micturates thus in harmony with the fringes of rain pouring from the roof tiles re-enacts first the creation of the world, as it was said to have been achieved by Eastern divinities who generated the entire world with their sperm, "spontaneously" ejaculating without benefit of a female body. Male creation myths demonstrating the sufficiency of a divine male fluid, and precluding the female role, exist in western tradition as well: The severed male member of Cronos, hurled into the sea, engendered the goddess Aphrodite, "born of the foam." The goddess Athene sprang fully formed from the head (i.e., penis) of her single parent, Zeus. And secondly, the act of micturition evokes the biblical flood, or any of the stories, Indian or Babylonian, of a great deluge that restored heaven and earth to its original chaos. Hence, destruction/creation are aspects of a single act for Wittig, necessary for the emergence of a new literature.

The scene that immediately succeeds this one recasts, in two sentences, the fall of man and the intercessive role of the Virgin Mary. "The women frighten each other by hiding behind trees" (as the serpent did in Eden). "One or another of them asks for grace" (the Virgin's dispensation). But the sense of the evil is neutralized and in fact reduced to a kind of game like blindman's buff, despite the "sounds of falling." "Cries" signal the fall, but "laughter" affirms the granting of grace.

Other familiar myths are alluded to, in which women assume independent roles. Throughout the novel there are drinking and dancing revels. Women drink together by the full moon from bottles of colored liquids. Each has permission to "fall dead drunk or lose her self control" (pp. 19-20). On another occasion, they "wander running through the avenues," while being offered colored sugary syrups (pp. 54-56). Later in fields of trampled poppies "the women say they are drunk." They dance, bare-armed and bare-legged. "Their loosened hair hides their cheeks, then, flung back, reveals shining eyes, lips parted in song" (p. 62). These are the frenzied and drug-inspired movements of the bacchantes, or maenads, in antiquity the female followers of Dionysus. Wittig draws attention to the parallel: "They shake their hair like the bacchantes, who love to agitate their thyrsi (the dionysian ivy-twined staffs)." But Dionysus himself is absent. Instead of swirling about the god, the women revel for themselves, and in fact dance in "homage to warlike Minerva," the goddess of wisdom (p. 93).

In classical mythology, Dionysus was said to have met his death by being torn, his body scattered. Wittig's women also assume the roles of sacrificial male gods. The entire narrative of *Les Guérillères* is punctuated (as was Wittig's first novel, *The Opoponax*) with a series of deaths. But here there are bleeding bodies, dismemberments as well, and ritual embalmings and entombings. The theme of tearing, crushing, dismembering is stated by an analogy—the crushing of poppy flowers, pinks, myrtle flowers, walnuts, and seeds, that thus yield rich and fragrant oils (pp. 36-37). The many martyrdoms of women are represented so as to parallel the ritual tearing and veneration of sacred male bodies: Osiris, Dionysus, Orpheus, Christ. One such story related by women in *Les Guérillères* features "the white face of the beautiful Marie Viarme" which "hangs detached from the trunk, torn across the throat. One sees the sudden streaming of blood on her cheeks" (p. 36). Or, there is a story about Iris Our, whose "severed carotid releases gushes of blood. There is some on her white garments. It has flowed over her breast, it has spread, there is some on her hands. . . . Clots have formed crusts on her clothes." And, women mourn the death of Julie (p. 82), publicly hanged on a gibbet, or strangled, or decapitated, or broken alive on the wheel. No one is sure of the mode of her death, but all agree as to the reason for her being put to death. It was the same as that of "the woman of whom it is written that she saw that the tree of the garden was good to eat, tempting to see, and that it was the tree requisite for gaining understanding." These sacrifices, and the dwelling with loving and fascinated detail on the flesh and blood of those slain, recall the attention customarily given to the martyrdoms of saints. The punishment accorded to Julie represents the punishment of all women throughout the ages for the "crime" of Eve, and links ritual slaughter (usually reserved for gods) to the quest for knowledge.

The quest for knowledge, in fact, the attainment of wisdom, is the subject of several transformed myths. There is the episode reminiscent of the Sphinx (p. 85). The Sphinx, it will be remembered, posed a series of questions (involving feet and walking) answerable only by a man who was, throughout his life, conscious of his feet. This was the lame Oedipus. The matching of questions to those who suffer in the terms in which the questions are asked is the name of the game. The questions "Who must never act according to their will?"; "Who is only an animal the colour of flowers?" and "Who must observe the three obediences and whose destiny is written in their anatomy?" all have the same painfully obvious answer. The only question whose answer might be "Man" in this episode is: "Who says, I wish it, I order it, my will must take the place of reason."

In a central episode, one that joins several myths, a story is told by Sophie Ménade. The name is significant, since Sophia is Wisdom; and a maenad, like a bacchante, was a woman devoted to the god Dionysus. But *Les Guérillères* tells the reader the the particular women who dance like bacchantes in fact follow the goddess of Wisdom, not Dionysus himself. Sophie Ménade, "Wisdom and a follower of divine wisdom," therefore, is about to tell a tale concerning women's quest for wisdom (pp. 52-53). Indeed, she tells of a woman who seeks knowledge by eating of a tree. The woman has a beautiful body and snake locks whose movement produces music. The favorite snake who advises her to eat is the god Orpheus. Snakes, instead of being the attributes of monstrous women (such as Medusa, or the Furies), or Eve's seducer, in other words destroyers in a male-ordered universe,[5] are here rendered musical and lovely. Snakes are kissed and venerated in *Les Guérillères*: the snake-cult is an "O" word—the Ophidians (p. 74).

By naming the snake Orpheus, representative of the divine art of poetry and song, Wittig elevates the serpent from its scriptural degradation, and identifies it with the god whose power of music moved trees and stones and liberated his wife, Euridyce, from the darkness of Hell. In addition, of course, he is a god commencing with the letter "O." Nor does the wisdom to which Orpheus encourages the woman of the story involve a punishing aftermath. Rather, it enables her to touch the stars. The episode closes in a joyous round dance in celebration of the blessed "O."

II

In revising the roles of female divinities, Wittig is striving toward an apotheosis of woman, that is, a recreation of woman as godlike rather than as an agent who carries out assignments in a male scheme of things. She leads into the apotheosis by alluding first to the role of female goddesses under the old dispensation. In an early scene of *Les Guérillères* during the "primitive" phase of the women's history, the powers of Artemis (or Diana) and Aphrodite (or Venus) are evoked. These were goddesses of the utmost importance in the primarily masculine pantheon of classical Greek, later of Roman religion. The passage reads:

> The huntresses have dark maroon hats and dogs. Hearing the rifle-shots, Dominique Aron says that the bird is still flying, the hare still running, the boar the deer the fox the wart-hog still afoot. It is possible to keep a watch on the surroundings. If some troop advances up the road raising a cloud of dust the women watch its approach shouting to those within for the windows to be closed and the rifles kept behind the windows. Anne Damien plays, Sister Anne do you see anything coming, I see only the grass growing green and the dusty road (p. 12).

The first sentence contains a concealed reference to Artemis, who was well known as a huntress and often a protectress of game. Thus, in Wittig's retelling, rifles are kept behind closed windows, and the game is still alive and running. Artemis, identified with the moon, also presided—perhaps through this link—over women's functions, such as menstruation and childbirth. Hence the dark blood-colored hats. Women in childbirth called upon Artemis to hasten their labor, and *in extremis*, to deliver them to a quick and merciful death. The silver arrows of Artemis thus dealt death to women, and in other instances, to the quarry of the field. A "virgin" herself, Artemis also stood as a kind of patroness of chastity.

The passage closes with the questioning of "Sister Anne." The line is a succinct evocation of the power of the love goddess, Venus. It refers to that tragic episode in Virgil's *Aeneid*, Book iv, where Dido is suffering hot anguish for Aeneas. Aeneas, having selfishly enjoyed her love, is now about to betray her. He and his men ready their ships on the beach, and shortly will set sail for Italy, where Aeneas has more important things to do. Dido confides in Anna, her sister, repeatedly sending Anna to plead with Aeneas in the hopes of getting him to abandon his plans and return to Dido's house. But the road remains empty and no Aeneas returns. Despairing, Dido will take her own life. Behind the agony and betrayal of Dido lies the powerful interference of Venus, who has willingly engineered the whole thing. Venus allows Dido to be sacrificed so that Aeneas (Venus's son, by the way), can leave her, refreshed and enriched, to prosper in Italy.

Both goddesses referred to in the quoted passage were in the habit of fulfilling assignments in a male cosmic scheme. They controlled the fates of women, with respect to love, birth, and death. They did so rather dispassionately, with goddess-like aloofness and caprice, unmoved by any particular benevolence unless it suited their higher plans. Aphrodite, of course, dealt love to men as well as to women, but the incident to which Wittig alludes shows Venus at her most cruel and "unsisterly."

Wittig modulates from this evil old dispensation to a newer one, featuring shining female divinities worthier of women's reverence. The deities

Amarterasu and Cihuacoatl (also a goddess of war) are sun goddesses; the third, Eristikos, is worshipped with fire. In the women's religion the sun, not the moon, is the star with which the women identify their strength. Valiant daughters who have fought well, according to a hymn, go to the "house of your mother the sun/where all are filled with joy, content, and happiness." At another point in the narrative when things are going well, the sun rises. The women's relation to the sun is expressed in a remarkable way. When they bare their bodies to the morning light, "one of their flanks is iridescent with a golden lustre. The rising sun does likewise. . ." (p. 15). "The women say that they expose their genitals so that the sun may be reflected therein as in a mirror. They say that they retain its brilliance. They say that the pubic hair is like a spider's web that captures the rays. They are seen running with great strides. They are all illuminated at their center, starting from the pubes the hooded clitorides the folded double labia" (p. 19). Their bodies shed a glare impossible for the eye to endure.[6]

In these allusions to the women's bodies as radiant suns, or reflectors of suns, lies a hidden myth in reverse. According to an ancient belief the sun, a male principle, had fecundating power. If it shonè upon the lap of a careless girl, it might quicken her womb with life. Danae, although locked in a tower, was made pregnant by Zeus when he poured over her in a "shower of gold." In Wittig's retelling, however, the sun is a female principle associated with three goddesses. Sunlight is reflected from, not absorbed into, female bodies, for their genitals are like mirrors. Radiating mirrors are weapons, sources of strength and ascendancy in Les Guérillères. The goddess Amaterasu possesses a circular mirror that, upraised, will "blaze forth with all her fires." The women in battle use the mirror, modelled on the goddess's as their "most formidable weapon." The mirror even serves as a kind of radio, since women use it to communicate among themselves by capturing the sun's rays in it.

The mirror is a complex symbol in classical and medieval lore, and I refer here to only a few of its meanings.[7] The mirror signifies the beginning of self-consciousness, as in the myth of Narcissus. Narcissus became enamored of his reflected image, but to his sorrow, for his infatuation caused him to drown in the brook that was his mirror. Self-consciousness is necessary for knowledge of self, which is, in turn, the beginning of wisdom. But the mirror is a double device, since it can both grant awareness and entice the beholder to a blinding and narrowing preoccupation with self.

Secondly, the mirror gives back to the beholder not only herself/ himself but an image of the whole world which is more perfect, more true than the ordinary world and in a somewhat exalted form. "The welter of human experience is clarified in a mirror," writes Goldin. During the Middle Ages, books in which the entirety of a subject was ideally, quintessentially contained, as in an encyclopedia or rule book, might bear the title of "Mirror." Some examples are A Mirror for Princes and A Mirror of Love, guidebooks in their respective disciplines. Alice "through the looking glass" finds a world which is a heightened version of her familiar world, but one in which some ordinary hypocrisies and absurdities are revealed. "Mirror, mirror on the wall" is the opening of a folklore query indicating the belief that a mirror is a source of absolute truth.

Thus the mirror is, as Goldin states, "an instrument of knowledge," both of the self and of the world. And naturally, any instrument of knowledge poses dangers of distortion if misread or misunderstood. At one point, Wittig alludes to a danger of the women's being imprisoned in their mirrors. Too great an absorption is self? The potential bondage of femaleness? The text, which presents the image of women sliding over a shining mirror surface to which their limbs cannot adhere, offers no clear clue (pp. 30-31). But more often the mirrors and symbolic mirrors in *Les Guérillères* are attributes of power. Mirrors form a bond of communication. The vulval mirror means radiance, identity. The women know themselves and one another through the mirrors of their bodies—their vulvas which they reveal in such a way as to capture and reflect the sun. The vulval circle, according to the novel's central mythology, reflects and repeats the female divinity, the sun, and is a paradigm of culture, tradition, the world, and the universe.

III

At the beginning and at the end of *Les Guérillères* are two poems printed in capital letters. Here Wittig's strategem of fracturing syntax reaches its most extreme form. Each poem is composed of words and images in clumps, not conventional sentence chains or even statements. However the fragmented syntax is not without meaning, for each poem focuses on the image of a bird. Let us examine the opening poem. We are aware of a sense of triumph. In fact, the war is over; the "time" is the end of the novel; peace has been established. Weapons are the jetlike glossy birds that are piled in the sun. Golden spaces, green deserts (an oxymoron signifying oases) are visible. Women sing in praise of the dead, commemorating those women heroes who fell. There is

INTENSE HEAT DEATH AND HAPPINESS
IN THE BREASTED TORSOS
THE PHOENIXES THE PHOENIXES
FREE CELIBATE GOLDEN
THEIR OUTSPREAD WINGS ARE HEARD

The Phoenix, as Ovid tells the story, is a legendary bird that lives five hundred years, feeding on incense and fragrant resins. When it is prepared to die, the Phoenix sets fire to its own nest, which it has made of myrrh, spikenard, and cinnamon, and perishes in the flames amidst the most delicious odors. From the ashes a new bird is born. The child bird, when it is strong enough, takes its nest and flies with it to the City of the Sun. It lays its nest before the doors of the sacred temple. Other redactors of the tale, like Herodotus and Tacitus, say the flight of the Phoenix is attended by flocks of other birds.

The resurgent bird as an emblem of the women's triumph is clear and eloquent. From this myth Wittig takes two motifs and develops them later in her narrative. One is the double fire/sun image, incorporated in her inventions about the three goddesses of sun and fire, together with the capturing of the sun in the mirroring vulvas of worshiping women. The second motif is that of the birds. Birds become attributes of the women's bodies, for the lips of the vulva are compared (in the feminaries, the women's "bibles") to the wings of birds, to doves, starlings, bengalis, finches, swallows. An early author doesn't know which beats with a faster wing, the swallow or the vulva (p. 44). Little girls collect birds and keep them as their playthings: goldfinches, chaffinches, linnets, and especially green canaries. When, however, their canaries die, a hundred thousand little girls mourn their deaths in the hundred thousand rooms of the hundred thousand houses (p. 18). Here is a literary allusion, writ large into the hundreds of thousands, to Catullus's poem on Lesbia weeping for her sparrow. All the little girls, then, in Wittig's evocation of the well-known poem become a hundred thousand "Lesbias."

The Phoenixes' dying and rising, the delicate punning allusion to Lesbia's sparrow from Catullus, transmuted to "lesbians' canaries," prepare for the development of a final double entendre in the book's concluding poem. There the Swan (*cygne*) emerges from its French homonym (*signe*), meaning Symbol. An initial portion of the poem has been translated:

NO/SYMBOLS TEARING
ARISE VIOLENCE FROM THE WHITENESS
OF THE UNDYING BEAUTIFUL PRESENT
WITH A GREAT DRUNKEN WING-BEAT

Here it will make clearer sense if we examine the lines as Wittig wrote them

NON/SIGNES DECHIRANT
SURGIS VIOLENCE DU BLANC
DU VIVACE DU BEL AUJOURD'HUI
D'UN GRANT COUP D'AILE IVRE

The French lines are recognizable as a variation on the first two lines of one of the best known of Mallarmé's sonnets

Le vierge le vivace et le bel aujourd'hui
va-t-il nous déchirer avec un coup d'aile ivre[8]

In Mallarmé's poem the controlling image is that of a swan (*cygne*) whose drunken wings beat vainly in an effort to escape from the ice in which he is imprisoned. Wittig adapts Mallarmé's language, in somewhat transposed order, to refer to symbols or signs (*signes*) that must also beat their wings against the medium that imprisons them. For both writers, though for different reasons, this icy medium appears to be the harsh rigidity of established language. Both Wittig and Mallarmé use the verb "to tear" (*déchirant/déchiré* in Wittig, *déchirer* in Mallarmé) to show that wings are torn when any force—bird or symbol—needs to liberate itself. It is the summation of Wittig's treatment of myth, to wrench it apart in order to create a significant object. Incidentally, by ending her work with an echo from a classical (and we may add, male) French poet, Wittig repeats a device she used at the close of *The Opoponax*, where she cites a line of a sixteenth-century poet, Maurice Scève.

Wittig thereby affirms her allegiance to salvageable myth and poetry, from antiquity through the present, provided that we as her readers will allow her the privilege of offering them to us in queenly tatters. With effort she has torn apart the conventional, and so with effort and willing erudition we may read her meanings. Triumphant creation and creative reading are achieved with some toughness of resolve. The Phoenix rising out of the refining fire is woman triumphant as she reaches the sun with which she can identify herself. But the Swan/Symbol tearing itself out of the ice is the woman as poet. These are the myth and the poem that Wittig chooses as her ending.

ST. JOHN'S UNIVERSITY

Notes

[1] References in this article are to the paperback English translation by David Le Vay (New York: Avon Books/Bard Edition, 1973).

[2] Erica Ostrovsky, "A Cosmogony of O: Wittig's *Les Guérillères*," in George Stamboulian (ed.), *Twentieth Century French Fiction: Essays for Germaine Brée* (New Brunswick: Rutgers University Press, 1975), p. 245.

[3] See Ostrovsky, p. 243. A similar observation was made earlier by Laura Durand in an essay review of *Les Guérillères*, "Heroic Feminism as Art," *Novel*, 8 (Fall 1974), p. 75.

[4] Mary Pringle Spraggins, "Myth and Ms. Entrapment and Liberation in Monique Wittig's *Les Guérillères*," *The International Fiction Review*, 3 (January 1976), p. 49. Margaret Crosland has also written about Monique Wittig in *Women of Iron and Velvet: French Women Writers After Georges Sand* (New York: Taplinger, 1976), pp. 211-17; and there is an intelligent review of *Les Guérillères* by Sally Beauman, in *The New York Times Book Review*, October 10, 1971, pp. 5, 48.

[5] Wittig's habit of neutralizing myths of feminine evil is also evidenced in her transformation of the Siren (p. 14). Not a menace, the Siren's green scales are enchantingly set off by rosy underarms, and her song is the magical "O".

[5] There is, in fact, an iconographic precedent for this image. A painted tray in the Louvre pictures Venus in the sky, being knelt to by the various lovers of history. Painted rays of gold stream from her whole body. Those beams which radiate from her thighs and genitals are the most conspicuous and touch the lovers' eyes and faces. The painting has been reproduced, most recently, in Robert P. Miller (ed), *Chaucer: Sources and Backgrounds* (New York: Oxford University Press, 1977), facing p. 275.

[7] The best scholarly source of mirror lore is Fredrick Goldin. *The Mirror of Narcissus in the Courtly Love Lyric* (Ithaca: Cornell University Press, 1967).

[8] Wittig's use of Mallarmé's poem is also noted by Durand, p. 74 and Ostrovsky, p. 250.

IV. Formalism

ON ONE CROSSING-OVER:
VALERY'S SEA INTO HART CRANE'S SCENE

Mary Ann Caws

Among all the possible textual passages on passage itself, none is odder than Hart Crane's quite singular poem, "Passage."[1] Marianne Moore, rejecting it for *The Dial*, called it a poem without simplicity or "controlling force," while contemporary critics call it a failed voyage in search of memory, a poem which fails "to communicate even an appropriate state of mind." Crane, however, thought it "the most interesting and conjectural thing"[2] he ever wrote, and I would be tempted to agree with him, because of the complex and unusual perception it permits of the interacts of spatial and temporal passage, as well as their own interaction with the literary one. Now admittedly, my choice is made by way of certain markers that impose themselves upon the reading and its sequels; in the re-reading here, another poem will join, as in the corridor of one reader's mind.

First Reading

Passage

Where the cedar leaf divides the sky
I heard the sea.
In sapphire arenas of the hills
I was promised an improved infancy.

Sulking, sanctioning the sun,
My memory I left in a ravine,—
Casual louse that tissues the buckwheat,
Aprons rocks, congregates pears
In moonlit bushels
And wakens alleys with a hidden cough.

Dangerously the summer burned
(I had joined the entrainments of the wind).
. . . .
. . .but the wind
Died speaking through the ages that you know
And hug, chimney-sooted heart of man!
So was I turned about and back, much as your smoke
Compiles a too well-known biography.

The evening was a spear in the ravine
That throve through very oak. And had I walked
The dozen particular decimals of time?
Touching an opening laurel, I found
A thief beneath, my stolen book in hand.

"Why are you back here—smiling an iron coffin?"
"To argue with the laurel," I replied:
"Am justified in transience, fleeing
Under the constant wonder of your eyes—."

He closed the book. And from the Ptolemies
Sand troughed us in a glittering abyss.
A serpent swam a vertix to the sun
—On unpaced beaches leaned its tongue and
    drummed.
What fountains did I hear? what icy speeches?
Memory, committed to the page, had broke.

In the beginning, within the edenic description, there is an implicit mixing of senses: for the opening lines bring the sound of the sea into the hearing of the listener, crossing over the land in exactly the place where he observes the tree beneath which he sits to rend the sky. The splitting apart of the spatial division may be deemed necessary for the sharpening of the hearing, as if indeed the wood of a cedar prow had carved its way by the delicacy of one leaf—standing metonymically for the whole tree—into the matter of the sky and then into the poetic consciousness, so that the sound of the water might pass by means of this vessel for a true transport of the senses. This reading will maintain that Crane's text is a double appeal to the senses, centered as much on sight as on sound,[3] for already at the beginning, the *eye* is twice stressed, phonetically, and stressed more vigorously still by the juxtaposition with the rhyming "sky": "I heard the sea./. . .I was promised. . . ." Thrice also the phonetic marker of poetic sight appears or, more properly, is heard: "*ce*dar," "*sea*," "infan*cy*," so the seeing, the seer, and the early scene are present even in this auditory passage, or perhaps, particularly in this passage. In an improved infancy, promised as the sapphire sea sets up its theatrical scene among the hills, in their own arena, this recreated unicity of childhood would indeed have sight included in the hearing. In the Mediterranean brightness, the past is temporarily shaken off and with it all the American memory—from buckwheat to bushels, rocks, and alleys. In his imagination, Crane seems to have exchanged the farm at Patterson on which he is in fact living—thus the pears and bushels—for the black and red "vine-stanchioned valleys" of Provence.

Yet the memory casually but effectively *tissues* the text—itself an etymological tissue or textile of woven forms—mothering the landscape with an all-enclosing apron, causing the disparate to congregate for another sort of American revival. To the speaker, now a poet freed of memory, a classic rebeginning has been promised, "in the sapphire arena" of those Mediterranean hills into which the color of the sea and sky has so clearly been absorbed: yet he is "turned about and back" in his own passage, subject to a peri-peteia, as a boat might be, becalmed after the initial passing of the cedar prow, with the dying of the wind. The tree is pierced once again for a crossing over—and this time not from hearing into sight—pierced rather by a time itself, by evening's lance, set pointing into the oak. Cedar, oak, and laurel: all these thrive in the poem's wood and have been signaled by the initial leaf. Here the passage is spatial, as was the initial crossing of the ship and of the sea into the ear of the land, and temporal, as was that of the wind, or the poet's breath, animating the ages. Here evening and memorized ravine pass into tree thriving: "that throve through a very oak." The very word is sharp, like the driving of the spear, as if, once more, some legendary and remembered Siegfried were to be summoned in order to remove the dagger from some natural object split open, as a tree might be, or then a stone, perhaps a written one, like Bonnefoy's *Pierre écrite*, for the finding of a text. Passing through the long evening of vigil and of night, those twelve hours or "dozen particular decimals of time" to make his epic gesture, he then questions the passage and the passing moment: ". . .And had I walked / The dozen particular decimals of time?"

In the moment of doubt, the gesture is of course only potential: no real or figured Siegfried pulls the dagger from out the tree. At the turn of the poem, the wind dies down under the heavy force of the ages, its transparent spirit succumbing to the usury of the soot and smoke. But the space of the poem will stretch from sun to sun, the turn sanctioned in the second stanza through this evening, spearing the ravine and the memory left there, now being questioned.

On then to the next day's sand—that other "arena" after the initial staging—and that glittering abyss and sun, where now the memory will recur for a fresh and final baptism. Here the laurel does not crown the end of triumph—no completed task, no ending passage—but rather and only the beginning, a tree spreading open until the leaves of the book are closed, on legend and on life. Yet the poem remains to signal the serpentine fleetness and the very transience of the heroic stepless passage across the "unpaced" and unpassed beaches, under the Egyptian sun of the Ptolemies, bright on emblems of eye and serpent, whose tongue of another language is unspoken, for the serpent only drums: the Egyptian hieroglyphics are here committed to memory and the modern page. But this sun, towards which the serpent swims, washes, and bleaches out the memory imprisoned now forever in the pages of the purloined and doubtless self-purloined book, stolen from experience, whose leaves lie idle like a ship becalmed, whose passage, at the conclusion of the poem, has found at last its closure. "Where the cedar divides the sky. . .": the final break of memory, negative in its undoing, or positive, like some break or day after a tedious vigil, refers back also to the opening or then the threshold division, parting, like a prow, its path through this supremely textual passage, thriving even through the page.

Second Reading

Le Cimetière marin (extracts)

Ce toit tranquille, où marchent des colombes,
Entre les pins palpite, entre les tombes;
Midi le juste y compose des feux
La mer, la mer, toujours recommencée!
. . . .
Masse de calme, et visible réserve,
Eau sourcilleuse, Oeil qui gardes en toi
Tant de sommeil sous un voile de flamme,
Ô mon silence!...
. . . .
La scintillation sereine sème
Sur l'altitude un dédain souverain.

Comme le fruit se fond en jouissance,
. . . .
Je hume ici ma future fumée,
Et le ciel chante à l'âme consumée
Le changement des rives en rumeur.

Beau ciel, vrai ciel, regarde-moi qui change!
. . . .
Je m'abandonne à ce brillant espace,
. . . .
L'âme exposée aux torches du solstice,
Je te soutiens, admirable justice
De la lumière aux armes sans pitié!
. . . .
Ô pour moi seul, à moi seul, en moi-même,
Auprès d'un coeur, aux sources du poème,
Entre le vide et l'événement pur,
J'attends l'écho de ma grandeur interne,
Amère, sombre et sonore citerne,
Sonnant dans l'âme un creux toujours futur!

Sais-tu, fausse captive de feuillages,
Golfe mangeur de ces maigres grillages,
Sur mes yeux clos, secrets éblouissants,
Quel corps me traîne à sa fin paresseuse,
. . . .
Non, non!...Debout! Dans l'ère successive!
Brisez, mon corps, cette forme pensive!
Buvez, mon sein, la naissance du vent!
Une fraîcheur, de la mer exhalée,
Me rend mon âme...O puissance salée!
Courons à l'onde en rejaillir vivant!

Oui! Grande mer de délires douée,
Peau de panthère et chlamyde trouée
De mille et mille idoles du soleil,
Hydre absolue, ivre de ta chair bleue,
Qui te remords l'étincelante queue
Dans un tumulte au silence pareil,

Le vent se lève!... il faut tenter de vivre!

> L'air immense ouvre et referme mon livre,
> La vague en poudre ose jaillir des rocs!
> Envolez-vous, pages tout éblouies!
> Rompez, vagues! Rompez d'eaux réjouies
> Ce toit tranquille où picoraient des focs![4]

Now in the rereading the passage is forged from one text to the other, if only in the reader's mind. Four years before Crane's poem was written, Valéry's "Cimetière Marin" appeared—whether Crane might have seen translated passages, or heard of it through his friends (very possibly Yvor Winters),[5] or absorbed its sense through the Provencal landscape which the poems concern, it matters little, for this present study is not meant to be of exterior source but of interior passage. And at the present, these two poems echo together like steps not lost, "pas perdus" and not meant to be, in the mental resonance of the corridor of reading, along the threshold between two perceptions, and toward one sensitivity to borders and exchange.

High noon at the Southern Coast then dazzles upon the sea which palpitates between the pines of Valéry's text, in whose foliage or grill the water is caught. Memory here too reposes in the calmest of abysses, awaiting some rejuvenated experience, some rebaptism by a waking water: after the fruit has melted in the mouth, the mouth is empty. But so far the flat sparkle of the surface is still: "Midi le juste y compose des feux/La mer..." The traditional pure vision is a mirror for the mind and yet its opposition, as in Mallarmé, Valéry's master: "Ce midi que notre double/Inconscience approfondit." Refusing human change and the defections of alteration, as the imperfections of memory are refused, the glass of this watching sea imposes self-study together with the prediction of non-being: In Crane's smoke, Valéry's has already blown, and the aroma of nothingness is heavy: "Je hume ici ma future fumée." Now the examination of Crane's own "Passage" in front of that other water, each mirroring each, guides this second and final stage of the present reading, itself a self-reading as contemporary criticism is often seen to be yet another mirror stage, to play on Lacan's language, whose surface lends itself to play. A reinterpretation may yield the key to an inner reading: what more can we be promised in the "improved infancy" which reading is? For noon contains in itself, quite as surely as night, all those "dozen particular decimals of time," as the just opening laurel of immortality still argues with transcience and the feeling of uselessness under the constant wonder of a watching eye: "Eau sourcilleuse, Oeil qui gardes en toi/Tant de sommeil sous un voile de flamme,/Ô mon silence!..." Might not these eyes, glanced at again—for the eyes have it, and indeed their wonder is wonderful to behold—be those of this sea freshly seen, so far the presumed stealer of the text, the sea whose glittering and unremembering perfection seems to will into silence even the garrulous book, where experience was formerly transcribed, as if it were only one more defect, like that "casual louse of memory" necessarily left behind? "Beau ciel, vrai ciel, regarde-moi qui change!/...Je m'abandonne à ce brillant espace." The phonetic superposition of "Eau/Oeil/Ô," linking water to eye to exclamation cannot be caught in the net of translation, but the stressed and liquid visibility of text is made therein, as in another sea. Eyes and water share the stage with hearing and conversation and voice in the Crane poem, with the past tense serving to distance our passage from his own. The coffin's cover shuts up the book in its silence, as motion is covered by the sea roof, glazed by Valéry's pitiless luminosity: "Je te soutiens, admirable justice/De la lumière aux armes sans pitié!" The book is then closed by the thieving sea, stealer of life and of the living body. The sand sifts over human transience, trackless and traceless, unremembering and unvital. But from the sibilants, or from the sand alone, rises a serpent in the hiss and undulations of the S shape: "La scintillation sereine sème/Sur l'altitude un dédain souverain" like the stunning triple S of Crane's fifth line: "Sulking, sanctioning the sun." He will pass from the sea to the sky, in another S thrice shaping the passage: "A serpent swam a vertex to the sun." This vertex is vertiginous like Valéry's Hydra of life reborn, as the wind lifts again its spirit, and the waves break on these dazzling pages, *rifled* by the breeze—thus, perhaps, was the book stolen or thieved—its pages now freed from the tomb of that unmoving perfection.

Some mysterious fountain in Crane's book, also, like a fountain of life or poetry, breaks now at last positively into the icy waste unlike that other imprisoning lake for some long-ago swan, glimpsed like a sign that "cygne" whose meaning passes by the corridor of its sound into another "signe," a sign marking the place where the wind of the word had once died down. Memory freed now, to be renewed by life, is loosed under the sun, in the rising wind resurrected, and into the rejoicing wave, thrusting against Crane's iron coffin and Valéry's deadly tranquil roof, towards a more vital passage:

> Non, non!...Debout! Dans l'ère successive!
> Brisez, mon corps, cette forme pensive!
> ....
> Le vent se lève!...il faut tenter de vivre!
> L'air immense ouvre et referme mon livre,
> ....
> Envolvez-vous, pages tout éblouies!
> Rompez, vagues! Rompez d'eaux réjouies
> Ce toit tranquille où picoraient des focs!

For the new epic to break into life, the causal and imperfect memory must be left behind, sick unto death, with its cough the opposite of poetry's most vigorous wind. And so the great wind of the word, blowing from the "ère" of ages to the "air" of air, is lifted in honor of renewed life, breaking into ice and tomb, like a wave of "improved" and childlike memory, rebaptised now in the most open sea with its possibilities freshly displayed.

Crane's book is closed, his path has been turned about, and the inspiriting wind formerly heard has died down. But then the poem is written in the past tense: Valéry's present air "opens and closes" the book once more, and still the wind lifts in the present tense, lifting the spirit with it: the final break here, supremely positive, now recasts Crane's other "passage" in its own light, for us. The last line fits back upon the beginning or initial *leaf* forming a circular frame, visible to those committed to the book but also to the breakers, as the rising and windy word turns leaf and page in this deeply self-reflecting spectacle of the sea. This last turn of the rereading, then, points the literary passenger's way linking the privileged sight of that sea and of that seeing to the inner seen, available to the eye trained, stubbornly and well, in and on the most open of passages, leading toward a double seascape.

THE GRADUATE CENTER
THE CITY UNIVERSITY OF NEW YORK

Notes

[1]"Passage," in *White Buildings. The Complete Poems of Hart Crane,* ed. Waldo Frank (Garden City, NY: Doubleday, 1958), pp. 90-91.

[2]In *The Letters of Hart Crane,* ed. Brom Weber (Berkeley and Los Angeles: 1952), p. 215, Marianne Moore rejected this poem which Crane had submitted to *The Dial,* with this reasoning: "Its multiform content accounts, I suppose, for what seems to us a lack of simplicity and cumulative force." Allen Tate cites its lack of controlling organization, and R. W. Butterfield in *The Broken Arc: A Study of Hart Crane* (Edinburgh: Oliver and Boyd, 1969) says: "In 'Passage' he began, and failed to complete, a journey in search, not of the heights of the spirit's potential, but of the deep recesses of memory and the past" (p. 107). Citing the widely differing attitudes of the critics, he concludes: "The poem has apparently failed to communicate even an appropriate state of mind" (p. 107). I will not be so impudent as to assume that this second reading will change, even for some readers, their opinion of this poem; but the comparison is rendered more interesting by the very contrast it brings into play between those other readings and the double image presented here.

[3]R. W. B. Lewis, in *The Poetry of Hart Crane: A Critical Study* (Princeton: Princeton University Press, 1967), maintains that the poem is centered on hearing. I take a different point of view. He sees Coleridge's own "Dejection" as hanging over this ode to dejection.

[4]"Le Cimetière marin," in Paul Valéry, *Oeuvres,* T. 1, ed. Jean Hytier (Paris: Gallimard, Bibliothèque de la Pléiade, 1957), pp. 147-51.

[5]My thanks to John Hollander for this suggestion.

LOS EFECTOS DE LA RESONANCIA
EN LA POESIA DE JOSE ANGEL VALENTE

Santiago Daydí-Tolson

Propio del estilo poético del español José Angel Valente ha sido, desde un principio, el tono contenido de la voz lírica, su sobriedad y concisión expresivas.[1] Directamente relacionada con esta característica está la concepción que el poeta tiene del objetivo del poetizar, explícitamente expuesta en sus ensayos teóricos: la poesía es un método de conocimiento de la realidad que, diferente al método científico, permite percibir la experiencia "en su compleja síntesis".[2] Sin entrar a comentar su poética personal es posible hallar por medio del análisis inmediato de los poemas una confirmación del esfuerzo de Valente por alcanzar dicha síntesis a través del lenguaje poético. Tal análisis lleva a descubrir en la obra total de este poeta un aspecto estilístico que responde cabalmente a su voluntad sintetizadora, esto es, el empleo abundante de variadas técnicas de resonancia. Se ha de entender como tales diversos procedimientos expresivos que, aunque difieren bastante entre sí, comparten al menos una característica común: la capacidad de suscitar ecos y correspondencias múltiples dentro del texto literario mismo, o entre éste y sus varios posibles contextos. Como podrá verse, todo caso de resonancia implica una síntesis expresiva en el poema. Estos procedimientos se encuentran en diversos niveles de la composición, muchas veces combinados entre sí, y sólo un análisis muy detallado podría dar razón de todos ellos. Baste como objetivo limitado de este trabajo la presentación y análisis de algunos casos ejemplares de resonancia en la obra de uno de los poetas españoles contemporáneos que mejor representa la conciencia crítica del lenguaje poético.

Un excelente ejemplo de las técnicas de composición del poema empleadas por José Angel Valente es el texto inicial de su primer libro, " 'Serán ceniza. . .' ",[3] poema que presenta una escena alegórica cuyo protagonista es el propio hablante:

> Cruzo un desierto y su secreta
> desolación sin nombre.
> El corazón
> tiene la sequedad de la piedra

y los estallidos nocturnos
de su materia o de su nada.

Hay una luz remota, sin embargo,
y sé que no estoy solo;
aunque después de tanto y tanto no haya
ni un solo pensamiento
capaz contra la muerte,
no estoy solo.

Toco esta mano al fin que comparte mi vida
y en ella me confirmo
y tiento cuanto amo,
lo levanto hacia el cielo
y aunque sea ceniza lo proclamo: ceniza.
Aunque sea ceniza cuanto tengo hasta ahora,
cuanto se me ha tendido a modo de esperanza.

La situación particular del hablante, su actitud y tono, constituyen la experiencia concreta comunicada, que bien podría racionalizarse como la conciencia del vacío existencial. En el plano de los significados, sin embargo, no hay ningún elemento que pueda entenderse como una idea abstracta si no se acude a las correspondencias alegóricas. El poema no comunica una idea, sino la actitud de un hablante que sintetiza lo abstracto de la concepción ontológica y la experiencia emotiva concreta. Se logra esta síntesis por medio de una serie de elementos de la composición que tienen la particularidad de suscitar en el lector un reconocimiento de parecidas experiencias anteriores. La acción narrada por el protagonista figura una escena tradicionalmente significativa: la alegoría del "Homo Viator". Esta interpretación resuena como un eco en la sensibilidad del lector. La situación particular del hablante y la más general de la alegoría se combinan en una sola impresión que recoge toda la valoración conceptual y emotiva de la escena tradicional.

La estrofa final del poema, y en particular sus tres últimos versos, representa importantes transformaciones del modelo alegórico:

> . . .y aunque sea ceniza lo proclamo: ceniza.
> Aunque sea ceniza cuanto tengo hasta ahora,
> cuanto se me ha tendido a modo de esperanza (vv. 17-19).

El marcado contraste con la escena tradicional hace más patente, en la comparación de los rasgos diferenciadores del motivo lírico, la actitud del protagonista: su decisión de aceptar la condición temporal y perecedera del hombre. Es evidente que en el plano de la anécdota la resonancia cumple una doble función. Por una parte despierta en el lector una serie de recuerdos de orden tradicional: la concepción cristiana del hombre como un peregrino. Un segundo momento de la resonancia se produce al contraponérsele a dicha concepción una voluntad nueva derivada de la concepción diametralmente opuesta: el hombre no está destinado a llegar a un lugar ideal y eterno, sino que, muy por el contrario, está condenado a la disolución total en la muerte; lo único que existe es el camino. Esta concepción materialista cobra mayor fuerza comunicativa en la resonancia temática de la escena alegórica. Pero las posibilidades de resonancia en este poema no se limitan al nivel de la representación. En otros niveles de la composición se dan también técnicas expresivas cuyo efecto principal consiste en producir en el lector un reconocimiento de elementos en relación.

Así, por ejemplo, los términos concretos de la escena alegórica (imágenes, símbolos, vocabulario) pueden entenderse como elementos de larga tradición cultural, e incluso como expresiones del habla común. "Desierto", "corazón" (que tiene "la sequedad de la piedra"), "luz remota", "mano" y "ceniza" se emplean en el poema en una relación que destaca sus valores simbólicos, suscitando así en el lector un reconocimiento que le ayuda a captar la serie de referencias tanto conceptuales como emotivas. La relación entre estos términos y la alegoría es estrecha, lo que permite hablar de concisión expresiva. Entre el nivel de la anécdota y el de las imágenes hay tal correspondencia que resulta difícil concebirlos como dos elementos estructurales diferentes en los cuales distintos procedimientos conducen a un efecto similar. Más aún, la exactitud de esta correspondencia se encuentra reforzada por la estructura métrica de la composición, en la que también hay que reconocer algunos efectos de resonancia.

Los aspectos rítmico y acústico de " 'Serán ceniza. . .' " se caracterizan por una versificación bastante regular y por sutiles relaciones sonoras. Ritmo y sonoridad se intensifican hacia el final de la composición, acentuando así la transformación comentada en relación con la escena alegórica. La primera estrofa es de metro ligeramente irregular (9, 7, 5, 10, 9 y 9 sílabas respectivamente) y contiene un encabalgamiento (vv. 1-2); también hay encabalgamientos en la segunda estrofa (vv. 9, 10 y 11), pero se advierte en ella una mayor regularidad métrica (11, 7, 11, 7, 7 y 4 sílabas respectivamente) que se hace más marcada en la tercera y última estrofa (13, 7, 7, 7, 14, 14 y 14 sílabas respectivamente). En las dos últimas estrofas es notorio además el uso de efectos acústicos en la repetición de versos y en el paralelismo, procedimientos que son evidentes en los versos finales del poema. En la estrofa inicial, en cambio, no se dan tales correspondencias acústicas, quedando en claro que la estructura total de la composición se basa en la intensificación progresiva. Este tipo de estructura, al apoyarse en los efectos de las relaciones rítmico-acústicas y sus ecos, destaca el valor emotivo de la voz lírica, y con ello el aspecto dramático de la anécdota.[4]

Los efectos de resonancia se producen en tres planos de la estructuración del poema: el de la representación anecdótica, el de las imágenes (o del léxico), y el acústico-rítmico. Aunque en cada uno de estos tres niveles tales efectos se consiguen por medio de procedimientos diferentes, todos ellos tienen en común el establecer relaciones y sugerir correspondencias entre elementos textuales, o entre éstos y otros del contexto cultural y lingüístico común al poeta y sus lectores. Todo caso de resonancia produce una armónica correlación entre varios elementos que se complementan y enriquecen unos a otros en la síntesis de su captación. Puede tratarse de la relación rítmica o acústica dentro de una misma composición (rimas, repeticiones, anáforas, paralelismos, aliteraciones) o de la repetición de ciertos términos del vocabulario; puede ser el uso de expresiones recogidas de la tradición literaria o del lenguaje común; puede tratarse también de símbolos o imágenes valorizadas desde antiguo, de situaciones típicas o motivos tradicionales. Las posibilidades son múltiples. En " 'Serán ceniza. . .' " las fórmulas de resonancia son centrales a su estructura; el propio título, tomado de un soneto de Quevedo,[5] formula ya un primer reconocimiento y prepara una actitud emotiva que se ve reforzada por la figura del hablante ficticio (su situación anecdótica y su tono) expuesta en términos de resonancia por medio de la alegoría tradicional y el discurso de intensificación rítmica y acústica.

Aunque no en todos los poemas de José Angel Valente se da un uso tan completo de los varios efectos de la resonancia, la abundancia de los mismos en su obra permite reconocerlos como caracterizadores del estilo sintetizador del poeta. El análisis de algunos casos aislados del procedimiento referidos a cada uno de los tres niveles establecidos más arriba dará una idea más clara de las posibilidades de la resonancia como forma de expresión lírica.

1. Nivel de la estructuración rítmico-acústica

Un aspecto del poema que Valente compone cuidadosamente en función de la unidad del mismo es el de las estructuras rítmica y acústica. En este nivel estructural las posibilidades de resonancia son muchas; José Angel Valente prefiere los paralelismos, las anáforas, las repeticiones, las combinaciones libres de versos tradicionales. Entre muchos poemas, sirva de caso ejemplar "Lo sellado" (p. 358). Dos breves estrofas iniciales imponen el metro de arte mayor (13, 13, 11) y contienen sutiles correspondencias de sonidos:

> Pero obremos ahora con astucia, Agone.
> Cerquemos el amor y cuanto poseemos
> con muy secretas láminas de frío (vv. 1-3).

La aliteración del primer verso y la repetición de tres formas verbales de primera persona plural con idéntica terminación son casos evidentes de resonancia acústica. Métricamente los tres versos combinan medidas que tradicionalmente se dan relacionadas. Este comienzo de equivalencias y combinaciones más bien sutiles se ve complementado por el resto del poema, compuesto de tres estrofas paralelas cuya estructuración es claramente repetitiva:

> Pasará el vendedor de baratijas
> y nada advertirá,
> pasará el traficante de palabras terciarias
> y nada advertirá,
> pasará el voceador de su estúpida nada
> y nada advertirá (vv. 4 y ss.).

Se dan en este ejemplo varios de los procedimientos preferidos de Valente: la combinación libre de versos tradicionales (11, 7, 14, 7, 13, 7), la repetición de un mismo esquema estrófico, la anáfora, y la repetición de sonidos y palabras (presencia obsesiva del fonema "a", repetición muy próxima de la palabra "nada"). Mirando el poema en su totalidad se advierte además la intensificación del procedimiento en la segunda parte. La composición del poema "De vida y muerte" (p. 56) se basa también en lo repetitivo y procede igualmente por intensificación del procedimiento en la segunda parte. A las dos primeras estrofas, en las que no hay mayores indicaciones de resonancias, las sigue una sección final donde se da la repetición obsesiva:

> Para morir,
> para vivir,
> para morir de cara.
> Para morir.
> Para vivir.
> Para morir
> de haber vivido.
> Y basta (vv. 9 y ss.).

El ritmo y la sonoridad insistentes establecen un tono cargado de emotividad. El efecto de las repeticiones sería el de comunicar por medio de tal emotividad la concepción de que la vida tiene un fin en sí misma. Esta interpretación no responde exclusivamente al efecto resonante de la estructura rítmico-acústica de la composición, sino que cuenta además con otras funciones de la resonancia que se dan coincidentemente en el poema reforzadas por la repetición. Las expresiones repetidas ("para vivir" y "para morir") se confunden en la alternancia, convirtiendo sus significaciones en una sinonimia. Las resonancias rítmico-acústicas pasan a afectar el nivel de los significados del poema al coincidir con un caso de resonancia de vocabulario.

2. Nivel de la estructuración de los significantes

En el plano de los significantes (vocabulario, expresiones, imágenes, metáforas, símbolos) la poesía de José Angel Valente se inclina por el uso de aquellas formas que suscitan en el lector un reconocimiento de algo conocido y valorizado previamente. Un poema como "La rosa necesaria" (p. 37) acude al símbolo tradicional de la flor y aprovecha de él todas las valorizaciones que pueda tener, sin indicar preferencia por ninguna en particular. En el poema " 'Serán ceniza. . .' " la alegoría del "Homo Viator" sufre una transformación reinterpretativa; en "La rosa necesaria" hay una concatenación de los significados que el símbolo suscita en la memoria del lector:

> La rosa no;
> la rosa sólo
> para ser entregada.
> La rosa que se aísla
> en una mano, no;
> la rosa
> connatural al aire
> que es de todos (vv. 1-8).

El término simbólico extiende sus significaciones en una designación más amplia que cualquiera de los distintos valores particulares que pueda tener en diversos contextos. Para entender la extensión del símbolo en este poema no se debe buscar una relación exclusiva entre el sustituyente y el sustituído. El término "rosa" despierta un amplio sector de resonancias; por una parte, las que aluden a la tradición literaria, que puede rastrearse desde la oposición "rosa-ceniza" propia de los poemas que tratan del tópico del "Carpe Diem", hasta la designación juanramoniana de la rosa estética; por otra parte está el valor sentimental que en el lenguaje común se relaciona con la flor. Todos estos significados coinciden en el poema, produciendo un reconocimiento impreciso que el lector capta como una síntesis. No se trata del proceso lógico de reconocimiento de un concepto, sino de la captación emotiva de una visión particular del mundo. El poema encuentra su significación en ese entender el símbolo como designador de tal concepción.

La concisión del poema no depende únicamente de las resonancias atraídas por el símbolo polisémico, sino que encuentra apoyo también en la estructura rítmico-acústica y en otros términos del vocabulario. Este último tiene resonancias del decir común en palabras como "plaza", "estancia", "casa" y especialmente en la expresión "de mano en mano":

La rosa que se da
de mano en mano,
que es necesario dar,
la rosa necesaria (vv. 11-14).

Este aprovechamiento de las expresiones del habla cotidiana es particularmente notorio en las primeras obras de José Angel Valente, y constituye un aspecto estilístico que comparte con otros poetas de su generación. Entre los muchos casos que podrían darse como ejemplo de esta característica en la obra de Valente destaca el empleo repetido de la expresión "estar en pie" en el libro *A modo de esperanza*. La resonancia es doble: por una parte afecta a la unidad del libro al usarse en varios poemas, y por otra se refiere al lenguaje común, enriqueciéndolo con una significación renovada.

En el poema "Lucila Valente" (p. 14) la frase común puede entenderse como la acción concreta que designa normalmente, aunque además alude a otra significación: "Estuvo en pie, vivió,/fue risa, lágrimas" (vv. 1-2). También alude a la vida en el poema "Como la muerte" (pp. 41-42):

Un hombre ha muerto, pero
díme que soy verdad,
que estoy en pie, que es cierto
el aire, que no puedo
morir (vv. 59 y ss).

El hecho de "estar en pie" se contrapone al yacer de la muerte. La misma expresión sirve en el decir común para indicar la permanencia de algo, su estado de existencia, así como también la recuperación de un enfermo que ha dejado la cama. Son estos valores aludidos los que hacen de la expresión un resonador, una fórmula rica en referencias significativas. La misma expresión se refiere a la personificación de la patria en el poema "Patria, cuyo nombre no sé" (pp. 31-33):

> Oh patria y patria
> y patria en pie
> de vida, en pie
> sobre la mutilada
> blancura de la nieve,
> ¿quién tiene tu verdad? (vv. 78 y ss).

La agregación del complemento "de vida" hace que la expresión original despierte resonancias de otro contexto: la frase "en pie de guerra". Como en este caso la expresión "de mano en mano" sirve en el poema "La rosa necesaria" de resonador del lenguaje común, a la vez que apunta a diversos usos del término "mano" en el libro. La frase hecha cobra así una valorización más compleja que la acostumbrada: hace referencia concreta a la idea de la solidaridad humana.

3. Nivel de la representación lírica

Otro aspecto de la resonancia en el poema "La rosa necesaria" se relaciona con la actitud del hablante lírico, que recuerda, ya que a ella se refiere, la actitud apostrófica del tradicional poeta del "Carpe Diem", tópico completamente transformado por el poema del español. Al analizar el poema " 'Serán ceniza. . .' " se advirtió que en el plano de la representación lírica la composición goza de un efecto de resonancia porque toma como base estructuradora la escena alegórica del "Homo Viator". El modelo para "La rosa necesaria" está en cambio en la actitud lírica del apóstrofe, actitud que también se encuentra como forma de resonancia de un tipo específico de composición en el poema "Lo sellado". El aprovechamiento de escenas tradicionalmente significativas y de actitudes líricas particularizadas puede darse en forma combinada en un mismo poema, aunque lo característico en la obra de Valente sea la elección de una de las fórmulas para cada composición.

Las anécdotas o escenas que sirven como base de la resonancia en algunos poemas de Valente provienen de diversos contextos. El monólogo de Hamlet en el cementerio es una referencia explícita en "La cabeza de Yorick" (p. 76). La historia de Abraham e Isaac (Génesis XXII, 1-14) sirve de asunto al poema "El sacrificio" (pp. 213-214) y representa un buen ejemplo del procedimiento. La crítica implícita en esta composición se comunica por la visualización de una acción y por la resonancia de la escena bíblica. Valente, atento al carácter mítico-religioso y al valor interpretativo de la anécdota elegida, logra el efecto de su crítica poniendo la narración en boca de un hablante omnisciente situado en una perspectiva opuesta a la del narrador bíblico. Desde su posición críticamente realista el nuevo hablante corrige la versión idealizada del primitivo narrador. Así, el sacrificio de Isaac tiene un final muy diferente al aceptado tradicionalmente:

> Al fin, sobre el desnudo torso

> brilló el acero al aire,
> puro como el ala de un ángel.
> Mas no era un ángel.   Súbita
> la fuerza entera de la vida
> paró el golpe senil.
> Irguióse Isaac terrible.
> Humillóse el anciano, mordió el polvo,
> suplicó y maldijo,
> para sumirse al cabo en la tristeza (vv. 17-27).

El reconocimiento de la escena original transformada constituye el aspecto más importante en la lectura de este poema. Es a través de tal transformación que se comunica un concepto de liberación. El reconocimiento del modelo es, sin lugar a dudas, un caso de resonancia. Ha de advertirse que por esta vía el poeta está no sólo haciendo uso de una posibilidad del lenguaje poético, sino que a la vez está introduciendo, de manera muy efectiva, su concepto central del poetizar como forma de captar en su esencia la realidad, siendo una forma de lograrlo la crítica o reinterpretación de la historia y la tradición, así como del lenguaje. Y son las técnicas de la resonancia las que en gran medida efectúan esta función.

Algunas composiciones de Valente escenifican concepciones míticas, conceptos tradicionalmente aceptados, dogmas sociales. Así, por ejemplo, "La respuesta" (p. 109) figura una escena objetiva que provoca una serie de relaciones interpretativas basadas en el reconocimiento de una situación similar que tiene un valor significativo en la tradición. La primera parte de la composición muestra a dos personajes contrarios enfrentados en una situación y espacio vagamente referidos:

> El hombre de la tierra
> miró mis manos, dijo:
> "No conocen el peso de la tierra."
>
> Escudriñó mis ojos: "No podrían
> distinguir las semillas."
>
> Alzóse hasta mi frente:
> "Ni el sol ni el aire la han sellado."
>   Dijo
> y volvióse a la tierra (vv. 1-9).

El paralelismo de los siete primeros versos es característico de la técnica de estructuración por resonancias. Los términos "manos", "ojos" y "frente" forman en la enumeración una caracterización del hablante gracias a sus valores representativos de lo esencial del hombre. Las frases negativas dichas por "el hombre de la tierra" plantean la oposición entre el campesino (hombre natural) y el hombre de la ciudad (hombre civilizado). Termina el poema con la narración de un acto que rompe el orden preestablecido:

> Largo tiempo
> la estuvo contemplando. Nadie
> mediaba entre los dos sino la tierra.
>
> Durante largo tiempo el hombre

la miró con cuidado,
luego vino hacia mí
solemne y simple,
como si al fin me hubiese
reconocido en ella (vv. 10 y ss).

La oración "Nadie/mediaba entre los dos sino la tierra" no sólo describe la escena, sino que además anota un factor fundamental de la idea contenida en el texto: la identidad de todos los hombres por encima de las clasificaciones establecidas. La escena, que parece narrar un acontecimiento real, expresa una idea. Los protagonistas son figuras muy generales, casi prototipos. Al oponer al yo del hablante la denominación bisémica "hombre de la tierra" el poeta insiste en una lectura que oponga a la figura del artista la del campesino que, en segunda instancia, representa al hombre arraigado en el mundo. La anécdota produce una vaga resonancia del tópico de la naturaleza opuesta a la civilización, y aunque el poema no se refiera directamente a tal aspecto, el efecto de dicha resonancia es esencial para la captación del motivo. Y, así como se ha indicado en relación con otros poemas, la resonancia no se limita al tópico literario; también se apoya en la repetición del término "tierra" y en la estructura paralelística que narra el encuentro.

El sistema de resonancias en este poema particular se apoya en un tópico literario que bien puede extenderse a una condición social presente en el mundo contemporáneo. Mientras este aspecto sin duda salta a la vista fácilmente, la referencia literaria, en cambio, puede resultar de más difícil reconocimiento para un lector común. Un reconocimiento aún más específico y especializado está en la base de la resonancia de la escena representativa en el poema "La cabeza de Yorick" (p. 76) que ya en el mismo título indica su antecedente literario:

La cabeza de Yorick
es pelada y redonda: examinemos
la cabeza de Yorick
el bufón, el alegre
cuenco donde el ojo bailó,
la frente donde
para siempre descansa el pensamiento (vv. 1-7).

Las referencias cultistas limitan el efecto de la resonancia a un público selecto y le dan a la obra de Valente un tono muchas veces marcadamente intelectual. Esto es particularmente cierto en lo que respecta al poema "Maquiavelo en San Casciano" (pp. 210-212), que pone en boca del político italiano sus comentarios decepcionados que le dictan la soledad y pobreza del destierro. El hablante específico e histórico cuenta con un lector-auditor también específico, como lo indica el epígrafe al poema, tomado de una carta de Maquiavelo a Francesco Vettori. Este dato determina sin vaguedades la circunstancia objetiva en la que se apoya el efecto de resonancia. En la lectura no se puede prescindir de este hecho, ya que en caso contrario disminuiría la significación del poema, perdiéndose el verdadero valor del tono de la voz, que depende directamente de la circunstancia histórica precisa por ser ésta la que establece el temple de ánimo del hablante y explica el sentido exacto de sus palabras:

> Los negocios de la República y los reyes
> de España y Francia
> o el Gran Duque lejos están;
> mas bueno fuera que alguien
> pagase en este tiempo aquel saber de entonces (vv. 10-14).

La resonancia responde en este caso tanto a la figura del personaje histórico simplificado en sus rasgos más característicos, como a la actitud del hablante definida por el género epistolar. De manera muy parecida el poema "Anales de Volusio" (p. 385), paráfrasis de la "Canción XXXVI" de Catulo, puede entenderse como una resonancia tanto en lo que se refiere a la identidad del hablante históricamente caracterizado como un tipo particular de persona, como referirse a la imitación de la forma poética misma:

> Sacrifiquemos Lesbia, adúlteros y alegres,
> a la terrible diosa que nos lleva
> papel inmundo, *Anales* de Volusio,
> *cacata carta*,
> la flor de lo obtuso (vv. 11 y ss.).

Del modelo latino Valente aprovecha la actitud y el tono del hablante establecidos desde antiguo como una tradición literaria y, como tal, distintamente valorizados. La forma poética del epigrama subyace como dato que ha de tenerse en cuenta en el momento de la lectura. El efecto de sarcasmo y burla se hace más patente al lector capaz de captar la resonancia.

El mismo procedimiento explica la efectividad expresiva de breves poemas en que José Angel Valente aprovecha una tradición más perdurable en las letras hispánicas: la imitación del lenguaje y estilo poéticos de la lírica galaico-portuguesa.[6] La resonancia de lo tradicional aporta en gran medida el tono emotivo de estas composiciones. Así sucede en "Mar de Muxía" (p. 262), poema que sirve, además, de modelo para los efectos de resonancia en el nivel de las estructuras métricas y acústicas:

> Quien pudiera andar
> sobre las aguas verdes
> de este mar.
>
> Y por el aire gris
> quien pudiera, mar grande,
> dejarse ir.
>
> Mar de Muxía
> que en sus barcos de piedra
> me llevaría.

El poeta contemporáneo no está copiando, detalle por detalle, un estilo particular de composición; del modelo presente en la memoria cultural de sus lectores, toma aquello que mejor lo representa y lo readapta a su propia expresión, cargándola así de una expresividad en gran medida heredada no tanto del modelo mismo como de la actitud del lector ante dicho antecedente. La resonancia consiste en este caso no en la imitación misma, sino en el reconocimiento del efecto sintetizador de emociones que tiene el empleo adecuado de ciertas fórmulas de alusión. En el caso particular de este poema, las resonancias son evidentes y directas, lo que no siempre se aplica a la obra de Valente.

El estudio, necesariamente limitado, de algunos casos del empleo de resonancias en la poesía de José Angel Valente aporta, por una parte, bastante luz respecto a su estilo y, por otra, abre una vía de análisis literario que, reconociendo las descripciones formalistas de ciertas técnicas poéticas, puede ir aún más adelante y explicarlas en relación estilísticamente significativa. No poca importancia cobran los aspectos contextuales y su dependencia del lector. En relación directa con el concepto descriptivo-analítico de resonancia están una serie de fenómenos que han interesado a la crítica desde antiguo, y que no por ello dejan de interesar al crítico contemporáneo que advierte las posibilidades de un planteamiento del problema desde perspectivas renovadas. La designación común de "resonancia" para referirse a una variedad de técnicas literarias que se aplican a aspectos diversos de la composición poética responde a una revisión crítica de ciertas cuestiones aparentemente tan dispares como lo son las categorías de imitación e influencia, los recursos de la alusión y la paráfrasis, las autorreferencias textuales, las técnicas de la versificación y la rima, las preferencias léxicas y temáticas.

La subdivisión metodológica del poema en tres niveles de estructuración permite reconocer la amplia gama de técnicas y procedimientos que alcanzan como efecto principal la resonancia, ese suscitar el reconocimiento de relaciones que en sí mismas son expresivas. Es al lector a quien le toca establecer tales referencias y advertir la serie de ecos que la producen. Cada poema se define como un resonador, una fórmula lingüística estructurada en base a claves de resonancia. En la obra de José Angel Valente estas claves se aúnan y combinan estructuradamente contribuyendo así a plasmar un estilo sobrio y expresivo. El efecto sintetizador de las técnicas de la resonancia explica en gran parte la concisión de un lenguaje poético capaz de comunicar líricamente una visión compleja de la experiencia cognocitiva del hombre contemporáneo de Occidente.

UNIVERSITY OF VIRGINIA

Notas

[1]En uno de los últimos comentarios acerca de la obra poética de José Angel Valente, el crítico José Olivio Jiménez resume así la continuidad estilística de su poesía: ". . .en los Treinta y siete fragmentos finales de *Punto Cero*, llevaba el poeta a extremos por igual de afinamiento y originalidad la nota intrínsecamente dialéctica y personal más característica de su decir, afirmada con los años: decantación y concisión

118   LA RESONANCIA EN LA POESIA DE VALENTE

apuradísma de la palabra". "Crónica de poesía: Bousoño y Valente", *Plural*, julio 1975, p. 62. Véase también: Emilio Alarcos Llorach, reseña a *A modo de esperanza*, *Archivum* 5 (1955), 190-193; Carlos Bousoño, "El arte de callar a tiempo. *A modo de esperanza* de José Angel Valente", *Indice de Arte y Letras* 79 (1955), suplemento bibliográfico sin numeración de páginas; José Luis Cano, "La poesía de José Angel Valente", *Insula* 163 (1960), 8-9; y José Angel Luvina, "Editorial", *Claraboya* 13 (1967), 5.

²"Conocimiento y comunicación", en Francisco Ribes, ed., *Poesía última* (Madrid: Taurus, 1963), pp. 155-161. Una versión corregida de este artículo se encuentra en: José Angel Valente, *Las palabras de la tribu* (Madrid: Siglo XXI, 1971), pp. 3-10.

³*A modo de esperanza* (Madrid: Ediciones Rialp, 1955), p. 9; también en *Punto cero* (Barcelona: Barral Editores, 1972), p. 13. En este trabajo se indica entre paréntesis al final de cada poema la página correspondiente a esta edición que recoge todos los libros de poesía publicados por Valente hasta la fecha.

⁴Para un análisis más detallado de un caso semejante, véase mi trabajo *Poesía social: Un caso español contemporáneo* (Valparaíso: Ediciones de la Universidad Católica de Valparaíso, 1969).

⁵Francisco de Quevedo, *Obra poética*, ed. José Manuel Blecua (Madrid: Castalia, 1969), I, 657.

⁶Dámaso Alonso y José Manuel Blecua, *Antología de la poesía española: Lírica de tipo tradicional* (Madrid: Gredos, 2a ed. corregida, 1964). Véase también: Eduardo Martínez Torner, *Lírica hispánica: relaciones entre lo popular y lo culto* (Madrid: Castalia, 1966).

V. Genre

EL HOMBRE Y LA MOSCA DE JOSE RUIBAL: TEATRO POETICO, TEATRO-CONCIENCIA

José A. Hernández

Signos

La obra alegórica *El Hombre y la mosca*[1] de José Ruibal se caracteriza por la presencia de signos de signos[2] y por la polisemia semántica de éstos. En ella el signo central es una gran cúpula que preside la representación total. Este signo visual realiza una función doble: es la alegoría de diversos significados centrales de la obra y es portador de la fábula que se desarrolla ante nosotros. Y así, en su primera función, representa el poder y la megalomanía personificados en el Hombre-dictador. "Toda la cúpula", dice el Hombre, "...es...¡la grandeza, la grandeza, la grandeza! ¡yo!" (pp. 45-46). Este delirio de poderío está basado en hechos ocurridos en el pasado y que se muestran visualmente en pinturas y decorados de batallas, fechas arbitrarias y trofeos de caza. La mole circular, según palabras del soberano, es "pieza a pieza una lápida de [su] glorioso pasado" (p. 45). Estos actos y fechas que ya no existen sólo perduran como recuerdos en la cabeza del Hombre, por lo que el cimborrio es también esa cabeza. Es, asimismo, jaula en donde viven los "dos pajarracos", es decir, El Hombre y el Doble (pp. 73, 30) y por analogía con el diálogo, es telaraña con su araña que chupa la sangre a las moscas (pp. 29-30).[3] Otros signos visuales escénicos son la pila de quejas escritas que evidencian la existencia de seres revolucionarios, los prismáticos electrónicos, muestra de que los avances científicos han invadido la vida estática de la cúpula, y los instrumentos del laboratorio del valor. Este, compuesto de anillas, trapecio, alambradas y arena es una combinación de gimnasio y circo y en él se va a efectuar la transformación del Doble en el Hombre. La historia del intento de esta transformación es la fábula de la obra y que queda expresada en la cúpula ya que la consecución de aquel propósito y el remate de la cúpula son la misma cosa.

Ahora bien, ya en estos signos visuales se hallan algunas bases del fracaso del dictador. Desde que pronuncia su primera palabra en escena, "¡Basta!" (p. 27), todo su esfuerzo va dirigido a parar el tiempo en esa omnipotente construcción esférica. Pero las pilas de papeles, los prismáticos electrónicos, el laboratorio cirquense y la imagen de los personajes-pajarracos nos van dando el tono incongruente y grotesco que impregna el intento de revivir un mundo ya inexistente. Por esto y otras razones que estudiamos a continuación no debe sorprendernos que la fábula de la araña y la mosca tenga un final insólito: el insecto volador destruye la cúpula-poder-telaraña-cabeza-jaula.

El lenguaje

En combinación con los signos visuales, el lenguaje, signo auditivo, complementa el mundo representativo de la obra. Roman Ingarden relaciona la lengua con las realidades objetivas que son mostradas al espectador (objetos, seres humanos, procesos)[4] y distingue el lenguaje que representa, completa y armoniza los signos presentes en el escenario y el lenguaje que representa realidades objetivas no mostradas en escena; en este caso, las realidades ausentes y relatadas concuerdan con lo visible. Una tercera posibilidad es la de aquellas obras cuyas realidades del pasado son idénticas a las mostradas en el escenario. Esta última es precisamente la que va apareciendo ante nosotros ya que concuerda con los planes del Hombre. La repetición a varios niveles temporales es constante en el transcurso de los hechos. El dictador relata sus hazañas bélicas ocurridas 70 años atrás y quiere reproducirlas en la actualidad. Asimismo, escenas ocurridas en un pasado reciente, fuera del escenario, son duplicadas al ser relatadas: "Y apreté con fuerza. (Suenan disparos lejanos)" (pp. 59-60). Estas reiteraciones van creando una angustiosa sensación de estancamiento que es reforzada por la repetición de ideas por parte del dictador.

Entre las funciones del discurso teatral, Roman Ingarden distingue la función de comunicación entre los varios personajes y la función de persuasión que se trata de ejercer sobre la persona a quien se dirige el discurso.[5] Ambas deben contribuir de manera decisiva a hacer progresar la acción. En *El Hombre y la mosca* a medida que el Hombre y el Doble van fundiéndose en uno, va disminuyendo la comunicación hasta que el monólogo de ambos al unísono y el monólogo final del Doble la elimina por completo. La función de persuasión va dirigida al cese de la comunicación. Se diría entonces que el lenguaje no nos da el progreso de la acción y que ni el pasado ni el presente pueden llevarnos al desenlace final. Sin embargo, el manejo del discurso teatral es tal que el público puede captar en él un segundo nivel de comprensión. Bajo el mecanismo de la ironía, el autor se confabula con los espectadores mientras los personajes centrales están, al parecer, ajenos a ello. La disemia lingüística, frecuente en la obra, expresa por un lado el camino hacia el punto negativo y por otro el desarrollo hacia la catástrofe final.

Estos dobles significados pueden dividirse en varias categorías:
1. Ironía. a. Casos en los que signos visuales y lingüísticos se combinan para dar el segundo significado: "Me he caído del burro" (p. 46). El discurso aquí toma el significado de la expresión idiomática. b. El caso en el que la expresión popular es entendida literalmente: "En dos patadas te he enseñado" (p. 80). c. En un tercer modelo de ironía, debido al uso del lenguaje se anuncia

el fallo de los planes del dictador: "él heredará el miedo" (p. 52), o se utiliza una frase hecha que expresa el triunfo del tiempo sobre el tirano: "funcionará como un reloj" (p. 58).

2. Las contradicciones ofrecen también la ambigüedad de la disemia. El "no" puede tener un significado afirmativo cuando el Hombre apunta: "No te digo que no" (p. 73). En otro tipo de contradicción, un vocablo elimina la verosimilitud de otro: "su futura Eternidad" (p. 49).

3. Por la depreciación del lenguaje se origina, en ocasiones, un caos lingüístico que es un reflejo de la mentira en el universo del dictador. La paz significa la guerra; la onomatopeya "¡Corrocotocó!" (p. 52) es, a la vez, el arrullo de la paloma de la paz y los disparos de la bélica ametralladora. En otro lugar, el amor es en realidad miedo: "me aman, pero con un miedo espantoso" (p. 54).

4. Existen también partes del discurso teatral que son presagios concretos de la muerte: "Ese es el sudario que tienes que imitar e incorporar a tu cuerpo" (p. 34). "No hable de la muerte. Su Eternidad, cuya vida guarde Dios muchos años,[6] puede..." (p. 41). "(mira el reloj) Ha llegado tu hora" (p. 44). Todos estos ejemplos nos dan un lenguaje engañoso que anuncia el derrumbamiento de los planes del dictador. Para éste, la mentira es "lo único verdadero que ha de haber en una política constructiva" (p. 33), pero en el "alambique de [su] sistema hablativo" (p. 58) le sale el tiro por la culata.

Así pues el discurso teatral lejos de mantenerse en "el espíritu de campanario" de que nos habla Saussure, se sitúa en el tiempo y en su dimensión diacrónica evoluciona junto al desarrollo histórico. Así mismo, los diversos significados se asocian a diferentes estratos sociales por lo que éstos quedan relacionados.

La mímica, otra parte fundamental de la representación, adquiere también, a menudo, un tono simbólico y polivalente que armoniza con los demás elementos escénicos. Así por ejemplo, al hablar de la paloma de la paz, el Hombre hace los gestos de una paloma mientras habla; y es a través de su lenguaje cuando comprendemos que esa paloma simboliza principalmente la opresión y la amenaza de violencia (pp. 52-53). En otra escena, el Doble, cuando da sus primeros pasos de dictador, camina como un niño ya que es un novato. Pero hay además otra razón, el aprendiz lleva los viejos trapos del tirano que le abruman y le hunden (p. 78). Los ropajes adquieren aquí función de signo y expresan el mundo gastado y deteriorado del Hombre.

Por último, las fotografías, el baile, la música, los ruidos y las luces son parte del mundo integrado de la representación total. La lucha entre ángeles y demonios, por ejemplo, va expresada por una confusa mezcla de música, resplandores y ruidos celestiales e infernales que acompañan a la acción (p. 88).

La forma polisémica de los signos llevan en sí el fondo de la obra y son, por lo tanto, parte del desarrollo de la misma. Los significados contradictorios de esos elementos representativos comparten el conflicto escénico que nos da por un lado la naturaleza y la vida y por el otro, la testarudez del Hombre que se empeña en acabar con ellas.

122   TEATRO POETICO, TEATRO-CONCIENCIA

El tiempo

El primer concepto clave dentro de esa oposición es el del tiempo. Este significa cambio y actividad en lo nuevo y hacia lo nuevo, lo cual es precisamente lo que el Hombre teme y trata de parar desde el primer momento. Su yo, que vive en el ayer es amenazado por los hechos que, en su exterior, ocurren en el presente. Junto al punto fijo espacial, pretende paralizarse en su pasado y eternizar la negación del tiempo. Su pretérito mental se compone de escenas seleccionadas por él. Sus cicatrices y heridas, huellas de las guerras, perduran todavía y ello junto con la ayuda de las diapositivas (p. 34) consigue la ilusión de la inmersión del pasado en el presente. El Doble adquiere las mismas cicatrices. El proceso se intensifica con el adiestramiento del "ojo trasero" del Doble. Este, que al principio no sabe aún retroceder rompe la cúpula (p. 44). El aprendiz de tirano no está listo todavía y los planes del Hombre pueden fallar. Pero una vez entrenado, como si fuera un cangrejo, puede caminar hacia atrás (p. 48), es decir, al pasado, y la construcción de la cúpula se va asegurando. Otra huella del ayer que el dictador salvó del olvido es el recuerdo de los muertos (p. 51); las "tercas efemérides" son las conmemoraciones anuales de su victoria guerrera setenta años antes.

Con todas esas bases, el presente alrededor de ellos es la nada (p. 50). Materialmente, el todo es la nada, y mentalmente, en un mundo sin vida, proyectos ni ambiciones, sólo encontramos la "muerte ideológica" (p. 51). "La muerte es abono y fermento de todo lo que vive" señala el déspota (p. 45) y este fermento no sólo va del pasado al presente sino del presente al futuro también. Para él las tres etapas son idénticas. Por eso "su Eternidad" puede predecir lo que vendrá ("Y lo será", 48) y decide cuándo va a morir (pp. 40, 81); para asegurarse de que no habrá cambios, exige al Doble que no adultere el futuro (p. 55). Al rematar la cúpula, el Hombre ve sus designios cumplidos y lo expresa en su canto: "Cuando yo me muera el presente estará conmigo...el pasado será revivido...el futuro dormirá tranquilo" (p. 76).

La historia

Intimamente ligado al concepto de tiempo va el de historia. El Hombre planea fijar los hechos que serán en el futuro considerados como historia. Piensa "gastar una broma a la historia" (p. 29) y de un botones de banca crea un doble para que éste prolongue y perdure su era introduciéndola de contrabando en la vida del pueblo (p. 58). Esa historia en la que se incluye su mentiroso curriculum vitae (pp. 38, 46) es la que va a seguir el doble "al pie de la letra" (p. 47). El dictador-historiador no es el único que falsifica los hechos; ya desde Carlomagno, o antes, se viene construyendo la Enciclopedia Universal del Valor que perpetúa el recuerdo de todos aquellos que amparados en su fama más que en sus actos impusieron su dictadura entre los que les rodeaban. Con esto se implica que las crónicas se escriben con fines políticos y propagandísticos. Los políticos-historiadores creen, con cierta frecuencia, que el futuro debe parecerse al pasado y sustraen a los seres humanos del presente, alejándolos así de las mudanzas del tiempo y reduciendo sus posibilidades de creatividad. Por lo tanto, la historia es una carga; esta es la imagen que nos da el Doble ahogado bajo viejas medallas y ropas usadas que pertenecieron al Hombre. "El peso de la historia" (p. 77) le impide andar. Ya solo en la cúpula, el nuevo tirano decide barrer el polvo allí acumulado. Pero esto equivaldría a una revolución porque el polvo es la huella de la historia y el símbolo del tiempo estancado y sin reloj, es decir, el no-tiempo. El tiempo matemático, el del reloj, no existe para el Hombre y su idea de la historia.

El "yo"

En el universo dictatorial en que transcurre la fábula surge con gran fuerza el problema de la identidad del ser. Porque si el Doble es el Hombre tanto para éste como para los súbditos, entonces ¿quién es el Hombre? o ¿quién es el Doble?; en otras palabras, ¿qué es lo que constituye el "yo" para ambos seres? Hallamos aquí un reflejo de la idea barroca del mundo como representación. Estamos ante la "comedia humana" en la que la existencia se reduce a papeles y nada más. Pero si en *El gran teatro del mundo* calderoniano era Dios quien confería los papeles, en *El Hombre y la mosca* el tirano se ha adjudicado ese don divino. He aquí otra razón por la que el Doble le llama, a veces, "su Eternidad" (pp. 51, 61). La idea de que ambos personajes no tienen vida propia se acentúa con su apariencia y actuación de marionetas a través de la obra. Su característica valleinclanesca culmina con la muerte del Doble-títere gesticulando de manera guiñolesca. Ahora bien, al mismo tiempo que son muñecos grotescos participan de la condición de entes trágicos atrapados en su papel sin ninguna otra alternativa. La cúpula-"jaula de pajarracos" es un mundo sin salida como el que presenta Becket en *Esperando a Godot*, Pedrolo en *Hombres y No* y Sartre en *Huit-Clos*.

El público-intérprete

Esos dos patéticos seres alegóricos de que venimos hablando no están solos en la escena. El público es también parte de la acción y, lo quiera o no, se convierte en público-actor. Esta idea estaba expresada visualmente en el estreno mundial de la obra celebrado en 1971 en la Universidad del Estado de Nueva York en Binghamton. La cúpula-escenario abarcaba toda la sala y nos cubría a todos los espectadores. El público puede ser también alegoría de la humanidad dominada por el Hombre, es decir, por el pasado muerto. Esta relación entre escena y pueblo es una gran innovación del autor que se diferencia de los esfuerzos anteriores por lograr la participación activa de la audiencia en la obra. En este aspecto destaca el teatro de Brecht. Si éste, para evitar la catarsis liberadora y motivar a la acción después de la representación, busca la no identificación de los espectadores con los personajes, Ruibal en *El Hombre y la mosca* pone al público dentro de la representación y este público-intérprete decidirá además qué desenlace tendrán las circunstancias problemáticas allí reveladas. Sobre todo, tendrá la oportunidad de elegir entre continuar bajo la opresión o liberarse y tener vida propia.

José Ruibal ha expresado en varias ocasiones su idea de "escribir contra

124   TEATRO POETICO, TEATRO-CONCIENCIA

el público".⁷ Para él, los espectadores acostumbrados al teatro realista que acuden a presenciar sus producciones teatrales no sólo no deben identificarse con la acción sino que además deben desecharla por irracional y por irreal o, mejor dicho, por aparentemente irreal. Pero ese rechazamiento será la chispa inicial que impulse al espectador a pensar y cambiar sus esquemas mentales que es lo que el autor buscaba.⁸ Volviendo a *El Hombre y la mosca*, oímos que en el escenario se habla despectivamente de los súbditos o público. El tirano los llama "rebaño de moscas" (p. 56) y señala en otra ocasión que los humanos tienen más capacidad mimética que unas botas (p. 39). Esta capacidad les permite adaptarse a las personas poderosas, que quieren agradar y a la vez pasar inadvertidos de sus enemigos. A este mimetismo servil se añade la pereza y la comodidad: aguantan al tirano porque "siempre será más cómodo sufrirle que echarle" (p. 74). Se trata de un pueblo sin ambiciones ni ilusiones y como señala el déspota en frase que resulta irónica "Un pueblo sin ilusiones es un cadáver" (p. 51). De todo esto resulta la poca halagadora imagen de una masa de borregos a las órdenes del dictador.

Pero, ¿cómo ha podido éste destacarse del grupo e instaurar la opresión? La clave está en que el miedo separa al Hombre del resto. Mientras el pueblo "va de susto en susto" (p. 63) el dictador "se ha curado de espantos" (p. 69), lo que constituye su mayor sabiduría. Esta es la desagradable verdad que el público se resiste a aceptar. Al mismo tiempo, en este sentimiento degradante reside el mecanismo promotor del desenlace final: el Hombre no ha podido traspasar su poder amedrentador al Doble por lo que éste no puede ser su sucesor. El temor es la fuerza que mantiene al uno y paraliza a los otros. Pero hay más, en el rico juego de polivalencias de la obra hallamos que en realidad el Hombre es el miedo ("El miedo y tu amo eran una y la misma cosa" [p. 97]) y el temor que insensibiliza al pueblo-público-actor es una alegoría que cubre toda la gama de los defectos de este público. Ya en la última escena cuando el Doble exclama "maldito sea el miedo" comprendemos que se refiere a su antecesor y al mismo tiempo, a la pusilanimidad de la mayoría. Esta compleja y rica imagen del miedo paralizador va dirigida a provocar una reacción mental en el espectador. Este comienza a comprender que se le ofrecen dos caminos principales: el primero, seguir como está, es decir, parecerse al Doble y en definitiva parecerse al dictador. En realidad esto no sería difícil para aquellos concurrentes-súbditos que tienen mentalidad de dictadores. "La mayoría de los hombres", apunta el tirano, "se creen predestinados para ejercer el poderío" (p. 43) y naturalmente "a todos les habría encantado ser capaces de haber levantado una cúpula" "como la del Hombre" (p. 45). Todo el proceso de pérdida del "yo" que el Doble sufre a través de la obra podría ocurrir en los espectadores y así éstos y aquél serían como una sola persona, una sola mente que acabaría convirtiéndose en un solo dictador. En este caso los planes del Hombre triunfarían por completo pues conseguiría reducir la existencia a un tiempo y espacio asentados en una sola cabeza-cúpula. El público no tendría "jamás una idea propia" (p. 55) y su eliminación sería completa. Esta cómoda postura implicaría también falta de responsabilidad.

Bajo la absorción del tirano el ser humano podría obrar impunemente e incluso transferir sus errores al dictador lo que constituiría un atractivo más para dormitar en la paralización: "DOBLE: Todas mis tonterías serán cargadas a su cuenta. Yo no existo. ¡Soy libre!" (p. 71). La decisión de seguir en esta primera tesitura constituye un acto de fe y la existencia del universo del Hombre se origina en la mente de los súbitos. Estos, por las razones de temor, comodidad y responsabilidad señaladas, creen en ese mundo y en definitiva son ellos quienes lo crean. En la noche de las calaveras el Hombre explica al Doble que si fuese ateo no vería nada de lo que le rodea (p. 66). El Doble cree en su Eternidad y todo aquello es su realidad. El espectador, por su parte, se preguntará si cree y acepta ese cosmos cupular o, si por el contrario, no existe para él y por lo tanto ni lo acepta ni lo ve.

La segunda posibilidad de elección encierra esfuerzo y obligación, es el camino que eligieron los tercos y aquellos que envían escritos. La lengua en su expresión oral y escrita representa aquí la fuerza de la oposición. El tirano lo sabe muy bien, por eso al iniciar su intento de paralización de la vida exclama "No me leas más" (p. 27) y en su ceremonia anual de comunión con la muerte quema la pila de quejas que han ido acumulándose.

Ante las alternativas que se le ofrecen, cada espectador decide la senda que ha de tomar. Con ello se reconoce el derecho personal a regir la vida propia. El derrumbamiento apocalíptico final de los valores de la cúpula se debe, entre otras razones, a un intento de individualización del Doble. Cuando éste comprende que es incapaz de atemorizar a los que le rodean decide tener sus propios muertos y hacer lo que le dé la gana con lo que precipita esa destrucción. Aunque dentro de un tono dictatorial parecido al de su antecesor, se despierta en él una iniciativa propia que apunta hacia un renacimiento de su propio "yo". La luz esperanzadora que nos da el desmoronamiento de ese mundo mortuorio queda, en cierto modo intensificada por este intento de individualización.

Teatro alegórico

Anudando muy sucintamente lo dicho hasta ahora, tenemos que el espacio-cúpula es la mente-cárcel del pueblo, es la jaula-prisión del carcelero y es telaraña que en el mundo de la obra será rota por la mosca-tiempo. Así mismo, los varios significados del texto dramático se entrelazan y armonizan con los signos visuales y comparten las contradicciones que llevan a la destrucción final. Se trata pues de un teatro poético con sus propias leyes y tensiones y su propio desarrollo. Para acercarnos a *El Hombre y la mosca* debemos olvidarnos del teatro realista e ir de la mano del arte alegórico como el que escribía Calderón, por ejemplo. Hablando de las diferencias entre sus producciones y las del teatro realista, Ruibal ha señalado que los dramaturgos de este último "se expresan a través de las formas de la realidad, dan imagen de la realidad frente a la cual toman una actitud crítica, pero esa realidad no cambia, sigue dominando y nosotros tratamos de destruir esa realidad."[9] Ahora bien que la obra constituya un universo específico único, no quiere decir que esté disociada de la realidad, al contrario. En primer lugar porque parte de una anécdota actual y en segundo lugar porque esa anécdota transciende a valores humanos universales que hacen que ese Hombre del título sea el ser humano quién es, en definitiva, el centro de la obra. Y en la anécdota-ejemplo que nos da el autor, ese ser humano que aparece en un ambiente de paz y contentamiento está en realidad bajo una amenaza de guerras y bombas atómicas (p. 53) y tiene como posibles soluciones la dictadura opresora o la economía actual de compañías multinacionales negadora del "yo". Si la araña-Hombre es inhumana, la mosca-pueblo ha de espabilarse para no quedar como idiota (p. 30). Sin duda ese primer derrumbamiento de la conclusión no es suficiente, tendrá que venir otro derrumbamiento, y otro, y otro. . .

Caducidad de valores

El enajenamiento del ser humano se debe también a que en su mente ha estructurado su propia realidad, basándose para ello en esquemas heredados. Vivimos en un mundo confortable, organizado "a priori" y que se fija muy poco, o nada, en la realidad circundante. Esas ordenaciones mentales se apoyan en conceptos morales que se nos inculcan. Son normas y prejuicios delimitadores del bien y del mal que rigen nuestras vidas, nuestras decisiones y nuestros enjuiciamientos. Frente a ello, Ruibal nos presenta un cosmos sin valores absolutos. Y así los conceptos de infierno y gloria son relativos ya que "en el más allá, al igual que en el más acá, todo está un poco revuelto" (p. 69). La calavera que perteneció a un terco se ríe al ser atacada por el doble de su asesino y llora cuando se le trata bien. Al mismo tiempo, el llanto de ella es una fuente de alegría para los visitantes (p. 69). En otro ejemplo de la relatividad de las cosas, los ángeles llaman tercos a los que mató el Hombre mientras que los demonios consideran inocentes a esos mismos muertos. Dentro del tono humorístico que impregna esta disputa entre los tradicionales representantes del bien y del mal, los ángeles son los entes totalitarios intransigentes ("Somos el todo o nada" [p. 83]) y cuanto les concierne "está pensado con antelación sempiterna" (p. 86), pero no contaban con la otra cara de la realidad, representada por los demonios. Cada uno de los grupos tiene que aceptar las demandas del otro y ambas parejas terminan repartiéndose el Hombre a medias. Los ángeles se van por un lado entonando, "Nosotros de lo absoluto contamos media verdad", en otra dirección caminan los demonios diciendo "Y aquí con media mentira tenemos leña de más" (p. 192).

En concordancia con esta demostración de la falsedad de mundos petrificados absolutos, el autor desbarata el lenguaje que encierra en sí la perduración de esos valores caducos. Sin el sostén de puntos fijos, se impone la mutabilidad de las cosas. El ser humano se enfrenta con la incertidumbre que exige de él responsabilidad propia y alerta constante. En esta situación vale más el consejo del enemigo (p. 93) que el halago del amigo. Ya no existen los héroes a seguir porque sus causas no son ni justas ni injustas. La experiencia de los antepasados no es válida y "nadie aprende en trasero ajeno" (p. 35).

El tiempo y el espacio

Si por un lado nos hallamos ante signos visuales y sonoros ricos en número y complejos en sus relaciones, por otro lado, el autor ha manejado una limitada gama de conceptos puros de la dramaturgia. La obra puede verse, entre otras maneras, como la problemática del Hombre-centro situado entre el espacio y el tiempo. Estas dos coordenadas básicas de la teoría teatral convergen y pugnan como dos protagonistas más en *El Hombre y la mosca* al mismo tiempo que transcienden a la humanidad. En la distinción bergsoniana entre tiempo mental y tiempo físico, el primero aparece alimentado por el pasado. Cuando recordamos lo pretérito en fragmentos integrados, éstos quedan fijos y nuestro "yo" desciende al espacio. Al obrar así no vivimos, todo se estanca y se convierte en piedra. En este caso, la mente puede descansar y continuar con sus hábitos mentales, se reduce a la contemplación y mantiene la ilusión de seguridad. El tiempo físico, el del reloj o "tiempo matemático" de Einstein, es el de la objetividad, implica progreso y creatividad. Cuando la mente del Hombre no encaja en el tiempo, va encontrándose mejor y mejor en el espacio y éste se va limitando a medida que el ser se aleja del tiempo. El Hombre es el ser anclado en la ilusión de seguridad que le dan el espacio y los recuerdos mientras es empujado por un tiempo que fluye constantemente hacia un futuro incierto, de ahí su tensión. La propia conciencia de estos hechos le proporciona su superioridad sobre los demás seres y constituye, a la vez, su condición de ente trágico. Esta tensión no parece existir entre los otros animales; por eso en la representación faúnica del drama que estudiamos, un objeto del reino animal, la telaraña, es el espacio y nada más y un animal de diferente especie, la mosca, simboliza el tiempo.

Conclusión

El Hombre y la mosca es un ejemplo de teatro total y poético en el que se armoniza la función de los elementos de que disponemos hoy día en el arte escénico. La obra tiene sus propias leyes que rigen la integración de las diferentes partes y que hacen de ella un mundo "per se". Ello significa una vuelta a las raíces de la dramaturgia pura.

Pero, además, esa escenificación simbólico-poética conlleva una filosofía. Lo que parece en principio el drama de un dictador moderno acaba siendo una interrogante trágica sobre el ser humano. La obra tiene tres bases fundamentales: cúpula, acción y concienciación que corresponden en nuestro cosmos a lugar, tiempo y responsabilidad. El avance del tiempo exige del Hombre cambio de espacio y responsabilidad ante lo incierto. Si la mayoría de la humanidad en el pasado y en el presente ha estado y está dividida en los falsos papeles de opresores y oprimidos, el comprometimiento y la revolución ofrecerán a los individuos la libertad con voluntad y vida propias. Obra pues de fondo relativamente optimista y dirigida a una amplia realidad humana que incluye política, moral, arte (demostrado por la construcción e ideas de la obra misma)...*El Hombre y la mosca* es un modelo de teatro-conciencia en el que el autor nos dice, ¡Liberemos al Hombre!

NEW YORK UNIVERSITY

Notas

[1]José Ruibal, *El Hombre y la mosca*. Madrid: 1977.

[2]Ptr Bogatyrev distingue entre "signo de signo" y "signo de objeto". "Les signes du théatre", *Poetique*, N. 8 (1971), 515-530.

[3]HOMBRE: Has encontrado una telaraña magnífica, idéntica a las de hace setenta años.

DOBLE: Era una araña asquerosa; estaba chupando la sangre de una mosca.

HOMBRE: ¿Y no le partiste el cráneo?

DOBLE: Las aniquilé a las dos de un machetazo.

HOMBRE: Brava acción de guerra. La araña murió por inhumana, la mosca por idiota.

DOBLE: De la panza de la araña salieron montones de arañitas.

[4] Roman Ingarden, "Les fonctions du langage au théatre". *Poetique*, N. 8 (1971), 531-538.

[5]*Ibid.*

[6]"Cuya vida guarde Dios muchos años". Esta fórmula obligatoria en instancias y documentos dirigidos a altas autoridades españolas, es un ejemplo más del uso paródico que hace el autor de expresiones lingüístico-sociales.

[7]José Ruibal, *Teatro sobre teatro*. Madrid: 1975, pp. 211-213.

[8]*Ibid.* Ver principalmente pp. 30-36.

[9]Ramón Chao, "José Ruibal en La Sorbona". En *El Hombre y la mosca*, Madrid: 1977, p. 131.

FROM THE IMPRESSIONIST
TO THE PHENOMENOLOGICAL NOVEL

Maria Elisabeth Kronegger

Nous sommes donc, au présent,
sur la scène de la parole.

Philippe Sollers, *Drame*

I. Impressionism and Phenomenology in Criticism

The physicist and philosopher Ernst Mach has diagnosed the widespread cultural phenomenon of impressionism. In *Die analyse der Empfindungen* (1885), Mach calls spaces and times sensations, as appropriately as one does colors and sounds. The unity of space and color sensation is, for Mach and the impressionists, an interplay of the individual's consciousness and the surrounding world. The reader is intended to seize the impressionist works spatially in a moment of time, rather than as a time sequence. Space is defined as the relationships which pieces of matter, in our experience, have with one another. Time, also, is the relationship between different occasions, again within the experience of the individual. In this allusive space and time, both human mind and physical objects have exactly the same ingredients, which from the point of view of psychology are sensations and from the point of view of physics, the constituents of things. With E. Mach and the impressionists, the antithesis of ego and world, sensation and thing vanishes. All that exists is in contact with everything else. The German critic Hermann Bahr calls Mach's views the "philosophy of impressionism."

The association of impressionism with phenomenology is most justifiable when used by critics, such as Gustave Geffroy in 1894, Bally in 1920, and Albérès in 1966 and 1970. Gustave Geffroy, in *Vie Artistique*, defines an impressionist painting as a kind of painting that approaches phenomenology, tending to represent the appearance and meaning of objects in space, and attempting to synthesize these things into the semblance of a moment. Bally, in *Mélanges d'histoire littéraire et de philologie offerts à M. Bernard Bouvier* (1920), distinguishes an "impressionist" or "phenomenological" and a "causal" or "transitive" form of perception. With the impressionists' perceptive experience, the reality of the novel changes; the traditional frozen forms of description set themselves into motion spatially. The protagonists see reality from several angles of vision at once and the objects are released without losing sight of their earlier positions. Seen at a distance, no object has any clear and detailed outlines, and thus, automatically, the subject itself is subordinated to the melodious effect of colors and sounds which then can be used to evoke a particular mood. Through unity of color, tint and tone, blurred outlines and vagueness of meaning, impressionist writers achieve musical effects. Referring to this new reality of the novel, the critic R. M. Albérès, when discussing the "roman artistique" and "roman phénoménologique" (1970), sees an analogy between phenomenology and impressionism in the contemporary works of Musil and Proust. Reality is seen as a harmony between subjects and objects, merging in terms of time and space during any act of the protagonists—that is, their states melt into one another. The act of perception is more important than either the perceived or the perceiver. No longer is there *Me* the narrator/protagonist, on the one hand, and that tree on the other hand; there is only my seeing, retaining, or remembering that tree. There is no separation between the narrator and the objects: there is a narrator seeing the objects, and without objects there can be no self, and without self there can be no objects. Impressionist writers share with recent investigators in phenomenology (such as Merleau-Ponty) the conviction that we cannot know reality independently of consciousness, and that we cannot know consciousness independently of reality: every act of consciousness is a consciousness of something, every act of love is a love of something. Impressionists don't return to the thing-in-itself (Kant's *noumenon*). They return to the thing which is the direct object of consciousness, to what Kant would have called appearance of reality in consciousness or *phenomenon*. Both impressionists and phenomenologists derive their conception of reality from sense impressions: it is in this context that there may be said to be an affinity between them.

Authors such as Flaubert, Gide, Proust, Claude Simon, Rilke and Joyce have powerfully demonstrated that their thought takes form only as they are writing. Gérard Genette, in his recent *Figures* and *Mimologiques*,[1] explores texts of works that find their essence only in the activity of reading a *mise-en-scène* of *écriture* rejecting the limits of their society's assumptions of the *vraisemblable* (its mental codes and expected norms of cultural models): Genette, and with him the new novelists, refute the Balzacian[2] concept of reality, its metonymic mode, a writing that traces the real in a potentially endless notation, representing and reiterating the society's forms of reality that it assumes to be real in a system of intelligibility, while language is lost in this monologue of re-presentation. The affirmation of two different notions, *parole* (speech) and langue (language) and an analysis of the correlation between them (the Geneva School) were extraordinarily fruitful for the science of language. Both structuralism and phenomenology in literature experience a shifting of conventional forms which threatens to abolish the causalism of the realist novel by establishing a dialectic of synchronic and diachronic experiences. Both the structuralist Gérard Genette and the phenomenologist Merleau-Ponty derive their theories of language from Saussurian linguistics. Saussure thought of the concepts of synchronic and diachronic linguistics as independent of *la parole* and *la langue*. Merleau-Ponty and Genette, however, institute a dialectic of perception to bring the diachronic and synchronic views into communication. Diachrony envelops synchrony; the dichotomy between impression and language is rejected by Merleau-Ponty who sees writing as bodily expression which is part of the ongoing primordial process of perception. The act of naming arranges a series of perceptual data, inaugurating rather than exhausting order. The written word indicates the presence of thought. Taking Saussurian linguistics as a basis for his argument, Merleau-Ponty hypothesizes an original utterance when *langue* is presented in its individual aspect as parole. Speech does not presuppose thought since *parole* has an innovative function and is not simply prefabricated from *langue*. Merleau-Ponty invokes Husserl's differentiation between the voluntary *intentionnalité d'acte* and the involuntary *intentionnalité opérante*. This division illustrates the automatic function of perception which conveys the natural unity of life and the world prior to its predication by a conscious act as objective knowledge. The *intentionnalité opérante* of the writer thus contains both his perception and expression. Communication through the written word constitutes a primary mode of perception that precedes the *intentionnalité d'acte* on the part of the reader. To indicate the direction of Genette's argument on Proust's "L'âge des noms," which is also the title intended for the first part of *A la Recherche du temps perdu* followed by "L'Age des mots" and "L'Age des choses," we may note that the definition of *la parole* responds to "l'image présentée par le nom propre,"[3] being internally dynamic (*confuse, indistincte, complexe*) in that it translates itself by means of its words. Genette proposes a linguistic concept of the *nom propre*, always linked to a geographical location, refuting *le Mot*—that is to say, ready made meanings within the experience of language. Genette, in his "L'Age des noms," in the footsteps of Merleau-Ponty, accentuates the internal power of the words themselves, a verbal experience in which the word carries a meaning that conveys a thought as a style, as an emotional value, as an existential mimicry rather than a conceptual statement, concluding with Proust that "ce n'est pas des noms qu'il faut partir pour connaître les choses, mais des choses elles-mêmes"[4] (the word's meaning is not in the sound, but in the modulation of existence enacted by the thing.) Marcel, however, takes the opposite road of apprenticeship: the shape of reality that gradually defines itself for Marcel is a shape determined primarily by the associations of words. His mental images are largely associations suggested by the words he hears, and in intense loneliness he both hesitates and struggles to make the associations fit into a coherent pattern closely linked to certain locations: ". . .les noms présentent des personnes—et des villes qu'ils nous habituent á croire individuelles, uniques comme des personnes—une image confuse que tire d'eux, de leur sonorité éclatante et sombre, la couleur dont elle peinte uniformément. . ."[5] Similarly, Swann discovers that the musical sounds are not the signs of musical meaning but the very substance of the sonata descending within him; and Marcel learns that La Berma is magically no longer the actress; she is Phèdre, the result of a perfect fusion of subject and object, of La Berma with Phèdre.[6] Roland Barthes makes what is essentially the same point when discussing the act of naming in Proust: "L'écrivain travaille, non sur le point de rapport de la chose et de sa forme, . . .mais sur le rapport du *signifié* et du *signifiant*, c'est-à-dire sur un signe."[7] It is as passive receiver rather than active interpreter that Marcel intuits synthetically the artistry of the actress. He has drawn closer to the signifier La Berma by appreciating the signified, her acting, as apprehended by his sense impressions rather than the event itself as a preordained work of art. He finally realizes, as Genette observes, the hopelessness of identifying sign and referent, signifier and signified at once. Marcel transforms this gap into the space of his literary exploration of reality as we shall see.

II. Impressionism and Phenomenology in Literature

Let us now turn to an investigation of affinities and contrasts between literary impressionism and phenomenological style in the works of Flaubert, Gide and Proust, Rilke and Joyce, and finally Claude Simon, taking into account the possible interference caused by the linguistic medium.

A word or an image placed in a particular context produces a particular effect. "The writer's work is a work of language rather than of thought" as Merleau-Ponty tells us in discussing Proust. "His task is to produce a system of signs whose internal articulation reproduces the contours of experience; the reliefs and sweeping lines of these contours in turn generate a syntax in depth, a mode of composition and recital which breaks the mold of the world and everyday language and refashions it."[8]

Poe, Joyce, Baudelaire, Rimbaud, and Mallarmé have initiated a movement in fiction to adapt changes of consciousness, feelings, or sensations to the power of words, inventing a new language that by itself will be capable of expressing the multiple nuances of the personality and feelings.[9] Proust and Gide were the first to acknowledge the aesthetic revolution of Flaubert's *L'Education Sentimentale* in which "impression" replaces "action." Detachment from the human character is a stylistic device: when Flaubert dispenses with character, naturally, he has to do away with plot, too. Characters simply *appear* in their pure physical reality; they are seen before their lives and thoughts are known. The reader sees Frédéric in successive portraits of fragmentary and progressive images of *anéantissement, abandon, oubli, dénouement, dépouillement, désagrégation, épuisement, dépersonnalisation*, and *dissolution*. The major impression of the book is the one of distance, of detachment, of discontinuity. Since each sensation is reflected by the mirror of the artist's consciousness, which is precisely located in space and time, no two impressions can be identical.

Flaubert's style reflects an impression that lingers for but a moment.

Characteristics of this style are devices which Flaubert shares with his impressionist successors: the strong verbs are often replaced by weak auxiliaries (*être, avoir*), by colorless verbs of perception such as *paraître, sembler, glisser, osciller*, by substantivized color adjectives, by quality nouns, by impersonal synthetic pronouns, by a predominance of color over objects, by subjective impressions and onomatopoeic overtones. There is a frequent use of ellipsis to express an absence; there are adverbial expressions to suggest a certain *Stimmung*, "mood," or "atmosphere." Flaubert initiates the use of present participles to suggest an illusion and indicate simultaneity. His composition by *tableaux* is most effective when he creates distance in the way French writers of the seventeenth century would create it: with the indefinite article, adverbs and prepositions (*avec, au-loin, par-derrière*). There are inversions, crescendo effects, a lack of outline, and a predominant shifting use of the present and imperfect.

Gide transformed the narrative of *La Nouvelle Education Sentimentale*, a short fragment and the original draft of *Les Cahiers d'André Walter* (1891), into the form of a diary, the form most used by impressionist writers. Also, when Gide wrote *Les Cahiers d'André Walter*, he felt many affinities with Flaubert's Frédéric Moreau and, even more, was deeply impressed by Flaubert's stylistic devices. The major purpose of his lyrical prose, Gide tells us, is to write not in French but in music. Phenomenologically, music is anterior to spoken language, and it is in the musical structure of Gide's lyrical work that language can appear. Language is no longer understood as thought and concept, but as sensation and sound image.

In this respect, Gide's *Les Nourritures Terrestres* (1897) appears to us as almost the gospel of impressionist lyrical prose. It is a hymn of joy, of spontaneity, of instantaneousness, of discontinuity, of detachment, of dissolution. All beings are judged according to their ability to receive light. The reflection of light on cities and landscapes creates the impression of distance, remoteness, and detachment. Reality for Gide's protagonist is a synthesis of pure sensations, modulated by consciousness, an impermeable surface which reflects vibrating light waves from a single instantaneous impression of matter in dissolution. The phenomenological consciousness may be likened to a prism that focuses the diverging impressions as they pass through its interior.

We find ourselves confronted with the problem of the relationship between the thing or reality as it appears, through a single perception, and the thing or reality as it really is: What is a visible thing for Gide's or Rilke's protagonist? What is it that makes that visible thing? And what is the visibility of the thing? Seeing is the act of perception taken as a vehicle of knowing a lived object; it is *Wesensschau, Schauen* for Rilke's Malte; it is the perceived perceiving, the speech speaking, the thought thinking, as Merleau-Ponty explains, "L'énigme tient en ceci que mon corps est à la fois voyant et visible. Lui qui regarde toutes choses, il peut aussi se regarder, et reconnaître dans ce qu'il voit alors l' "autre côté" de sa puissance voyante.

Il se voit voyant, il se touche touchant, il est visible et sensible pour soi-même."[10]

In Rilke's *Die Aufzeichnungen des Malte Laurids Brigge*, sickness and death adopt, as Malte tells us, the characteristics of the person they attack. He contrasts personal death with a hospital death where sickness becomes anonymous and cannot express the person. Thoughts of death fuse with the surroundings of Malte's grandfather, Christoph Detlev, in harmony with the broken rhythm of sentences that describe the fall of objects and lead to the major effect, the death of Chamberlain Christoph Detlev Brigge; the repetition of key words suggests, in ever louder and penetrating rhythm, death. The passage conveys the impression that death emerges from the world of broken and falling objects as a necessity. Even structure and images reflect a "coloration" of death which penetrates and dissolves both subject and object simultaneously. The crescendo of key words, obtained by an elaborate arrangement of rhythms and images, creates the effect of a musical elegy. The predominant sound effects excite our soul, conveying the impression that these sounds live.

In Joyce's *Dubliners* and *A Portrait of the Artist*, intellectual associations are completely dispensed with whenever Joyce wishes to capture the ephemeral, translucent atmosphere of Dublin. Joyce seems to be going beyond form to seize, for a moment, the peculiarly sensual qualities of light playing havoc with the staid objects of the outside. In one passage, Stephen is journeying to cork by the night mail train. His window is his frame on life, and outside objects flash by with kaleidoscopic effect, revealing only their essence in the repeated and momentary flaring up of tiny grains of fire. Joyce creates the impression of blurred images passing before his eyes in total silence by repetition of key words such as flung, and by his use of the gerund and adjectival participles. Words take the place of objects: darkening, slipping, passing, glimmering, twinkling, etc. This blurring of images is an essential part of Joyce's technique, and so often his frame of reference is the window picture frame, as with Flaubert who also used it with preference.

A la recherche du temps perdu reflects the transitional process from impressionist to phenomenological vision and from geometrical to lived perspective in the act of literary creation. Both Genette and Merleau-Ponty take Proust's writing as an example of the primordial expression which precedes logical formulation. Stating that language can never be a mere purveyor of received ideas, he describes Proust's expression of ideas as an integral part of vision. Genette shows that the farther we go into Proust's *A la recherche du temps perdu* the more daringly abrupt become the uses of ellipsis, as a counterpart to the fact that the scenes in between, though they cover shorter and shorter periods of story time, contain greater and greater detail. The whole effect is of an ever-growing discontinuity between discourse time and story time. The formal structure of Proust's work reflects only a choice of interpretation which is arbitrarily imposed upon the tissue of perception. The present engages in constant dialogue with the multiplicity of individual impressions which constitute the past. Proust's rendering of reality through art is achieved by portraying the prismatic refraction of impressions which takes place in the reflective consciousness, rather than by a simple reflection of the impression. The interconnecting patterns of perception create a constantly shifting prelogical perspective.

Each impression is located in a time/space continuum and is modulated by Marcel's individual point of view, the nuance of emotion renewing each memory and creating new associations. The book written by Marcel is that action of consciousness in which author and reader communicate not with each other, but with their own feeling of existence. It is a necessary correlative to self-observation in a phenomenological mode. The functions of his self seem to be taken up by a variety of interpersonal systems that operate through it. Thus the text, as the following passage illustrates, is an exploration of both writing and reading. It is about Marcel's becoming a writer, about his learning to see his world clearly and understand it, about his structuring his vision of his world in a way that will enable him to write the book we are reading. Time arises from Marcel's relation to things. It is a network of intentionalities that are a product of spatial positions. We may be warned by W. Iser: "the reader, in establishing these interrelations between past, present and future, actually causes the text to reveal its potential multiplicity of connections."[11] A reader approaching a Proustian sentence expects a coherent whole but actually sees many fragments which he must reconstitute into a coherent whole.

Nous ne pourrions pas raconter nos rapports avec un être que nous avons même peu connu, sans faire se succéder les sites les plus différents de notre vie. Ainsi chaque individu—et j'étais moi-même un de ces individus—mesurait pour moi la durée par la révolution qu'il avait accomplie non seulement autour de soi-même, mais autour des autres, et notamment par les positions qu'il avait occupées successivement par rapport à moi. Et sans doute tous ces plans différents suivant lesquels le Temps, depuis que je venais de le ressaisir dans cette fête, disposait ma vie, en me faisant songer que, dans un livre qui voudrait en raconter une, il faudrait user, par opposition à la psychologie plane dont on use d'ordinaire, d'une sorte de psychologie dans l'espace, ajoutaient une beauté nouvelle à ces résurrections que ma mémoire opérait tant que je songeais seul dans la bibliothèque, puisque la mémoire, en introduisant le passé dans le présent sans le modifier, tel qu'il était au moment où il était le présent, supprime précisément cette grande dimension du Temps suivant laquelle la vie se réalise.[12]

In this particular sentence, Proust secures, isolates, and immobilizes Time. He presents the past, the present, and time as an element of duration: "the past," "the present," "Time." He also gives examples of each: "while I was following my thoughts alone in the library," "in this last hour," and "all these different planes within which. . .I had recaptured it [Time]." He also includes the preterite, present, and continuous tenses of verbs (equivalent to past, present, duration) as well as the infinitive and conditional. Thus, he has managed to include in one sentence the three dimensions of lived time and lived space. At this point Marcel gives the linear life of the present the rich orchestration of the past, the full temporal and spatial consistency of a life lived in time. Time and space are inseparable coordinates of existence: spatial vision directs the reader to grasp the harmonious whole of the book. Space is the means whereby the positing of things becomes possible. Just as he is able to compress many angles of a person, seen almost as many different people, into one character, Proust is compressing, here, many sentences into one sentence. At the same time, he is compressing many times into one Time, a Time which is itself immobilized in the sentence. He can present various planes of time without distorting perception.

When Marcel attempts to seize the identity of others or of himself, they seem to dissolve simultaneously into a multiplicity and succession of selves in space and time. He contrasts *psychologie plane* (two-dimensional psychology) with *psychologie dans l'espace* (three-dimensional psychology), perhaps to be understood as the difference between flatness in pictures and that of three-dimensional volume in sculpture or architecture.

Finally, as Genette observes, Time is abolished: "le temps retrouvé, c'est le temps aboli."[13] The notion of *espace* (space) is introduced as a necessity: with the notions of space, time, individuality—all the conditions and limitations of ordinary life—suspended together; eternity and infinity become a physical experience in the privileged moment of heightened awareness. Writing stops Time (it gives a text a limitless duration of time) in order to allow not just a surface perception, but a unified vision, a vision which, by being written (captured or recaptured), can be perceived and comprehended by another, the reader.

Claude Simon introduces phenomenological elements into the act of writing, completing the break between primordial and secondary forms of expression. The comforting activity of reorganizing impressions upon which Marcel embarks in *Le Temps Retrouvé* is for the narrator of *Histoire* a discomfiting primordial expression of his own reflective consciousness. The vain attempt at architectural symmetry of composition yields before the insistent prelogical promptings of a mind preoccupied by a mythomanic paranoia of lived experience. In the novel of Claude Simon, a radical transformation of narrative perspective has occurred. The narrator is no longer free to divorce himself from his impressionist point of view, but must interpret it phenomenologically. His conception of reality becomes the expression of his *écriture* (as he observes the interior dimensions of his reflective consciousness. With *Histoire* the narrator's retreat into the interior space of the novel becomes more pronounced. Memory rather than sensory perception becomes the *intentionnalité opérante*. The exterior world is progressively reduced to a series of objective correlatives, the postcards serve as generators for the *écritures* as the narrator relives his past. As the eye of the narrator turns inwards, so he reveals the obsessive, mythomanic equality of his consciousness. The reduction of the exterior world to a photographic representation which is phenomenologically counterfeit is mirrored by the expression of the narrator's consciousness through language. The final words of the text bring the narrator to an awareness of his own psyche. The day has come to an end, the narrator has closed off perception of the exterior

world and has confined himself as the product of his *écriture*, he is the un-willing witness of his own transformation, a Kafkaesque metamorphosis.
Similar to the Hollandais who unsuccessfully attempts to include himself in a photograph which he is taking, the author's attempt at inward appraisal is defeated by the prismatic space of the *écriture*. The narrator can only perceive himself phenomenologically as an unrecognizable monstrosity un-predicated by rational analysis.

We may conclude with Genette: "Critique de langage, triomphe de l'écri-ture."[14] The intellectual organization of the work of art is subsequent and subordinate to the impression. It is a complement to the more immediate awareness of reality. The interest of the narrator in disengaging truths from experience leads him to accept both the phenomenological and epistemo-logical modes of expression in *l'écriture*. It seems to us that structuralism, a method based on linguistics, must take its place within phenomenology.

MICHIGAN STATE UNIVERSITY

Notes

[1]Gérard Genette, *Figures I* (Paris: Seuil, 1966); *Figures II* (Paris: Seuil, 1969); *Figures III* (Paris: Seuil, 1972); and *Mimologiques* (Paris: Seuil, 1976).

[2]Michel Butor, "Research on the Technique of the Novel," and "Balzac and Reality," *Inventory*, ed. Richard Howard (New York: Simon and Schuster, 1968), pp. 146-84.

[3]"L'Age des noms," *Mimologiques*, p. 315.

[4]Ibid., p. 328.

[5]Marcel Proust, "Du côté de chez Swann," *A la recherche du temps perdu*, I (Paris: Gallimard-Pleïade, 1954), pp. 387-88, quoted in *Mimologiques*, p 315.

[6]Maurice Merleau-Ponty, "The Problem of Speech," *Themes from the Lectures at the Collège de France 1952-1960*, translated by John O'Neill (Evanston: 1970), p. 25.

[7]Roland Barthes, "Proust et les noms," *Le degré zéro de l'écriture* (Paris: Seuil, 1953 et 1972), p. 113.

[8]Maurice Merleau-Ponty, *Phénoménologie de la perception* (Paris: Gallimard, 1945), pp. 213-14.

[9]Maria E. Kronegger, *James Joyce and Associated Image Makers* (New Haven: College and University Press, 1968), and *Impressionist Literature* (New Haven: College and University Press, 1973).

[10]Maurice Merleau-Ponty, *L'Oeil et l'Esprit* (Paris: Gallimard, 1964), p. 16; Käte Hamburger, "Die phänomenologische Struktur der Dichtung Rilkes," *Rilke in neuer Sicht* (Berlin, Köln, Mainz: Kohlhammer, 1971), pp. 83, 59; and E. F. N. Jephcott, *Proust and Rilke*, The Literature of Expanded Consciousness (London: Chatto and Windus, 1972), pp. 155-75.

[11]Wolfgang Iser, "The Reading Process: A Phenomenological Approach," *New Literary History* 3 (Winter 1972), p. 238.

[12]"Le temps retrouvé," *A la recherche du temps perdu*, III, p. 1031.

[13]*Figures II*, p. 47.

[14]*Mimologiques*, p. 328.

THE ENCOUNTER OF GENRES:
CYMBELINE'S STRUCTURE
OF JUXTAPOSITION

Joan C. Marx

Dr. Johnson dismissed *Cymbeline* as "unresisting imbecility," and only slightly politer versions of his opinion held sway until the 1930's when Shakespeare's last plays (*Pericles, Cymbeline, The Winter's Tale, The Tempest*) were first considered as a group and admired for their optimistic romantic vision, their reconciliations of kingdoms and families, of man and a beneficient Providence.[1] Yet *Cymbeline* is still regarded as the group's bewildering poor relation. E. M. W. Tillyard, one of the first supporters of the late plays, viewed *Cymbeline* as a mixture of disparate elements which blurred and ran together in a "welter of unreality," and after seeing a 1974 Royal Shakespeare production, Frank Kermode suggested that we no longer know what structure the first audience ever found in the play: "the loss of some code. . .[can] make something that was originally well formed look like an untidy mess."[2]

It is not my purpose to argue that a minor Shakespearean drama has the power and beauty of a major play, but rather, by employing the method of genre criticism, to suggest that *Cymbeline*'s structure is quite different from what it has been assumed and that a clearer perception of this structure will make the play livelier and more coherent than modern critiques and productions allow.

As a drama whose plot elements include the machinations of a wicked stepmother Queen, the lustful pursuits of a court fop, the Welsh mountain life of two kidnapped princes, Jupiter's descent from the sky, the hero's testing in an Italian jealousy plot like *Othello*'s, the princess' disguise as a pageboy, and the invasion of Britain by Imperial Rome, *Cymbeline* gives cause to those who find it a mixture of disparate elements. Yet I will argue that the play has seemed inchoate because its actual structure consists in juxtaposition, in unmediated and sharp contrast not only of characters but of scenes. These scenes are so distinct in nature and so discretely rendered that we are justified in calling them bits of different genres. It has been the attempt to blur these different genres—among them fairytale, satire, Italian intrigue, chronicle, and pastoral romance—into a uniform whole which has created the sensation of welter. For *Cymbeline*'s energy and coherence lie in the contrast of its different genre worlds.

As a technique, juxtaposition is common to all Shakespeare's plays: the Porter's sleepy muttering of Hell after Duncan's murder, Antony's majestic declaration, "Kingdoms are clay," just after Philo scoffs at him as a strumpet's fool." These are only two among countless instances in the plays when a new action or view supplies a fresh and striking context to the scene before. But to find juxtaposition serving as a play's major structural device, as it does in *Cymbeline*, is rarer; we see it in *Love's Labour's Lost* and *As You Like It*, two plays where there is almost no plot action and the energy and sense of movement are largely created by thrusting together contrasting characters and scenes.[3] What makes *Cymbeline* remarkable is that, unlike the other two plays which use juxtaposition as their structure, it also has plot events to move its characters from one action and place to another, from Wales to Italy.

Let me describe *Cymbeline*'s structure more precisely by comparing two moments in *Cymbeline* and *As You Like It*, a comparison which will help to make clear *Cymbeline's* contrasts of genres and the abruptness of those contrasts. In both plays, characters with different, discrete styles are allowed to interact, Touchstone with Corin in Arden and Cloten with Guiderius in Wales, and our pleasure lies in hearing the encounter of their styles.[4] In *As You Like It*, Corin asks, "And how like you this shepherd's life, Master Touchstone?" and Touchstone replies:

> In respect that it is solitary, I like it very well; but in respect that it is private, it is a very vile life. Now in respect that it is in the fields, it pleaseth me well; but in respect it is not in the court, it is tedious (III.ii.15-18).[5]

Then Touchstone asks in turn for the shepherd's "philosophy," and, hearing that he has never been to court, pronounces him "damn'd." So in *Cymbeline* when the courtly Cloten and the pastoral Guiderius meet in the Welsh mountains, they too question each other, though this time it is the pastoral figure who has the best of it. Cloten demands, "What slave art thou?"; Guiderius returns, "What art thou?" Cloten responds with a puff of his garments, "Know'st me not by my clothes?" But Guiderius only laughs at "the tailor. . .thy grandfather."

However, the encounters of *As You Like It*, its contrasts of characters, take place within a unified whole; the play establishes the likeness of its two worlds, court and forest, and it rings with a single tone. *Cymbeline* uses none of the same techniques to establish one mellow world; instead, its juxtaposition is like a force of gravity, pulling together objects of unlike mass as the play speeds towards its end.

In *As You Like It*, the forest's special tone of leisure and civility silvers the air. Touchstone and Corin stroll together,/stroking out their differences without a spark of acrimony, rather with a pleasure in the parley. Touchstone pricks at Corin's descriptions of country manners with "Instance, briefly; come, instance," and when Touchstone pronounces, "You are damn'd," the shepherd counters, "For not being at court: Your reason." They are gracefully fencing in the manner of Lyly's characters, who rejoice in their debates, even though, unlike Lyly's characters, they have wide differences in viewpoint.

Moreover, though the court's ingratitude separates it from the forest, Arden shares its civility of style and manner with the court, as Orlando's exaggerated fears of the alien "desert" help to make clear. After charging the Duke's feast with drawn sword, he appeals to the desert inhabitants by whatever touch of civilization they may have known, if they have been "where bells have knoll'd to church," and his appeal calls forth the ceremonious echoes of the Duke, his reply that he has "with holy bell been knoll'd to church." Their shared language, these echoes in themselves, are the sign of their shared manners.[6]

Cymbeline, on the other hand, is not blended into such a whole. When Cloten and Guiderius encounter each other, they clash together as two very different qualities; their encounter lacks the light tone, the civil play, that mediates between Touchstone and Corin. Since Cloten and Guiderius see each other, challenge, and then duel, they are bound to give the effect of division, but their language further reveals their isolation.

Gui.   Say what thou art:
    Why I should yield to thee.
Clo.   Thou villain base,
    Know'st me not by my clothes?
Gui.   No, nor thy tailor, rascal,
    Who is thy grandfather; he made those clothes,
    Which, as it seems, make thee.
    . . . .
Clo.   To thy further fear.
    Nay, to thy mere confusion, thou shalt know
    I am son to th' Queen.
Gui.   I am sorry for't; not seeming
    So worthy as thy birth.
Clo.   Art not afeard?
Gui.   Those that I reverence, those I fear—the wise:
    At fools I laugh, not fear them   (IV.ii.80-97).

Unlike Orlando, Cloten keeps expecting that the pastoral world will be like the court. But whereas Orlando's tentative claims were reassuringly echoed, knolling bell to knolling bell, Cloten's terms are neatly opposed. His clothes mean nothing to Guiderius and to his "I am the son to th' Queen," comes "I am sorry for't; not seeming / So worthy as thy birth."

The two characters step forward from quite different worlds, which they seem to pull behind them. We recognize these two worlds, for each has earlier occupied whole scenes: there have been short scenes of Cloten, the court dandy and fool, bowling and swearing (I.iii, II.i, II.iii), other scenes of Guiderius and his fellows in Wales, bowing to the sun and returning from the hunt (III.iii, III.vii). And in these scenes Cloten and Guiderius have set and controlled the tone of the scenes in a way that single characters in *As You Like It*, Touchstone and Corin, for example, never have.

Indeed in *Cymbeline* we are watching the extraordinary confrontation of two genres, the comic butt of satire, Cloten, and the hero of pastoral, Guiderius, meeting at swordpoint, each gesturing in the most conventional terms of his genre and finding his mirror image responding. The foolish satire butt is flaunting his elegant clothes, the sign of rank, a moment made for a satiric commentator who could flay the world that allows such a discrepancy between worth and birth. Guiderius, solidly noble in the simplest of clothes, completely ignores the flap of Cloten's clothing and as simply as he is dressed, declares his allegiance to moral categories that discard social rank: "Those that I reverence, those I fear—the wise." As the hero of the pastoral romance, his worth is completely consistent with his birth, but he has been temporarily divested of social recognition.

In fact, the question with which Guiderius judges Cloten, "Art thou 'so worthy as thy birth'?"—a demand that moral worth equal social rank—is fundamental to both pastoral and satire. The two genres are mirror images of each other,[7] each asking the same question but from polar perspectives. Thus the encounter makes us perceive the difference and likeness between two genre worlds, their fundamental values and the relationship of those values.

Since Cloten and Guiderius step forward from distinctly different, neatly opposed worlds, and there is no mediation between them, they seem, as we have said, to pull those worlds behind them; it is as if their two genres have clashed. This effect of the abrupt juxtaposition of qualitatively different worlds is typical and essential in *Cymbeline*. Cloten and Guiderius' particular encounter is uncommon only in that this effect arises from the meeting of two characters. For, although there are other such meetings, such as that of Roman Lucius and pastoral Fidele, the Italians and the British knight, the play is constructed so that unmediated juxtapositions are usually felt between two scenes rather than two characters.

Typical of *Cymbeline* is the opening of the play with the First Gentleman's lament of Posthumus' banishment, a sorrow stirred by the absolute value of Posthumus' person and character: "I do not think/So fair an outward and such stuff within/Endows a man but he." All the court is of his mind, he says, although the King and Queen mistakenly preferred Cloten, "a thing/Too bad for bad report" as the bridegroom. When the scene shifts to Rome, again it opens with a discussion of Posthumus, his marriage, his banishment: "We had very many there [in France] could behold the sun with as firm eyes as he." Surely, Iachimo suggests, his banishment has been a sentimental temptation to excuse his ordinary character and the princess' mistake. Rome sounds quite different, cynical, shaded, doubting. Philario's protest only underlines the way in which the opinion of the First Gentleman and all the British court is being reshaped: "You speak of him when he was less furnished than now he is with that which makes him both without and within." In effect Philario has already accepted a modified judgment of the young Posthumus. We seem to have shifted worlds—the same man, the same issues, but quite differently received.

Or the worldly travelers of the Italian novella, visiting Philario with their talk of thieves, accomplished courtiers, reputation, and the sale of "ladies' flesh," withdraw from the stage, and we hear, "While yet the dew's on ground, gather these flowers." It is the stepmother Queen in her garden, preparing to make her fairytale poisons. Or Cloten chatters crudely of "fingering" and "penetration" in a morning of court satire which follows Iachimo's midnight, hushed veneration of "Cytherea." The pastoral hunters withdraw and the Roman senators appear. Posthumus rages offstage at the climax of the Italian plot swearing his revenge on Imogen, and the state council of a chronicle scene begins. Or there will be two scenes not immediately juxtaposed but borne together by their similarity: Iachimo adores Imogen at midnight in the sensuous Ovidian mode; her body creates the aura of a "chapel" around her in which he worships the rubies of her lips, the eyelids "azure lac'd." Then Belarius, in daylight, moves toward the cave and finds Imogen, and he too marvels; he sees "an angel," an "earthly paragon."

Thus Cymbeline's justaposition causes different worlds, fairytale Britain and Italianate Rome, pastoral Wales and the Roman Empire, to meet up without attempting to mitigate, indeed exploiting, their differences. Each supplants the other in the play's progress, and since these shifts are not ruled by one tone or set of attitudes, as were the juxtapositions in As You Like It, each new scene demands that the audience choose its viewpoint, or at least recognize its tone and attitude, as a new alternative.

For as the play thrusts these different genres together, we are made to recognize the differences in their perspectives. Both the Queen and Iachimo love secrecy, poison, intrigue, but the power of the Italian indirection is much greater than the lucid fairytale evil. The Queen fools only her husband; Imogen and the entire court perceive her "dissembling courtesy" immediately. Therefore, when the Italian courtiers leave the stage and the Queen appears with her poison in the garden, we are right to feel that this is a "morning" evil, much easier to take and less threatening than a shrug which assumes women unfaithful and their infidelity indiscernable, than the bitter distillation of gossip and resentment in Rome.[8] Or we see that the moral pillars, the clear, absolute judgments of a thing too good, a thing too bad, of the fairytale opening are simply not part of the structure of the Italian novella world. There is no idealizing in that cynical world—with one exception. Shakespeare endows Iachimo with the Ovidian tongue to intensify our vision of the Italian marvelling before the body, the one unguarded adoration allowed in the Italian novella genre. Belarius is struck by the same beautiful body, but his pastoral romance admiration is for the spirit he sees. In his genre, the body declares the spirit.[9] Posthumus' angry refusal to continue to "pay tribute" to Imogen and his fervid wish that men no longer be dependent on women are part of his proud insistence on independence; after sorrowing at his fierce, mistaken anguish on Iachimo's return, we cannot help but question the national independence proclaimed by the Queen in the council scene which follows.[10] Yet in the chronicle genre complete independence is a possibility for nations as it can never be for the lovers of a novela.

If the play is produced with each scene played distinctly, each genre given its due, we will be able to mark *Cymbeline*'s structural continuities and the play of values against one another: the repetition of the first scene, the versions of idealizing, the visions of indirect evil. The Queen and her doctor can both be played as fairytale figures; there is no need to make this stepmother "sultry" or to muffle the perfect click with which Cornelius, the good servant, supplies missing, needed information to the finale.[11] But on the other hand, their clear absolutes of good and evil belong to their particular genre: there is also no need to blur other genres in the play to accord with theirs, to suppress Iachimo's wonder at Imogen's beauty, for example, as the 1974 Royal Shakespeare did, or to choreograph the chronicle battle, or to cut out Cloten's small-minded, static scenes of court satire.[12] Granville-Barker's notion of "artlessness" which "displays art," perceptive and important as it is, has proved a particular critical temptation to stir all the genres of the play together.[13] The recent Royal Shakespeare production, for instance, concentrated on the play as a self-conscious "fictional construct"[14] and, to dramatize this focus, used Cornelius as a presenter figure throughout it to smooth out all disjunctures and difficulties. According to Frank Kermode, Cornelius would continually call to the audience "by means of interpolated speeches, winks, shrugs, and leers," to make them recognize that "the whole thing is actually meant to be naive or absurd."[15] The result—the play appeared "an untidy mess."

Cymbeline is a play which consists of our looking out from one genre to another and our learning to recognize their different visions, to feel the air of their different worlds. It is a minor Shakespearean play because each of the genres remains simple, its plot and characters stereotyped, but acted as it is written, the play offers bare, exciting glimpses of genres' essential and differing values, and these views juxtaposed form a clear and lively whole.

DENISON UNIVERSITY

Notes

[1]Samuel Johnson, "*Cymbeline*," *Samuel Johnson: Notes to Shakespeare*, ed. Arthur Sherbo, 3:2 (Los Angeles: Univ. of California, 1958).

[2]E. M. W. Tillyard, *Shakespeare's Last Plays* (London: Chatto and Windus, 1938), p. 76; Frank Kermode, "*Cymbeline* at Stratford," *TLS* (5 July 1974), p. 710. For other examples, see Arthur Kirsch on the play's lack of "coherency," in "*Cymbeline*" and Coterie Dramaturgy," *ELH* 34 (1967), pp. 285-306; Emrys Jones on its "central fumbling"; Murray Schwartz's judgment that it is "unsatisfying drama," in "Between Fantasy and Imagination: A Psychological Exploration of *Cymbeline*,"

Psychoanalysis and Literary Process, ed. Frederick Crews (Cambridge, Mass.: Winthrop Pub., 1970), p. 283.

³Harold Jenkins, "*As You Like It*," *Shakespeare Survey* 8 (1955), rpt. in *Shakespeare: Modern Essays in Criticism*, ed. Leonard F. Dean (New York: Oxford Univ. Press, 1957), pp. 108-27.

⁴*Ibid.*, pp. 125, 121. "Encounter" is Jenkins' term.

⁵All Cymbeline quotations are from the Arden edition, ed. J. M. Nosworthy (Cambridge, Mass.: Harvard Univ. Press, 1955). All other references to Shakespeare's plays will be to the edition of Peter Alexander: *William Shakespeare: The Complete Works* (London: Collins, 1951).

⁶From a lecture by Donald Friedman, Univ of California, Berkeley, 1964.

⁷Northrop Frye similarly remarks on a mirroring of irony and romance in *Anatomy of Criticism* (New York: Atheneum, 1957), pp. 162 ff.; satire and pastoral are their respective sub-genres.

⁸*Shakespeare and the Comedy of Forgiveness* (New York, Columbia Univ. Press, 1965), p. 151.

⁹See Edmund Spenser's *The Faerie Queene*, III, v, p. 35 and VI, ix, pp. 11 ff. for other examples of this convention.

¹⁰D. R. C. Marsh discusses this relationship of isolation between the two scenes in *The Recurring Miracle* (Pietermaritzburg: Univ. of Natal Press, 1962), pp. 50 ff.

¹¹Joan Miller played a "sultry" Queen in the Straford 1957 production, according to J. C. Trewin, *Shakespeare on the English Stage 1900-64* (London: Barrie and Rockliff, 1964), p. 238. J. R. Brown discusses the laughter Cornelius' pat timing can cause in *Shakespeare's Plays in Performance* (London: Edward Arnold Ltd., 1966), p. 108.

¹²Frank Kermode reported Iachimo's exchange of "turbulence" for "banter" in the bedroom scene, in "*Cymbeline* at Stratford," *TLS* (5 July 1974), p. 710. The Old Vic staged a battle with "eurhythmic movement" in 1932, according to J. C. Trewin, *Shakespeare on the English Stage 1900-1964*, p. 140, and Derek Traversi wishes there were fewer Cloten scenes in *Shakespeare: The Last Phase*, p. 58. In contrast, James Edward Siemon suggests the need for all the court satire scenes by pointing out neat parallels between Cloten's actions and Posthumus', in "Noble Virtue in *Cymbeline*," *Shakespeare Survey* 29 (1976), pp. 55-61.

¹³"*Cymbeline*," *Prefaces to Shakespeare*, II, p. 94.

¹⁴From the program note.

¹⁵"*Cymbeline* at Stratford," p. 710.

VI. Linguistics

LANGUAGE AS PROTAGONIST IN SARDUY'S *DE DONDE SON LOS CANTANTES:* A LINGUISTIC APPROACH TO NARRATIVE STRUCTURE

Sharon Ghertman

In his discussion with Rodríguez Monegal,[1] Severo Sarduy comments that language is the intermediary between the author and reality in his second novel, *De donde son los cantantes.* Sarduy, however, understands language as a binary opposition when he notes, "Sería más bien en la oposición binaria compacto/difuso utilizada por Jakobson, donde veríamos el paragrama de lectura más adecuado."[2] It is my contention that Sarduy uses this theory of language as a structure of continuum versus discontinuum, of expansion and contraction, as a narrative device through the transformation of oppositional syntactic relationship into characters, nominalized as the protagonists Auxilio and Socorro.

This synonymic relation Auxilio-Socorro is a starting point for the novel in "Curriculum cubense," its introduction. Auxilio represents the contextual, continuous function of language, which in terms of the narrative means that she attracts other people into her sphere, acquires a paradigmatic arrangement, and allows for expansion. Socorro then moves in the opposite direction, toward a structural zero, to be filled in the final chapter, "La entrada del Cristo en la Habana." She represents the contrastual, discontinuous function of language, as she stops the action, changes its course, or diverts it into another area. Sarduy, aware of this process, defines text as: "Texto que se repite, que se cita sin límites, que se plagia a sí mismo; tapiz que se desteje para hilar otros signos."[3] In the transformations throughout the novel, Auxilio and Socorro at times appear on the same syntactic level, at times on opposing syntactic levels, relating to each other as paradigm and syntagma, or vertical diachrony and horizontal synchrony.[4] In "Curriculum cubense," both the convergent and divergent relationships are operative. The subtitle in itself comprises a binary opposition essential to language structure: *curriculum* the noun indicates a continuum or series, while *cubense* the adjective delimits and controls its extension. This pattern is a base from which more complex relations derive, a process called "la lectura radial del texto,"[5] commencing with the title *De donde son los cantantes.* *Donde* stands for a displaced antecedent; it is a kind of void,[6] to be replaced with the titular structure composed of a place name and a referent to person: "Junto al río de Cenizas de Rosa," *Cenizas de Rosa* being a substitute for the illusive *Flor de Loto*, the Shanghai Opera singer "La Dolores Rondón," marked by the absence of place, a means of contracting the pattern. The last chapter restores the original arrangement, "La entrada de Cristo en la Habana." Thus the title of the novel becomes a syntactic chain setting forth a dominant organizational pattern for the remaining titles, each realization leading toward new sets of internal relationships. Let us now examine the syntactic patterns in "Curriculum cubense" and view the ways in which they influence the narrative direction of the text.

I distinguish two opposing levels of discourse. The first is the contextual system of continuation, realized as a nominal series plus a displaced antecedent or pronoun in association with *ser* or with its omission as an ellipsis. The second level is the contrastual system of discontinuation, realized as a series of negations, imperative verbs, exclamations, and insults, providing an internal means of textual closure.[7] Changes in the pattern and shifting from one level to another are frequent occurrences, furnishing a dynamic for the text as well as a model for deciphering it.

The first paragraph of the novel is a highly contextual system, a description of Auxilio and the writing process itself, replete with impersonal objects and chance associations. All signs of continuum are present, including an affirmation *sí*: "Plumas, sí, deliciosas plumas de azufre, río de plumas arrastrando cabezas de mármol, plumas en la cabeza, sombrero de plumas, colibríes y frambuesas." Omission of the verb is characteristic of this level of syntactic arrangement in which Sarduy reverses any preconceived notion about nominal forms being discontinuous and static.[8] This nominal system points to analogies between dissimilar objects by forcing them into similar syntactic forms. The first expansion of *plumas, deliciosas* plus a noun modifier *de azufre*, unites the animal with the mineral. In the next set of nouns, *plumas* modifies *río* in connection with a present participle, *arrastrando*, and its object *cabezas de mármol*. However, *plumas en la cabeza* marks a return to the first combination only to produce *sombrero de plumas*. The remaining noun couple, *colibríes y frambuesas*, concludes the segment as equivalents to *plumas*, for *frambuesas* and *azufre* are used for their ability to perform an imagistic, adjectival function rather than a logical one. The text does not proceed in a linear fashion but in a radial one, emanating from *plumas* as a base. The noun used as adjective becomes a recognizable underpinning for this lectura radial, as the nominal group moves the text foward by relating *plumas* to different semantic components while preserving the same syntax.

The formula *río de* plus noun has other reverberations in the novel as a sign of continuum. The title of Chapter 1, "Junto al río de Cenizas de Rosa," is one example. Also, Socorro's first appearance without Auxilio is marked by this equivalence and the omission of the verb *ser*:

> ¿Pero cómo no equivocarse? Eran miles. Miles de piececillos. Manitas carcomidas. Aquel chirrido. Platos de lata y cucharas. Salían verdosillos y arremetían contra las ollas. Sirena y aparecían. Chirrido, y desaparecían. Al mismo tiempo. Salía una mujer a cada uno de los vidrios. Y en cada uno sacudía un mantel negro. La fachada desaparecía detrás de una cortina de migas de pan. Río de plumas (p. 13).[9]

The *migas de pan* become a *río de plumas*, an aquatic metaphor of continuum that is transformed once more into hyperbole with: "Las migas de pan han blanqueado la copa de los árboles, el césped negro. ¡Es como nieve!" (p. 14). Further, in the last chapter, the snow scene is composed in a similar nominal sequence, with the dialogue of Auxilio and Socorro reminding the reader of the repetitive system of continuation: "Cortinas de migas de pan— Auxilio —¿Quién en lo alto sacude sus manteles?— Socorro" (p. 146). The aquatic image, however, finds its final expression in a destructive context as it shifts the noun *nieve* to a verb phrase counterpart, *llovió*: "Ya iban alcanzando los portales cuando desde los helicópteros, llovió la balacera" (p 149). Thus we have an interrelating system of nominal forms that explain or contradict one another, and in this manner provide a recognizable pattern for the text.

Textual re-elaboration emerges in the first paragraph of the novel, as the second part, beginning with *desde él*, explains the first part, *Plumas sí:*

> desde él caen hasta el suelo los cabellos anaranjados de Auxilio, lisos, de nylon enlazados con cintas rosadas y campanitas, desde él a los lados de la cara, de las caderas, de las botas de piel de cebra, hasta el asfalto la cascada albina. Y Auxilio rayada, pájaro indio detrás de la lluvia.

The vehicle of connections is created by the series of prepositional phrases from *caen hasta el suelo* to *hasta el asfalto la cascada*. Yet the sequence begins with the pronoun *él* referring to *sombrero*. Nominal analogues appear in rapid succession: *cabellos anaranjados* reworks *plumas de azufre*; *enlazados con cintas rosadas y campanitas* refers to *arrastrando cabezas de mármol*, with the equivalence *cabezas—campanitas*. The paragraph closes with an ellipsis, comparable to *colibríes y frambuesas*: "Y Auxilio rayada; pájaro indio detrás de la lluvia." This final equation, *Auxilio* and *pájaro*, completes and interprets the relationships between parts one and two of this segment. The noun *plumas*, a synecdoche for *pájaro, colibríes*, and Auxilio herself, begins the radial sequence, expanding with noun modification and then contracting with the ellipsis. The combination *pájaro indio detrás de la lluvia* is a re-elaboration of *río de plumas*, a controlling contextual image of the entire work, becoming the "imagen deshilachada y móvil" of Chapter 1 (p. 27). Thus the transformational possibilities of language, through the integration of dissimilar semantic components into similar syntactic structures, becomes a formal basis for the peregrinations of Auxilio and Socorro in their various nominal equivalents.

Now let us examine the second structural pattern in Sarduy's use of language. According to the structural theory of binary oppositions, the system of continuum must be accompanied by a system of discontinuum. If we read Sarduy metalingually, a term used by Jakobson for signs pointing to the internal structure of language,[10] we find: "Bueno querido, no todo puede ser coherente en la vida. Un poco de desorden en el orden, ¿no?" (p. 28). It is Auxilio, however, who introduces the system of discontinuum or contrast after the first paragraph of "Curriculum cubense" with a negative verb that effectively causes a break in the pattern at a point at which one would expect a continuation of it: "¡No puedo más! —chilla y abre un hueco en las migas de pan." Even the gestural symbol of breaking bread indicates discontinuity of the nominal descriptive system. It is Socorro's function to negate what has gone on before with the following verbal series:

> —¡Revienta! —es Socorro la que habla— Sí, revienta, aguanta, muérete, quéjate al estado, quéjate a los dioses, *drop dead*, cáete abierta en dos como una naranja, ahógate en cerveza, en frankfurter chucrute, jódete. Conviértete en polvo, en ceniza. Eso querías (p. 11).

It is not the pattern of seriation that explains this conflicting relationship between Socorro and Auxilio but the polarity between nominal description and verbal dynamics. In response to this verbal attack, Auxilio retorts with the formulaic equation of the continuous system: "—Seré ceniza, mas tendré sentido. Polvo seré, mas polvo enamorado." As a contrastual device, Sarduy integrates non-hispanic terms like, *drop dead*, or Socorro's response to Auxilio's Quevedian equation: "—Tu me casses les cothurnes! (en français dans le texte)," again a verbal negation.[11] This entire first segment of the novel is composed by alternating the two syntactic levels with Auxilio and Socorro on opposing levels. Yet when Auxilio begins her harangue on Socorro, the nominal series of apostrophic insults, "—Crápula. Granuja. Rana," progressively builds up to the series of verb clauses, integrating Socorro's system into her own: "Que te trague el Ser. Que te aspire. Que se te rompa el aire acondicionado. Que a tu alrededor se abra un hueco" (p. 12). After this convergence of the two systems, the narrative takes a new turn, leading to the separation of Auxilio and Socorro.

The next sequential arrangement I will examine appears in "Self-Service." Auxilio and Socorro appear on the same organizational level, joined in a convergence with a series of nominal substitutional names that unite the pair: *Deidades amarillas, pájaros flavios, Gamos, Las Floridas, Las Siempre-presentes.* "Self-Service" fluctuates between two oppositional levels, as Auxilio retains her function as a structure of continuum, characterized by the overturned plate of potatoes: "Papa por papa, papa por papa las recoge" (p. 15). Auxilio, however, reintroduces the contrastual system, emphasizing contraction and change, closing the text in upon itself: "—¡Quiero desaparecer!— Ya no es ardilla sino topo: se hace una esfera, esconde la cabeza" (p. 16). It is with the *tableau vivant* that the structural convergence point becomes operative in the text. Socorro and Auxilio re-unite in a nominal chain in a triangular arrangement with the outside world.

The convergence point is a kind of structural knot or stopping place:

> Ya están las dos sentadas, compuestas, ante una ventana de celuloide. Ni una mancha, ni un solo cabello desplazado, ni una gota de salsa de tomate en las mejillas. Fijas: las cabezas, separadas por unos centímetros, coinciden con el cruce de las diagonales del paisaje—domos azules perforados de ventanas, un campo de aviación de donde se levantan mosquitos y bimotores—, las manos pálidas sobre el pecho. Ni siquiera se mueven, pero es inútil, todo el mundo las mira. Se saben acusadas (p. 16).

Here we have an example of what Sarduy calls "la geometrización del espacio"[12] with the synonymic pair integrated into a geometric environment, as indicated by the verb *coinciden* and the noun phrase *con el cruce de las diagonales del paisaje*. Sarduy juxtaposes a metaphoric equivalent for the pair as a means of re-elaborating this relationship. The visual effect of the two heads coincides with a diagonal crossing in the landscape seen through a window. Thus we have *cabezas* as equal to *domos azules perforados de ventanas*, whereas *un cruce de las diagonales* equates to *un campo de aviación*. As this diagonal crossing is seen through a window, two levels emerge: *bimotores* lift off the diagonal air strip outside, while *mosquitos* remain inside. The convergence point illustrates the way in which similar linguistic relationships, here the contextual system of nominal equivalents, change function to produce stasis in the text. The solution to this absence of movement is once again seriation, as Auxilio presents the fifty photographs of her in varying poses. Her statement "Tengo una idea" (p. 16) serves as a pronominal form, replacing *idea* with a multiple sequence of photos. Finally, the segment closes with a dialogue composed on the contrastual, negative level of Socorro: "Espera. Olvidaba la hoz" (p. 18). The nominal image *la hoz* becomes integrated into the horizontal function of contrastual finality, as Socorro reiterates this syntactic pattern of negativity through imperative verbs.

The third realization of the oppositional pattern, Auxilio versus Socorro, appears in the last segment of "Curriculum cubense." Nominal seriation expands into a more complex set of relations: the subordinate clause plus a pronoun. In "Una nueva versión de los hechos: parca y general," Auxilio attracts the General into her sphere.

> Que ella lo enredó con sus guedejas de champán, que él la pinchó con el broche abierto de una de sus medallas, que la confitura de cereza cayó sobre el kaki carmelita del uniforme, que él la cortó con un galón, que se enredaron ambos, que se callaron por cortesía, que se insultaron, que los espárragos a la crema quedaron entre las condecoraciones, que el pírrico invocó a la patrona de los artilleros, la invencible Changó, que ella respondió apelando a la reina del río y del cielo, su antídoto y detente: no se sabe ya nada. (p. 19).

This passage, composed of ten clauses plus a contrastual negation, *no se sabe ya nada*, re-elaborates the section on the self-service. Even the title, "Una nueva versión de los hechos," indicates its re-elaborative function. Subordinate clauses introduced by *que* constitute a system of substitutions of the pronoun by a noun. The first pronoun *ella* is replaces by *confitura de cereza* in the third clause and *espárragos* in the eighth, both referents to the spilt food in the self-service. *Ella* recurs in the tenth clause, closing the sequence of continuum through a circular arrangement. *El* appears in the second and fourth clauses, replaced once with *el pírrico* (clause 9). In the fifth, sixth, and seventh clauses a convergence appears, marked by reflexive pronouns. This fusion is reinforced by the nominal series:

Allí están los dos —serpientes emplumadas— *cheek to cheek*, pegados uno a otro, pegadas a las bandejas. Hermanos siameses forcejeando. Murciélago de la Bacardí, mancha de tinta, animal doble, ostra abierta, cuerpo con su reflejo; eso son Auxilio y el General (p. 19).

This third realization of patterned syntax in Sarduy serves the function of integrating new material into the text. The structure of continuum characteristically transforms and expands using the same basic syntactic arrangement, while introducing a new character, the General, into the framework of the narrative. At this point, however, Socorro demonstrates her role as a discontinuous component in her metalingual comment: "Yo lo que quiero es que acaben de sacar a Auxilio de este enredo." The authorial first person remarks, on the contextual level: "Hija mía, ¿No ves que si el general se quita sus quincallas sería como el pájaro pinto de Lacan?" Yet if Auxilio escapes the continuous *enredo*, the novel will end. Socorro objects to the affirmation, "Ya volverá a su casa, modosa, presumida, casta" (p. 20), with a criticism of structures of continuum: "Oigan esto. Tres adjetivos de un golpe. En mi tiempo no era así. A dónde va la joven literatura. . . ." The text provides its own dynamic structures, while, as Sarduy states, "es tapiz que se desteje para hilar otros signos."[13] These contrastual structures called "characters" in the narrative are aspects of the same linguistic phenomenon: "Cuatro seres distintos y que son uno solo." Language itself is the model for the narrative organization of *De donde son los cantantes* because of its capacity to transform and expand and yet remain a unified whole.

In conclusion, the present essay is an attempt to view the synonymity of Socorro and Auxilio as an ordering device in the text. The syntactic arrangements for these characters give a formal basis for what Sarduy calls *la lectura radial*. I have examined those syntactic systems in "Curriculum cubense" that are responsible for textual cohesion, recurring at crucial points in the narrative development. The work establishes its own internal ground rules but then changes the function of the pattern from continuous to discontinuous. The search for this underlying model in linguistic patterning is both the technique and the objective of the author in his quest for *cubanidad*.

The search for identity is in itself an underlying theme in *De donde son los cantantes*; even the title reflects a preoccupation with origins. Yet perhaps what is significant for the discipline of literary criticism is that Sarduy uses linguistic theory, the binary structures of opposition, as a creative mechanism for the narrative. In "Curriculum cubense" he lays the groundwork for the syntactic relationships that contract and expand in the novel to shape its course and direction. His innovative use of Auxilio and Socorro is the *Siempre-presentes* in the entire work. Auxilio is first a contextual system of continuum, while Socorro is her counterpart as a contrastual system of discontinuum. Thus the hypothesis that the text is a network of interconnections, demanding a "radial reading" rather than a linear one, becomes poetic practice, poetic in the Greek sense here, with the dual protagonists Auxilio and Socorro:

> Las dos mujeres ilustrarían aquí dos vertientes de la hispanidad —en el tapiz, la Fe y la Práctica—, opuestos que imantan los continuos virajes del texto: si el comienzo evoca cierta fastuosidad, Zurbarán, pronto aparecen las *vanidades*, Valdés Leal; si Socorro quijotiza, Auxilio es un refranero sanchesco (p. 152).

Further, this relation between Auxilio and Socorro is not only thematic but syntactic, as the nominal system introduced by Auxilio is contrasted and severed by the verbal system of Socorro. These opposing functions, however, are not fixed values in the text but are subject to change, providing a dynamic for the work. When Socorro enters the *Domus dei*, "la casa de Dios" in "Curriculum cubense," her first separation from Auxilio is characterized by her integration into the contextual system of nominal expansion. Thus the process by which linguistic signs, here syntactic relationships, change their function becomes a narrative device that influences the development of literary structure. In the last chapter, Auxilio assumes a horizontal, discontinual function, analogous to her search for the material object, the potatoes in the "Self-Service," while Socorro in representing faith moves vertically in a continuous function, reversing her role in "Curriculum cubense." Sarduy is indeed aware of the ever-changing linguistic sign, "Cada frase tuya, que parecía banal y gratuita, cobra un gran sentido, se integra a una maquinaria precisa" (p. 78). Each new contextual combination then changes the interpretation of the statement and refers to the underlying binary model of language, integrating the surface complexity of the text with narrative devices. Thus it is not enough to document isolated linguistic forms in a text in order to determine their literary function, for it is essential to understand not only what the signs are but what they become.

UNIVERSITY OF SOUTHERN CALIFORNIA

Notes

[1]Severo Sarduy, "Las estructuras de la narración," *Mundo Nuevo*, 2 (agosto 1966), p. 17: "El arte me sirvió de intermediario con la realidad, como en la segunda novela, el lenguaje ha sido el intermediario."

[2]Severo Sarduy, *Escrito sobre un cuerpo* (Buenos Aires: Editorial Sudamericana, 1969), p. 49.

[3]*Ibid.*, p. 66.

152   A LINGUISTIC APPROACH TO NARRATIVE STRUCTURE

⁴Sarduy, p. 83: "Auxilio (agitando sus cabellos anaranjados, de llamas, aspas incandescentes, vinílicas) —Querida, he descubierto que Lezama es uno de los más grandes escritores.— Socorro (pálida, cejijunta, de mármol) —¿De La Habana? — Auxilio (toda diacrónica ella) —¡No hija, de la HISTORIA!" Here we have another use of linguistic terms as metaphor.

⁵Phillipe Sollers, "La boca obra," in *Severo Sarduy* (Madrid: Editorial Fundamentos, 1976), p. 116.

⁶Roberto Gonzáles Echevarría, "Memorias de apariencias y ensayo sobre *Cobra*," in *Severo Sarduy*, ibid., p. 72.

⁷Cervantes understood this combination of negation and nominal series; *Don Quijote de la Mancha*, ed. Martín de Riquer (Barcelona: Editorial Juventud, 1968), p. 227: "Y fue esta negación añadir llama a llama y deseo a deseo." For the term closure, see Barbara Herrnstein Smith, *Poetic Closure: A Study of How Poems End* (Chicago: University of Chicago Press, 1970).

⁸Rulon Wells, "Nominal and Verbal Style," in *Style in Language*, ed. T. Sebeok (Cambridge, Mass.: M. I. T. Press, 1968), p. 217: "Nouns are static, less vivid than verbs."

⁹The number in parenthesis refers to the page of Sarduy's *De donde son los cantantes* (México: Joaquín Mortiz, 1970). All quotations are from this edition.

¹⁰Roman Jakobson, "Linguistics and Poetics," in *Style in Language, op. cit.*, p. 356: "A distinction has been made in modern logic between two levels of language, 'object language' speaking of objects and 'metalanguage' speaking of language."

¹¹Ferdinand de Saussure, *Cours de linguistique générale* (Paris: Payot, 1969), p. 168: "La langue est pour ainsi dire une algèbre qui n'aurait que des termes complexes. Parmi les oppositions qu'elle comprend, il y en a qui sont plus significatives que d'autres; mais unité et fait de grammaire ne sont que des noms différents pour désigner des aspects divers d'un même fait général: le jue des oppositions linguistiques." Also Severo Sarduy, *Escrito sobre un cuerpo, op cit.*, p. 52: ". . .el lenguaje aparecerá como el espacio de la *acción de cifrar*, como una superficie de transformaciones ilimitadas. El travestismo, las metamorphosis continuas de personajes, la referencia a otras culturas, la mezcla de idiomas, la división del libro en registros (o voces) serían, exaltando el cuerpo —danza, gestos, todos los significados somáticos—, las características de esa escritura."

¹²Severo Sarduy, *Barroco* (Buenos Aires: Editorial Sudamericana, 1975), p. 32.

¹³Sarduy, *Escrito sobre un cuerpo, op. cit.*, p. 66.

LE VARIANTI COME ESPRESSIONE
DEL PROCESSO CREATIVO

Hermann Haller

La civiltà letteraria italiana è segnata sin dalle origini da una fortissima preoccupazione per l'elaborazione formale, dovuta in gran parte alle incertezze linguistiche, e alla frammentazione culturale. Petrarca, Ariosto, Leopardi, Pirandello, Palazzeschi, Ungaretti[1], poeti e prosatori, tutti hanno riscritto o ritoccato le loro opere, spesso più di una volta. Questa tradizionale passione degli scrittori, antichi e moderni, ha generato la critica delle varianti, un metodo fertilissimo che ha ottenuto saldi e utili risultati soprattutto in Italia. Le varie redazioni manoscritte e stampate, insieme alle correzioni autografe, costituiscono un ricco patrimonio testuale, che permette di seguire la metamorfosi dell'opera singola o dell'opera complessiva di un autore. Di natura essenzialmente dinamica e diacronica, tesa verso l'opera *in fieri*, verso l'atto più che il dato poetico, la variantistica s'intende come metodo complementare della descrizione caratterizzante[2], tecnica fondata sulle opposizioni interne dell'opera. L'interesse è dunque tutto nel processo *creativo*, più che nel prodotto "creato," nel testo non finibile—che chiamerò *metatesto*—, più che nel testo finito.

L'analisi dinamica, favorita dal postsimbolismo francese, specialmente dalla scuola uscita da Mallarmé e Valéry[3], è stata sviluppata e teorizzata da due esponenti della critica formalista italiana: Giuseppe de Robertis e Gianfranco Contini. E' comune ai due critici la convinzione che si debba studiare l'opera *in sé (l'oeuvre en soi*, come propose già Flaubert), invece di interpretarla dal punto di vista dell'esperienza vissuta dell'autore. La variante assume allora, per De Robertis, il valore di prova "d'un'acuta e, alla fine, vittoriosa ricerca dell'espressione, in una infinita scala di gradazioni; oltre a far quasi toccar con mano il graduale alleggerimento, fino a sparire, del mezzo dell'espressione."[4] In netta opposizione al Croce, De Robertis, basandosi sull'analisi dei valori formali, si accinge a penetrare nel segreto dello scrittore, nella storia interna del testo, e cioè nel processo acquisitivo della progressiva perfezione. Si badi bene all'espressione *vittoriosa ricerca*, punto di vista centrale che si ripete nel saggio derobertisiano "Sull'autografo del canto *A Silvia*" (1946)[5], nell'ormai famosa frase "Leo-

pardi non è di quei poeti che si diano mai torto, correggendo." Polemiz-
zando contro questa visione unilaterale e generica del processo creativo
in una risposta intitolata "Implicazioni leopardiane" (1947)[6], Contini de-
finisce invece le varianti come "spostamenti in un sistema" in cui "tout se
tient," spostamenti cioè, che "involgono una moltitudine di nessi con gli
altri elementi del sistema e con l'intera cultura linguistica del correttore."[7]
Basti un esempio per illustrare i due punti di vista. La trasformazione di
sovvienti (ed. Piatti, 1831) nel primo verso del canto *A Silvia* di Leopardi,
a *rammenti* (ed. Starita, 1835), e poi a *rimembri* (correzione autografa nella
stessa edizione), secondo De Robertis si spiega dalla mancanza d'interio-
rità di *sovvienti*;[8] secondo Contini invece questa correzione è dovuta all'
intenzione del poeta di evitare la ripetizione del verbo *sovviemmi* nel v. 32[9],
cioè allo spostamento nel sistema.[10]

Il metodo della variantistica, che ho applicato finora all'opera novel-
listica di Pirandello e alla narrativa di G. Bassani[11], pur ispirandosi ad
alcune componenti centrali proposte dai due antecedenti critici, ha come
oggetto non un solo metatesto, bensì una varietà di opere dello stesso
autore, studiate in tutte le redazioni successive, senza includere lo studio
di autografi. Al lavoro filologico che consiste nello spoglio microcosmico
di un'enorme quantità di varianti, segue una prima valutazione statistica
che permette di ottenere risultati circa la relativa intensità delle revisioni,
e circa il rapporto numerico tra eliminazioni, sostituzioni, aggiunte nei
vari rifacimenti. La quantificazione dei materiali linguistici, giustificata
forse nella lettura dinamica della prosa più che in poesia, rivela le correzioni più ricorrenti, quelle che chiamo le *costanti* o i paradigmi di varianti.
Nelle *Novelle per un anno*, p. es., il raffronto statistico illustra come il nu-
mero delle eliminazioni prevalga di gran lunga su quello delle sostituzioni
e aggiunte; inoltre come la soppressione delle parti descrittive costituisca
una costante nelle revisioni pirandelliane che suggerisce la tendenza verso
uno stile ellittico, di cose e non di parole, stile che risulta infine nel silenzio
dello spazio bianco.

L'analisi delle correzioni, compiuta nelle dimensioni del tempo e dello
spazio, cioè non solo in un singolo testo, permette conclusioni abbastanza
sicure sull'evoluzione artistica, spesso tormentata e antitetica, di uno scrittore, sulle nuove direzioni, sui suoi dubbi e pentimenti, tutti elementi
preclusi allo studioso del testo storico.

Dopo aver stabilito le costanti, le varianti vengono interpretate in
chiave della storia linguistica, e anche discusse e verificate sullo sfondo di
dati biografici e di dati della critica stilistica statica. Nell'analisi linguistica
si tratta di separare gli aggiustamenti grammaticali, richiesti dalle nuove
esigenze dell'istituto linguistico—per cui si avranno *lui/lei* in luogo di
egli/ella, questo invece di *questi* al caso soggetto; ritocchi ortografici, er-
rori rimediati—dalle variante individuali[12], che esprimono l'aspirazione
dello scrittore alla maggiore corrispondenza tra forma e contenuto, tra
idea e espressione.

Per quanto riguarda le correzioni individuali, si pensi a Pirandello, le cui correzioni rivelano la sua ricerca antimanzoniana di una lingua comune italiana, non di tipo fiorentineggiante. Si pensi a *Il dio di Roserio* di Testori, testo che da una lingua letteraria fortemente dialettale è stato traslitterato in un italiano milanese nell'edizione 1958[13], e che risulta in uno stile più modesto e meno vistoso. Si pensi, infine, al lavorìo per un lessico più comune e colloquiale nella preparazione dell'edizione einaudiana delle *Cinque Storie ferraresi* del 1953, in cui Bassani si scosta decisamente dalla prosa d'arte rondista delle prime redazioni. Questa tendenza verrà contrastata in seguito non solo dalla maggiore concisione lessicale nel *Romanzo di Ferrara* (1974), ma anche dall'introduzione di parole più scelte e letterarie—*discorrere* invece di *parlare, comunicare* per *dire*, interrogatori *svoltisi*, non *fattisi* in questura, il *coniugio* che si sostituisce al *matrimonio*, l'*eloquio farcito* in luogo del *modo di parlare*. Sorprende anche l'insistenza con cui Bassani elimina, riduce o trasforma i frequentissimi avverbi in *-mente*, di sapore giornalistico, dalle pagine dell'intero *Romanzo di Ferrara*. In tutti questi casi, l'analisi delle varianti in chiave dei molteplici registri linguistici si rivela particolarmente feconda.

Altre correzioni si muovono su un piano piuttosto estraneo alla lingua e allo stile dell'opera, tali le precisazioni onomastiche e toponomastiche, specie nei rifacimenti delle *Storie* di Bassani, che sono spie dell'approssimarsi a un maggiore realismo documentario attraverso una più puntuale descrizione del mondo ferrarese.

Nell'ultima fase della mia analisi delle varianti, l'enfasi passa dal microcosmo al macrocosmo, dall'attenzione al particolare alla discussione dell'evoluzione artistica quale si manifesta attraverso tutte le revisioni.

L'applicazione del mio metodo di variantistica porta, in conclusione, a due risultati:

a) Le varianti non vanno in una sola direzione; non sono cioè in ogni caso l'espressione del perfezionamento del testo da una relativa "informità," come voleva De Robertis. Il paragone delle redazioni insegna invece che sono parecchi i casi in cui allo scrittore non è riuscito l'approssimarsi positivo al valore poetico, a una maggiore identità tra forma e pensiero[14]. Si può vedere, così, come in Bassani la ricerca di uno stile più letterario tenda a volte a decadere nell'esoterico e pedantico. —D'altra parte, in Pirandello si nota spesso il pentimento di una correzione e il successivo ritorno alla redazione iniziale.

b) Nelle varianti d'autore non si riesce a stabilire un sistema determinato in senso strutturale. Al contrario, le varianti sono in reciproco conflitto, e non solo nel corso delle varie redazioni: Bassani, p. es., dopo aver creato uno stile meditativo nel *Romanzo di Ferrara*, tramite la tecnica dell'isolamento di singoli membri della frase, sembra ritornare a un ritmo più fluido nell'edizione del *Giardino dei Finzi-Contini*, posteriore di due anni[15]. Invece, questa tensione tra codici opposti coesistenti si può identificare anche all'interno della medesima revisione.

Come già accennato, frequentemente in Bassani, si oppone alla tendenza verso uno stile più letterario la variante di livello stilistico comune. E sono numerosi i momenti nelle revisioni delle *Novelle per un anno* in cui l'attenuazione dell'enfasi contrasta con la generale tendenza di Pirandello verso un testo più drammatico e dialogato, colmo di esclamazioni. Questa mancanza di struttura sembra di voler modificare la tesi continiana, secondo cui *tout se tient*, tutto è spostamento in un sistema.

Tolta dunque la punta sottilmente esteticizzante nel metodo derobertisiano, e moderato il rigore sistematico di ispirazione continiana, la variantistica fornisce risultati complementari ed ausiliari non solo per il giudizio critico del testo non finibile, in trasformazione, ma anche per la comprensione dell'evoluzione artistica dello scrittore.

QUEENS COLLEGE OF THE
CITY UNIVERSITY OF NEW YORK

Note

[1]Cfr. a modo d'esempio, gli studi di G. Contini, "Come lavorava l'Ariosto," in *Esercizi di lettura* (Nuova edizione, Torino, 1974); I. Baldelli, "Dal *Codice di Perelà* all'*Uomo di fumo*," in id., *Varianti di prosatori contemporanei* (Firenze, 1965), 1-23; id., "Dello stile di *Corse al trotto*," ib., 24-45; nonché il mio saggio "Stylistic Trends in the Making of Pirandello's *Novelle per un anno*," *Italica* 52 (1975), 273-90.

[2]Termine coniato dal Contini, *op. cit.*, 233.

[3]Per lavori di variantistica nella letteratura francese, v. p. es. G. Contini, "Sulla trasformazione dell'*Après-midi d'un faune*," in id., *Varianti e altra linguistica* (Torino, 1970), 53-67; A. Feuillerat, *Comment Marcel Proust a composé son roman* (New Haven & London, 1934); L. Pierre-Quint, *Comment travaillait Proust* (Paris, 1929).

[4]Prefazione a G. Ungaretti, *Poesie disperse*, a cura di G. De Robertis, cit. da S. D'Arco Avalle, *L'analisi letteraria in Italia. Formalismo, strutturalismo, semiologia* (Milano-Napoli, 1970), 50.

[5]*Letteratura* 8 (1946), 1-9; ora ristampato nell'appendice antologica di Avalle, *L'analisi letteraria*, 178-90.

[6]G. Contini, *Varianti...*, 41-52.

[7]Ib., 41.

[8]P. 187.

[9]"Implicazioni leopardiane," *Varianti...*, 45s.

[10]De Robertis esprime cautamente il suo scetticismo di fronte al metodo sistematico di Contini: "Non corri rischio di livellare un poco, pianificare i dati espressivi; sottrarre qualcosa all'individualità dell'espressione?", v. "Biglietto per Gianfranco

Contini," *Letteratura* 9 (1947), 117-18; ora nel volume di Avalle, *L'analisi letteraria*, 202-04.

[11]V. il saggio già citato N. 1, nonché "Da *Le Storie ferraresi* al *Romanzo di Ferrara*: Varianti nell'opera di Bassani," in *Canadian Journal of Italian Studies* 1 (1977), 74-90.

[12]Contini distingue tra *compensi attigui* e *compensi a distanza*, varianti che rinviano ad altri passi del medesimo componimento o a passi dell'autore fuori del componimento presente; oppone queste varianti alle correzioni che rinviano a abitudini culturali dell'autore. —Meno convincente mi sembra invece la distinzione qualitativa, proposta dal Devoto, in varianti *sostitutive* ("quelle che definiscono un mutamento e un avviamento graduale al Testo definitivo, in un affinamento") dalle varianti *instaurative* ("quelle che consistono in un brusco mutamento delle realizzazioni espressive"), cfr. G. Devoto, *Nuovi studi di stilistica* (Firenze, 1962), 127s. Tra le instaurative si elenca l'eliminazione di esotismi, che, a mio parere, è pure motivata esteticamente.

[13]I. Baldelli, "La traduzione di Testori," *Varianti...*, 76-91.

[14]V. p. es., le correzioni sveviane considerate infelici dal Devoto, "Italo Svevo," in *Itinerario stilistico* (Firenze, 1975), 253 ss.

[15]V. l'eliminazione frequentissima della punteggiatura nell'edizione Mondadori 1976 del *Giardino dei Finzi-Contini*, che era stata introdotta nel *Romanzo di Ferrara* 1974 per isolare i vari complementi di luogo, tempo, specificazione ecc., con l'intento di creare un'andatura di prosa più calma e riflessa.

EMILY DICKINSON'S
FRACTURE OF GRAMMAR:
SYNTACTIC AMBIGUITY IN HER POEMS

Robert L. Lair

Speaking of the few lyrics which Emily Dickinson had sent him for examination and criticism, Thomas Higginson wrote in his *Atlantic Monthly* essay:

> She almost always grasped whatever she sought, but with some fracture of grammar and dictionary on the way. Often too she was obscure, and sometimes inscrutable; and though obscurity is sometimes, in Coleridge's phrase, a compliment to the reader, yet it is never safe to press this compliment too hard.[1]

Thomas Bailey Aldrich, a less sympathetic critic, writing in the same periodical within a year of Colonel Higginson's pronouncement, stated his opinion of the "poetical chaos" of her grammar somewhat more sharply:

> The English critic who said of Miss Dickinson that she might have become a fifth-rate poet "if she had only mastered the rudiments of grammar and gone into metrical training for about fifteen years," the rather candid English critic who said this somewhat overstated his case. He had, however, a fairly good case. If Miss Dickinson had undergone the austere curriculum indicated she would, I am sure, have become an admirable lyric poet of the second magnitude. . . . .
>
> Miss Dickinson's versicles have a queerness and a quaintness that have stirred a momentary curiosity in emotional bosoms. Oblivion lingers in the immediate neighborhood. . . .
>
> . . .an eccentric, dreamy, half-educated recluse in an out-of-the-way New England village (or anywhere else) cannot with impunity set at defiance the laws of gravitation and grammar.[2]

Even those critics who believed most fully in the power of Miss Dickinson's "versicles," I mean those courageous persons who edited them for publication, had serious doubts about the acceptability of certain enigmatic or downright erroneous usages in the lyrics. Mabel Loomis Todd and Thomas Wentworth Higginson were careful to "correct" instances of "substandard" grammar when they prepared the first collection in 1890. The difficulty is complicated because we have these 1,775 poems only in draft stage. Had Miss Dickinson prepared her own manuscripts for publication, what might she have done to "set the grammar in order"? We can never know, so slightly had she developed a theory of poetry, having sung, as she herself had urged, "as a boy does by the burying ground, because I am afraid." Her *ars poetica* she had stated succinctly and enigmatically to Colonel Higginson:

> If I read a book and it makes my whole body so cold no fire can ever warm me, I know that is poetry. If I feel physically as if the top of my head were taken off, I know that is poetry. These are the only ways I know it. Is there any other way?[3]

And when she wrote of her literary craft within the poems themselves, she was equally cryptic: "Tell Him—I only said the Syntax/And left the Verb and the Pronoun out—."[4]

George Frisbie Whicher devoted several pages of his *This Was a Poet: Emily Dickinson* to the "dislocations of syntax and other verbal abnormalities." He insisted that Miss Dickinson's idiosyncratic diction was "normal" in a creative artist, however:

> If we examine Emily Dickinson's apparent lapses from grammatical convention, we shall soon discover that nearly all spring from one or another of the following causes: her preference for vernacular idiom, her old-fashioned training, her use of poetic mannerisms which she did not employ in prose, and her omission of verbal connective tissue in the effort to secure the utmost condensation of thought.[5]

Confronted by the necessity of concluding one of two things—either that the idiosyncratic syntax results from imprecision of expression or that it is a part of a poetic technique deliberately embraced as the means to conscious ends—, we must inevitably decide that the latter is true—that Emily Dickinson strove with intelligence and artistic sensitivity for the realization of specific syntactic goals. These explain the grammatical abnormalities, the instances of syntactic ambiguity.

Take, for example, the instance of her substitution of the adjective for the adverbial form, a frequent, syntactically ambiguous occurrence in her poems. Note, for example, the following stanza from one of the very early lyrics:

> But I tug childish at my bars
> Only to fail again—(77).

We have, in English, two ways of determining syntactic function: inflection and slot. The word "childish" here, inflected as an adjective, appears in an adverbial slot. One must determine therefore whether to honor the inflection or the placement in interpretation of the lyric. If we take the inflection as primary, "childish" is an adjective modifying "I": "But I, childish, tug at my bars/Only to fail again". If, however, we appeal to the force of placement, "childish" appears a foreshortened adverb, somewhat akin to "slow" which, because of a synchronic development from two different older forms, often rivals "slowly" for adverbial status. Now the lines read: "But I tug child-ish[ly] at my bars/Only to fail again."

There is, however, a third choice—one that I prefer. One may see in the syntactic ambiguity a slight enlargement of modification, an enlargement of meaning. Why could not the word "childish" be thought to function as both adjective and adverb, serving as a double modification? "But I, childish, tug childishly at my bars/Only to fail again." Now it is both *the speaker of the poem* who is childish, deluded by fantasies of escape when she knows her imprisonment is secure, excited unreasonably by the thought of liberation, and *the action of the tugging* which is engaged in childishly. Two syntactic functions are then compressed into the single word "childish"; it is both adjective and adverb, doubling the semantic force of the word. And, I believe, while the mind may not work logically through the ambiguity, the two-pronged effect does suggest itself even unconsciously. Examples of this species of syntactic ambiguity are legion in the Dickinson canon.

It is a fairly simple matter to make the emendations of the text required to comprehend the syntactic relationships when the simple adjective form "childish" is substituted for the adverb "childishly." However, the necessary syntactic correction is somewhat more complex in the comparative and superlative forms; it is no longer the shortened "childish" for "childishly," but something like "preciser" for "preciselier" or "more precisely." There is an example in the lyric entitled "There is a finished feeling."

> By Death's bold Exhibition
> Preciser what we are
> And the Eternal function
> Enabled to infer

Here the inversion, the ellipsis, the comparative form of the adjectival-adverbial ambiguity all work together to add to the difficulties of interpretation. A prose reading of the stanza might explain the ellipsis in this way: "[When confronted] by Death's bold Exhibition, [we are] enabled to infer preciser (i.e., "more precisely," if read adverbially) [both] what we are (i.e., the meaning of our existence) and the Eternal function (i.e., the purpose which a concept of eternity serves in human experience)."

However, we may prefer to read "preciser" as an adjective functioning substantively in an ellipsis: "By Death's bold Exhibition [we are given a] preciser [sense of] what we are, and [are] enabled [by that knowledge] to infer the Eternal function." The ellipsis requires us to expand, either consciously or unconsciously, the syntactic framework. Whether we honor the inflection or the placement will determine to a large extent the modification of elements and may very well change the meanings of individual passages.

Particularly in her poems treating the subject of death, semantic ambiguities begin often to arise out of the ambiguities of syntax. In lyric 804, for example, the poet watches a woman confronted by death's gaze: "And met the gaze—direct—." One may either accept the adjectival inflection of the word "direct" and speak of "the direct gaze of death," or one may accept the force of position to say that she met death's gaze "directly." In the first reading, emphasis is upon the figure of death, staring unflinchingly at his victim; in the second, it is upon the woman, who, fearless in the face of death, looks unflinchingly back to him. Perhaps both meanings are implied—death and the woman in direct confrontation. I do not think the *double entendre* necessarily bad in poetry.

There is here, as in others of my examples, an important ancillary factor at work—a heurism of meter which forces the dropping of the adverbial marker *-ly*. In Emily Dickinson's day it would have been called "poetic license" in the exploitation of an available "flat" adverb form. Nonetheless, the device produces an ambivalence with both implications at work. In the one instance, the central focus is upon death itself; in the other, upon the heroine's courageousness in the face of death. Thus the poem gains in semantic dimension through syntactic ambiguity.

Getting on to other kinds of syntactic substitutions, let me suggest that Emily Dickinson frequently uses nouns as adjectives or adjectives as substantives. For example, in lyric 98, a significant difference in interpretation of the entire poem depends upon one's decision between reading "pomp" as a noun, as its inflection argues, or as an adjective, as its placement after "how" argues: "How pomp surpassing ermine. . . ." Reading the first line of the last stanza with "pomp" retaining its noun function, one may expand the ellipsis in the following manner: "How [great a] pomp [there will be at my death, even] surpassing ermine (i.e., the pomp which attends the burial of kings)." The lyric's meaning then seems obvious. No matter how lowly the circumstances of a man's life, no matter how trivial his person, there is one grand and dignified event awaiting him: he will be treated regally in death. The brilliance of the lyric lies in the manner in which Miss Dickinson provokes it all to vivid sensuous life: the coach, the footmen, the chamber in which we lie in state, the throng of mourners, the somber bells which resound as we are borne along toward the grave, the stiff ceremoniousness of those who stand alongside the casket, the grandeur and solemnity of the funeral service itself—all are evoked in steady, yet rapid, sequence. All is shrouded with the proper reverence of tone. Ant there is almost a rhapsodic note in the voice when we arrive at the concluding stanza: "How great a pomp there will be, even surpassing the ermine of kings!"

However, unless we become dogmatically partial to our first reading of that line, there is another interpretation which is likely to suggest itself. The "how" preceding "pomp" has an urgency which compels us to consider the noun form a possible compression of the adjectival "pompous": "How pompous an event that will be, even surpassing the pompousness of kings in their ermine." Many readers must sense this ironic contrast almost instinctively. Yet there is a great deal of connotative difference between the two words "pomp" and "pompous." While pomp may be a legitimate show of splendor, a pompous display is usually an excessive parody of grandeur. Thus the meaning of the entire poem may hinge upon the syntactic interpretation of the single word "pomp." If read as a compressed adjective, the subject is the hypocrisy and excess of the funereal gaudiness which usually accompanies the putting away of bodies in death. The dignity is no dignity at all, but a rancid mockery of the proper respect which one expects to be paid at the ending of human life.

The question will arise in some minds whether two such disparate meanings can comfortably coexist within the same passage or whether the resultant ambivalence is only confusion in need of clarification. It appears to me that the paradoxical statement in the lyric is adequately justified and is as precise an account of our ambiguous attitudes about the ceremonies of death as one will find anywhere. All who have stood at a graveside know how essential reverence is to the occasion; yet paradoxically, we have been struck as well by the embarrassing hypocrisy which often characterizes the rite. Emily Dickinson has compressed this paradox into the very syntax of her lyric.

Often in her interchange of adjective and noun functions, Miss Dickinson seems bent upon utilizing the qualitative nature of the adjective and the more tangible character of the noun—I refer here, of course, to the concrete noun—. In "As sleigh Bells seem in summer," for example, she describes those lost in death; they seem distant, remote, fictitious, fairylike in her memory. But she uses the noun for the last of these qualities: "So fairy—so fictitious/The individuals do [seem]." The noun "fairy" here suggests greater tangibility than the adjective "fairylike," which bears a more essentially dependent function.

In "An awful Tempest mashed the air," we have a contrary circumstance: "A Black—as of a Spectre's Cloak/Hid Heaven and Earth from view." The lyric describes a storm so frightful that it appears to be a supernatural invasion. It may be possible to read "black" as an adjective, modifying "cloak," though the placement is strange, if that be true. However, it appears "black" is instead a foreshortened form of the noun "blackness." Now the syntax is normal despite the compression. What has Miss Dickinson achieved? Primarily she has avoided the conventional picture of the storm as evoked in the blackness of the night, and has given it an eerie, almost necromantic substantiality, suggesting that it is palpable, a mystic entity, and not a mere quality. It is the black itself which hides heaven and earth from view.

What about verbs? In prose, as in poetry, an enormous weight of meaning is entrusted to the verb. Carefully devised prediction can eliminate wordiness and misconstruction in the writing of the English sentence. Miss Dickinson makes three species of verbal substitutions regularly in her poems: (1) she frequently uses the active for the passive forms; (2) plural for singular forms; (3) subjunctive for indicative forms.

In considering the substitution of the active for the passive voice, let us look at a specific example: "Agony that enacted there/Motionless as Peace."

However, to do so is to nullify the active implication of "enacted," a subtle point perhaps, but one which makes the agony itself, and not the mere suffering human creature, an active agent transcending the fleeting motions of men now dead. The agony itself acted out the tragedy and now lies motionless as peace—something more than simple personification, I believe. It is an ambiguity worth preserving.

The second species of verb substitution, the use of the plural for the singular form, is more puzzling. Interestingly enough, there are examples of this same usage in the letters. Yet, at times Miss Dickinson achieved an unusual effect with it in the poems. Note its use in "The Robin is the One," for example:

> The Robin is the One
> That interrupt the Morn. . . .
>
> That overflow the Noon. . . .
>
> That speechless from her Nest
> Submit. . . .

Here the consistency of the effect makes it seem deliberate, evoking the conjecture that Miss Dickinson uses the singular form of the noun to "single out" the robin from all other birds, to individualize him, while she uses the plural form of the verb to suggest the large number of robins assembled to interrupt, to overflow, to submit. Such an assertion can be speculative at best, but it seems reasonable in view of the recurring pattern.

The third verb interchange is that of subjunctive for indicative forms. "Triumph may be of several kinds," for example, builds its quality of ambiguity upon this substitution of subjunctive for indicative forms.

> When that Old Imperator—Death—
> By Faith—be overcome—. . .
>
> When Truth—affronted long—
> Advance unmoved—. . .
>
> A Triumph—when Temptation's Bribe
> Be slowly handed back—. . .
>
> Severer Triumph by Himself
> Experienced—who pass
> Acquitted from that Naked Bar—

On the surface, the poet appears self-confident. There are several kinds of triumph: that of conquest over death through faith, that of truth over error, that of resisting temptation, and that of acquittal before the judgment of God.

But Miss Dickinson's casting of the four main verbs in the subjunctive mode tends to raise some doubt about the matter. Upon careful rereading, one hears: "There is triumph in the room when death is overcome by faith— if indeed death can be overcome by faith at all," etc. The subjunctive undercuts the ringing assurance of the Calvinistic sermons Miss Dickinson had heard and reveals the poet's timorousness in the face of so awesome a metaphysical spectrum as is evoked by talk of death, of truth, of temptation, and of final judgment. The grammar conveys the hesitation.

Let me conclude by suggesting that, in my own study of the lyrics, I found well over 2,000 of these instances of syntactic oddity—I have selected only a few examples to suggest ways in which I believe they enrich particular poems. Taken together, these examples reveal an extraordinary awareness of the potential of language when freed from its narrowest conventional confines. They show too a sensitivity and, at times, even an intellectuality, which baffled her reader so totally that they revised her "weaknesses" out of existence or denounced them as the wanton defiance of inexorable grammatical "laws" by an ill-prepared schoolgirl who should have preferred yeast and lily to the rigors of the mind. My own conclusion is that she did know what she was doing—that she was often striving for second and third meanings superimposed upon the more obvious renderings through syntactic ambivalence.

And I believe she succeeded.

MALONE COLLEGE

Notes

[1]"Emily Dickinson's Letters," *Atlantic Monthly,* 68 (October 1891), 444-456.
[2]"*In re* Emily Dickinson," *Atlantic Monthly*, 69 (January 1892), 143-44.
[3]"Letters," *loc. cit.*
[4]All quotations from the poems are from *The Complete Poems of Emily Dickinson*, ed. Thomas H. Johnson (Boston: 1960).
[5]George Frisbie Whicher, *This Was A Poet: Emily Dickinson* (Ann Arbor: 1957), p. 231.

SPLIT SIGNIFIERS IN
LA PASION DE URBINO

John M. Lipski

Among the lesser known specimens of the *nueva narrativa latinoamericana* figures *La pasión de Urbino*, by the Cuban Lisandro Otero. Conoisseurs of Cuban literature perhaps recall this work as the novel which lost the Biblioteca Breve prize to Cabrera Infante's *Tres tristes tigres*, but in most instances when Otero's name is even mentioned at all as a contemporary novelist it is in connection with his earlier novel *La situación* or his more recent montage venture *En ciudad semejante*. And yet *La pasión de Urbino*, whose fewer than ninety pages barely qualify it as a novel, is by far the most tightly structured of Otero's works, and it offers a variety of opportunities for the employment of structural techniques of literary analysis. The text is extremely compact, highly charged with symbolism, connotation, and allegory—all topics deserving of in-depth investigations. Nonetheless, in the interest of brevity and coherence, the present study will focus solely on structural aspects of the text, in particular the various deformations to which the signifying function has been subjected.

Banned in Spain due to official Catholic censorship, *La pasión de Urbino* deals, on the superficial level, with the adulterous affair between a Cuban priest, Antonio de Urbino, and his sister-in-law Fabiola. Their relationship, always apparently a warm one, reached the heat of passion during a trip to Florence by Antonio, his brother Guido, and the latter's wife, Fabiola. Upon returning to Havana, both Antonio and Fabiola engage in a process of soul-searching and reflect upon the nature of sin, the existence of God, and the dual role of the priest as human being and emissary of God. Intertwined with the main threads of the narrative are direct or indirect references to several peripheral "passions," including the secret love of the Urbino's housekeeper, Sibila Mayerburg, for her master, Guido, and the adolescent infatuation of the black servant boy Trifino Candá for Fabiola. The overall web of conflicting emotions is characterized by a number of non-reciprocal relationships: Sibila regards Guido as a basically mild-mannered and non-aggressive individual who would be content to tend his stamp collection but for the machinations of his socially ambitious wife. Fabiola, in turn, regards Guido with ambivalence, and feels that she has, in fact, been responsible for saving him from a life of mediocrity and destitution by forcing him to assume control of his late father's business emporium. Guido presumably loves his wife in his own rather passive fashion. Doña María, Fabiola's mother-in-law, considers Fabiola to be guiltless and regards Sibila as a conniving woman set on luring Guido away from his lawful wife and family. Trifino, in turn, idolizes Fabiola, creating an almost saint-like mental image of his patroness, as does his aged mother, Tata Candá, who tended the Urbino brothers from their birth. Fabiola lavishes her affection on her sole child, Machayo, in a bizarre, over-protective fashion that repels Sibila. The feelings of Antonio Urbino are left unspecified by the author, although one is left to assume the details of his "passion"; Antonio is thus set apart as an isolated pole in a conglomerate of emotional relations, the recipient of overly stated feelings, but himself excluded from the expression of such explicit emotions. Antonio may thus be considered the structural center of the novel, about whom all the other relations revolve. These relations may be depicted schematically as follows: (+) indicates positive emotion; (-) indicates negative emotion; (±) indicates ambivalence; and the arrow signals the direction of the emotion in question.

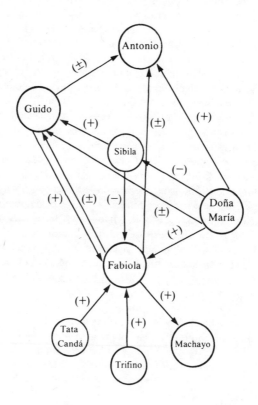

The second half of the novel presents the most striking technical innovations, which are also inextricably bound up with the narrative structure of the text. Reference is made, at about the half-way point (p. 45) to Antonio's supposed embezzlement of stocks from the Urbino business, a robbery discovered by the company bookkeeper and reported in a memo which Guido is keeping for blackmail purposes. Guido's opinion is that Antonio should leave the country immediately, provided with money and a passport which the former is willing to furnish, in order to repair the tarnish to the family honor. During Guido's absence, Antonio sneaks into his brother's study and forces open a drawer which he supposes contains the auditor's report. The drawer contains, in addition to the memo, a loaded pistol, which falls to the floor and discharges, killing Antonio. The following chapter begins, "La muerte del padre Antonio no alteró la bien establecida rutina de la casa Santacruz." Two pages later, however, we are suddenly confronted with the unheralded sentence "El lunes por la mañana el padre Antonio acudió como de costumbre a la casa Santacruz," and the narrative continues, as though the earlier scene had never taken place. The suspicion that author Otero is tampering with narrative reality is further reinforced by two other "deaths" and subsequent "resurrections" in the remainder of the novel, each event with its concomitant plot details. The second part of the novel begins with an argument between Antonio and Guido in which the former complains about mismanagement of his inheritance through Guido's business ventures and announces his decision to leave the country. Guido in turn replies that "No estimamos que existan razones sólidas para esa decisión," to which Antonio retorts, somewhat apocryphally," No entienden nada. No saben de qué se trata." Guido's comeback is "Debo hacerte notar, Antonio, que eres el primero de los Urbino que abandona sus deberes." Two chapters later, Guido and Antonio meet in their sleeping mother's bedroom, where the former accuses the latter of the robbery and insists that he leave the country. The following chapter begins with the identical opening paragraph, but this time Doña María awakens and, while Guido leaves on an errand, announces to Antonio that Guido is robbing the company and plans to run off with Sibila. The subsequent chapter, two pages later, returns to the previous situation, with Antonio informing Fabiola that the bishop has denied him permission to leave. This scene is followed, several pages later, by one in which Fabiola, portrayed as Jezebel, kills Antonio by beating him over the head with a crucifix in the sacristy of his church. In the next chapter, Antonio, during an interview with the dying bishop, is given permission to leave Cuba, and upon leaving the audience, he encounters his own funeral on the street, as if in a dream. A few pages further along, Antonio, after reviewing the unhappy events which have led him to the decision, stabs himself to death, after which Guido and Sibila run off, as if fulfilling Doña María's prophecy, and Fabiola is rumored to be sleeping with Trifino. On the following page, Antonio appears again, once more without any overt textual indication that anything is amiss, and the novel ends with Antonio, Fabiola and Guido planning a trip to Florence "to get to know one another better."

It is thus apparent that the novel, whose brevity and innocuous beginning conceal a great inner complexity, represents a structural pattern which departs from the norm in traditional Spanish narrative fiction and even stands apart from other current Latin American novels. The introduction of the multiple versions of Antonio's death, and the surrounding events, appears in the text without any overt signals, being inserted into an otherwise coherent narrative flow. The startling effect engendered by such manipulations results in a loss of textual continuity and creates a disconnected text which may be reconstructed only by each individual reader using the interpretation he has chosen for himself, for the author provides no further clues as to the unravelment of the puzzle. "¿Dónde termina el sueño y empieza la vigilia?" asks the publisher's introduction to the novel, and the question is indeed pertinent to an overall interpretation of this most unusual literary creation.

In order to approach the technical fabric of the novel, we shall have recourse to two notions from structural linguistics—one, the "syntagm-paradigm" dichotomy and the other, the nature of the signifying function. The term "paradigm" refers to the underlying system of possibilities, or related elements, which may be placed in a single slot or position. In the case of a verb, for example, the paradigm is the entire conjugation, while in the system of food, the paradigm would be all those items that are inter-changeable on the menu for a particular course, such as entrée, dessert, and so forth. The "syntagm," on the other hand, represents the concrete realization of the paradigm, in which one choice is made from the paradigm or system for each slot of the syntagm. Jakobson[1] has used the term "simultaneity" to characterize the paradigm, since all potential values are simultaneously present until one is chosen. On the other hand, the word "successivity" best describes the syntagm, for elements occur one after the other in succession in order to form a corpus of data. Applied to a narrative, the paradigm refers to the underlying set of all possible variants on a particular set of semantic structures, whereas the syntagm is the concrete text under discussion. It is not uncommon, however, for the paradigm to be in some sense extended onto the syntagm—i.e., for several associational entities to appear in an actual text. In addition to obvious cases such as metaphor, rhyme, and puns, a variety of other creative possibilities exist. Roland Barthes notes that it is "as if perhaps there were here a junction between the field of aesthetics and the defections from the semantic system. . . . It therefore seems that it is always on the frontiers of the two planes that creation has a chance to occur."[2]

It is not uncommon, among modern Latin American novels, to encounter examples of paradigmatic overlapping or interpenetration in which the author has presented within the expanse of a single text, paradigmatic variants which would normally entail mutual exclusion. The use of such a literary device runs the gamut from Cabrera Infante's *Tres tristes tigres*, in which the text abounds with word games, through Vargas Llosa's *Conversación en la Catedral,* in which the constantly shifting narrative perspective provides a prismatic view of reality, to Donoso's *El obsceno pájaro de la noche*, in which studied use of ambiguity and contradiction has been employed to create a novel and its antithesis within the confines of the same text. In each case, the structural function of the paradigmatic overlapping is somewhat different, and yet there remains a fundamental unity of purpose, which is that the reader follow for himself the process of authorial creation and reconstruct a version of the text under consideration, or perhaps several versions.

The text of *La pasión de Urbino* is clearly characterized by a number of instances of paradigmatic overlapping, so many in fact that the entire text may be regarded as nothing but a set of juxtaposed paradigmatic variants. An enumeration of the various paradigmatic possibilities presented in the text will therefore facilitate an overall structural interpretation.

The most obvious point of paradigmatic interpenetration involves the multiple versions of the death of Antonio Urbino. At no point in the text is it made clear whether these events are the result of the dreams or imagination of Antonio, Fabiola, Doña María, or one of the other characters or whether perhaps one of the death scenes is real and the others merely hypothetical alternatives. Each death scene and Antonio's subsequent returns to the pages of the narrative is introduced without reference to altered states of consciousness or cognition, and even a shifting temporal reference is absent from the textual meanderings, except in the final chapter, where the narrative turns upon itself like a circle and returns to the events preceding the novel's opening chapters. Thus the portrayal of Antonio's death, in each case the violent result of his passion, provides the central framework for the novel, around which are interlaced the remaining paradigmatic sections.

Inseparably related to the death scenes are the various versions of the embezzlement, in which Antonio and/or Guido are implicated, as well as the conflicting opinions of Fabiola, Sibila, and Trifino and Antonio's plans to leave the country, which are alternately permitted or thwarted by Guido and/or the bishop. Such events all occur embedded in the larger context of a death scene and must thus be analyzed in relation to the larger frame of reference of the entire text.

In the course of Antonio and Fabiola's conversations and self-analyses, a number of fundamental religious and moral tenets are brought up for discussion, and in several instances Antonio is led to offer contradictory remarks, which indicate the internal torments which ravage him and offer yet another instance of multiple paradigmatic variants in the same text. About halfway through the novel (p. 51) Antonio, after some preliminary breast-beating about his affair with Fabiola while the two are sunbathing on a beach, makes the remark that despite all appearances to the contrary, sensuality is not a sin. This statement, coming from the mouth of the tormented priest, sounds more like wishful thinking than a carefully reasoned opinion, and the ensuing discussion touches on the dichotomy of good and evil: Antonio declares, "El hombre concentra el Bien y el Mal en una sola entidad. Aun Cristo no pudo evitarlo. Al expulsar a los mercaderes les hizo un Mal que era un Bien para otros." The reverie is broken by Fabiola's remarking as to what the extremely chaste and traditional Doña María would think if she knew of their actions at that moment.

Somewhat further along, during Antonio's audience with the bishop, the former remarks, somewhat paradoxically, "Todo se llegará a entender. Nada será comprendido," upon which the bishop explains the magical significance of the circle: "El rectángulo es categórico, explícito, toda una obvia declaración. El círculo, en cambio, es infinito, pasa y repasa sobre sí mismo, no termina nunca ni empieza en ningún lugar." With these words the bishop has characterized the structure of the novel itself which, as noted above, is completely circular, offering a linearly ordered paradigmatic display, turning about itself like a ferris wheel, in which each of the passengers passes successively before the eyes of the observer, in an eternally recurring progression. Following the bishop's remarks, Antonio replies, "La Iglesia tiene las fuerzas necesarias para aceptar el desafío del círculo." Again, this statement represents a fundamental paradox, for neither Antonio nor the bishop, both representatives of the Church, seems able to fully confront "el desafío del círculo." Antonio is torn by doubts regarding the existence of God, the nature and boundaries of sin, and his quite corporeal relations with Fabiola. The bishop, in his old age and moribund state, has lapsed into a mysticism which borders on sorcery, speaking of circles and cabals, a state which appears to alarm even Antonio. It is at this point in the novel that one may claim to have reached the epicenter, for it is this fundamental dichotomy, which is never resolved in the novel's endless circular progression, that defines the narrative fabric of the text. On the following page Antonio remarks, "Nuestro reino no es de este mundo," to which the bishop replies, "Es y no es."

Another related pattern concerns Fabiola's supposed infidelity to Guido. Aside from her rather bizarre relationship with Antonio, she is not demonstrated to be an adultress; rather, the text contains several contradictory passages which form a dynamic tension or opposition characterizing Fabiola's dual nature, both toward Antonio and toward other men. Towards the beginning of the novel (p. 12) Fabiola thinks, "¿Cómo podía recibir el cuerpo de Dios con tantos estigmas sin purificar? ¿Por qué Guido y no otro? Y ¿por qué los otros?" The following pages contain an unusual interchange between Antonio and Fabiola:

> Recuerda que no debes tener amistad con hombre alguno—aconsejó el sacerdote.
> —¿Y contigo?
> —No soy un hombre.
> —Sí eres.
> —No olvides quiénes somos.
> —No lo olvido.

Two chapters later, Antonio accuses Fabiola of infidelity to Guido, an insinuation which she flatly denies. The next chapter begins with the passage:

> ¿Por qué dijo aquello el padre Antonio? ¿Por qué mintió? ¿Por qué quiso calumniar su probada castidad? Ella no se había contaminado jamás con el contacto de otro varón que no fuera aquel a que Dios la destinó. ¿Por qué el padre Antonio dijo la verdad tan brutalmente? ¿Por qué la enfrentó, de repente, a su lascivia?

Here we are confronted once again with the basic split in Fabiola's nature; whether or not she committed adultery in reality is irrelevant. The significant point is the constant tension between Fabiola and Antonio and also the ambivalent nature of her relations with Guido, which lead her to her disastrous encounters with Antonio and perhaps with other men.

In order to probe more deeply into the function of the paradigmatic interpenetrations in *La pasión de Urbino*, it is necessary to briefly discuss the nature of the linguistic sign. According to Saussure[4] a sign is composed of two elements, the "signifier" and the "signified," which are related by the sign function itself. Thus a sign is in fact a dynamic entity that creates meaning by its very existence. Hjelmslev[5] symbolized a signifying system as a plane of expression E and a plane of content C united by a relation R; thus, each such system may be depicted as $E\ R\ C$. Hjelmslev and Barthes[6] later considered the possibility of staggered systems—that is, systems whose plane of expression, or content, or both, were in themselves entire signifying systems; a system whose expression plane is a signifying system is called a "connotative semiotic," while one whose content plane is a complete system of signs is a "metasemiotic." Other, more complex systems have also been discussed, particularly with respect to certain works of literature,[7] and there is in theory no limit to the degree of complexity that can be attained by a set of signs.

Of central significance to the present endeavor is the possibility for bifurcation in the process of signification.[8] The most commonly noted bifurcation results in a split in the signified, or the content plane of a semiotic system; such, for example, is the case with various works of Alfred Jarry, and may be graphically represented as:

$$E \qquad R \diagup\!\!\!\!\diagdown \begin{matrix} C_1 \\ C_2 \\ \cdot \\ \cdot \\ C_n \end{matrix}$$

Put in simpler terms, a split in the plane of content means that the plane of expression, in this instance the text, does not refer to a unique referent on the plane of content, but rather is linked to several. An example would be the title of the novel under consideration: *La pasión de Urbino*. Superficially, one may take this title, representing the plane of expression to have as referent the relationship between Antonio and Fabiola although the "passion" is stated almost exclusively from the latter's viewpoint. It is also possible, however, to include in the same sign the feelings of Sibila for Guido, as well perhaps, as Trifino's love for Fabiola. Thus the normally unique referent of the title has been ruptured to admit a number of other elements on the plane of content. The structural function of this multiplication of signifieds is to offer an implicit relationship among superficially disparate entities and thereby to create a tighter narrative foundation.

The reverse process, i.e., the possibility of a split signifier, has rarely been mentioned explicitly, perhaps because in the most common occurrences to do so would be trivial. In a normal text, there are frequently a number of references to the same person, place or event; for example, each time a particular character is named, one may add a further signifier to the list of occurrences, each of which is related to a single signified, who is the character himself. It is in fact the absence of such multiple signifiers that would be bizarre, for texts are developed and plots are woven through repeated reference. There are, however, more interesting possibilities, in which the split signifiers play a non-trivial role.

In *La pasión de Urbino*, the use of multiple paradigmatic varients gives rise to a series of split signifiers, but in a fashion radically different from the trivial configurations mentioned above. Let us take as an example the most striking case, the supposed death of Antonio Urbino. Clearly, it is impossible for a man to experience death more than once, regardless of the circumstances; therefore, we must postulate that at least two of the three death scenes depicted in the novel are, in fact, devoid of real content as applied to Antonio. The precise nature of these spurious scenes is open to interpretation, but in any case they allow the reader to participate in the construction of the labyrinth of relations which describes the narrative structure of the novel. Moreover, it is entirely possible, given the circular structure of the text, that Antonio does not meet death in *any* of the scenes listed in the novel, but rather that all three descriptions are purely hypothetical, serving ancillary functions in the development of the narrative. Whatever the case may be, however, it may be deduced that the actual signifying *function* in each of the death scenes is in some sense distinct from the other two, for it is impossible for a single signified or content element to be "referred" to by mutually contradictory signifiers. In order to accommodate the split signifiers within the general semiotic framework of the narrative, it is consequently necessary to posit not only multiple signifiers but also multiple relations of signification between the plane of expression and the plane of content. Schematically, this configuration is:

$$E_1 \quad R_1$$
$$E_2 \quad R_2 \rightarrow C$$
$$E_3 \quad R_3$$

In each instance the "meaning" attached to the signifier denoting the death of Antonio Urbino is different because a separate reality is defined in each scene, and it is impossible to force the individual frames of reference to coincide, even for a moment.

Another example of a split signifier occurs near the beginning of the novel, when Fabiola sits in church, looking at a crucifix and pondering her relations with Guido and Antonio. As she stares at the cross, the face of Christ is suddenly replaced by that of Guido, in all its details, and later returns to the face of Christ. While it is hinted at that this hallucination is the result of Fabiola's feelings of guilt about her (real or imagined) adultery, the fact nevertheless remains that, as expressed in the text, the content level signified, i.e., the image of the crucifixion, is depicted by two signifiers, the face of Christ and the face of Guido Urbino. The relations which link these signifiers to the single signified must therefore be of two different natures: one, a straightforward reference to the normal image associated with a crucifix; the other, a hallucinatory and allegorical relation which links Guido's face to the same image.

Split signifiers also figure in the various paradoxes posed by Antonio and Fabiola. For example, although the true nature of Fabiola's adultery is never textually revealed, the novel contains a split signifier which alternately affirms and denies the possibility of infidelity. One may also include at this point the paradoxical views characterizing Antonio's religious vocation. Originally, Antonio was not drawn into the priesthood by a true religious vocation. Rather, he was forced by his mother, who had made a promise to the Virgin of Lourdes during a serious childhood illness which almost claimed Antonio's life. At one point, Antonio tells Fabiola that he actually accepted the spiritual life of the priesthood for a while in the seminary, but his later views are strikingly distinct from those expected of a man of God. Thus Antonio goes through a series of spiritual oscillations, alternating between the poles of spiritualism and faith in God and an antagonistic agnosticism that not only condones sensuality but also taints Antonio's entire life with unmitigated cynicism. Both elements of the figure of Antonio are depicted in the text without overt indication of the transition from one state to the other. Therefore, we must consider this dually portrayed aspect of Antonio to be yet another example of a split signifier.

La pasión de Urbino is in reality not one novel but rather several paradigmatically related but nonetheless distinct and logically incompatible narratives. The rather extraordinary use of paradigmatic overlapping has given rise to split signifiers, in which the normally unique relation between expression and content in a narrative is ruptured along the axis of expression. As an independent literary device, the paradigmatic interpenetration of the syntagmatic flow of the narrative would tend to produce a series of mutually independent works, but the unifying force provided by the split signifiers with unitary signifieds serves to bind the paradigmatic alternatives into a single coherent text. As well as containing a number of individual signs, a literary text may in itself be considered a closed semiotic system.

La pasión de Urbino is, through the use of multiple signifiers and signifying relations, provided with a ready means of uniting the several disparate narrative propositions. It is the splitting of the relations between expression and content, rather than the mere juggling of elements on one plane or the other, that gives *La pasión de Urbino* its unique structure, and it is this semiotic innovation which provides a vitalizing force in what would otherwise be a rather absurd literary venture.

MICHIGAN STATE UNIVERSITY

Notes

[1] R. Jakobson & M. Halle, *Fundamentals of Language* (The Hague: Mouton, 1956), pp. 58-81; R. Jakobson, *Studies on Child Language and Aphasia* (The Hague: Mouton, 1971), pp. 49-94.

[2] R. Barthes, *Elements of Semiology*, tr. A. Lavers & C. Smith (Boston: Beacon Press, 1967), pp. 86-88.

[3] Cf. J. Lipski, "Paradigmatic overlapping in *Tres tristes tigres*," *Dispositio* 1 (1976).

[4] F. de Saussure, *A Course in General Linguistics*, tr. W. Baskin (New York: Philosophical Library, 1959).

[5] L. Hjelmslev, *Prolegomena to a Theory of Language*, tr. F. J. Whitfield (Madison: University of Wisconsin Press, 1961).

[6] Barthes, *op. cit.*.

[7] Cf. in particular M. Arrivé, "Structuration et destruction du signe dans quelques textes de Jarry" in *Essays de Sémiotique Poétique*, ed. A. J. Greimas (Paris: Larousse, 1972), pp. 64-79; also *Les Langages de Jarry* (Paris: Klincksieck, 1972).

[8] The possibility of bifurcation on either the expression or the content plane is a direct violation of the "First Canon of Symbolism" of C. K. Ogden and I. A. Richards, *The Meaning of Meaning* (New York: Harcourt Brace & Co., 1923), p. 88. The First Canon states that "one symbol stands for one and only one referent." In the realm of literature, however, it is not necessary that such characteristics of the physical universe apply at all times. Moreover, even in the real world, recent work in physics indicates the existence of topological singularities or 'black holes" in the universe, around which the normal laws of physics break down, causality may be reversed, and, in effect, anything can happen. Cf. S. W. Hawking & G. F. R. Ellis, *The Large Scale Structure of Space-Time* (Cambridge: Cambridge University Press, 1973).

VII. Psychoanalysis

IN SOME CASES JUMPS ARE MADE: "AXOLOTL" FROM AN EASTERN POINT OF VIEW

Jerome S. Bernstein

The short story "Axolotl" appears in Cortázar's *Final del juego*.[1] It has been the subject of a good deal of critical commentary and has received a fine analysis from Antonio Pagés Larraya.[2] At the end of his quite comprehensive study, Pagés notes that his analysis suggests only some of the "gama amplísima de interpretaciones" that the story lends itself to. This essay is an attempt to read "Axolotl" from an Eastern point of view. While it is certainly true, as Noé Jitrik points out, that Cortázar's stories deal with recurrent and complementary themes,[3] and that they gain from a critical reading which relates one to another, it may not be amiss to treat "Axolotl" individually. If my conclusions are sound, they will perhaps fit into a larger frame and be applicable to several other stories as well. In any event, my reading may help to round out a future "complete" interpretation of the story, if indeed the polyvalency of its meanings can ever be thoroughly explored.

The events of the story are easily summarized. The narrator stops at the Jardin des Plantes one day and, neglecting the favorite animals he would usually visit, he happens upon the axolotls in their aquarium (p. 161). He returns the next day to see them again, and soon he is able to think of nothing but the axolotls. His visits increase in frequency and duration, until the point where he spends hours in front of the aquarium, contemplating the axolotls. Suddenly, his face pressed to the glass, he feels that he has entered into the axolotl in the aquarium, taken the bodily form of the axolotl whose golden eyes have held his attention for so many hours. He acknowledges that he has become the axolotl—indeed he tells us this fact in the first paragraph of the story—and for a while he is able to watch a man come to observe him through the glass of the aquarium. Soon, the man comes to see him less often and finally does not come any more.

The narrator stresses the involuntary nature of his attraction to the axolotls and mentions that he feels linked to them through some obscure kinship: "desde un primer momento comprendí que estábamos vinculados"

(p. 162). Although he experiences fear as a result of the obsession which daily takes him to the zoo (p. 165), he does not stop his visits. Nor is he concerned with any of the daily routine of his life when he is not an observer of the animals. Contrary to some stories by Cortázar, e.g., "La noche boca arriba," there is no sense of anguish at the fate which befalls the narrator. In the many transformations into animals that occur in Cortázar's fictional world, some would see a sinister or bizarre element.[4] If a sinister element is seen in this story, it is perhaps because we project one onto it.[5] In point of fact, the narrator give no hint after his transformation into an axolotl that he has gone through any sinister ordeal. There is perhaps an element of the marvelous in the story, which is common to the stories in *Bestiario*, and *Historias de cronopios y de famas*.[6]

Since the story is about the transformation of a man into an axolotl, this transformation is properly the object of our attention. The importance of the theme of transformation in Cortázar's work has been studied extensively by critics, particularly in connection with *Rayuela*. As is the case with other pivotal themes in his work, e.g., the *figura*, the mandala, the bridge, transformation permits the fictional character to get across to "the other side," to the sanctuary which is a "zona sagrada" free from the orderly rationality of bourgeois existence.[7] Commenting on the surrealistic elements in his fiction, Graciela de Sola notes "un realismo profundo, mágico" in Cortázar's stories.[8] And of surrealism itself, Cortázar has said:

> es sencillamente una vivencia lo más abierta posible sobre el mundo, y el resultado de esa apertura, de esa porosidad frente a la circunstancia, se traduce en la anulación de las barreras más o menos convencionales que la razón razonante trata de establecer entre lo que considera real (o natural) y lo que califica de fantástico (sobre-natural). . . .[9]

James E. Irby gives a proper emphasis to the matter when he says, "Cortázar whole-heartedly continues, in his own fashion, surrealism's vast dream of undoing the whole rational machinery and routine of Western thought and regaining man's true spiritual abode."[10] Can we doubt the presence of a highly serious and revolutionary intent behind (or alongside) the humor, the antic hellraising and hectic insanity in Cortázar's fiction? Let there be no mistake about the revolutionary and visionary intent in our author's games and game playing; if his fictions can move us off the comfortable dead center of our daily routines, then truly we may become transformed.

Insufficient attention has been paid to the nature of the animal into which the man is transformed. Most readers properly take the animal to be an amphibious reptile, and searches in dictionaries will reveal its scientific name: *Ambystoma*, a genus that has several species most of them native to North America. Among them are the Eastern Tiger Salamander, found as far west as Texas and as far north as central Ontario, and *Ambystoma tigrinum*, the adult form of our own Mexican axolotl.[11] Perhaps the chief peculiarity of the axolotl, as Bridges tells us, is that "after weeks or months in water, the young go to land for their adult life. In most western subspecies, however, the young may fail to transform and breed while in the gilled stage. A larval form that regularly breeds at that stage is the Axolotl, common near Mexico City and sold for food there." The axolotl's failure to transform is worth some further comment. In a discussion of larval forms, Adam Sedgwick remarks:

> development consists of an orderly interaction between the organism and its environment. The action of the environment produces certain morphological changes in the organism. The changes enable the organism to move into a new environment. . . . The essential condition of success in this process [adaptation through change in response to a new environment] is that the organism should always shift into the environment to which its new structure is suited, any failure in this leading to impairment of the organism. In most cases the shifting of the environment is a very gradual process, and the morphological changes in connexion with each step are but slight. In some cases, however, jumps are made, and whenever such jumps occur we get the morphological phenomenon termed metamorphosis.[12]

The arrival of the first axolotls in Paris in 1863 occasioned considerable interest. Within five years the six original specimens had given birth to nine or ten thousand larvae, enough for the Jardin des Plantes to supply zoos and individuals throughout Europe. The animals' ability to propagate in the larval state was the subject of research over the years, and the axolotl's failure to emerge from its watery habitat into land where it would transform into the *A. tigrinum* salamander gave rise to consternation among naturalists. In Gadow's opinion,

> the constant abundance of food, stable amount of water, innumerable hiding places in the mud, under the banks, amongst the reeds and roots of the floating islands which are scattered all over [Chalco and Xochimilco Lakes], —all these points are inducements or attractions so great that the creatures remain in their paradise and consequently retain all those larval features which are not directly connected with sexual maturity. There is nothing whatever to prevent them from leaving these lakes, but there is also nothing to induce them to do so. . . . Nevertheless, in the axolotl the latent tendency can still be revived. . . .[13]

To summarize the characteristics of this animal which I take to be significant for our purposes here: it develops into the larval state in which, lacking any spur to transform into the mature adult salamander, it may remain for years and even reproduce itself. Given the epistemological framework of our biology, an inducement to emerge from the water onto land is to be sought strictly in changes in the marine habitat. For all we know, with the increasing contamination of the natural habitats of these animals, more and more of them are or will be emerging, and transforming into the mature form. In Cortázar's story, however, the epistemological constraints of biology need not be faithfully adhered to. In "Axolotl," it seems to me, there are inducements other than biological ones for the axolotl to emerge and change places with the man. Are we to assume that in a perfectly symmetrical transformation such as the one in our story there is only a one-sided motivation? If the man is moved to transform, for reasons I shall presently touch on, it seems fitting for us to understand that the axolotl is also moved.[14] There is one concrete detail of a biological or environmental sort that provides a clue: mention is made of the crowding of the axolotls in their aquarium. Perhaps the spur toward transformation lies in that. The crowding serves at least the function of discouraging the axolotls from moving about in the aquarium, and this helps explain why they are mostly immobile (p. 163). Their lack of movement is an important factor in providing for the transformation, because, if the axolotl is still, the narrator can fixedly observe the animal with which he will change places.

However, if we admit that motives other than those stemming from biology may operate in the story, then I would suggest that the inducement for the axolotl to change places with the man, for the larva to emerge from the water and assume a mature, adult form—albeit, not the form of an adult salamander—lies precisely in its having been chosen by the man for that lengthy, meditative encounter that unites them. It is enough that another being has stood, hours on end concentrating deeply on him and communicating his longing (for the long-lost kinship), for the axolotl to recognize its opportunity and "make the jump" to another developmental state. I take it that the axolotl has transformed into a "higher" or more advanced stage, since, at the end of the story, the axolotl which was a man tells us: "Y en esta soledad final, a la que él [the man who was an axolotl] ya no vuelve, me consuela pensar que acaso va a escribir sobre nosotros creyendo imaginar un cuento va a escribir todo esto sobre los axolotl" (p. 168). Becoming a man is an evolutionary advancement for the axolotl; it has made an enormous jump. In his new form, he will perhaps write a story, believing that he has imagined the event. Evolutionary theory teaches that life emerged from the waters; the axolotl-become-man, Cortázar says, will perhaps retain an unconscious memory trace of his watery origin. We note here the suggestion of the sort of infinite regress that Cortázar exploits in other stories, e.g., "Continuidad de los parques." As a matter of fact, the biological memory trace of its adult salamander form that Gadow tells us the axolotl still retains fits the events of the story also. The man who walks away at the end of the story retains the ancestral memory of the larval stage from which he emerged. In perhaps writing a story about it—the story we have in hand—he imagines that it is only a story, i.e., that he himself was never an axolotl. Biological memory traces and imagination fuse in a Jungian gestalt: an endless cycle of changes. The fact that the axolotl can tell us that if the man does write a story about axolotls it will be while believing something untrue—that he has imagined, instead of lived through, the experiences he writes about—indicates that the axolotl at the end of the story has a superior understanding of what has happened than does the man. In this sense, the man who becomes the axolotl also advances, although not now biologically; he advances spiritually or intellectually, because, in knowing the "truth" about what the other will imagine he has invented, his is the superior wisdom.

I should note here an aspect of this transformation that strikes a distinct note of modernity, as against the surrealistic elements which tend to bring us back to an avant garde tradition whose high point was in the 1920s and '30s: the transformation in this story is an example of inter-species communication, in so far as the two beings' biological forms are concerned. At a point in our history when we are beginning to learn how to communicate with chimpanzees by teaching them a form of English through Skinnerian conditioning, and when we are making serious attempts to learn the language of the dolphins and whales, Cortázar's story looks forward to even more refined forms of communication between the species.

A sustained note in Cortázar's work is an antipathy to Western rationalism which is rooted in more than a surrealist's attitude or a romantic's delight in kicking the middle class in the pants. "Toda la obra de Cortázar es un esfuerzo por trascender ese *homo sapiens*, o, como se nos dice a lo largo de *Rayuela*, por 'ir más allá del criterio griego de verdad y error'. . .más allá de 'la gran máscara podrida de occidente'. . . ."[15] Cortázar has written,

> Cuanto más violenta fuera la contradicción interna, más eficacia podría dar a una, digamos, técnica al modo Zen. A cambio del bastonazo en la cabeza, una novela absolutamente antinovelesca, con el escándalo y choque consiguiente, y quizá con una apertura para los más avisados.[16]

With these indications in mind, we can perhaps turn to a perspective on "Axolotl" that comes from the East, specifically from Buddhism.

The principal end of Buddhism as a religion is the enlightenment of every person. Zen and other schools of Buddhist thought place great emphasis on meditation. Meditation can be of various kinds, sitting meditation (*zazen*), yoga *asanas*, breath control, chanting, long-distance running, archery, and the baking of bread, to take some few examples. The object of meditation in whatever form it is practiced is to still the drunken monkey of the mind, to focus the awareness on a single point, the present ("El tiempo se siente menos si nos estamos quietos" [p. 163], to achieve one-pointedness of mind. In general, it is when the awareness is riveted in the present moment that the individual is receptive and perceptive enough to "get through it to the other side" of the phenomenal universe he inhabits, to come into direct awareness and understanding of the actual nature of existence. The actual nature of existence underlying all the ephemeral cultural structures and learned behaviors of mankind is the divinity in each form of life. A glimpse of this fundamental reality, a breakthrough that carries the person beyond *maya*, the deceptive, illusory phenomena that Western thought takes to be "Reality," is a *satori* experience. *Satori* is not enlightenment; it is an illumination, an epiphany, an insight, in which one suddenly gets an inkling of the true nature of being beyond and beneath *maya*.

Cortázar's fiction is designed to do at least two separate things: to relate a character's experiences of breaking through some Western illusions, and to permit the reader, using the fiction as a mediation aid, to make his own breakthrough. For Oliveira, in *Rayuela*, the "glimpse of the Forbidden Kingdom" is *satori*; the "kibbutz of desire" is *satori*. For the reader of the novel, its hypothetically infinite number of different readings, stemming from the intricacies of the "Tablero de Dirección" for reading the novel, provides one who is seeking it a mandala, a device for fixing the mind meditatively so that enlightenment can enter. I don't suppose that many

Western readers of the novel have used it for this purpose; I myself have not. But its potential for such use is clear.

For additional light on Buddhism's contribution to our thinking on these matters, let us turn to an enlightened master, Rajneesh:

> At the center you are God; at the periphery you are the world—and the world is ugly. . . . You have to be very courageous to pass through the periphery to be a witness. And if you can enter this periphery, this society, this history, then at the center you are God himself. . . . But to reach that, you have to pass through all the ugliness. The whole history of man has to be crossed. . . . You have to move through fire, and only in that fire will your ego drop. Looking at the whole ugliness of it, it drops automatically. . . . You have passed through history, and you have come to a point, here, to this moment you have come. . . . Because a meditation means returning to the source. You have come up to this point in time; you will have to go back, you will have to regress, you will have to reach the original point from where the journey started.[17]

In "Axolotl," the narrator stands and stares; he is a witness, a man doing Vipasana meditation. Perhaps he is not aware that this is what he is doing, it matters very little. He is called to witness himself witnessing the axolotls.[18] Their immobility facilitates the concentration of his awareness; everything is excluded from his awareness except the golden eye of the larva. True, there is an occasional interruption from the aquarium guard. . . but the narrator is only momentarily distracted.

If the axolotls are immobile witnesses of his witnessing (the lidless, golden eye), then on the level of awareness there is in actuality no distraction between them. They are both performing the same "actions" in the story, playing the same meditative role. Only the glass of the aquarium separates them in physical space; nothing separates them in spiritual terms. They are both parts of the same being, what we could call a witnessing presence, a unified being with one-pointedness of mind and total awareness. At the moment when the narrator reaches this knowledge, he has a *satori* experience, has taken a step on the path of enlightenment. The transition is painless, although preceded by some fear; Rajneesh says one must be very courageous. The narrator confronts his fear, and continues visiting the aquarium. Only literal-minded readers are likely to wonder what circumstances of his practical life outside the zoo permit him to disregard the ordinary claims on his attention, for example, the need to earn a living.

Confronting the fear he is able to understand that it comes from within himself and not from the situation. Dropping the fear then he is able to recognize—i.e., to know again—the beast before him, to acknowledge his kinship with that animal. As this takes place, he insensibly passes into the aquarium and into the shape of an axolotl. He passes insensibly in that no attention is paid at all to the experience of passing through the glass.[19] In more traditional readings of the story this fact is dealt with as an aspect of magical realism. In my reading, there is no trauma associated with passing through the glass because the glass is part of the phenomenal world (*maya*), thus it is an illusion. He takes on the larva's being and impassively watches the "man," now inhabited by the axolotl, come less and less to the aquarium;

he watches the "man" fade away. The metaphor is saying: only through the fearsome transition to another state of awareness—through meditation, through witnessing—can a man drop his ego, his socially conditioned self, and reach a higher level of being.[20]

One of the puzzles in this interpretation is that in his transformation to what Westerners would ordinarily consider a "lower form of life," the narrator reaches a "higher form of existence." All our socially conditioned antipathies to reptiles—the axolotl is called a "lagarto" (p. 162)—are at work in our feelings of revulsion at the transformation. None of us, I think, would voluntarily undergo the transformation in question, which is why the narrator's attraction to the axolotls is described as a matter of fate or inevitability. He does not "will" it; it simply happens to him, through him.[21] The narrator does seem to wish to "save" the axolotls (165). He projects onto them a plea for salvation; that is, he wants someone to save *him* from imprisonment in his body, from total silence and "reflexión desesperada," i.e., from the drunken monkey of his mind. He answers the extrojected plea with "palabras de consuelo," and undergoes the transformation which "saves him."[22]

Part of the impact of Cortázar's story stems from its reversal of the ranking of the man and the axolotl. We believe that reptiles are an "inferior" form of life, and our belief rests on certain assumptions that are built into our way of interacting with the phenomenal universe. Our culture stresses *homo sapiens'* use of reason, language, and his opposable thumb, and so far as is known, the salamander enjoys the use of none of these things. In our present arrangements, we "rule the roost," and use our superiority to decide upon the hierarchy in the animal kingdom which seems most appropriate to us. But if my assumption is correct, if the man advances or ascends to a higher state of awareness by his transformation into a "lower" form of life, the author is perhaps suggesting that we can profitably revise our ranking of life forms. This brings us to another element of the story worth noting: its ecological understanding.

Since Ecology has become fashionable there is a temptation to dismiss it as to popular or too current to be of value in an understanding of art and the forms of high culture. Yet, from Aesop down through the medieval bestiaries, to the modern concerns with the preservation of endangered species (among whom some would wish to place man), the relationship of our species to the rest of the biological forms that share our planet has been a subject of keen interest. In "Axolotl," the lowly salamander (or whatever he is) has been exalted to a position of preeminence over the man. And the man in the story advances to a higher level of awareness, surrendering his ego and all the Cartesian coordinates of his everyday life. There is in this exaltation, none of the note of doom which can be seen in Capek's *War with the Newts*, and none of the personal, psychological frenzy of Kafka's "Metamorphosis." Instead, there is the simple statement, uttered in reflective, meditative calm, that the salamander too participates in a being of which man is also a part. That is, we are brothers under the skin.

In sum, "Axolotl" is of a piece with the bulk of Cortázar's fiction in its use of the double, the estrangement of man from his everyday life, and its surrealistic insistence on the "higher truth" lying beyond the phenomenal universe. To the readings critics have previously given this story, I have suggested another: that in the light of Buddhism, the story describes the transformations of two beings who are part of the same entity. Each of them advances in their respective evolutionary paths: each makes a jump that brings enlightenment nearer.

UNIVERSITY OF CALIFORNIA, LOS ANGELES

Notes

[1](Buenos Aires: Editorial Sudamerica, 1964), pp. 161-68. I will be quoting from the 3rd edition, 1965; numbers in parenthesis in my text refer to this edition.

[2]"Perspectivas de 'Axolotl'', cuento de Julio Cortázar," *Nueva Narrativa Hispano-americana*, 2, 2 (1972), pp. 7-24.

[3]"Notas sobre la 'zona sagrada' y el mundo de los 'otros' en *Bestiario* de Julio Cortázar," in *La vuelta a Cortázar en nueve ensayos*, eds. Sara Vinocur de Tirri and Néstor Tirri (Buenos Aires: Carlos Pérez, 1968), pp. 13-20.

[4]Don E. Wood, "Surrealistic Transformation of Reality in Cortázar's 'Bestiario'," *Romance Notes*, 13 (1971), pp. 239 and 242.

[5]Cf. Lanin A. Gyurko, "Hallucination and Nightmare in Two Stories by Cortázar," *MLN*, 67 (1972), esp. pp. 561-62. Gyurko sees an anguished protagonist. In "La fantasía como emancipación y como tiranía en tres cuentos de Cortázar," *RI*, 40 (1975), pp. 230 and 231, the same critic tells us that the protagonist leaves "la parte negativa de su yo, sus frustraciones y sus ansiedades, atrapada dentro del cuerpo de uno de los animales," and that he ends up in "una esquizofrenia permanente."

[6]Manuel Durán, "Julio Cortázar y su pequeño mundo de cronopios y de famas," in *La vuelta a Cortázar en nueve ensayos*, p. 32, remarks that "más que lo maravilloso metafísico le interesa [a Cortázar] lo maravilloso biológico. . . ." A reaction to the axolotl that attempts to deal with its reptilian nature through humor can be seen in the following poem, from *The Mad Frontier*, ed. Mad Magazine (New York: 1962). I am indebted to Prof. Stanley Robe for bringing it to my attention.

I Wandered Lonely as a Clod

by William Wordswords

I wandered lonely as a clod
Just picking up old rags and bottles,
When onward on my way I plod,
I saw a host of axolotls;
Beside the lake, beneath the trees,
A sight to make a man's blood freeze.

Some had handles, some were plain;
They came in blue, red, pink, and green.
A few were orange in the main;

The damedest sight I've ever seen.
The females gave a sprightly glance;
The male ones all wore knee-length pants.
Now oft, when on the couch I lie,
The doctor asks me what I see.
They flash upon my inward eye
And make me laugh in fiendish glee.
I find my solace then in bottles,
And I forget them axolotls.

[7]Cf. Rubén Benítez, "Cortázar: 'que supo abrir la puerta para ir a jugar'," *RI*, 39 (1973), p. 490. See also Cortázar's "Del cuento breve y sus alrededores," *Ultimo round* (México: 1969), pp. 35-45.

[8]*Julio Cortázar y el hombre nuevo* (Buenos Aires: 1968), p. 72.

[9]Mario Vargas Llosa, "Preguntas a Julio Cortázar," *Expreso* [Lima], 7 February 1965, *apud*, Juan Loveluck, "Aproximación a *Rayuela, RI*, 34 (1968), pp. 89-90.

[10]"Cortázar's *Hopscotch* and Other Games," *Novel*, 1 (1967), p. 64.

[11]William Bridges, *The Bronx Zoo Book of Wild Animals: A Guide to Mammals, Birds, Reptiles and Amphibians of the World* (New York: 1968), p. 248. See also the entry in the *Encyclopedia Britannica*, 11th edition, 1910-11, s.v. 'axolotl.'

[12]*Ibid.*, s.v. 'Larval Forms.'

[13]H. Gadow, "The Mexican Axolotl," *Nature*, 67 (1903), p. 331; Antonio Planells, "Comunicación por metamorfosis: 'Axolotl', de Julio Cortázar," *Anales de Literatura Hispanoamericana*, 5 [1976], pp. 291-301, also refers to the biology of the axolotl.

[14]Pagés, *art. cit.*, p. 12, remarks: "Hay una búsqueda cognoscitiva tanto desde el narrador al axolotl como a la inversa y esa inquisición escapa al orden racional." This reciprocity of motive is seen also in the technique of the story; Pagés, p. 13, notes the repeated shifts in the point of view in the story. Such shifts betoken a shared narrative perspective, hence, a shared interest in the unfolding events of the story.

[15]Jaime Alazraki, "Homo Sapiens vs. Homo Ludens en tres cuentos de Cortázar," *RI*, 39 (1973), p. 617.

[16]*Rayuela* (Buenos Aires: 2a ed., 1965), p. 490, *apud* Loveluck, *art. cit.*, p. 83. Although James E. Irby correctly notes Oliveira's desire for "a new cosmology made of given elements, an illumination, a kind of *satori*," he labels Cortázar's interest in non-Western philosophies "a modish pose," *art cit.*, pp. 66-67.

[17]Bhagwan Shree Rajneesh, *The Hidden Harmony: Discourses on the Fragments of Heraclitus*, Swami Amrit Pathik and Ma Yoga Anurag, eds. (Poona: Rajneesh Foundation, 1976), pp. 74-79 *passim.*

[18]Cf. Marta Morello-Frosch, "El personaje y su doble en las ficciones de Cortázar," *RI*, 34 (1968), p. 330: "el yo se observa a sí mismo, . . .se sitúa, en suma, fuera de la materia literaria en la enajenación más total; no obstante, retiene su facultad observante y narrativa. . . ." The protagonist is led by his curiosity. Cf. Durán, *art. cit.*, p. 42: "Lo extraño, misterioso y desconocido puede ofrecer dos vertientes: si nos creemos amenazados nos inspira terror; si nos creemos libres de toda amenaza, nos inspira curiosidad. . . ."

[19]Pagés, *art. cit.*, p. 13, notes that changing places "no manifiesta ruptura alguna en la identidad del yo." If there is no break in the identity of the two beings after their transformation it means there was none before they transform. This is their kinship.

[20]Benítez, *art. cit.*, p. 494: "Porque el absurdo no está en esos estrañamientos sino en la cotidianeidad que dejamos de lado; el absurdo es la costumbre, la falta de excepciones en el orden."

[21]Other ways of reading this story may point out that although his visits to the aquarium are not willed, the narrator is indeed unconsciously motivated to visit it. A psychoanalytic reading could even suggest a desire in the narrator to return to the womb, for the man "returns to the water," to the embryonic uterine existence through which he had passed before his birth. He may, as an axolotl, await another transformation when another being devotes to him the meditative attention he has lavished on the axolotl.

[22]Cf. Julio Matas, "El contexto moral en algunos cuentos de Julio Cortázar," *RI*, 39 (1973), p. 603.

A PACK OF CARDS

Rosette C. Lamont

In the course of his book-length *Entretiens* with Alain Schifres, when queried by the interviewer about the writer who might have influenced him during his formative years, Arrabal replied without hesitation, "Un auteur qu'à l'époque je ne pensais pas être un écrivain véritable: Lewis Carroll. Il me rappelait ces pièces que j'inventais tout enfant pour un théâtre en carton, avec des figurines découpées."[1] As a child of five or six, Arrabal had built this theatre for his mother. In his autobiographical novel, *Baal Babylone*, the dramatist describes his creation, and suggests its deeper meaning as an instrument of incantation and possession:

> L'intérieur était éclairé par deux bougies dissimulées. Au début, je mettais beaucoup de décors peints dans chaque pièce. Comme après je n'en avais qu'un—juste ébauché—tu n'avais plus à attendre que je les change. Elisa n'aimait pas lire le texte et je me chargeais de tous les rôles en contrefaisant ma voix....Chaque personnage était placé sur une baguette en bois et alors je pouvais les mouvoir du dehors....Ni Elisa, ni tante Clara, ni grande-père, ni grande-mère n'assistaient aux représentations. Il n'y avait que toi qui y assistais. A présent, comme tu n'es pas ici, j'en fais pour moi tout seul.[2]

When the family moved from Villa Ramiro to Madrid, the seven-year-old boy carried his "treasure" by hand onto the'train. In Madrid, he built another model, made of wood, one his mother liked even more. In 1949, Arrabal discovered a trunk full of letters and documents relative to his father's arrest and imprisonment. Since no one had mentioned these events, suppressing the memory of the dead father, the adolescent boy imagined that this kind, devoted mother was in reality a monster, a woman who had denounced her own husband. Passionate love for her changed to hate tinged with despair, itself yielding to an ambivalent love/hate. From that time on, images of betrayal, of prison torture, and executions began to fill the neo-baroque theatre of the dramatist. Yet, the violence of the stage imagery is tinged with childlike innocence and couched in the babble of child's talk. Arrabal's sources are *Alice in Wonderland*, Kafka, Dostoyevsky—he discovered the latter two at the Madrid *Ateneo*—and the films of Chaplin and the Marx brothers which he would watch all day, cutting his classes at the Military Academy.

In her perceptive article, "From Tweedledum and Tweedledee to Zapo and Zepo," Irmgard Zeyos Anderson uncovers the basic *Alice* myth underlying *Pique-nique en campagne* (1952; Engl. tr., *Picnic on the Battlefield*, 1967). In their happy ignorance of military operations, their games of dressing-up, their family merry-making, and above all their boyish innocence, the soldiers Zapo and Zepo are a reincarnation of Lewis Carroll's enantiomorphs. Indeed, since we are speaking of mirror images, one could say that Arrabal's message mirrors Alice's stand, namely that "one should be ashamed of fighting."[3] As Alain Schifres has detected and brought out, the same influence prevades *Le Tricycle* (1953; Engl. tr., *The Tricycle*, 1967), and many other plays, such as *Fando et Lis*, and *Le Couronnement*. "Tout vient de Lewis Carroll,"[4] admits Arrabal.

In no play, however, is the texture of *Alice in Wonderland* more apparent, nor more intimately woven into the vocabulary and structure of the play, than in the 1975 *Jeunes barbares d'aujourd'hui (Today's Young Barbarians)*. In fact, whole scenes have been literaly lifted and transcribed by the dramatist, as though he wished to lay claim to the very substance of Carroll's world, making it his own flesh and blood. *Jeunes barbares* is an *auto sacramental* in the modern mode. In it, bicycle racing has become the metaphor for the cruel absurdity of worldly ambitions, and of those ready to exploit them. This Eucharist play presents a legend at once secular and sacred in which a unification occurs between the mock-heroes who are the protagonists and the innocent characters from the universe of fables and romance which they re-enact. Thus, Arrabal's *auto* constitutes a confession culminating in a communion between the eternal child in the dramatist and the childlike mathematician-logician who photographed pre-pubescent girls and spun tales for their private delectations, fables which became classics of the literature of the fantastic.

In *Jeunes barbares*, we find ourselves once more in "a metaphysically sealed world."[5] If this is true of the play Louise Fiber Luce singles out for discussion, *Cimetière des voitures* (1957; Engl. tr., *The Car Cemetery*, 1962), it can most certainly be applied to *Le Labyrinthe* (1956; Engl. tr., *The Labyrinth*, 1967), *Les Deux Bourreaux* (1956; Engl. tr., *The Two Executioners*, 1962), or even to Arrabal's masterpiece, *L'Architecte et l'Empereur d'Assyrie* (1966; Engl. tr., *The Architect and the Emperor of Assyria*, 1969) which takes place on a desert island.

The dramatist's "organic theatre"[6] evolves within the confines of the impenetrable universe of childish sado-masochistic games and rituals, obsessive in their recurrent matricidal wish-fulfillment patterns, a reflection of Arrabal's "inverted Oedipal relationship"[7] with the pious, conservative woman who was never able to forgive herself for having loved an army officer of Republican sympathies. Thus, the enclosed space of Arrabal's dramatic enactments, call it nightmare, wonderland, or "a waste land of blighted. . .psyches,"[8] is the concretization of the cloistered atmosphere of the Terans household—the home of his maternal grandparents—as well as that of the parochial school at Getafe where the priests inflicted subtly cruel punishments on their young charges. Nor did the feeling of confinement leave young Arrabal in Madrid where his classmates at the Military Academy mocked him for his dwarf-like body topped by a disquietingly large head. Later still, in France, he was forced to enter the sanatorium of Bouffémont where he was treated for a severe case of tuberculosis. It was at Bouffémont, alone, fearing death, that the young man must have re-lived in his mind the incarceration of his father at the fortress of El Hacho and the political prisoner's transfer to a psychiatric ward from which he escaped in January of 1942, barefoot, and wearing only his pajamas. The father's mysterious disappearance still haunts the imagination of the dramatist; it is the source of many of his oneiric plays, some of which were composed at the sanatorium.

Just as *Alice in Wonderland* mirrors a crisis, a *rite de passage* from childhood into adolescence, so do the plays which are linked to Arrabal's private dream world. They are naive in expression, and yet strangely sophisticated, rejecting as they do the easy dichotomies of Good and Evil. The dramatist credits the philosopher Jankélévitch with opening his eyes to a new way of judging human action. In 1967, Arrabal heard the author of a famous book on irony give a course on sincerity at the Sorbonne. Jankélévitch stated that, to his way of thinking, fidelity, truth, sincerity were flat, non-vital notions, and that the child becomes interesting from the moment he tells his first lie. Arrabal makes a connection between this notion and the surrealist trial of Barrès.

> Il y eut, à un certain moment, un échange de répliques entre Breton et Tzara, où Breton se plaçait sur le terrain de la morale: "Barrès est un salaud, etc..." et Tzara sur le plan de l'humain: "petits salauds, grands salauds, nous sommes tous des salauds."[9]

This lecture brought Arrabal back to the world of his own childhood which is that of his works. There nothing can be called clear cut. His characters attempt to be sincere, good, faithful, but they do this with a kind of mechanical, inhuman precision, as though following dictates that are to them meaningless, drained of significance. They experience the temptation of goodness, but when they put it into practice it turns into *ennui*. It was Jankélévitch who reinforced in the writer "certaine méfiance. . .pour les 'valeurs nobles.' "[10]

Even before the 1967 lectures, Arrabal was developing a cosmic vision of life forces. In 1962, he met the Mexican director, Jodorowsky, and with the assistance of Topor and Sternberg, the group which had assembled at the Café de la Paix, decided to found the Panic theatre. The term "Pan" suggests an all-embracing, grotesquely beautiful, comic and terrifying form. Theatre, when it is poetic, oneiric—Arrabal equates poetic dramaturgy with dream images—must issue from excess. A spectacle is a race between the writer and the director, but it is one they must win together. In trying to define for Schifres the difference between the artist and the average man, Arrabal explains that the latter works on a finished product, "l'achevé," while the artist "jette un regard sur ce qui va être fait."[11] Thus, it is up to the artist to reveal the future, and this can be achieved only by means of what appears as an absurd, extravagant, panic creation.

Jeunes barbares d'aujourd'hui has been called "the class struggle seen through its reflection in the fun house mirror of Alice in Wonderland."[12] It is also possible to see it as an *opera mundi*, not unlike the phantasmagoric visions of *Don Quixote* and the comic nightmares of *Alice*. Lewis Carroll once said that the fairy tale is the love gift, and Mircea Eliade calls it an initiatory scenario. As Bruno Bettelheim explains in his study, *The Uses of Enchantment*, fairy tales address us in symbolic language, and so "their deepest meaning will be different for each person, and different for the same person at different moments of his life."[13] It is this fertile ambiguity Arrabal wishes to recreate.

In this short play, we meet three characters vaguely reminiscent of the Marx Brothers: Dumpty, without the Humpty, who has had a great fall and is blind as the result of it; Chester, a mystical epileptic; and the sadistic Tenniel whose name reminds us of the magnificently cruel illustrations of Carroll's book. Chester and Tenniel are champion bicycle racers in the employ of a team leader as invisible in the play as the *deus absconditus* of the Jansenists. Snarck—his name, like that of most of the characters from the play comes right out of the Lewis Carroll *oeuvre*—is a monstrous slave driver, a blood-thirsty Dracula. Although Arrabal's Snarck has issued from "The Hunting of the Snark," the comparison with Dracula lends great power and life to this cruel divinity. For Arrabal, Dracula is the true anti-hero. The dramatist explains:

> On tente de faire oublier la mort par des moyens publicitaires, mais il reste que la représentation la plus atroce de notre civilisation est Dracula. Dracula, voilà un héros pour moi: l'homme qui ne meurt pas, qui dort le jour et vit la nuit, l'homme qui procure la vie éternelle. Si Dracula existait, je voudrais qu'il me morde tout de suite. On a fait de Dracula un monstre atroce. Tout ce qui empêche la mort de venir est représenté dans notre civilisation sous les traits les plus horribles. Frankenstein aussi est un être magnifique, mais on s'est arrangé pour le haïr. Notre société cherche à démontrer en toute occasion qu'il faut donner sa vie, qu'il existe des valeurs supérieures à soi et plus fortes que la mort. C'est alors que la survie peut devenir une grande morale, la plus destructrice de toutes.[14]

Man becomes dangerous to society in direct proportion to his determination to survive. "Je n'ai aucune sympathie pour le 'héros' traditionnel," Arrabal declares, "pour moi, le héros c'est le déserteur, celui qui lutte pour se sauver."[15] Snarck is deeply subversive because he represents man's hidden instinct for survival. The bicycle race symbolizes our ambitions and struggles.

In order to groom his team, Snarck makes use of his servant, the blind Dumpty. The latter is the *masseur* whose function it is to put Chester and Tenniel "together again," by relaxing their muscles between races, and to prepare them for the ultimate test, "the queen race."[16] We recognize here Alice's frantic running, hand in hand with the Red Queen. There also the wind is whistling around the racers as they go faster and faster. In "The Garden of Live Flowers," however, "it takes all the running you can do, to keep in the same place," and "you must run twice as fast as that"[17] if you want to get somewhere. Whether life is a bicycle track or an enormous chessboard, it is equally difficult to win any victories or simply to retain tiny gains. Dumpty must make sure that "all the king's men" will continue running. Dumpty's state of blindness suggests the utter darkness at the center of the cosmic egg. It is from this *nigredo*, however, the condition of undifferentiated matter, that the process of alchemical transmutation begins. As Joseph Campbell points out in *Creative Mythology*, Orphic bowls are in the shape of the cosmic egg. Dumpty's massage parallels some of the initiatory rites of the Orphic-Dionysian cult. Tenniel and Chester are initiates, which would account for the question Chester asks at the beginning of the play: "Où se trouve la lumière?"[18] Dumpty, the Tiresias or shaman of the play, enlightens the champions by ministering to their naked bodies and their minds. The latter process is achieved by means of strong doses of amphetamines which have a double effect on Chester: physically, they turn his urine blue—this phenomenon suggests the metamorphosis within the *vas Hermeticum* of the *urina puerorum*, or *aqua permanens* which, heated from below, undergoes vaporization so as to enter the adjoining flask containing the winged dragon biting its own tail, *Hermafroditum*—[19]; spiritually, the drugs alter his consciousness, in a manner rather similar to the effect the huge mushroom has upon Alice's perception. Like Alice, Chester finds himself in a universe of blue, hookah-smoking caterpillars where he can see "le chat à chevelure d'argent (a relative no doubt of the Cheshire cat), la girafe aux éternuements mélancoliques."[20] In this magic, womb-like world, Chester, having regressed to an unborn state, is able to escape from the materialistic schemes of Snarck. Addressing Tenniel, who has assumed for a time the role of the Great Mother, Chester begs, "Mets-moi dans ton ventre, Maman, et garde-moi toujours enfermé comme si j'étais ton veau de fumier."[21] This form of escape is illusory for the race must continue and be won. Tenniel, the illustrator of their lives, describes the existence of the bicycle racer with mounting bitterness:

> Tous les jours à suer, à courir, épuisés, sans tam-tams ni arc-en-ciel...et pourquoi? Quelles sont nos vies? Nous avons couru pour la gloire, puis pour l'argent et maintenant pour ne plus nous arrêter comme des automates morts. C'est comme si la vie était une fête dont nous serions absents, comme si les horloges, les roues, les feux d'artifice s'emplissaient de poussière et d'absence en nous contemplant. Comme si c'était un théâtre où nous ne jouerions jamais le moindre rôle.[22]

Jeunes barbares d'aujourd'hui starts within the theatre space, with the actors making their way to the stage through the aisles. Once they reach the curtain and pull it open, hoping to see some of the denizens of Wonderland, "la reine de coeur peignant les roses en rouge et les huîtres espiègles invitant à dîner le morse gourmand"[23] or perhaps "des dragons, des tortues célèbres et un jardin de fleurs vivantes,"[24] the enactment becomes a play within the play.

This inner play, conceived in the best neo-baroque tradition, is a side show, an act in Kafka's circus, the Grand Circus of Oklahoma which provides *Amerika* with a grotesquely tragic ending. It is clear that for Arrabal *Jeunes barbares* is a play about living in literature. He developed this ability early in life, spending days in the *Centro Ateneo*, a Catholic library in Madrid. It was there that he discovered Kafka, Dostoyevsky, Camus, Faulkner, Steinbeck. He says, "En deux ou trois ans, j'ai lu constamment, à un rythme accéléré."[25] The bout at the Centro taught Arrabal how to inhabit the space of literature, how to remain himself and yet become the characters he was meeting in books. He brought some of this knowledge to the surrealist games he played with Breton. One of them was called *L'un dans l'autre*, and he describes it in the following manner:

> Un joueur sortait et décidait de jouer un personnage: par exemple un poupée. Quand il rentrait on cherchait à deviner ce personnage. Par exemple on lui disait "tu es un perroquet". Alors il devait faire le perroquet et, en même temps, suggérer qu'il était un poupée.[26]

Game playing allows the artist to unveil the mechanism of creation; it is an element of exploration. Through games and rituals, the writer casts a light upon the dark inner regions of the psyche, his own, and the collective psyche of his audience. Arrabal's *dramatis personae* are constantly assuming roles or exchanging personalities. In *L'Architecte et l'Empereur d'Assyrie*, the Architect takes turns impersonating the Emperor's wife, mother, brother, and numerous torturers. The play has been called "a philosophical *pas de deux*." In *Jeunes barbares* it is the cruel Tenniel who is willing to play the mother role for Chester, and this very fact reveals Arrabal's ambivalence with regard to his own mother. We need not go so far as to espouse Dr. Phyllis Greenacre's view of Alice as a symbol of Lewis Carroll's mother[27] to see that for both the author of *Alice in Wonderland* and the dramatist who used this book as the skeleton of his *Jeunes barbares*, the unresolved attachment to the mother lies at the bottom of the nightmarish atmosphere of their tragi-comic creations.

There are two women in *Jeunes barbares:* the beautiful singer Ecila, a Jocasta figure, and the erotic adolescent Kitty, half-Alice, and half Alice's many cats. It is Kitty who will participate in a wild version of "The Mad Tea Party." As the audience enters the theatre, the first thing they see and hear is Ecila, a kind of *anima* figure. Like the blind Salome of C. G. Jung's archetypal fantasies, Ecila is the soul in the primitive sense. She sings as the spectators file in, and her voice is still heard when the lights go out. Ecila is the mouthpiece of the unconscious, and one might even venture the hypothesis that it is she who emits the spectacle which issues from the mythopoeic matrix. As she lingers in the room where Tenniel and Chester are trying to sleep, a room which looks more like a hospital room than a hotel, with its rolling beds and stretchers, she appears as some Great Mother/Nurse figure floating over the bodies of wounded, suffering men. Her mysterious, ancient cantilena speaks of the reconciliation of opposites:

Voulez-vous que vérité vous dise?
Il n'est jouer qu'en maladie
lettre vraie qu'en tragédie
lâche homme que chevaleureux
horrible son que mélodie
ni bien conseillé qu'amoureux.[28]

Kitty is pure Eros, the concretization of Tenniel's erotic delirium arising
from being massaged by Dumpty. Tenniel's extraordinary monologue
evokes Tantric temples, a cosmic round of love-making, or the love feasts
of deviant early Christian sects. Although it begins in the most banal fashion,
with Tenniel imagining that he picks up a stranger in a movie theatre, it
gathers speed, rises, unfolds, imitating in its stylistic motion the great wave of
universal desire, *Kama*, the power central to existence:

> Je me place sur une roue qui tourne et je suis comme écartelé et l'une après
> l'autre, elle viennent se poser sur ma bite roide et se tiennent immobiles tandis
> que je tourne, ayant pour axe mon sexe plongé en elles, l'une après l'autre des
> centaines, des milliers de femmes, des millions d'archanges.[29]

If Tenniel practices a form of Tantrism, a meditational system that aims at
the experience of the highest bliss in physical and spiritual meditations, one
could say that Ecila and Kitty taken together are inciters of rapture and
Dumpty, the High Priest of this form of cosmic worship.

Eros leads to Thanatos. At the end of this modern *auto sacramental*
the spinning wheel of cosmic time turns into the whirling sails of windmills
seen by Chester and Tenniel as they race their bicycles along the edge of a
precipice. They dream of re-enacting the greatest Spanish literary myth, the
mock-heroic charge of Don Quixote and Sancho Panza. Earlier, Tenniel
had proclaimed, "Nous serons les jeunes barbares d'aujourd'hui!"[30] This
statement echoes the famous exhortation of the radical Spanish leader
Emilio Lerroux. It is a stirring call to freedom and revolution. Yet, like
Lerroux's visions, Tenniel's dreams of glory will be dashed upon the rocks.
Paralleling Dumpty's fall, Chester's tumble in the course of the "queen race"
deprives him of his sight. As Tenniel picks up his companion, he speaks to
him once more in the voice of the Mother, the voice of the dead Jocasta,
"Mon enfant tu es couvert de sang."[31] Is Chester Oedipus? Is this a symbol of
Spain? Arrabal's chastely confessional play raises questions but will not
provide us with an answer.

Despite the somber coloring of *Jeunes barbares*, the play ends on a note
of faith as the five characters huddle together for warmth and comfort,
each carrying a taper of eternal light. Chester exclaims in a profoundly joyful
voice, "Oh! quel bonheur, comme ça je vois avec les yeux de la foi et je peux
ensemencer d'imaginaire tous les mots que j'entends."[33] Having transcended
human longing and human pain, the postulants are ready for their final
initiation. The ceremony has come full circle since the light they were
seeking at the beginning can now be found in their innermost being.

At the absurd trial with which Book I of Alice's adventures comes to an
end, Alice dismisses the outrageous happenings by shouting defiantly,

"You're nothing but a pack of cards!"[33] As she comes to the realization that the creatures she was taking so seriously are flat, she is ready to step into adulthood and to return home. A pack of cards suggests a pack of lies. Yet, it can also be said that all creation is a house of cards, and that literature is a structure of lies, sublime lies of course. To go back to Jankélévitch's assertion about a child becoming interesting only from the time he tells his first lie, we can interpret these words to mean that a child becomes interesting from the moment he discovers his own imagination. Then only is he able to remake himself and his world. Fragile though it may appear, Arrabal's house of cards is a mansion in which those who, like Jarry, exclaim about certain life adventures, "C'est beau comme la littérature!" would be happy to dwell.

"The greatest influences on my life and work have been those of Artaud and Lewis Carroll," Romain Weingarten confessed to me on a cold winter day in 1961, the year I met him in Paris. Weingarten looks a good deal like a lean, black cat, and indeed he played the role of Le Chat in his own *Akara*. In a brief essay, "A propos des chats," published February 1967, Weingarten discusses feline creatures both in *Akara*, his first play, and in his 1966 whimsical stage poem, *L'Eté:* "Le chat d'*Akara* est un homme-chat, les chats de l'Eté sont des chats-hommes."[34]

Poets have often been drawn to these silent, sensuous, mysteriously independent companions. Who can ever forget Baudelaire's cat, walking within the poet's brain, as much at home there as in an apartment of which he, the feline ruler, would be sole owner? Perhaps the same creature made its way on silent, velvety paws through the sleepless night of Tennessee Williams when the American dramatist wrote the following lines of poetry: "I am a furtive cat, unowned, unknown,/a scavenged sort of blackish alley-cat. . . ." Cats, Weingarten explains, have kept something of "l'antique sauvagerie,"[35] held tame within the confines of a home or a garden. He goes on to say, "Quand je parle de sauvagerie je ne pense pas tant à la cruauté, à la violence brutale que le mot évoque, qu'à la libre jouissance de soi, au pur jaillissement de l'instinct dont le nom est: Paradis."[36] Both *L'Eté* and the more recent *Alice dans les Jardins du Luxembourg* take place in the enclosed space of a garden, one not unlike that of the deanery where the Liddell girls, Lewis Carroll's young friends, played croquet under the watchful, admiring, and slightly envious eye of Christ Church's sublibrarian. As his smiling face peered from an upstairs window he must have looked a good deal like the Cheshire Cat.

In his 1974 play *La Mandore* (*The Bandore*), Romain Weingarten introduces the viewer into the self-contained universe of a small but singularly busy apartment building. Since the facade has been removed, exposing the inner structure of the house, one is able to watch the peculiar goings-on throughout the five-story dwelling. The set suggests the stand-up cut-outs of children's books, and, on a deeper level of interpretation, it evokes both the Tower of Babel and the Tree of Life. Like the latter, it is an *axis mundi*, rooted in an underworld peopled by snakes and dragons and rising through the human realm to that of winged spirits, heroes, and gods. It symbolizes, as do the Nordic ash, Yggdrasil, and the sacred birch of the Tungus of Manchuria, the process of individuation, the unfolding of human personality. Mircea Eliade states that every human habitation is projected to the center of the world, making the ascent to heaven a potential reality. Here also, the inner flights of stairs and outer ladders enable mythical birds and spirits to visit human beings, and, in turn, make possible the ascent of shamans and their initiates.

In *La Mandore*, more than in any of his preceding plays, touched though they may be with the poet's imagination, Weingarten has allowed quotidian life to be permeated by magic. Indeed, one might say that the dramatist has set for himself the task of weaving an intricate tapestry composed of fables, fairy tales, and myths. These co-exist with modern mythologies based on popular awe for scientific investigation tinged by *angst* in the face of a possible apocalypse. The visual vocabulary of *La Mandore*, as well as its lexical texture, is an amalgam of bourgeois mores and clichés, with the stuff and nonsense of science fiction cartoon strips, or television detective thrillers.

The title of the play is a cluster of signifiers—the sleeping lover, the dormant soul, the golden lover, the golden soul, razor blades made of gold—which point to the signified: the alchemy of dreams whereby base metals can be transmuted, base emotions transcended, and both transformed into the rare substance of poetic imagination. As the play begins, we hear the gentle plucking of the strings of a rare instrument, a lute which disappeared in the early part of the eighteenth century. Thus, this haunting, nostalgic sound lures us onto another plane, that of the sacramental reality. The bandore invites us to step through the gates of dreaming.

The cast of characters is given floor by floor: on the ground floor (le rez-de-chaussée), the *concierge*, Gaston, and his wife, Marjorie; on the second floor (le 1er étage), a family made up of Albert, the father; his wife, Marguerite, a young, attractive woman; her aged aunt, tante Solange (a mannequin which constantly falls off its chair as though to testify mutely to the lumpness of old age); the grandmother, who is a kind of ancestor figure; and Charles, a brat who could be kin to Vitrac's Victor. The third floor harbors a young couple, Julien and Juliette, with their seven children (rag dolls), all different races and therefore colors, not unlike the brood adopted by Josephine Baker; an old couple, Edgar and Honorine, live on the fourth floor, and, above them, there is an old scarecrow in a wheel chair, La Fée, and her fifteen year old daughter, Annabelle, whose name suggests that she might be a cross between Belle of "Beauty and the Beast," Peau d'Ane, and Cinderella. This microcosm is invaded by a foreign professor who seems involved in mysterious research on the macrocosm and his sensuous, licentious daughter, Maria. There is also L'Homme d'Or, a kind of Superman, who turns out to be an outer space assassin, an Inspector and his assistant, Casimir, and a young photographer, Richard, who might feel more at home in Cocteau's *Les Mariés de la Tour Eiffel*. There is also a huge dog, ironically named Puce, which, as we find out at the end of the play, serves as a body mask for L'Homme d'Or.

The play opens in an atmosphere of sleep and dreaming. A peculiar light bathes the room of Edgar and Honorine. It is composed of the silver glow of the full moon and the golden shimmer of an orb floating in the sky. The latter awakens in the viewer a chain of mythical and scientific associations: the golden sphere of the fairy tale "The Frog King"; the solar boat of Dogon legend, sent by the deity Nommo to instruct his people; Apollo's chariot; space stations; flying saucers. As the phenomenon floats out of Edgar's ken, he sits down at his desk to record its passage in the ledger he is keeping. Meanwhile, Honorine, who got out of bed to watch the mysterious planet, returns to their bedroom. Her "je vais dormir"[37] echoes the signifier "globe d'or"[38] (orb of gold). Later, in scene three, still in the old couple's apartment, the radio begins to emit strange static. Could this indicate the coming of a storm, or are these distant rumblings of an impending apocalypse? Pointing with great solemnity to his writ, Edgar utters, "Tout est noté...là."[39] Edgar's book seems to be "the Book," the cosmogony wherein the history of creation is recorded.

The following night—the play is divided into seven days and eight nights, thus favoring the shadowy realm of the fantastic—L'Homme d'Or enters the house. He is seen by Gaston who, having stepped out of his *loge*, flashes a light upon the intruder. The latter, however, does not register fear or surprise. He merely comments on the beauty of the golden knob, or pommel (in French the word is pomme), of the staircase railing. Here again the word echoes with associations, particularly those which suggest the fruit of the Tree of Knowledge. Death and Sin enter the house with the arrival of the stranger. Leaving the *concierge* wordless, L'Homme d'Or proceeds up the stairs, enters the room where Edgar and Honorine are half asleep, and strangles them in their bed. Edgar's last words to his wife, spoken before he has time to realize that she lies dead by his side are: "Comme on est bien!... Honorine? Tu dors? Je crois que je vais m'endormir aussi."[40] Later, when Gaston discovers the bodies, with the assassin still at hand, the latter says, "Ils dorment! De mort naturelle."[41] Thus, sleep and death are fused to make this violent end appear as a natural phenomenon. Also, one could say that sleep is a kind of death and death a final form of sleep. L'Homme d'Or would then be an envoy of Death, a golden archangel.

To divert Gaston's attention, the mythical murderer tempts him with the discovery of the hidden treasure of the old couple. In the best of ancient French traditions, Edgar and Honorine hoarded their money and perhaps that of their ancestors. Guided by the stranger in the gold suit, the *concierge* finds a cache of gold louis under the seat of the armchair, a veritable nest of golden eggs. Like the sound of the bandore, this ancient currency issues from a fabled past. We are reminded of the Brothers Grimm's "The Two Brothers," in which we meet an evil brother, a goldsmith, and a kind, poor brother who is rewarded for his goodness with the find of a golden bird. By eating the heart and liver of the bird, the good brother's twin children acquire the ability to find a piece of gold under their pillow every morning. The evil brother, however, persuades the father of the twins that his sons are possessed by the devil and that he must drive these wicked spirits out of the house. In a parallel way, Gaston's lucky find proves to be cumbersome evidence of a crime he did not commit. Urged by Marjorie (her name also contains the words *or*) to hide the coins, he pours them into the drainage pipes of the house where they make a merry, jingling sound, golden music.

Gold may be power, but Zeus found out when he fell in love with Danae, it can spell erotic domination. Marjorie is facinated by Golo, L'Homme d'Or. His name rings with the sound of gold—most French people know enough English to make the association—but it also echoes with rich legendary and Proustian meaning. We recall that the narrator of *A la recherche du temps perdu* whiles away some melancholy evenings spent in the company of his aunt by having her project tales from a Merovingian past by means of a magic lantern. Thus, his bedroom is temporarily transformed by the appearance on the wall and then on the floating white curtains of frightful Golo riding his horse in the direction of fair Genevieve de Brabant's castle. Like L'Homme d'Or, Proust's Golo is impelled by the yellow of "le château et la lande," and above all by the "sonorité mordorée du nom de Brabant."[42] According to Allan H. Pasco, "the yellow range (in Proust)—*blond, jaune, or,* and *doré*—accompanies organizing factors"[43] in the novel. Pasco claims that "legend and mythology are associated with these hues."[44] As to Proust's Golo, his body and that of his mount seem to be of supernatural essence, and thus can interiorize any object in their path. The narrator tells us that the door knob can thus become part of Golo's skeleton as his body traverses the door; familiar objects are metamorphosed into Golo's astral body. Since the Golo of *La Mandore* is summoned by the old witch, La Fée, a caricature perhaps of Proust's tante Léonie, he may be a supernatural projection. For Weingarten's audience, brought up on Proust as was the dramatist, L'Homme d'Or issues from legend, and from the pages of the greatest work of fiction ever written. Such are his titres de noblesse, those of a character composed of literary text.

The charm of *La Mandore* lies partly in the fact that all the *dramatis personae* have had a pre-existence whether in fable, legend, literature, the cinema, comic books, cartoon strips, detective novels, newspaper stories. Once this becomes clear, one can no longer be amazed by the co-existence of strange humans and beasts or their constant metamorphoses.

On the top of the house, as close to heaven as possible within this given structure, lives the shrewish, helpless woman who calls herself La Fée and claims that her lovers were birds who instructed her in the art of flying. According to Chinese legends, birds actually taught certain women to fly, a secret passed on later by Taoist priests. Through the greater part of the play, La Fée acts as a cruel mother, almost a stepmother, to her fifteen year old virgin daughter, an uncomplaining Cinderella who spends her time fixing the old woman's broken magic wand or wheeling her about their room in a gilded wheel chair, the caricature of a fairy tale chariot. The chair, La Fée tells her hapless daughter, is nothing less than the girl's father. Whether the young woman believes this cosmogonic myth or not, or whether it simply suggests many virgins' fantasies about pregnancy resulting from sitting in the chair used by a man they love, Annabelle is stirred by the old woman's promise that she will be initiated into womanhood by a "feather guest," an event which takes place at the end of the play. Nor does the girl register undue surprise when, in the course of the Fourth Night, La Fée dressed in an eighteenth-century travel costume, flies out the window. She will return on the Seventh Night in the form of a saurian. Her reptilian mask suggests the African myth about God sending men a chameleon to tell them they would be immortal, and a lizard to inform them of their condition of mortality; the lizard having won the race, death became part of the human condition. Here, however, since La Fée's mask is ambiguous, it is not impossible to feel that death and the promise of eternal life are fused.

Magic and science are one in the universe of *La Mandore*. Thus, we have a bizarre scientist, a kind of cross between Dr. Caligari and Dr. Strangelove. Paralleling his research in space travel, there is Julien's passion for electricity. This inveterate *bricoleur*, an Einstein raté has set up a system that allows him to blow the fuses throughout the house. To one of his numerous children, he explains, "Quoi? L'électricité: Ben oui, la petite bêbête qui court! Je cherche, c'est ça! Je cherche."[45] The little animal on the run—one of the leitmotifs in the play—reminds one of the "furet" of the well-known children's ring game accompanied by the chant: "Il court, il court, le furet. . . ." Moreover, the comparison between currents racing along wires and the running "bêbête" serves to strengthen the links between the world of science and that of art, connecting both to the universe of the child. By reminding his audience of the ever-renewed wonder of search and discovery, Weingarten follows Mallarmé's precepts to treat all great human endeavors as a form of game, the Supreme Game. Nor must we think that scientific geniuses are impervious to a sense of mystery. There is the famous anecdote about Einstein being driven by a friend through a thunderstorm. Einstein stuck his head out of the car window and threw out a question which seemed to address itself to the cosmos: "What's lightning?" It was his friend who gave the obvious answer: "Electricity." Looking puckish, the great physicist retorted, "That's what you think."

The banal and the fantastic mingle in the household of Albert, and as a result the viewer undergoes what Tzvetan Todorov calls a hesitation "entre le réel et. . .l'illusoire."[46] One enters a zone "où naît un sens que ne peut exister nulle part ailleurs,"[47] a feeling which has to do with unnamable terror. The latter, according to H. P. Lovecraft (Supernatural Horror in Literature) is basic to the experience of the fantastic. Here, however, terror stems from the character of the supposedly protective grandmother. Charles, her grandson, claims that he loves her "grandes dents. . .[her] dents d'or,"[48] but he also cries out, "J'ai peur."[49] His fear may not be unjustified since we see the old woman, on various occasions, standing very still and brandishing a huge knife. Is she protecting her immediate family from the assassin who lurks in the house or defending the whole building? At any rate, she can be said to combine what Bruno Bettelheim calls the wolf's "selfish, asocial, violent, potentially destructive tendencies," and the hunter's "unselfish, social, thoughtful, and protective propensities."[50] Her male grandchild, however, is no innocent chaperon Rouge. The stealthy but active rival of his father, Charles makes passionate erotic overtures to his mother. The *rites de passage* of puberty are played out in most explicit terms, and presided over by an encouraging grandmother:

> Charles: Je ne me rappelais pas que vous étiez si belle!
> Marguerite: Tu m'étouffes!. . .
> Charles: Vous repoussez un fils!
> Grand-Mère: Ce n'est pas gentil!
> Charles: Il faut que tout soit clair! Qu'on devienne grand!
>   Cri de Marguerite[51]

This is the story of Cupid and Aphrodite in reverse; we witness a wicked boy's rape of his half-willing mother. She who was called earlier by her would-be poet of a son: "Le chèvrefeuille et le jasmin, la neige et le nénuphar,"[52] will be laid upon the ground, or at least the living room floor, and covered with flowers like Ophelia's corpse. The rites of puberty seem to parallel those of Spring as mother and grandmother play out the Kore/ Demeter union:

> Marguerite (to Charles):   Non, non, pas ici.
> Grand-Mère: Si! Si! Par terre! C'est bien par terre!
> Charles: Un lit de fleurs![53]

If this incarnation of pure id acts out the subconscious desires of every adolescent boy, one must also say that love and lucre are commingled in his nature. Like the monstrous child of *Victor ou les enfants au pouvoir*, Charles is aware of the power of money, and he demands from the *concierge* the latter's ill-gained "louis d'or," knowing full well, however, that "un loup y dort."[54]

La Mandore is a dramatic poem in which reality and imagination intertwine, and all metamorphoses are possible. Puce, the dog, makes love to Marjorie, *la concierge*, while her husband "rampe, aboie, grogne, puis va ramasser les effets (de sa femme) avec les mains, les dents."[55] The Professor changes into a rat and is killed by L'Homme d'Or who issues from Puce's furry body, a mask for his own beastliness. We recognize here the pattern of animal-groom stories. These are also connected to the Cupid/Psyche myth. As Bruno Bettelheim explains, there is a significant feature all of these have in common:

> The groom is absent during the day and present only in the darkness of night; he is believed to be animal during the day and to become human only in bed; in short, he keeps his day and night existences separate from each other. . . .The female, despite the ease and pleasure she enjoys, finds her life empty: she is unwilling to accept the separation and isolation of purely sexual aspects of life from the rest of it. She tries to force their unification.[56]

Or, as Weingarten writes in one of his poems, "la Fête":

Une partie homme, une partie bête
Une partie qui se dresse
Une partie qui se traîne,
laquelle?
....
Et je ne savais pas si c'était la bête qui
tendait affreusement vers l'homme
ou l'homme qui revenait vers la bête
car l'un et l'autre sont le même moment
d'avant ou après,
le moment de la ligature
lorsque la bête dut parler
et lorsque l'homme perd la parole.
L'un et l'autre à ce moment
ôtèrent leur vêtement,
vêtement du sexe.[57]

It must not be forgotten that guides of the dead such as the Greek Hermes Psychopompos assumed the forms of a dog or wolf. The jackal-headed Anubis performed a similar function for the Egyptians. Most of the time, however, it is the bird symbol that is associated with the soul and the soul's voyage to the beyond. On a Greek vase painting, the soul of Patroclus, killed in the Trojan war, is seen carried by two winged deities Hypnos (sleep) and Thanatos (death). Thus, when at the end of *La Mandore*, on that *Huitième Nuit* which must be the night of miracles, Richard, the photographer, appears at Annabelle's window "en costume d'oiseau,"[58] we know that he is not only the celestial messenger promised by La Fée in the course of The Third Night ("Un grand oiseau va venir"[59]), but also a messenger of death. After all, La Fée, who must be considered in the context of the symbolism of death and secret knowledge, had also announced, "Un jour, vous aussi, vous entrerez dans la lumière douteuse d'une nouvelle naissance."[60] In his final scene, Weingarten presents the universe of the between, a realm where the living meet the shades emerging from "la trappe,"[61] one of the entrances to the Underworld. As the latter issue to partake of salvation, they fill the stage with the sound of the bells they hold. There is a strong suggestion of the most solemn moment of the Mass, that of the Eucharist. One is reminded of Auden's magnificent statement: "Art is breaking bread with the dead."

By making use of myth, fairy tales, children's stories for the texture of their plays, Weingarten and Arrabal have concretized upon the stage the dark, dreaming aspect of the human psyche. To understand their form of theatre, one must apply a method of study which reveals the functioning of the imagination. These dramatist-poets have taken on the role of story tellers, Scheherazades who must enchant us so that they may live another day, and give us life in turn, that greater, deeper life which is the work of art.

GRADUATE CENTER OF THE
CITY UNIVERSITY OF NEW YORK

Notes

[1]Alain Schifres, *Arrabal* (Paris: Editions Pierre Belfond, 1969), p. 31.

[2]Bernard Gille, *Arrabal* (Paris: Seghers,1970), p. 9.

[3]Irmgard Zeyos Anderson, "From Tweedledum and Tweedledee to Zapo and Zepo," *Romance Notes*, 15 (Winter 1973), p. 220.

[4]Schifres, p. 35.

[5]Louise Fiber Luce, "The Dialectic of Space: Fernando Arrabal's *The Automobile Graveyard*," *Journal of Spanish Studies: Twentieth Century*, 2, 1 (Spring 1974), p. 33.

[6]Ibid., p. 36.

[7]Allen Thiher, "Fernando Arrabal and the New Theatre of Obsession," *Modern Drama*, 13 (1970-1971), p. 176.

[8]Luce, p. 32.

[9]Schifres, pp. 131-32.

[10]Ibid., p. 132.

[11]Ibid., p. 42.

[12]Jean Decock, "Arrabal. *Jeunes barbares d'aujourd'hui*," *The French Review* (Creative Works edited by Stefan Max), 50, 1 (October 1976), p. 191. The sentence has been translated from the French by the writer of this essay.

[13]Bruno Bettelheim, *The Uses of Enchantment* (New York: Alfred A. Knopf, 1976), p. 12.

[14]Schifres, p. 137.

[15]Ibid., p. 134.

[16]Arrabal, *Jeunes barbares d'aujourd'hui* (Paris: Christian Bourgois Editeur, 1975), p. 35. The author of the essay translated this particular expression from the original, "l'étape-reine," to establish clearly the connection with *Alice in Wonderland*.

[17]Lewis Carroll, *The Annotated Alice* (New York: Bramhall House, 1960), p. 210.

[18]Arrabal, *Jeunes barbares*, p. 8.

[19]This process is carefully described by Joseph Campbell in *The Masks of God: Creative Mythology* (New York: The Viking Press, 1970), pp. 278-81.

[20]Arrabal, *Jeunes barbares*, p. 13.

[21]Ibid.

[22]Ibid., p. 22.

[23]Ibid., p. 8.

[24]Ibid.

[25]Schifres, p. 30.

[26]Ibid., p. 155.

[27]Phyllis Greenacre, *Swift and Carroll* (International Universities Press, 1955).

[28]Arrabal, *Jeunes barbares*, p 20.

[29]Ibid., p. 16.

[30]Ibid., p. 41.

[31]Ibid., p. 46.

[32]Ibid.

[33]Carroll, *Annotated Alice*, p. 161.

[34]Romain Weingarten, *L'Ete, Akara, Les Nourrices* (Paris: Christian Bourgois Editeur, 1967), p 330.

[35]Ibid., p. 331.

[36]Ibid.

[37]Romain Weingarten, *La Mandore* (Paris: Gallimard, Le Manteau d'Arlequin, 1974), p. 13.

[38]Ibid.

[39]Ibid., p. 16.

[40]Ibid., p. 39.

[41]Ibid., p. 40.

[42]Marcel Proust, *A la recherche du temps perdu* (Paris: Gallimard, Bibliothèque de la Pléiade, Tome I, 1954), p. 9.

[43]Allan H. Pasco, *The Color-Keys to "A la recherche du temps perdu"* (Genève-Paris: Librairie Droz, 1976), p 118.

[44]Ibid., p. 119.

[45]Weingarten, *La Mandore*, p. 15.

[46]Tzvetan Todorov, *Introduction à la littérature fantastique* (Paris: Seuil, 1970), p. 29.

[47]Ibid., p. 105.

[48]Weingarten, *La Mandore*, p. 19.

[49]Ibid.

[50]Bettelheim, *Uses of Enchantment*, p. 172.

[51]Weingarten, *La Mandore*, p. 97.

[52]Ibid., p. 21.

[53]Ibid., p. 98.

[54]Ibid., p. 47.

[55]Ibid., p. 101.

[56]Bettelheim, *Uses of Enchantment*, p. 294.

[57]Romain Weingarten, *Poèmes* (Paris: Christian Bourgois Editeur, 1968), pp. 41-42.

[58]Weingarten, *La Mandore*, p. 168.

[59]Ibid., p. 94.

[60]Ibid.

[61]Ibid., p. 170.

JOHN WEBSTER:
A FREUDIAN INTERPRETATION OF
HIS TWO GREAT TRAGEDIES

George Whiteside

As you read Webster's two great plays, you cannot help noticing that Flamineo is facinated by his sister's sexuality and Ferdinand thinks constantly of his sister's body. Each thinks his sister lascivious: "her coyness? that's but the superficies of lust," says Flamineo (*White Devil* I, 2) to his master Brachiano; "you are my sister; this was my father's poniard, do you see?...And women like that part which, like the lamprey, hath never a bone in't," says Ferdinand (*Duchess of Malfi* I, 1) to the Duchess. She has done nothing unchaste, but still he imagines her lust and warns her to curb it. Later, when her learns that she is pregnant, he is enraged beyond all reason and obsessed by thoughts of her with the other man. Ferdinand behaves like a jealous lover, not a brother. Flamineo, too, is obsessed by the spectacle of his sister with Brachiano. But instead of being like a jealous lover, he is a voyeur. Instead of *imagining* that she is with his master, Flamineo arranges the liason, *watches* them together, and urges Brachiano on: "Hand her, my lord, and kiss her," he says (IV, 1) as he watches Brachiano lean over the bed. His interest in his sister's sexuality is intense. He, like Ferdinand, is infatuated with his sister. Both have fairly obvious incestuous feelings, and people who write about the plays sometimes point this out.[1]

However, I have found no one who gives a Freudian explanation of these incestuous feelings. In fact, I have found little explanation of them all. William Empson provides one. He says these feelings are a kind of proud self-love: in loving one of his own—his sister, his twin—Ferdinand is loving himself.[2] That may be true, but it does not explain why he is sexually attracted to her. For he does not only love his sister proudly, possessively; he also lusts for her, thinking lewdly about her all the time. Flamineo does the same. So we have to account for incestuous sexual desire. A simple Freudian explanation would be that oedipal desire for the mother has been deflected into the sister; or else—what amounts to the same thing—Webster has created mother figures whom he puts in sister roles. Either way, the idea is that certain men in his plays feel toward some women as a little boy feels towards his mother. It is a simple idea, and what I propose to do in this paper is try it out, see how much it explains. I would hardly claim that it explains everything; I am well aware that there are a number of ways of understanding Webster's art. The reader shall decide whether this Freudian way is idiosyncratic or, instead, is one of the permanent views of Webster's two tragedies that we can take.

John Webster collaborated on a number of plays, but the first we have that was his own is *The White Devil; or, The Tragedy of Paulo Giordano Ursini, Duke of Brachiano, With the Life and Death of Vittoria Corombona, the Famous Venetian Curtizan,* published in London in 1912. Brachiano and Vittoria had really existed; in the play, Webster was dramatizing events that had actually happened in Italy a quarter century earlier. The real-life Brachiano had abandoned his wife, Isabella, for Vittoria, and the murders and revenge had ensued. We do not know what account Webster had of these events, so we cannot tell to what extent Webster's characterizations are his own inventions nor to what extent the pattern given the events is his own.[3] All we can do is look at the pattern.

Before I search for oedipal feelings and the like, I will describe the pattern of the play, for it can be made evident without resort to any special ideas, Freudian or otherwise. The title calls this the tragedy of Brachiano: the depiction of his fall. At the start, still married to Isabella but infatuated with Vittoria, he is poised between two women. When he tells his wife, "Henceforth I'll never lie with thee" (II,1) and gives himself up to his passion for Vittoria, he falls. The white devil of the title is Vittoria, for it is her white beauty that lures him to his damnation. Isabella, conversely, is a white angel; as Webster portrays her, she is the perfect wife. And Vittoria is the perfect courtesan. They are two types: the angel and the whore; she who offers licit love, and she who offers illicit.

Similarly, the other characters of the play divide into two groups: those with a licit place in society and the intruders. Those with a permitted place in society are: the Cardinal, later Pope, who presides; Isabella, who incarnates its goodness; her brother the Duke of Florence, who has its power; Ludovico, who is his instrument; the boy Giovanni, who inherits the power; and the Cardinal's nephew Camillo, who lets the intruders in. These intruders are the Corombonas together with Zanche the Moor. Camillo let them in when he brought Vittoria, penniless, from Venice: "You came from thence a most notorious strumpet, and so you have continued," says the Cardinal (III, 1), and then he, as presiding judge, decides that she, a corruptor that has entered the society, must be cloistered where she can corrupt no more.

His decision reveals the way in which this society handles evils: its presiding judge, the future Pope, does not try to extirpate evil or banish it but only tries to put it under control. He is a Pope who keeps the names of criminals in a black book instead of arresting them. Thus, the society has a good surface and evil depths. Both good and bad, white angel and white devil, licit and illicit, lawful members of society and lawless are kept here.

The order of things is disturbed only when the lawless obtrude and the lawful sink.

The protagonist of a tragedy sets forces in motion, and then they overwhelm him. He disturbs the order of things, and then that order, reasserting itself, crushes him. So when Brachiano—husband of society's goodness, brother to its power, father of its inheritor—sinks, succumbs to Vittoria, it is a lawful part of society that has sunk, and society reacts. First, the Cardinal tries to put the cause of passion, Vittoria, under control. But next, he lets the Duke of Florence see his black book and use lawless force to destroy Brachiano. In using it, Florence becomes lawless himself. (His disguise as a Moor signifies as much, for the Englishmen of Webster's time thought blacks were instinctive, unruly.) And so, destroying his brother duke, Florence destroys himself, and the power of both dukes passes to Giovanni. He, with the rightful power of society, and the Cardinal, new Pope and the guardian of its law, together will reconstitute things.

This summary should make clear that the play was meant to be a moral drama about what happens when one duke succumbs to illicit passion (Vittoria) and another gives rein to lawless force (Ludovico).[4] The moral, quite evidently, is that lawlessness is dangerous: that the instinctive and the unruly in a person or society must be kept down. I suppose Webster meant the play first of all to point this moral and he would expect us to make moral judgments of the characters. We should see, for example, that the Cardinal did right to cloister Vittoria and wrong to permit Ludovico to roam free. We should view him, as well as Ludovico and Vittoria and the dukes and Isabella, in this moral way. But of course this should not be the only way we look at the characters. Vittoria, for instance, is a white devil; she is bad news, from a moral point of view, and anyone who decides otherwise misinterprets the play. But it is not enough to decide she is bad news; we must also succumb to her appeal. It is not enough to make moral judgments; we must also engage our emotions.

Here a Freudian view of the play comes in, for it reveals the characters in such a way that we can see why they engage our emotions. They do so because they re-enact, onstage, the drama of oedipal desire and punishment. We, or at least men, can re-experience that drama, feel arising in us again the love and fear and fury, the intense passions that we knew as little boys. Thus, men in the audience who submit to Webster's art will identify with Brachiano first of all, for the latter will be acting out their oedipal passion. The Cardinal-Pope will be il Papa, who watches this passion, cloisters the desire-arousing mother figure from view, and then finally gives rein to the power that will punish. As Brachiano pursues his desire even into the cloister, men in the audience will know again the little boy's deep disquiet, sense of wrong, and identify with the indignation of Florenco. He, the older brother who wields the punishing power and attacks in the hero's own home, will be their conscience—Papa's prohibition internalized within their own breasts. And Ludovico, who adores Isabella, will be the savage retribution they visited on themselves for hurting the adored mother. Thus, men whose oedipal feelings can be re-aroused—most men's can—will re-experience the savage anger, the sense of wrong, the presence of Papa in the background as well as the desire itself. In the grip of Webster's art, they will relive the oedipal drama in one of its common forms.

In that form, mother has two aspects: she is adored and she arouses desire. But for the boy to act out his desire for her is to kill the adored figure. Then, horrified, the boy furiously punishes himself. In this play the doer of the deed and the punishers are separate characters, so men in the audience identify first with Brachiano, then with Florence and Ludovico. First, they are attracted to Vittoria, then indignant at Brachiano's crime, and ultimately feel primitive fury welling up at the spectacle of lovely, vulnerable Isabella being snuffed out. This fury—the kind of rage arising in a helpless child, an aggression which respects no law—is Ludovico.

As I see this play, then, it is emotionally powerful because certain men in it, mainly Brachiano and Ludovico (and Flamineo), feel toward two women, Isabella and Vittoria, as a little boy may feel toward his mother, and we identify with these men. If I am right and this play gets its power from thus re-awakening oedipal emotions, then women in the audience must be unable to feel its full force or must experience it differently from the way men can. It would be interesting to know what women think of Isabella and Vittoria, the two figures or aspects of mother.[5] Isabella is the perfection of lovely sub-missiveness: she is pure, yet warmly receptive to her husband; she forgives him his sins without a murmur; and she dies in the act of worshipping him, kissing an icon of her lord. To women, she may seem an absurd, unrealistic figure. I think that a man, however, will not find her absurd, for she will accord with his earliest imagining of a lovely, yielding woman who absorbs his aggressions meekly and arouses the great protective feeling that is their concomitant. Conversely, a woman in the audience might find Vittoria a normal lady, good-looking and not bashful but hardly the white devil, the seductive whore, that she is meant to be. Webster calls her "the famous Venetian curtizan," and to Englishmen of his day Venice was the voluptuary of Europe, the sink of sensuality as Italy was of wickedness in general. The "famous courtesan" of Venice would indeed be the ultimate seductress. What, women might ask, makes Vittoria so seductive? I would say, the fact that she resists and then yields to a man before our eyes. Her spiritedness, then pliancy (for instance, IV, 1) and demureness that soon give way to her "blood" (I, 2)—these excite us as we watch in the same way that a mother may excite her little boy if he imagines or observes her resist, then yield to some man.

It is Flamineo who is the observer of Vittoria with a man. In the scenes mentioned above, it is he who watches her with Brachiano and urges her to yield, and it is his fantastic lascivious descriptions that virtually conjure up the image of her that men in the audience will have. The scenes are his crea-tions, much as that between the typist and young man carbuncular is Tiresias' creation in *The Waste Land*. Men in the audience who are excited by Vittoria will have identified with Flamineo and be for a while, along with him, the little boy watching mother with a man. For it seems clear to me that Flamineo's attitude toward Vittoria is that of a boy toward a mother who has aroused him.

At the start of this paper I said that Flamineo is aroused by Vittoria's sexuality. I would add now that he has the whole range of oedipal feelings and acts them out. Thus, he kills his good brother, Marcello, leaving his good mother, Cornelia, to mourn the loss, and it is as if in doing so he wanted to show his feeling that he is bad. It is as if with this act he were saying: "See, mother, I am a bad boy; your good little boy is dead." I am devoted to the bad Vittoria (whom Cornelia had cursed) and a good son no more. Clearly, Flamineo feels he is wicked. And he acts out a common Freudian pattern for men who feel so: such men, fixated in the oedipal attitude that their sexual urge is wicked, will inhibit it toward women they consider good and release it only toward "bad" women. They see women as either angels or whores, untouchable or promiscuous, and are attracted only by the latter, whom they revile and degrade. In reviling Vittoria, and in expressing desire only for her maid, Zanche the Moor, who, because black, would be thought instinctive and promiscuous, Flamineo carries out the pattern. But finally, at the end he seeks—and gets—a kind of *Liebestod* with Vittoria during which he tells her, "Thou'rt a noble sister! I love thee now" (V, 6). In other words, his last act is to plan a death with Vittoria (and Zanche); and only when they are dying together does he cease revilement and proclaim his love. A *Liebestod*, in which the punishment for oedipal passion falls at the moment of its consummation, expresses the negative and positive oedipal feelings—the sense of deserving punishment and the love, the fear and the release—in one action. It is fitting that Flamineo, who has that range of feelings, should end so.

Flamineo is, I think, one of the great literary embodiments of oedipal feeling. He is not a principal in the main events but an observer of them. Nevertheless, the observer of a tragedy—Quentin of *Absalom! Absalom!*, for instance, or the chorus of the *Agamemnon*—may be the most important character, and I think Flamineo is. The principals, enacting legends and desires that grip men's imagination, are creatures of men's imagining, larger than life. The protagonist of this play, for example, as he carries out the oedipal wish, is a creation of the wishers who watch: he is a figure in a myth. Those who watch him, on the other hand, are more real. Flamineo is what a real man would be who dredged up, felt again, and gave utterance to his oedipal emotions. His is a full embodiment of the emotions—desire, fascination, disgust, bitterness, rejection, hopeless attachment—of a boy aroused by his mother. Brachiano's deeds and their consequences stir us as they stir Flamineo. But it is Flamineo's utterance that, like Hamlet's, brings us most fully in touch with all the oedipal feelings. His lewd, sardonic, and anguished speech creates the atmosphere of the play.

Webster's tragedy of *The Duchess of Malfi*, the second of his plays aside from collaborations, was written in 1613 or 1614. Like *The White Devil* it dramatizes events that had actually happened in Italy, in this case about a hundred years earlier. We know the account that Webster had of these events—a novella in William Painter's *Palace of Pleasures*, principally—and can see how he altered it to suit his purposes. Thematically, the main alteration is that Webster changed "the wanton widow of. . .Painter" into a woman of "purity and integrity."⁶ Structurally, he made Antonio, the chief male of the novella, into a figure less important than the Duchess' two brothers and Bosola. In Painter's book these three are little more than mentioned so their characters are Webster's invention. He made them so vivid, in fact, that we attend to them more than to Antonio.

These three, the Cardinal, his brother Ferdinand, and the spy Bosola, bring about the Duchess' downfall just as the Cardinal, Florence, and Ludovico brought about Brachiano's. The patterns of the two plays are very similar. In both, a protagonist indulges passion not accepted by society and is punished for it. The Duchess, protagonist here, sets forces in motion when she marries Antonio just as Brachiano set similar forces in motion when he chose Vittoria. The Cardinal here presides over society as the Cardinal in *The White Devil* did; Ferdinand wields society's power as Florence did; Bosola is the instrument of punishment as Ludovico was; and the Duchess' son inherits power at the end just as Brachiano's son did. The only character important in the main action of *The White Devil* who has no counterpart here is Isabella; I will explain why shortly.

The division between licit and illicit exists here as it did in *The White Devil*. In the eyes of the Cardinal and the other established members of this society, Antonio is a social upstart, intruding as much as Vittoria did in the previous play. There as here, the society permits lawless men a place in it but considers those who intrude on it—Vittoria and Antonio—impermissible, illicit.

In both plays, society takes two actions. First, its Cardinal separates intruder from protagonist. Then, its duke (Florence, Ferdinand) uses the lawless men (Ludovico, Bosola) to destroy the protagonist. In doing so, that duke destroys himself too, after which a boy inherits the power and will reorder society. Thus, the main action of the two plays is similar.

There are, however, two important differences that point to a moral lesson. First, the Cardinal of *The White Devil* survived to preside over the new order, whereas the Cardinal here is killed at the end. Second, Brachiano murdered his wife whereas the Duchess commits no crimes. The lesson I draw from this is that the guilty protagonist, Brachiano, was defeated, the Cardinal of the play prevailing, while the innocent protagonist, the Duchess, triumphs morally when the Cardinal here dies. In short, Brachiano was wrong, but she, I think, is in the right.

We cannot be sure, however, that Webster meant us to call her right. He seems the sort of playwright who makes moral judgments, yet toward the Duchess he is ambiguous. Clifford Leech has argued that "on the surface of Webster's mind" there was disapproval of the Duchess but "with part of his mind" he was sympathetic to her.⁷ That may be. At any rate he was certainly of two minds about her. The action of the play vindicates her, her evil opponent sinking to defeat as she rises to nobility of character; so with part of his mind Webster surely approved of her. However, as Leech says, with another part—and not the surface, I think—he felt that her passion was wrong.

Such ambivalence is, of course, a commonplace oedipal phenomenon, and *The Duchess of Malfi*—with phallic objects (a poniard, a cut-off limb), spying on pregnancy, a kind of sibling rivalry (between the brothers-in-law Antonio and Ferdinand), a remorseless Cardinal as father figure—has commonplace attributes of an oedipal story. The action begins when the lady of the house invites the good one of her household, Antonio, into her room in secret. Before then, bad brother Ferdinand has shown her his father's poniard to scare her from inviting anyone and has set Bosola to spy on her. For a whole act Bosola tries to get at her, see if she is pregnant, uncover the secret. Then Ferdinand enters the bedroom to spy and give her the poniard. Later he imprisons her in her house and for a whole act sadistically tortures her, brings a cut-off limb to her, and finally has Bosola strangle her in her room. Both he and Bosola are then sorry, blame each other for killing her, also blame the Cardinal, together kill the Cardinal, and kill each other. Only the Cardinal has not been sorry and has continued to hunt down the one who shared her bed secretly.

Webster gave this Freudian shape to the action; his source, the novella in Painter's book, does not have it. For instance, Webster, not the novella, has Ferdinand threaten the Duchess, set a spy on her, and imagine her lustful, all before she has done anything. Webster invented most of the spying, including Cariola's in I, 1 and Ferdinand's when he hides in the Duchess' bedroom (and gives her the poniard there). It was Webster, also, who had Ferdinand inflict mental torture and give the Duchess, in her room in the dark, a cut-off hand he first pretends is his and then pretends is Antonio's. And it was Webster who showed Ferdinand crazed with remorse for his sadism toward the Duchess and Bosola also repentant. Webster, too, invented the deaths of Ferdinand, Bosola, and the Cardinal. And he thought up the relationship among these three according to which the Cardinal presides and directs from a distance. Webster also created the curious scene (III, 2) in which Antonio, with Cariola, plays a boyish prank on his lady. Finally, in depicting the relationship between the Duchess and Antonio, Webster showed her deciding everything and him just obeying like a dutiful boy, while in the novella Antonio is the one who decides that they should part.

Webster, then, created this oedipal configuration: the lady of the house in her chamber; the dutiful one admitted secretly; two others jealously approaching, spying, finally entering and sadistically taking her; their remorse and destruction afterwards; and the remorseless father figure directing their sadistic attack from a distance and hunting down the one who first entered her room. The pattern of movements is toward that room and the Duchess. Antonio enters first; Ferdinand and Bosola then approach, look, and at last enter. This pattern has an evident sexual meaning of

approach and penetration. It is the kind of meaning—latent, symbolical—
that events in a dream have. By his art Webster had made a dream in its
latent, wish-fulfilling shape come alive onstage, so that men in the audience
can re-experience the same excitement, and fear, that they have known in
past dreams.

This is the dream of fantasy of the unattainable beautiful lady suddenly
becoming amorous. The fantasier imagines his astonishment—until she
makes it all right. Then he enjoys a short-lived bliss until rivals take her or she
betrays or abandons him, at which point he either pines away or dies defiant
toward his tormentors. This dream—with interesting variants in many times
and places, from *Sir Gawain*, for instance, to Wagner's *Tristan*—fulfills a
little boy's wish that mother should choose him, take him to her bed, and
make it all right. He knows, however, that it is wrong, that punishment will
come, so the rest of his dream is his imagining of how doom will fall. Thus,
when men in the audience watch the Duchess choose Antonio (in I, 1), reveal
her amorousness, and make it right by marriage, they will, if they let this
great scene revive old emotions, feel how vulnerable the couple are and
dread the outcome.

The ambivalence in this oedipal-wish fantasy is obvious: the dreamer
wants to feel his wish is right but knows it is wrong. So he senses its goodness,
then senses its wickedness, then senses its goodness again. By the way
Webster arranged the series of scenes, we experience this emotional alternation, so that we see the Duchess one way, then the other, and back again.
First, she is all goodness, loveliness: "She throws upon a man so sweet a
look," Antonio says (I, 1). Then, in the closet scene of I, 1 she becomes
sexually exciting too. We—men in the audience, anyway—will identify with
Antonio there and become sexually aroused by her. Once aroused, however,
we will be susceptible to Bosola's view: watching her in a "loose-bodied"
gown, imagining "the young springal cutting a caper in her belly" (II, 1), we
will share for a while his lewd, wicked-feeling thoughts about impregnating a
woman, his little boy's peeping-tom curiosity about pregnant mother. And
now, feeling like the infant who sees mother as bad, we will be ready to share
Ferdinand's jealous fury: "Damn her! that body of hers, While that my blood
ran pure in't, was. . .worth," but now it is sullied, he exclaims (IV, 1). His
sense that she is physically part of him, his shock at the thought that
another's "blood" has impregnated her, his belief that her goodness, her
purity is gone—these are feelings an infant may have about mother. We can
relive them in all their power. However, we will not retain them—we will not
remain in Ferdinand's emotional state—very long. For Webster has made us
feel Antonio's impression of the Duchess, so that we soon repent having had
these unworthy emotions. I think that any man watching the play quickly
rejects lascivious thoughts about the Duchess, though they do arise in him,
and likewise rejects the feeling, aroused by her pregnancies, that she is not
pure.

He returns, then, to his sense of the Duchess' goodness and affirms that
her love for Antonio—that his dreamed-of wish—is right. However, he

knows the rest of the dream will be played out—Ferdinand and Bosola will attack—so from Act One on he is expecting and dreading this. But *The Duchess of Malfi* is great not because it merely awakens dread but because it arouses horror. That is the spectator's emotion as he watches Ferdinand and Bosola close in on the Duchess and strangle her. It is horror because Webster by his art has made the spectator share for a while the feelings that drive Ferdinand and Bosola on and then has made him reject these feelings. Horror is the emotion when what one experienced and rejected, what one knew and tried to kill, still lives on. This play is great because it awakens a man's bad feelings about mother, gets him to repudiate these, and then forces him to watch as they nevertheless persist and destroy her.

A number of readers of this play have felt that the events after the Duchess' destruction—that is, all of Act Five—are anti-climactic and would have been better omitted. However, these events—the repentance of Ferdinand and Bosola and their deaths together with the Cardinal—are a needed relief: what the spectator had tried to kill in himself earlier is finally killed. His good feeling about mother—his sense of the Duchess' goodness—is finally affirmed.

The White Devil has two images of mother. One is an infant's earliest imagining: a mother who ministers to his needs, absorbs his aggressions, cares and decides for him—in short, a ministering angel. The other, fantasied somewhat later by the boy in the oedipal stage, is the beautiful woman who is at first demure and then passionate—a creature who seems bad because tempting him to go wrong. There are no separate Isabella and Vittoria in *The Duchess of Malfi* because the Duchess is both. She is angel and temptress. She has the enormously appealing qualities of Isabella, including devotion to her husband and that vulnerability which awakens men's protective feelings. The Duchess also has the spirit, as well as the passion, of Vittoria. Since she has the attributes of both, the alternating views of her are possible. As she is both angel and temptress, all the adoration as well as the desire converge on her. She awakens all, not half, of men's deepest feelings for women. Just as Flamineo expressed, she evokes the complete range of oedipal feelings. That is why she is Webster's great creation in this play as Flamineo was in the other.

"Man, woman, child (a daughter or a son), That's how all natural or supernatural stories run." Thus Yeats, in "Ribh Denounces Patrick." Father, mother, son—that's how Webster's stories run. The father is a Cardinal, in each play. He is calculating and controlling but remains aloof, not punishing the son himself but letting others punish. These others— Florence and Ferdinand, Ludovico and Bosola—are the conscience of the son, I would say. Florence and Ferdinand embody that indignant sense of wrong that comes from internalizing parents' prohibitions. Ludovico and Bosola embody the much more primitive rage of the helpless infant, a fury which later is, as psychoanalysts say, put in the service of the superego. This primitive fury may take over the superego. It takes over Ferdinand as he becomes more and more sure the Duchess' goodness is lost, for it is an infant's rage at the loss of his good ministering mother.

The son in these plays, then, is three separate characters. Filial conscience, filial fury, and filial desire are embodied in Florence, Ludovico, and Brachiano respectively and in Ferdinand, Bosola, and Antonio, rather than all in one character. *The White Devil* has a character, Flamineo, who combines this guilt, rage, and lust in one, but he is an observer voicing these feelings, quite distinct from the trio who act them out. Nevertheless, he is more memorable than that trio, in my opinion, just because he is a mixture of emotions whereas each of them enacts only one. *The Duchess of Malfi* has an observer, Delio, but (like Horatio in *Hamlet*) he is emotionless; all the filial feelings are voiced by the trio. And each, unlike his counterpart in *The White Devil*, is a mixture of emotions. Thus Antonio, unlike Brachiano, is not just desire but adores his lady also. And Ferdinand, unlike Florence, is not pure indignation but is infected with fury and lust for the Duchess as well. Bosola, too, is infected with lust as well as with fury at the loss of goodness—rage with despair of regaining good—that characterized Ludovico.

In Webster's two great plays, the mother is killed after her good aspect seems lost: after Isabella dies; after the Duchess proves passionate. The killer is infantile fury at the disappearance of the good mother. Mothers in oedipal dramas—Jocasta, Phaedra, Gertrude, Isolde, for example—generally die, but I can think of no other plays in which this rage is their killer. Ludovico and Bosola, who enact it, are therefore unique creations of Webster's. Outsiders who crave to be in, creatures without self-direction, who are cruel one moment and then sorry the next, beings cynical because despairing and helpless—they remind us of many characters in modern literature, embodiments likewise of an anger and a frustration deeper than the sexual. But I can think of no modern oedipal drama in which that kind of anger is a prime force. Indeed, it is uncommon to find any oedipal drama in which struggle against father takes a back seat to demand for a good mother, as it does here.

In *The White Devil* Webster assumed that a good woman and a passionate one are two separate types. True, Isabella is not cold, and Vittoria has decency in her. If the former were solely good and the latter solely sexual, they would not be reminiscent of real mothers at all and hence would not awaken our deep feelings. Still, they are distinct types enough so that the filial characters devoted to Isabella (Florence and Ludovico) are moved not at all by desire but solely be demand for goodness, whereas the one attached to Vittoria (Brachiano) is all desire and kills goodness. It seems clear, therefore, that Webster intended a moral statement: he was saying that purity is separate from passion, that passion destroys it. A little later, however, when he wrote *The Duchess of Malfi*, Webster said the opposite: there he created a heroine who is passionate as well as pure. In that play all three filial characters love her with a mixture of emotions, so that the conflict between them is a battle between rivals more than a case of conscience punishing desire. The moral, therefore, is less clear. Nevertheless, I do believe one is present: the forces of conscience (Ferdinand and Bosola), with their belief that a good woman cannot also be a passionately loving one, with their feeling that the sexual is the whorish, destroy goodness. It is they, not Antonio—conscience, not passion—that Webster ultimately condemns in *The Duchess of Malfi*: just the opposite of his message in the former play. I think that when Webster wrote *The Duchess of Malfi*, he was imagining the way things ought to be: with an ideal maternal figure who fulfills our demand for goodness and for love. *The White Devil*, on the other hand, with its picture of women as either too pure for passion or too whorish for respect, is probably his despairing view of the way things actually are.

YORK COLLEGE OF THE
CITY UNIVERSITY OF NEW YORK

Notes

[1]See, most notably, Elizabeth Brennan, "The Relationship between Brother and Sister in the Plays of John Webster," *Modern Language Review*, 58 (1963), pp. 488-94. Most others remark on Ferdinand's incestuous desire but not Flamineo's. See, for instance, McD. Emslie, "Motives in *Malfi*," *Essays in Criticism*, 9 (1959), pp. 391-405; Clifford Leech, *John Webster* (London: 1951) and *John Webster: The Duchess of Malfi* (London: 1963); and Robert Reed, Jr., *Bedlam on the Jacobean Stage* (Cambridge: 1952).

[2]William Empson, "Mine Eyes Dazzle," *Essays in Criticism*, 14 (1964), p. 85.

[3]The sources and dates of both plays are given in F. L. Lucas, ed., *The Complete Works of John Webster* (London: 1928).

[4]What it was meant to be and what it actually is may be different things, of course. The question whether Webster's plays are moral has been debated at enormous length and is too complex for me to deal with here. I have no doubt Webster thought he was teaching moral lessons (in *The White Devil* obedience to law, for instance). But whether his vision of existence nullifies these lessons is a question I will not try to answer. For an opinion that it does, see Travis Bogard, *The Tragic Satire of John Webster* (Berkeley: 1955). For an opposite opinion see David Cecil, *Poets and Storytellers* (London: 1949). For a summary of the debate see Don D. Moore, *John Webster and His Critics, 1617-1964* (Baton Rouge: 1966). A first-rate scholarly treatment of this and other matters is Peter B. Murray, *A Study of John Webster* (The Hague: 1969).

[5]Una Ellis-Fermor, *The Jacobean Drama* (London: 1958), speaks of Vittoria's "nobility" and "courage, even if it be Satanic" (p. 184). But she does not say whether she feels Vittoria's satanic power or just accepts that Vittoria is supposed to have it. Neither she nor any woman writing about Webster has addressed herself to the question whether women apprehend his plays differently from the way men do. I find it an interesting question.

[6]So Elizabeth Brennan believes, and I agree with her. The quoted words are hers. See John Webster, *The Duchess of Malfi*, ed. Elizabeth Brennan (New York: 1965) p. xii.

[7]Leech, *John Webster*, pp. 108, 78.

VIII. Rhetoric

CORTAZAR'S RHETORIC OF
READER PARTICIPATION

Robert Y. Valentine

In his four novels, as well as in essays and interviews, Julio Cortázar calls for a reader-accomplice who is willing to enter his fiction at the moment of interpretation in an act of co-creation. By participating in the creation of the novel in a duplication of the author's difficult quest, the reader identifies with the author's search for himself within the artistic vocation. Cortázar suggests that this results in self-knowledge for both the reader and the author: "Lo que el autor de esa novela haya logrado para sí mismo, se repetirá (agigantándose quizá, y eso sería maravilloso) en el lector-cómplice."[1] The novel, according to this view, is a ritual typical of earlier literary modes in which the teller and hearer identify closely with particular events or beliefs. In an attempt to overcome resistance to belief, Cortázar pleads for this ritual participation; however, in fact, as a novelistic technician he creates pattern, a net which he stretches to avoid losing readers.[2] With the pretense of seeking reader participation, Cortázar actually creates a complex system of controls over the reader's involvement in the author's fictional world. Among these, the call for collaboration itself is a rhetorical device used to exploit specific reader interests and to draw the reader more effectively into his novels *Los premios* (1960), *Rayuela* (1963), *62, Modelo para armar* (1968), and *Libro de Manuel* (1973).[3] In essence, on one level Cortázar disclaims entrapment and thus entraps.

Most successful writers since Cervantes have been concerned with readers' reactions to their fiction. Many writers have divided their readers into two or more camps.[4] In the "alternative" section of *Rayuela*, Cortázar, through the notes of his fictional creation Morelli, states that the only character who interests him is the reader, and describes three types: *lectores-alondra, -hembra,* and *-cómplice*. Cortázar says he wants an active, interested, involved *lector-cómplice* who is willing to undertake "otros rumbos más esotéricos," in contrast with the traditional response of lazy readers:

Yo creo que un escritor que merezca este nombre debe hacer todo lo que esté a su alcance para favorecer una 'mutación' del lector, luchar contra la pasividad del asimilador de novelas y cuentos, contra esa tendencia a preferir productos premasticados. La renovación formal de la novela debe apuntar a la creación de un lector tan activo y batallador como el novelista mismo, de un lector que le haga frente cuando sea necesario, que colabore en la tarea de estar cada vez más tremendamente vivo y descontento y maravillado y de cara al sol.[5]

But Cortázar recognizes that most readers prefer tidy novels that "te llevan de la punta de la nariz," according to a character in his first novel (*LP*, p. 248). These *lectores-hembra* demand sequential ordering of time and space within the novel: "Pero no había que fiarse, porque coherencia quería decir en el fondo asimilación al espacio y al tiempo, ordenación a gusto del lector-hembra" (*R*, 109:533). Also, the *lector-hembra* seeks protective detachment: "No quiere problemas sino soluciones, o falsos problemas ajenos que le permiten sufrir cómodamente sentado en su sillón, sin comprometerse en el drama que también debería ser el suyo" (*R*, 99:500).

Similar to the *lector-hembra* is the *lector-alondra*, who identifies himself with characters in the novel, which serves as a mirror to keep the reader happy with his own reflection (*R*, 21:115; 112:539). These readers, Cortázar suggests through various characters in his works, do not seek an intimate author-reader relationship (*R*, 112:539); instead, they respond to forms which have dominated the majority of traditional novels, especially those of Latin America.[6]

Cortázar's call for ritual participation by the reader is also made throughout his essays. In 1954 he wrote that "la evolución regionalizante del hombre ha eliminado progresivamente la cosmovisión mágica."[7] He implies a loss on man's part because of his new allegiance to rational or scientific epistemologies. The poet or writer, he believes, should remain closer to the magician. He quotes from Lucien Levy-Bruhl on the nature of ritual participation: "La esencia de la participación consiste, precisamente, en borrar toda dualidad; a despecho del principio de contradicción, el sujeto es a la vez el mismo y el ser del cual participa."[8] Cortázar wants a story to evoke predictable emotional responses in the teller and the hearer. But he recognizes reader resistance to participate in his ritual, or fictional reality. In his essay "Situación de la novela," published after he wrote many of his stories but ten years before his first novel, Cortázar demonstrates an historical awareness of the genre and confesses his ambition to write a special kind of novel.[9] These writings expose Cortázar's political and social concerns, the need to bring men closer together—as suggested by Lukacs, Goldman, and Sartre—by returning somehow to more primitive modes. He builds his essay on the notion (perhaps too obvious) that the novel has always been a means for self-knowledge. The origin of the word *lector-cómplice* emerges in this essay from the idea that there no longer can be characters in the modern novel, only accomplices:

Cómplices nuestros, que son también testigos, y suben a un estrado para declarar cosas que—casi siempre— nos condenan; de cuando en cuando hay alguno que dé testimonio en favor, y nos ayuda a comprender con más claridad la exacta naturaleza de la situación humana de nuestro tiempo (*SN*, p. 224).

Cortázar wants to do away with the novel as "recreación (en el sentido doble del término)" in order to produce a literature that is no longer interested in what man is, "sino la manifestación activa del hombre mismo" (*SN*, p. 235). He seeks identification with "la acción del hombre, con su diario batallar" (*SN*, p. 237), in order to produce "el estado de las cosas mismo. . .que busca desde hace tiempo ser en cierto modo la situación en sí, la experiencia de la vida y su sentido en el grado más inmediato" (*SN*, pp. 238-39). Cortázar admits, however, that "los hombres capaces de esta confrontación son pocos" (*SN*, p. 239).

The heroes of Cortázar's novels, Persio, Horacio, Morelli, Juan, and Andrés are self-conscious writers who frequently resemble Cortázar himself and who wrestle with their creative tasks from cover to cover. In contrast with *lectores-hembra* and *-alondra*, the ideal reader would experience their situation as his own without necessarily seeing himself as the character portrayed. Cortázar wants to establish the sincerity of his artistic venture by causing his novel to unfold simultaneously to the author and to the reader without pattern. The process is described in *Rayuela*:

> No engaña al lector, no lo monta a caballo sobre cualquier emoción o cualquier intención, sino que le da algo así como una arcilla significativa, un comienzo de modelado, con huellas de algo que quizá sea colectivo, humano y no individual (*R*, 79:454).

Morelli, again speaking for Cortázar in *Rayuela*, wants to

> hacer del lector un cómplice, un camarada de camino. Simultaneizarlo, puesto que la lectura abolirá el tiempo del lector y lo trasladará al del autor. Así el lector podría llegar a ser copartícipe y copadeciente de la experiencia por la que pasa el novelista, en el mismo momento y en la misma forma (*R*, 79:453).

The result of the reader's participation is a duplication of the author's confusing and difficult artistic quest. According to these statements, by participating in the creation of the novel the reader becomes a participant in the author's search for himself within the artistic vocation.[10] Cortázar wants the reader to experience his vision, not just read about it. In another essay he writes:

> Detesto al lector que ha pagado por su libro, al espectador que ha comprado su butaca y que a partir de allí aprovecha el blando almohadón del goce hedónico o la admiración por el genio. ¿Qué le importaba a Van Gogh tu admiración? Lo que él quería era tu complicidad, que trataras de mirar como él estaba mirando con los ojos desollados por un fuego heracliteano. Cuando Saint-Exupéry sentía que amar no es mirarse el uno en los ojos del otro sino mirar juntos en una misma dirección, iba más allá del amor de la pareja porque todo amor va más allá de la pareja si es amor, y yo escupo en la cara del que venga a decirme que ama a Miguel Angel o a E. E. Cummings sin probarme que por lo menos en una hora extrema ha sido ese amor, ha sido también el otro, ha mirado con él desde su mirada y ha aprendido a mirar como él hacia la apertura infinita que espera y reclama.[11]

In these and many other declarations, Cortázar directs the reader to
forget that the novel is an object to be admired, at least until he has
finished reading it, in order to subject himself to the experience or situation
through which the narrator is going or has gone. The true *lector-cómplice*
will say, "This is real and I believe."

All of Cortázar's pleas to readers have led to the appealing (but hard to
explain) idea that the reader collaborates directly with the author in the
creation of the novel. Osvaldo López Chuhurra writes:

> Autor y lector constituyen así los dos términos de una dualidad; la obra es hija
> de un ser que sustantiva la creación, en la cual participa otro ser que adjetiva
> con la fantasía un posible y multiforme acontecer. El creador hace "aparecer"
> una cosa (cosa, tal como la considera Heidegger) que antes *no era*, en cambio el
> lector "elabora" a partir de la cosa que aparece. Si fuese capaz de provocar una
> aparición aprovecharía la energía de su espíritu para crear sus propias obras.[12]

A variation of this notion is offered by Julio Ortega [*La contemplación y la
fiesta* (Lima: Editorial Universitaria, 1968), p. 14.]:

> La nueva novela latinoamericana quiere ser una novela abierta porque
> entre el tiempo del lector y el tiempo del autor no se reconstruye un mundo, no
> se lo arma para entenderlo, sino que se organiza aquella geometría que el
> lector mismo establece convirtiendo en otro arte su acción de leer.

Although partially accurate, these assessments decry the novelist's powers
to create pattern to control his audience. In reference to the contemporary
novel, Guillermo de Torre clarifies this problem reminding us that reader
participation is not a new idea:

> La confusión, la desmesura sobre la posible participación del lector se confunde
> con el desprestigio recaído sobre el llamado autor "omnisciente," quien
> imponía su visión de las cosas por modo "absolutista y autoritario" a los
> leyentes. La ambigüedad, inclusive la multiplicación del punto de vista es cosa
> distinta, y, frente a todas las apariencias, sigue corriendo siempre a cuenta del
> autor.[13]

The entire question becomes more confusing when we discover that many
narrators limit privilege or "omniscience" in their novels. Yet even authorial
silence, the nearly total effacement of a guiding presence to help the reader
along, used extensively by Cortázar and other novelists, is, paradoxically, an
effective rhetorical control on the reader's response to the novel.

The actual author-reader relationship is indeed a difficult matter.
Helpful to an understanding of this complex interaction is the concept of the
implied author proposed by Wayne C. Booth.[14] Any author invents an
implied version of himself, or second self, as he composes each of his
novels—that is, an implied author whose character changes according to the
specific nature and demands of each work. A similar transformation takes
place in the active reader who must create a second self distinct from the self
who "goes around paying bills, repairing leaky faucets, and failing in
generosity and wisdom" (Booth, *Fiction*, p. 137). The creation of a second
self in the reader is necessary because "the implied author of each novel is
someone with whose beliefs on all subjects [the reader] must largely agree if

[he is] to enjoy [the] work" (Booth, *Fiction*, p. 137). But this does not mean that the reader is independent in the creation of his second self. On the contrary, the implied reader must coincide with an image of the reader in the author's mind.

> The author creates, in short, an image of himself and another image of his reader; he makes his reader, as he makes his second self, and the most successful reading is one in which the created selves, author and reader, can find complete agreement (Booth, *Fiction*, p. 138).

The image Cortázar has of the ideal *lector-cómplice*, then, must coincide with an image the reader has in mind of his own role. If the reader is unwilling to subject his second self to the particular demands of each of Cortázar's works, then Cortázar's plea for a *lector-cómplice* has no purpose from the outset. Yet implicit in Cortázar's plea, but unfortunately misunderstood by some critics, is the recognition that fiction is an action that authors and readers perform together.

This is easier for the reader to accomplish in Cortázar's stories than in his novels. For instance, in "Carta a una señorita de París" the narrator tells of vomiting little rabbits from his mouth until they overpopulate the apartment. The reader is drawn in and participates willingly in a briefly narrated fantastic experience. The intensity of this kind of participation is more difficult to achieve and to prolong within the form of the novel.[15] The reader must view the materials in the novel for an extended period with the same degree of detachment or sympathy felt by the implied author.

In the novel *Los premios*, the reader's second self accepts the initial passivity of the passengers on board the Malcolm as they confront a series of mysteries. A *lector-hembra* would ask, "Why do these adults sit quietly without protest under such strange circumstances?" A *lector-alondra* would declare, "I wouldn't put up with that situation. It is neither tragic nor plausible." The *lector-cómplice*, however, suspends judgment in order to identify with the experience of the novel. He forgets about verisimilitude as he reads *Los premios*, understanding that the author's purposes lie elsewhere and that he must adopt a particular attitude toward the work at hand. Implausible novelistic situations are rejected by some readers, who throw the novel down in disgust. For others, Cortázar's true accomplices, obscurities and difficulties demand a clarification and ironic communication that plunge these readers deeply into the ultimate meaning of the works.

In an essay on the difficult Cuban writer Lezama Lima, Cortázar suggests that in some novels a variety of reader poses is needed. Criticizing the majority of readers today, Cortázar says that

> éste tiende hoy a adoptar una actitud especializada según lo que esté leyendo, resistiéndose a veces de manera subconsciente a toda obra que le proponga aguas mezcladas, novelas que entran en el poema o metafísicas que nacen con el codo apoyado en un mostrador de bar o en una almohada de quehacer amoroso (*VD*, p. 137).

Not knowing whether Lezama Lima's monumental work *Paradiso* is a novel, poetry, or anthropological study, Cortázar calls for a *lector-diagonal* willing to adopt the numerous poses required by a multifaceted work. Indirectly, and in agreement with Booth, Cortázar is saying the same thing about the reader's approach to his own novels, especially *Rayuela*. A reader must adopt different poses for Cortázar's different works, often a variety of poses within the same work.

The range of narrative and structural devices by which an author controls the reader's responses and participation in his novels is fully illustrated by Booth in *The Rhetoric of Fiction*. Cortázar and most novelists manipulate various categories of reader interests to grasp their public. No great work of art relies on any single interest. Booth emphasizes that an author exploits these interests according to his ability. He suggests three general groupings: (1) "Intellectual or cognitive: We have, or can be made to have, strong intellectual curiosity about 'the facts,' the true interpretation, the true reasons, the true origins, the true motives, or the truth about life itself." (2) "Qualitative: We have, or can be made to have, a strong desire to see any pattern or form completed, or to experience a further development of qualities of any kind. We might call this kind 'aesthetic,' if to do so did not suggest that a literary form using this interest was necessarily of more artistic value than one based on other interests." (3) "Practical: We have, or can be made to have, a strong desire for the success or failure of those we love or hate, admire or detest; or we can be made to hope for or fear a change in the quality of a character. We might call this kind 'human' if to do so did not imply that 1 and 2 were somehow less human" (Booth, *Fiction*, p. 125). All of these devices, and more, are used by Cortázar to control his reader's responses to his novels. His appeals for reader participation given within the novels exploit intellectual and qualitative reader interests. Literary critics of Cortázar's works need not concern themselves, then, with whether or not Cortázar subjects his readers to pattern, but rather with the types of rhetorical devices and reader interests he actually does employ as a novelist. This critical stance sees literature as an action upon the reader and not just as a message. In other words, the *meaning* of Cortázar's novels results from his *doing*. The critic looks at his works not just as a "poetic" but as a "rhetoric."

Wellek and Warren also deal with the notion that a literary work is the experience of the reader and warn that the psychology of the reader, "however interesting in itself or useful for pedagogical purposes, will always remain outside the object of literary study—the concrete work of art." Acceptance of the idea that the reader's experience is commensurate with the literary work, they continue, leads to the absurd conclusion that the work of art is non-existent.[16] But since the work of art is both an analyzable object as a "poetic" and an author's intention as a "rhetoric," no matter how many pleas to the contrary, there is a vast difference between reader involvement through the second self and reader co-authorship. The latter is never fully achieved unless the author provides blank pages between two covers with other writing, as in the case of Laurence Sterne, from whom Cortázar probably purloined the term "female" reader, and more recently the French novelist Michel Butor.[17]

Willingness to subject oneself to the purpose of the novel at hand is not co-creation or even participation in the creative process. Unless the reader experiences the same literary birth pangs, the anguish of the blank page, any attempt to depict or to approach a duplication of the author's creative quest falls into the category of intellectual interest, one of the manipulative devices of pattern used to forestall the reader's escape. Pure ritualistic commonality can be established to a limited degree only among other writers for whom the described processes or surfaces have a basis in shared experience. Otherwise the novel would resemble a ritual *tertulia* in which established authors exchange impressions of the delights and horrors of the craft of fiction.

Cortázar's plea for reader-accomplices attempts to court the reader on another level by establishing a sympathetic relationship with him. He no doubt seeks the reader with an intellectual interest in the making of a work of art, an interest exploited by writers as similar and diverse as Sterne, Cervantes, Proust, Gide, Henry Miller, Unamuno, Pirandello, and Anais Nin. By creating self-conscious, dramatized narrators, usually writers who are primary characters in his novels, Cortázar's implied author in each of his works attempts to get the reader on "the side of the honest, perceptive, perhaps somewhat inept, but certainly uncompromising author in the almost overwhelming effort to avoid falsehood" (Booth, *Fiction*, pp. 214-15). In this way, the implied author in each work makes the reader part of the battle, not by allowing him to create his own art, but by controlling his responses to the novel. Although the meaning of his works might be considered the experience itself—an attempt at ritual commonality through a duplication of the writer's quest—control over the reader is still demanded if fiction is Cortázar's goal. No matter now hard an author tries to remove controls from his fictional work, some will remain.

Cortázar is a consummate technician, as he admits directly and indirectly throughout his non-fictional works. Without manipulation there is no art. Technique is "any form or rhythm imposed on the world of action; by means of which, it should be added, our apprehension of the world of action is enriched or renewed."[18] Cortázar's technique causes the reader to participate willingly in a fictional experience. It is not a matter of whether or not the creative experience is contained within the pages of the novel but whether or not the reader is.

Technique and control also lead to intimate contact with the reader. If Cortázar understands co-participation to mean the establishment of intimate contact with a highly sophisticated reader, then as critics we must deal with his consistent use of irony throughout his novels. Ultimately, the establishment of a special relationship with the *lector-cómplice* hinges on the success or failure of his ironic communication. A large measure of pattern is achieved by Cortázar by means of his extensive use of stable irony, a complicated literary device clarified by Booth in *A Rhetoric of Irony*.[19]

To be a *lector-cómplice* in many ways is to have a sense of irony in key with that of Cortázar, to yield to his pattern qualitatively by stepping onto his ironic platform. In fact, only the reader who shares ironies with Cortázar will glean intended hidden meanings from the texts of his novels. Booth writes:

> Often the predominant emotion when reading stable ironies is that of doing, of finding and communing with kindred spirits. The author I infer behind the false words is my kind of man, because he enjoys playing with irony, because he assumes my capacity for dealing with it, and—most important—because he grants me a kind of wisdom; he assumes that he does not have to spell out the shared and secret truths on which my reconstruction is to be built (Booth, *Irony*, p. 28).

Failure to understand Cortázar's irony is manifested by several critics who accept all of his fictional and non-fictional statements unquestioningly, without penetrating his real intentions or rhetoric. But those who reconstruct his irony enjoy a wider degree of reading pleasure.

In spite of the fanfare by Cortázar and others, the reader's role is a traditional one. Mary E. Davis recognizes that Cortázar and Nabokov descend from the master of literary tricks, James Joyce. Assuming that the "open" novel removes controls on the reader, she states that, compared with *Don Quijote, Tristam Shandy,* and *Moby Dick,* Cortázar's (and Nabokov's) works are not revolutionary. "La red o malla del estilo desplegada por estos novelistas sirve para enredar a los esquivos personajes, como también al lector."[20] This assessment must be compared with that of Richard F. Allen, whose praise for Cortázar's revolutionary prose and "completa metafísica novelesca propia" leads one to wonder if he has read Joyce and others.[21] Mauricio Ostria González insists that the structure of *Rayuela* permits the reader freedom to approach the novel according to his whims and personal "invention" by breaking with traditional rhetoric, such as refusal to comment, lack of descriptions, and lack of sequential coherence.[22] This critic forgets that these "omissions" have been used by other novelists to control the reader.[23] Silverio Muñoz Martínez correctly points out that the random order of the alternative chapters of *Rayuela,* rather than leading to reader freedom, "instaura una singularidad que en ningún caso podría ser alterada."[24] And according to a recent detailed study by Lucille Kerr, the "movement of reduction" that results from the suggested reading orders "eventually undermines or subverts the freedom which the Table first appears to offer."[25]

Lida Aronne Amestoy accepts Cortázar's direct plea for ritual participation and suggests that studying the tricks of an author "es una garantía de fracaso." Emphasizing the participatory nature of *Rayuela,* she suggests that the reader learn how to "play" because "*Rayuela* quiere ser un puente, y, al desmenuzarla para reconocer sus materiales malogramos su función, nos condenamos a quedarnos de este lado."[26] Readers have always been required to suspend some beliefs as they read the novel and to "play" along with the author, yet the discernment of pattern appeals to qualitative reader interests and has always been part of the reading experience. She lists several statements by Cortázar in support of her assumptions, succumbing in the process to one of his rhetorical tricks, which she claims should not be analyzed. On the other hand, Fernando Alegría admires Cortázar's ability to control the reader: "yo me puse a leer *Rayuela* y dejé la puerta abierta por si acaso. A las cien páginas, más o menos, Cortázar me la cerró y no me di cuenta. Supe que estaba preso y no hice nada por escaparme."[27] Osvaldo López Chuhurra also points out Cortázar's exploitation of reader interests: "Si un libro de Cortázar 'interesa' a un lector, es porque en la obra existen ciertos elementos capaces de modificar—con su participación—la marcha interrumpida de su existencia."[28] But when the reading is completed, the reader's primary self re-establishes control and goes about his daily business, although his second self may want to man the barricades, or engage in a passionate love affair, or do as one famous reader did—"desfacer tuertos."

The author's intentions, his desire for ritual participation as discussed in the preceding pages, are always commentaries that must be taken into account but recognized as part of the author's rhetoric. Cortázar is the first to insist that "no bastan las buenas intenciones"; what is needed, he says, is the "oficio de escritor" to transform "conmociones" into art.[29] In Cortázar's case, his intentions are used for control and thus are part of pattern. Although Cortázar attempts to affirm the independence of his readers, he creates a complex system of controls over his readers' fictional world. Cortázar is aware that the success of his fiction centers on his ability to control his readers by causing them to join in the process through his exploitation of intellectual, qualitative, and practical reader interests and other deliberate rhetorical ploys. It is not a matter of whether or not Cortázar's reader is controlled, but rather in what ways he is controlled. Indeed, Cortázar's rhetoric has more than a little to do with our admiration of his novels.

UNIVERSITY OF NEBRASKA

Notes

[1]Julio Cortázar, *Rayuela* (Buenos Aires: Sudamericana, 1963), p. 452. Future references to *Rayuela* are from this edition and will be indicated in parentheses with the letter *R* followed by chapter and page.

[2]The contrast of pattern and ritual participation is discussed by David I. Grossvogel, *The Limits of the Novel* (Ithaca: Cornell University Press, 1968). Pattern in the novel is also discussed by E. M. Forster, *Aspects of the Novel* (New York: Harcourt, Brace and World, Inc., 1927).

[3]Julio Cortázar, *Los premios* (Buenos Aires: Sudamericana, 1960). Future references will be indicated in parentheses with the letters *LP. 62, Modelo para armar*

(Buenos Aires: Sudamericana, 1968), *Libro de Manuel* (Buenos Aires: Sudamericana, 1973).

[4]Referring to Cortázar's classification of readers, Edna Coll, in "Aspectos cervantinos en Julio Cortázar," *RHM*, 24 (1968), pp. 596-604, points out Cervantes' dislike for the *vulgo* as reader and compares it to Cortázar's dislike of *lectores hembra*.

[5]"Sobre las técnicas, el compromiso y el porvenir de la novela," *El Escarabajo de Oro*, 1 (1965), p. 3. He continues: "Por eso, y sin ocuparme ahora de los resultados conseguidos, admiro el esfuerzo de los escritores de la llamada 'nueva novela' francesa. Se ve perfectamente que han comprendido la necesidad de quebrar los hábitos mentales de una sociedad acostumbrada a la gran novela psicológica, y quebrarlos de la manera más agresiva, ácida y hasta maligna imaginable. Más que libros, están haciendo lectores."

[6]Ignacio Iglesias, in "Novelas y novelistas de hoy," *Mundo Nuevo*, 28 (octubre 1968), pp. 84-88, says that the "new" Latin American novel was destined to be read by a small group of *iniciados*. Antonio Pagés Larraya, in "Tradición y renovación en la novela hispanoamericana," *Mundo Nuevo*, 34 (abril 1969), pp. 76-82, responded that these novels "no suponen un lector pasivo, sino un lector despierto y avisado" (p. 77).

[7]"Para una poética," *La Torre*, II, 7 (1954), p. 124.

[8]Quoted by Cortázar on page 126 of "Para una poética" from Lucien Levy-Bruhl, *Las funciones mentales en las sociedades inferiores* (Buenos Aires: Lautaro, 1948), p. 346. In reference to these statements by Cortázar, Saúl Sosnowski, in "Los ensayos de Julio Cortázar: pasos hacia su poética," *RI* 39 (1973), p. 663, says that participation on the reader's part means "llevarlo a la acción" and that "cada línea es re-escrita con cada lectura."

[9]"Situación de la novela," *CA* III, 4 (julio-agosto 1950), pp. 223-43. Subsequent references to this essay will be indicated in parentheses with the letters *SN*.

[10]Typical of many critics who accept this invitation at face value is Rubén Benítez, "Cortázar: 'que supo abrir la puerta para ir a jugar,' " *RI*, 39 (1973), p. 485: "El lector reproduce así el mismo ritual de conocimiento que el escritor y sus personajes. Busca, simple busca, sin solución definitiva. Cortázar no nos impone dogmáticamente su idea de la realidad sino que nos proporciona un método para descubrirla."

[11]"Morelliana, siempre," *La vuelta al día en ochenta mundos* (México: Siglo Veintiuno, 1969), p. 208. Future references will be listed as *VD*.

[12]Osvaldo López Chuhurra, "Sobre Julio Cortázar." *CHA*, 71, 211 (julio 1967), 12.

[13]Guillermo de Torre, *Ultraísmo, existencialismo y objetivismo en la literatura* (Madrid: Guadarrama, 1968), pp. 308-9. Not attempting to evaluate lazy readers, he continues: "¿No será pues, un espejismo afirmar que 'el lector se ha convertido en protagonista activo de la creación literaria'? ¿No supondrá ello extender al lector común—que es el específico lector de novelas—una virtud sólo adscribible al minoritario, al lector crítico? Pero tal actitud, tal creencia supone más exactamente tanto una ingenua supervaloración de los poderes del lector como una afligente disminución de los poderes del autor, en este caso, concretamente, del novelista."

[14]Wayne C. Booth, *The Rhetoric of Fiction* (Chicago: University of Chicago Press, 1961). Future references to this edition will be indicated in parentheses with the designation "Booth, *Fiction*," followed by the page number. Germán Gullón, "La retórica de Cortázar en *Rayuela*," *Insula*, 26, 229 (octubre 1971), p. 13, makes brief use of Booth's concept of "implied author" to distinguish the novelist from his narrators in *Rayuela*.

[15]In an essay entitled "Del cuento breve y sus alrededores," *Ultimo round* (México:

Siglo Veintiuno, 1969), pp. 42-44, Cortázar deals with the author-reader relationship in the short story: "*Ellos* respiran, no el narrador, a semejanza de los poemas perdurables y a diferencia de toda prosa encaminada a transmitir la respiración del narrador, a *comunicarla* a manera de un teléfono de palabras. Y si se pregunta: Pero entonces, ¿no hay comunicación entre el poeta (el cuentista) y el lector?, la respuesta es obvia: La comunicación se opera *desde* el poema o el cuento, no *por medio* de ellos. Y esa comunicación no es la que intenta el prosista, de teléfono a teléfono; el poeta y el narrador urden criaturas autónomas, objetos de conducta imprevisible, y sus consecuencias ocasionales en los lectores no se diferencian esencialmente de las que tienen para el autor, primer sorprendido de su creación, lector azorado de sí mismo."

¹⁶*Theory of Literature*, 3rd ed. (New York: Harcourt, Brace and World, 1956), pp. 146-47.

¹⁷In *Tristam Shandy* (New York: Random House, 1950), p. 60, Laurence Sterne's narrator says: "I wish the male reader has not passed by many a one, as quaint and curious as this one, in which the female reader has been detected." Sterne's narrator continually chides "Madame" reader to pay attention to the work and to forget her quest for adventures instead of erudition.

¹⁸Mark Shorer, "Technique as Discovery," *Myth and Method: Modern Theories of Fiction* (Lincoln: University of Nebraska, 1960), p. 88.

¹⁹*A Rhetoric of Irony* (Chicago: University of Chicago Press, 1974). Future references will be indicated in parentheses with the designation "Booth, *Irony*."

²⁰"Cortázar y Nabokov: La estética del éxtasis," *Homenaje a Julio Cortázar*, ed. Gelmy Giacoman (New York: Las Américas, 1972), p. 487. Silverio Muñoz Martínez, "Otra mirada sobre *Rayuela*," *RI* 39 (1973), p. 558, reaches a similar conclusion: "Cortázar no hace más que integrarse a una forma narrativa configurada primero por Sterne."

²¹"Temas y técnicas del taller de Julio Cortázar," *Homenaje a Julio Cortázar*, p. 299.

²²Mauricio Ostria González, "Concepto e imagen del lector en *Rayuela*," *Chasqui*, II, 2 (February, 1973), p. 23.

²³For instance, Wolfgang Iser, *The Implied Reader* (Baltimore: The John Hopkins University Press, 1974), p. 33, refers to "gaps" in the text that control the reader by heightening awareness, forcing him "to discover for himself the divergencies from the established repertoire."

²⁴Muñoz Martínez, "Otra mirada," p. 568.

²⁵"Leaps Across the Board," *Diacritics* (Winter, 1974), p. 31. With no reference to Kerr's study, John S. Brushwood joins those who emphasize reader participation: "*Rayuela* is a kind of standard fiction that invites the reader's participation, most specifically because its structure is in process rather than predetermined, and because the novel has no definite end." He says the novel is endless because we do not know what happens to Horacio. *The Spanish American Novel: A Twentieth Century Survey* (Austin: University of Texas Press, 1975), p. 267. By concluding that we do not know what happens to Horacio, Mr. Brushwood has passed over the references to his recovery and his subsequent writing of the novel.

²⁶*Cortázar: La novela mandala* (Buenos Aires: Fernando García Cambeiro, 1972), p. 13. She recognizes Cortázar's use of clarity and confusion to control his reader: "Violando técnicas, intercalando recursos inusitados, confrontándolo con incidentes absurdos y desenlaces inesperados, desconcierta al lector, lo saca literalmente de sus carillas. Y lo fuerza así a observarse, a tomar conciencia frente a sí mismo y frente al mundo" (p. 97).

[27]"*Rayuela*, o el orden del caos," *Homenaje a Julio Cortázar*, p. 83.

[28]López Chuhurra, "Sobre Julio Cortázar," outlines some of these deeply felt interests present throughout Cortázar's works—i.e., time, duality, and death.

[29]"Algunos aspectos del cuento," *CHA*, 85, 255 (marzo 1971), p. 411.

IX. Semiotics

FROM *EL OBSCENO PAJARO* TO *TRES NOVELITAS BURGUESAS:* DEVELOPMENT OF A SEMIOTIC THEORY IN THE WORKS OF DONOSO

Sharon Magnarelli

José Donoso's most recent work, *Tres novelitas burguesas*, published in 1973, represents a prolongation and subsequent amplification of the topics and themes begun and at times already well-developed in *El obsceno pájaro de la noche* of 1970. In spite of the fact that *Tres novelitas* evidences a return to the shorter genres exercised and apparently preferred by Donoso before the appearance of his masterpiece, *El obsceno pájaro*, this later work in no way implies a retrogression to early themes. On the contrary, the major thrust of the trilogy (like that of *El obsceno pájaro*) is art and the effect art exercises on bourgeois society.

In the coming pages, I hope to show that the three basic activities dramatized in "Chatanooga Choochoo," first novella of the collection, are basically the same activities performed throughout *El obsceno pájaro* and that each of these three activities reflects the texts' preoccupation with language and art, and in turn with the sign. Even the title of each of the three stories or novellas designates some type of artistic creation. "Chatanooga Choochoo," of course, denominates an American song of the "big band" era. "Atomo verde número cinco" is the title of a painting executed by the protagonist of the second story, and "Gaspard de la nuit," title of the third story, denotes the title of a composition by Ravel.

Although the analysis will specifically treat only the first story of *Tres novelitas*, the theories and conclusions are easily applicable to the other two stories as well. All three works concentrate on the bourgeoisie of Barcelona in a contemporary setting, and, while each is autonomous, the three are closely interrelated in that the protagonists of each reappear as secondary characters in the other two stories.

"Chatanooga Choochoo" recounts some of the events in a week of the life of two Barcelona couples: Ramón del Solar, his mate, Sylvia Corday, and their friends Magdalena and Anselmo Prieto. The action of the story (although not the narrative itself) begins at a social gathering; Sylvia and Magdalena, identically dressed, perform a song and dance number to the tune, "Chatanooga Choochoo." The story concludes a week later at a similar gathering when Anselmo and Ramón, also identically attired, do the same song and dance number.

The first activity which predominates in both the text of *El obsceno pájaro* and "Chatanooga Choochoo" is the endeavor to create a face. Face, of course, became a metaphor for a unique personality or identity in *El obsceno pájaro*, but the faces which the protagonists wished to invent there were but masks, guises ultimately reducible to artistic-linguistic conglomerations—to signifiers which composed an identity.[1] In *El obsceno pájaro* both don Jerónimo and Mudito continually sought to devise faces for themselves, or in Mudito's words—to be somebody. Mudito tried to generate a distinctive identity for himself by means of the book he wrote (the book with the green cover, parts of which are included within the text of *El obsceno pájaro*). And, perhaps more importantly, the identities of the characters in *El obsceno pájaro* were formulated by the rumors surrounding them, by the mystic each character succeeded in creating.

In a parallel manner, within just a few pages of "Chatanooga Choochoo," we are already enmeshed in the "se dice," in the floating rumors, and we are offered nothing to measure the extent to which we are to accept or reject these rumors. "Poseía, sobre todo, una enorme destreza para echar a correr rumores sobre ella. . .rumores tan sabrosos. . .decían las malas lenguas. . .y hasta se murmuraba. . ." (p. 15).[2] Clearly, there is little necessity here to quote the rumors; the important fact is that we and the characters are surrounded by them. Our knowledge of the characters, as well as their supposed familiarity with each other, is formulated and regulated by these rumors, these floating words with neither origin nor proprietor. As Mudito esteemed don Jerónimo in *El obsceno pájaro*, Anselmo, the narrator here, also admires these "people" who, like don Jerónimo, have been able to fashion an identity, an existence, from the rumors: "Como siempre he sentido gran admiración por la gente que sabe crearse un aura, transformando las cosas y anexándoselas como por arte de bírlirbirloque aunque la calidad de esa magia sea discutible. . ." (p. 17).

The principal difference between the rumors and gossip of the two works is the nature of the myth created by these linguistic shadows. In *El obsceno pájaro* the hearsay produces a myth about witches and saints, while in *Tres novelitas* the rumors are directly related to a bourgeois world which would *appear* to be more easily identifiable with some form of origin or referent. Nonetheless, the rumors function in exactly the same manner by forging a myth which ultimately can be neither confirmed nor denied. Although the gossip of "Chatanooga Choochoo" constructs a social aura, a social illusion which directly parallels the one in which we live rather than producing a myth of supernatural powers, in both cases the rumors, the words, the "se dice" create the character and the personality. In spite of the fact that the words, ultimately, are without origin, these rumors become directly related to the question of "face" or individual personality.

But the attempt to invent a face becomes less abstract and even more overt in "Chatanooga Choochoo" when we discover that Sylvia's face can be totally re-fashioned, redesigned, at any moment. Her face is completely erasable; one wipe with Elizabeth Arden Vanishing Cream leaves it a blank, white, smooth surface (a tabula rasa, so to speak). On this "superficie lisa y plana como un huevo" (p. 18) or "pobre rostro ovoide y bello completamente anulado" (p. 30), the man at hand can apply cosmetics and paint or compose the face (chosen from *Vogue* magazine) which pleases him most.

This blank, white ovoide, of course, evokes the *imbunche* of *El obsceno pájaro*, but at the same time it is important to recognize that the painting of Sylvia's face directly effectuates an artistic and linguistic composition not very different from that produced by the rumors. As her creator puts on her cosmetics, he formulates her and assigns her qualifying signifiers. In as much as she is even called "una mujer adjetiva," there obviously is little difference between the symbolic act of painting her face, making her up— and in this sense, providing her with specific modifiers—and that of fashioning her through the medium of rumors or language, again supplying her with adjectives which restrict and specify. Just as an adjective is "any class of words used to limit or qualify a noun or other substantive,"[3] formulation of a face for Sylvia limits and qualifies the possibilities open to that "superficie en la que se proyectaban distintas realizaciones de la belleza" (p. 30). Thus, the invention of Sylvia's face overtly parallels the efforts of each character to generate a face or personality by attributing to himself selected and very specific signifiers.

It becomes evident then that, reduced to its simplest terms, the creation of a face, either through the rumors or cosmetics, is simply the grouping and subsequent denomination of a set of signs. The individual facial features selected from *Vogue* magazine have no relationship to Sylvia until they are grouped and labelled "Sylvia." Whether the characters use words or pictorial representation, they are simply selecting a group of signifiers, assigning them a specific name (or proper noun), and thus, hopefully in this manner, creating some degree of importance, meaning, or significance. (And, of course, this is true of the process of creation of any literary character—the author chooses a group of signifiers and gives them a name.) Although the characters of both the Donoso texts seem naively to believe that these groups of signifiers are unique, the texts themselves emphasize the non-unique nature of these signifiers and the resultant entities. Because adjectives are finite in number and must be shared and repeated, the result is an entity that is neither totally distinctive nor unique as Derrida has noted.[4]

A similar linguistic theory is demonstrated in the second major activity of the two works. The dismantlement and subsequent reconstruction of the literary character becomes a major preoccupation of both texts. Of course this activity is dramatized to some degree in the erasure and re-invention of Sylvia's face, but it becomes more conspicuous in other places. We recall, for example, the scene towards the end of *El obsceno pájaro* when the old women go to the desecrated chapel and begin to redesign statues of saints by joining already used, fragmented remains (signifiers if you will). Similarly, during the week in which the action of "Chatanooga Choochoo" transpires, Sylvia teaches Magdalena the technique of totally dismantling her husband when he becomes vexatious or superfluous. Once disassembled, the men can be stowed away in a suitcase until the women need them or are ready to reassemble them. In this dramatic way the character is overtly reduced to simple components which may be combined at will, and each segment may be substituted by another if desired (each woman can borrow certain characteristics to give her husband when she reassembles him).

It seems particularly relevant to recall that when Anselmo thinks of dismantling his secretary and storing her away, he notes, "pensé, no sin una especie de mareo de ilusión, que seguramente de haberlo querido yo también podría borrarle las facciones a esta mujer y desarmarla como a Sylvia, y cuando me hartara, guardarla, clasificándola pieza por pieza en el Kardex verde. . ." (p. 59). His wish to deposit her in the Kardex implies the possibility of reducing her to words on note cards; it demonstrates the nature of the literary character, which is reducible to linguistic signs that can be filed away, brought out, and reassembled at will, just as the pieces of the saints' statues could be arbitrarily joined to form new saints.

The basic difference between the treatment of the literary character as a composite of signifiers in the two works is that in *El obsceno pájaro* the objects dismembered and reconstructed are already presented as works of art; they are already recognized as signs of signs.[5] In other words, they are never presented as anything but artistic creations; the statues of the saints are easily acceptable and recognizable as re-creations, as composites of signifiers. However, in *Tres novelitas burguesas* the creation which is de-constructed and then reconstructed is not overtly presented as artistic creation, as something which holds potential for that type of treatment (although, ultimately, it is just that). Not only is this literary creation presented as a person, an animated being, but one of the creations de-constructed is our very narrator (an act we will discuss in detail at a later point). This dismemberment of the narrator not only undermines our willing suspension of disbelief, but it also converts the notion of narrative center into a game. The narrator that until the moment of dismemberment has been readily accepted as the narrative center is suddenly destroyed and negated (as in *El obsceno pájaro*). To this extent, the disassembly of the narrator not only undermines the possibility for any authority (authorial or narrative) within the text, but it also underlines our position, distant from any potential origin or referent. The entire movement of the text, then, continually emphasizes the Derridian notion of language and the sign as repetition. Each aspect of this text is overtly already repetition: the song, the rumors, the cosmetics, etc., and, to this extent, all are without identifiable origin. In these texts, then, the literary character is explicitly shown as a repeated conglomeration of verbal signifiers that can be filed or stored away and reassembled.

We must note, however, that in both works this formulation of an identity by means of either of the two activities is contingent upon an artistic or linguistic relationship with the other (another entity of one form or another). The character cannot and does not construct this face or composition in isolation, without the complicity of the other, nor without some type of semiotic interchange. Just as don Jerónimo was dependent on Mudito's eyes, so also is each character subject to the artistic-linguistic attention of the other (within the fiction that other is another character; outside the fiction that other is the reader). Such a dependency on the other is demonstrated in the rumor as well as in the character of Sylvia. The vague other produces the rumors, without origin or ownership, which create the self, while in the same manner the other invents Sylvia's identity, an identity over which she has only peripheral control. In these works, identity and existence are reduced to the notion that as you paint me, as you name me, as you assign me signifiers, I exist; as your attention focuses on me and you speak of me, I also exist. As Anselmo notes, it is as if "la falta de atención de todos me negara la existencia" (p. 101). To this extent, then, we see that the creation of an existence is directly related to a theory of language, which seems to suggest that existence and naming are simultaneous processes—that is, an object cannot exist for us until we find a name for it, and, simultaneously, the naming of it confirms and reaffirms its existence.[6] Thus, to a greater or lesser extent the text implies that I am what our mutual language, our common set of signs perpetrated by our interchange, makes me. Naming, then, is dramatized in its most abstract and theoretical context: to name is to assign a proper noun to a more or less arbitrarily selected group of adjectives, qualifiers, or characteristics.

Interestingly and, I believe, significantly, this process of naming occurs twice in "Chatanooga Choochoo"; Anselmo is named once by Sylvia and once by Magdalena. In each case the utterance of his name contradictorily signals his subsequent effacement. Sylvia labels him at the start of a series of events which ends with her usurpation of his masculinity, and Magdalena names him as she is dismembering him and stowing the pieces in a suitcase. As we consider the significance of the two instances of denomination, we cannot but recall Derrida's theory of naming and the violence and effacement implied by the act of labelling:

> Il y avait en effet une première violence à nommer. Nommer, donner les noms qu'il sera éventuellement interdit de prononcer, telle est la violence originaire du langage qui consiste à inscrire dans une différence, à classer, à suspendre le vocatif absolu (*De la grammatologie*, p. 164).

At an earlier point in the same text, Derrida noted:

> C'est parce que les noms propres ne sont déjà plus des noms propres, parce que leur production est leur oblitération, parce que la rature et l'imposition de la lettre sont originaires, parce qu'elles ne surviennent pas à une inscription propre; c'est parce que le nom propre n'a jamais été, comme appellation

unique réservée à la présence d'un être unique, que le mythe d'origine d'une lisibilité transparente et présente sous l'oblitération. . . (p. 159).

Thus, just as the painter or writer has the power to erase what he has created, so also it would appear that the namer has the power to efface that which the name creates. We must wonder then if this artistic-linguistic complicity on which the character depends is not simultaneously the first step in the usurpation and effacement of that same "identity" which the complicity creates.

The ultimate paradox demonstrated in "Chatanooga Choochoo" is that this same energy which creates, this same power which forges Sylvia and upon which she is dependent, is enslaved by her—an enslavement which results in the master/slave dichotomy already begun in *El obsceno pájaro*. The relationship between the creator and the creation, the master and the slave, is most clearly demonstrated in the following passage when the armless Sylvia stops before a closed door which Anselmo gallantly and generously opens for her. She continues to stop before each door but develops an increasingly commanding attitude until she commands him to open the drapes.

> Se detuvo ante la puerta cerrada, yo me di cuenta de su problema, y galantemente se la abrí. Ella sonrió y siguió camino. Ante cada puerta, como una reina, iba deteniéndose para que yo se la abriera, pero su primera sonrisa ante la primera puerta que le abrí se fue transformando a medida que le iba abriendo puertas sucesivas, en una expresión autoritaria. En su habitación me ordenó. . .(p. 49).[7]

Thus, what had begun as generosity here is soon converted into slavery.

Of course, this generosity/slavery paradox directly reflects the linguistic functions of the characters of this story. One is not forced to name, to create, to give linguistic identity, just as Anselmo does not have to paint Sylvia. For the most part, one is not inherently obligated to speak or to write, but one does. One does speak, write, participate linguistically, perhaps in a display of generosity or perhaps in order to subjugate. But once said, once written, the words seem to own and enslave in reverse. In other words, language here is produced contradictorily out of a sense of generosity and a desire to master, but results in subjugation of the producer.

We must consider the creative power of language and the theory that once produced the word itself creates and gains power. We have seen this process dramatically displayed in *El obsceno pájaro*; each character not only creates (Humberto writes his book, don Jerónimo constructs the Rinconada, and Inés elaborates and perpetrates the myth), but each believes in his creation, becomes enslaved by it and is eventually destroyed by his own fabrication. It seems clear that the dramatic point being made in the texts of Donoso is that language, which begins as our slave, our servant, which we produce only out of generosity or our desire to humble others, soon converts into a tyrannical master which enslaves us and makes us its victims.[8] And, conversely, the works suggest that the language generated by others, because it creates us, even more definitively subjugates us. This power of the word is alluded to in "Chatanooga Choochoo" when Anselmo wishes to make love and Sylvia begins murmuring about breakfast and hunger; soon Anselmo discovers that "al hacerlo me sorprendí al comprobar que en este momento comenzó a primar en mí el habitual hâmbre de la mañana más que el deseo, que ahora bien se podía aplazar durante una hora" (p. 48).

Thus, in both works, language, power, and sex become closely and immediately related. Both language and sex are means of power, and congruently, both power and sexual activity are generated by language. Anselmo finds Sylvia sexually attractive as a result of the power he has over her and his creation of her, as demonstrated when his painting of her face becomes an erotic activity charged with overtones of domination and language:

> Sí, bórrame primero las cejas. . .así, así. . .y luego el color de las mejillas. . . suave. . .sí, así, mi amor, qué bien lo haces, qué bien, mucho mejor que Ramón, mucho mejor. . .(p. 51).

Of course, ultimately, the whole question of language and power and the master/slave opposition returns us to the creator/creation dichotomy considered by many authors—Unamuno and Galdós, among others. As Augusto Pérez says to Unamuno, "No sea, mi querido don Miguel. . .que sea usted y no yo el ente de ficción, el que no existe en realidad, ni vivo ni muerto. . .No sea que usted no pase de ser un pretexto para que mi historia llegue al mundo. . . ."[9] Similarly, Anselmo notes, "Yo no existía, no era más que el maquillador de Magdalena" (p. 77).

And, the text demonstrates that nothing escapes this paradoxical subjugation. Even Anselmo, our narrator, is dismantled and stored away. This is particularly relevant since the third major activity of the text centers around him. The text of "Chatanooga Choochoo," in effect, is based on Anselmo's interpretations of events and his efforts to understand their meaning. Or more abstractly, the text centers on the potential significance inherent to each sign or group of signs and the plurality implicit in them.

When the story opens, Anselmo has gone to spend a weekend at the Solars' weekend home. In the very first paragraph the following event takes place: "Una mariposa nocturna, gorda, blanda, torpe, chocó contra el trozo de espalda que la blusa *folk* de Sylvia dejaba desnuda. . ." (p. 11). What follows in the text is a series of interpretations of the potential significance of this apparently minor, irrelevant incident. The principal procedure of the text is to describe an episode and then offer multiple commentaries or "translations" of that occurrence, giving no explanation more value nor authority than another. The story is filled with words which either suggest possibility and conditional status or which offer contradictory interpretations: *Quizá, sin embargo, pero, me pareció, a pesar de, como si, casi como, aunque, por otra parte,* etc.

These conditional words suggest two things. First, each sign is plural in nature and has multiple referents. Second, the literary sign is plural because it is arbitrary, and, conversely, it is this very arbitrariness which produces the multiplicity of referents. Were there a more concrete, more exigent relationship between the signifier and the signified, multiplicity of significance would not be a possibility; each signifier would demand a single referent, a single relationship, a unique interpretation. But, our language is not based on that type of singularity and simplicity, and the word or signifier almost inevitably becomes arbitrary. For example, when Anselmo tries to explicate the words of Sylvia, "Y Magdalena tiene tan buen gusto. . ." (p. 13), his first thought is to wonder when Sylvia had tasted her. His successive thoughts continue to underline the multiplicity of connotation potential to the statement and to emphasize the lack of a one-to-one relationship between the words and their meaning.

Ultimately, then, this arbitrary and multiple relationship between the signified and the signifier produces several results. First, the search for origin or referent becomes inevitable as a result of the very plurality of the sign. And, this same plurality makes this origin impossible to discover. What we have then is a text that strongly resembles the detective novel; the protagonist seeks out the clues and tries to discover their significance in an effort to solve the "mystery" (all the while recognizing the possibility of multiple interpretations). Our text in this respect becomes what the character of *El túnel* defined as the perfect detective novel. We recall that in Sábato's text one of the characters wished to write a detective novel whose relationship to the genre would parallel that of *Don Quijote* to the chivalresque genre. His idea was to devise a character who would be a narrator, detective, and murderer all in one. It is apparent that it is this very type of relationship which is concretely worked out in "Chatanooga Choochoo." Anselmo, the narrator, not only functions as the detective, ferreting out information and trying to discover the mysteries of creation, but in the end he, too, is de-constructed and reconstructed, just as the signs he endeavors to explicate.

It cannot be ignored that in many ways the investigatory activity of Anselmo directly corresponds to that of the literary critic. The latter's sole function, like that of the detective, is to read signs and those elements which he sees as signs. But, as the text of "Chatanooga Choochoo" notes, the critic's or detective's function is not as simplistic as it seems, for he not only "reads" the signs, but he supplements them as well.

Thus, as was suggested at the start of this study, both *El obsceno pájaro* and *Tres novelitas burguesas* might be seen together as the development of a semiotic theory. This theory begins with a recognition and dramatization of the concept that each sign and/or signifier refers but to another signifier, is already duplicative. This layering of signifiers in turn inevitably leads to an incessant search for origin, a search which is doomed to failure from the beginning. Because each signifier becomes the sign of another signifier, *ad infinitum*, the impossibility of discovering the origin or referent is implicit. I would suggest, as has Tzvetan Todorov, that this search and ultimate failure are inevitable in fantastic literature and, in turn, that fantastic literature predominates during those historic periods when the sign becomes less simply and immediately related to its referent or some type of presence.[10] It is in fantastic literature, especially, where we overtly recognize that language cannot be taken at its face value, a recognition which causes us futilely to search out meaning, a referent, a symbolism, an origin. While the search for a referent and origin is always implicit in any literary work, it is in fantastic literature where this search becomes explicit.

There are many examples in "Chatanooga Choochoo" of this layering effect and multiplicity of signs that but point to other signifiers. Perhaps the most overt example is in the very title of the story, "Chatanooga Choochoo." First, the title of the story is a Spanish sign of English words which are the sign of an American song, the referent of which is a specific train that, in turn, becomes a symbol of a desire to return home (return to the origin), which signifies the universal search for origin and desire to return to that which is past. To this extent, the title of the work, because it reflects a desire to return to origins, again underlines the movement of language back towards some type of original referent, back to some type of past which is ultimately fiction. All this multiplicity is indicated by merely the title.

The song itself, parts of which are included in the text, indubitably reflects the plurality of any artistic creation. The song first intimates power; it not only seems to transform the characters singing and performing it into mindless "muñecas," but it also suggests the powers of the North American culture, as portrayed in its devouring context (the Barcelona couples are totally caught up in imitating this culture). In spite of the fact that the characters of this story neither lived the epoch of the song, nor are a part of the North American culture which produced the song, they are familiar with it and have at least indirectly been affected by that same dominant North American culture. The song, in turn, evokes various aspects of that culture. A war-time song about a man returning home, it hints at the power and might of the military giant. It evokes the post-depression economy as reflected by the song's concern for sufficient money: "I've got my fare / And just a trifle to spare." It simultaneously reflects the repression of the black Americans as the singer demands a shoe shine from the "boy," and it conjures North American slang with "Gimme a shine."

Perhaps the most significant aspect of the song is the theme of time. Time is portrayed in terms of hours—the hours at which specific activities are performed or will be performed—and, in a more spatial sense, hours at which the train will arrive at certain destinations. To this extent, the passage of time becomes a movement in space. Principally, time is portrayed as a return to an origin, a return home, which becomes both a spatial and a temporal journey. Thus, the hours spent in the train suggest a simultaneous progression and retrogression, culminating in that past golden age.

All this is conjured by the old song, but the performance of the song, in its own way, suggests and dramatizes many of the same things. For instance, the very performance of this song in the early seventies evidences the nostalgia sweeping society: the same nostalgia and desire to recapture that past golden age that the song itself and, in effect, all language reflects. Also, as the song underlines the power held by the United States, the performance of the song becomes a power play and portrait of the control of one character over the other. And, finally, just as the song and its journey imply both progression and retrogression, so also does the performance of that song: retrogression in the sense of a pseudo-return to that past era, and progression to the extent that the performance continually advances toward the end of the song and the end of the story.[11]

Returning circularly to where we began, then, the song underlines the multiplicity of the signifier which points but to another signifier. We have demonstrated the multilayered condition of the story's title and we must additionally note that the very act of entitling a story with a sign which points to another work of art emphasizes the disposition of the story as literature based on other literature, repetition of repetition. Todorov, of course, has noted that all literature must be founded on other literature,[12] and it is clear that Anselmo is creating his "life" from literature. I merely list some examples of this duplication of other written texts: "Elementary, Watson!" (p. 37); "Masters and Johnson curan estos traumas" (p. 56); "García Lorca llamaba el sitio del pecado" (p. 63); "la idea de tener que leer a Hesse otra vez" (p. 72); "I'll think about it tomorrow, in Tara" (p. 83); "como Swann la sonata de Vinteuil" (p. 86); "para leer *El juego de los abalorios*" (p. 87); "Charles Addams en la época de oro del *Esquire*" (p. 97). Again, we must recognize that just as it was impossible to encounter totally new signifiers or adjectives for Sylvia, so also it is difficult (if not impossible) to find a work of art which does not, to a greater or lesser extent, take into account and reproduce previous creations. Decidedly, this tendency is more salient in "Chatanooga Choochoo" than in other texts.

Reduced, then, to its very simplest terms, "Chatanooga Choochoo," like *El obsceno pájaro de la noche*, portrays a complex and sophisticated theory of the sign. Recognizing that ultimately the textual discourse is almost exclusively supplemental, the text demonstrates the triple movement of this fluid sign. For example, *choochoo*, baby-talk for train, is, of course, onomatopoeic and, to this extent, not a totally arbitrary sign. In the course of the novella, however, we watch its repetition and movement away from the signified until the term becomes but a signifier of another signifier. To this extent, the text accentuates the inevitable, eternal absence of a signified (which is always necessarily past and simultaneously future, both temporally and spatially). It is the possibility of re-assembling these units of meaning and recreating which produces their arbitrary nature. And, each reassembly, each recreation, necessarily entails additional supplementation. Thus, it is the supplementation that produces both the power and the danger that we previously spoke of: power to the extent that the creator has various options, various combinations open to him and thus he has the power to control; danger to the extent that the supplement—fraught with power—consistently and continually threatens to efface and erase the signified (and in effect does). It is because of the continual repetition and supplementation that the signifier loses the potential for any immediate and direct relationship to a signified. Just as in both works the small elements of the characters can be reunited, separated, and joined again in a new way, so also' in language can we recombine each and every element, down to the smallest phoneme, and each reassembly would appear to produce greater power, greater danger, and greater distance from that mythical origin.

The ultimate paradox is that it is the very drive and motivation to find that "origin" (e.g. Anselmo's search for meaning, significance, and the signified in the words of others) that leads us away from that destination because of the power, persistence, and inevitability of our own supplementation which is a part of that very same drive.

ALBERTUS MAGNUS COLLEGE

Notes

[1] This whole notion of "face" bears great resemblance to the ideas expressed by Borges in *El hacedor*, where being, the mask, and literary, linguistic creation are directly related: "ya se había adiestrado en el hábito de simular que era alguien, para que no se descubriera su condición de nadie. . . .La identidad fundamental de existir, soñar y representar le inspiró pasajes famosos." See Jorge Luis Borges, "Everything and Nothing," *El hacedor* (Buenos Aires: Alianza, 1972), p. 60.

[2] All page references are from the first edition of *Tres novelitas burguesas* (Barcelona: Seix Barral, 1973).

[3] *Webster's New World Dictionary* College Edition (New York: World, 1962), p. 18.

[4] As we have noted, Derrida maintains that proper nouns are not proper at all but shared: "On ne nomme donc jamais: on classe l'autre." See Jacques Derrida, *De la grammatologie* (Paris: Minuit, 1967), p. 160.

[5] Derrida has noted that everything is necessarily already repetition and reproduction: "Tout commence par la reproduction. Toujours déjà. . . ." See "La scène de l'écriture," *L'écriture et la différence* (Paris: Seuil, 1967), p. 314. In *Grammatologie* he notes, "il n'y a jamais eu que de l'écriture" (p. 228).

[6] Even Saussure suggests the possibility that ideas do not necessarily pre-exist words. See Ferdinand de Saussure, *Course in General Linguistics*, trans. Wade Baskin (New York: McGraw-Hill, 1966), p. 65. Obviously, Derrida's notion of the absence of origin suggests a similar interrelationship between the object and the name (see *Grammatologie*).

[7] It would not be fortuitous to note that this passage is closely related to *El obsceno pájaro* in that Mudito's enslavement to Iris in the latter text began with the opening of a door.

[8] Nevertheless, this "original innocence" of language may be as much a myth as the "innocence" of Levi-Strauss' primitives. See *Grammatologie*, pp. 149-202.

[9]Miguel de Unamuno, *Niebla* (Madrid: Espasa-Calpe, 1968), p. 149.

[10]Both Todorov and Foucault have suggested similar concepts. See Tzvetan Todorov, *Introduction à la littérature fantastique* (Paris: Seuil, 1970) and Michel Foucault, *Les mots et les choses* (Mayenne: Gallimard, 1966).

[11]Additionally, the song provides a certain neat, circular structure to the text, which portrays Sylvia and Magdalena at the beginning in the same manner as it portrays Anselmo and Ramón at the end.

[12]*Introduction*, p. 97. Equally relevant, of course, is Derrida's observation (already noted) that all language is, in fact, the possibility of repetition.

X. Sociology

ALL FOR LOVE
AND THE THEATRICAL ARTS

Margaret Lamb

Neo-Classical drama is famous for its rules. Yet a Neo-Classical play must, like any work intended for the stage, owe much of its success to its suita-bility to contemporary actors and stages, and its acceptance by the specta-tors. Any purely literary study of a successful dramatic work has to leave out a great deal: the theatre is a notoriously impure, or mixed, art.

John Dryden's *All for Love* is often considered the finest English example of Neo-Classical tragedy on the French model. Certainly it is very different from the heroic plays—including Dryden's own—that were popular after the Restoration. As a stage piece, *All for Love* outlasted the heroic drama; *All for Love* was still a staple of the Patent theatres in Samuel Johnson's time, when Neo-Classical dramatic theory was in decline in England. In fact, *All for Love* is sometimes thought to have driven—or kept—Shakespeare's *Antony and Cleopatra* from the stage for almost a hundred years.

Because Dryden was such a great poet and literary critic, later critics have naturally emphasized the literary values and classical standards exemplified in *All for Love*. Yet the success of Dryden's play and the eclipse of Shakespeare's version were at least partly dependent on non-literary arts. These other influences included: the performance style of such actors as Thomas Betterton and Barton Booth; Restoration stage decor and the increased stress on the visual aspects of the English theatre after 1660; and the enormous change—from the pre-Civil-War period to Dryden's time—in audience sensibilities and expectations. That is to say, the great actors who succeeded as Dryden's Antony and Cleopatra were technically more suited to Dryden's language than to Shakespeare's; also, the triumph of change-able scenery and the preferences of Restoration audiences are closely related to the pace, dramatic structure, and stage directions of *All for Love*. In the Augustan and early Georgian theatre, the standards of English tragic acting, decor, and language did not change very much from Dryden's time.

Theatre practice has not been so prominent in comparative studies as literature, the visual arts and philosophy. The problem, naturally, is lack of records. Not only does the theatrical art itself disappear, but its practitioners—particularly the actors—rarely theorized about their work before the nineteenth century. There are only fleeting references to performances of *All for Love*. Yet theatrical sources do help to explain why *All for Love* held the stage from 1667 for about a hundred years and why *Antony and Cleopatra* remained the *only* Shakespearean tragedy which was not performed in some version during most of that time.[1]

In his famous preface to *All for Love*, Dryden set forth his dramatic principles with Neo-Classical clarity—such clarity that the play's success has sometimes been attributed to its illustration of the rules. In summary, Dryden's reasons for reworking Plutarch's Antony had to do with morality, propriety, classical dramatic theory, and standards of poetical language. Like some later critics, Dryden felt that Shakespeare's treatment of the story showed a lack of decorum and a corresponding lack of high moral tone: " 'Tis true, some actions, though natural, are not fit to be represented; and broad obscenities in words ought in good manners to be avoided." Although he regretted the awkwardness of bringing Octavia to Alexandria to confront the lovers, Dryden was pleased with the resulting unity: *All for Love* was, its author declared, "the only [play] of the kind without episode, or underplot; every scene in the tragedy conducing to the main design and every act concluding with a turn of it."[2] In another essay, Dryden criticized Shakespeare for undue geographic "leaping" and for creating dramatic characters who are "composed of mighty opposites."[3] Like most English writers of the time, Dryden regretted the "superfluities of expression" of Shakespeare and other "old" dramatists; Dryden preferred regularity of plot, latinity in language, and smoothness in versification.[4]

Such a summary, like the preface to *All for Love*, leaves out Dryden's artistic complexity and his great admiration for Shakespeare; it only makes obvious that every one of Dryden's points contradicts Shakespeare's practice in *Antony and Cleopatra*. (Shakespeare's version of the story has, of course, more changes of location than any other single play he wrote; it has the most hyperbolic language, a leisurely time scheme, and so forth.) Yet it seems likely that the actors' preferences also helped to keep Shakespeare's *Antony and Cleopatra* off the stage after the Restoration. The London theatres were reopened in 1660, but *All for Love* did not appear until 1677; during these seventeen years, thirteen of Shakespeare's plays were performed—often undergoing great changes—in the new Patent theatres.[5] Actors are naturally conservative, especially in the wake of troubled times for the theatre; it is likely that the Shakespearean plays first revived after 1660 were those that the older actors remembered seeing or performing during Charles I's time.[6] Charles Hart, for example, had been a child actor before 1642; Hart's company owned the rights to Shakespeare's *Antony and Cleopatra* after the Restoration.[7] Yet when Hart played Antony, it was in Dryden's play. This was in the first production of 1677, with Michael Mohun as Ventidius (Antony's sturdy Roman conscience and chorus). Betty Boutell, a blonde actress who usually played innocent young ladies, seems to have been miscast as Dryden's Cleopatra.[8] This first production was not a great success.[9] The play found more favor after 1684, when Thomas Betterton, the great Restoration actor, played Dryden's Antony and Elizabeth Barry played Cleopatra. *All for Love* did not really become a great hit until the 1718 revival with Barton Booth and Nance Oldfield.[10] After that, *All for Love* was a repertory staple until the 1750s. During this long period the very different play of Shakespeare's that had inspired Dryden was not produced in any form.

In the hundred years that followed the Restoration, tragic actors had a particular affinity for smoothness and regularity in language. Of course, the adaptors like Nahum Tate were used to taming Shakespeare's more extravagant flights; but the actors also helped in this smoothing-out process. For example, Thomas Betterton had to perform in *The Rival Queens*, which its author, Nathaniel Lee, had modeled after Shakespeare's *Antony and Cleopatra*. In his performance in *The Rival Queens*, Betterton employed "the Charms of harmonious Elocution" to tone down the playwright's "unnatural scenes and flights of the false sublime."[11] (The quotations are from Colley Cibber, an actor of the next generation who greatly admired Betterton's ability to curb the excesses of a playwright.) Perhaps Betterton would have given Shakespeare's *Antony and Cleopatra* the same treatment he gave *The Rival Queens*.

Betterton's and Dryden's mutual distaste for eccentric and rough language was shared not only by the Augustan play adaptors but by the following generations of eighteenth-century actors. As late as 1752, the editor of a popular Shakespeare quotation book apologized for the "turgid" and over-realistic language of Shakespeare's Antony.[12] Thus Antony's indelicate reference to "dungy earth" in *Antony and Cleopatra* was considered rough soldier's talk.

It seems likely that English Neo-Classical actors also had technical reasons for preferring Dryden's version. The more lavish, specific, and eccentric the dramatic language, the less likely it is to yield to a chanted delivery. "Chanting" or use of a "dramatists' twang" was a marked characteristic of English acting style from Betterton to James Quin; the delivery seems to have been influenced by the tragic speech of the French theatre.[13] Colley Cibber compared the actor's art to that of the singer: "The voice of a singer is not more strictly tied to time and tune than that of an actor in theatrical elocution: the least syllable too long or too slightly dwelt upon in a period depreciates it to nothing."[14] Dryden's Antony was particularly congenial to Betterton's talent, to judge from accounts of his performance in other plays. Contemporaries remarked on Betterton's arresting voice and his effective yet economical use of gesture. Colley Cibber remembered the great Betterton as neither ranting nor falling into a monotone. "Betterton kept his passion under, and showed it most. . . when stifled."[15] Betterton had an almost hypnotic power of holding an audience with his voice. Dryden, too, in *All for Love*, may be said to have "kept his passion under," showing strength through restraint.

Actors in the Betterton tradition were clearly more at ease with the "smoothed and harmonious numbers" of Neo-Classical dramatic poetry than with Shakespeare's extravagant language. (Actors in the old Elizabethan theatre employed, it is thought, a rapid speaking voice with greatly varied pitch.[16]) In contrast to the old public-theatre style was the new speech of a Restoration actress like Elizabeth Barry. Mrs. Barry's performance as Dryden's Cleopatra was much admired for its dignity. Mrs. Barry "ran into a tone" when she was young and unskilled; yet she was later praised for her becoming manner of drawing out her words.[17] Shakespeare's mercurial Cleopatra could not have employed such a drawl any more than his Antony could have exhibited passion "kept under." Like Mrs. Barry in her youth, some actors overdid the chanting. Barton Booth, who played Antony in the successful 1718 revival of All for Love, was sometimes accused of ranting.[18] Yet the principle was clear: in tragedy, as Colley Cibber wrote, "the manner of speaking varies as little as the blank verse it is written in."[19]

The restrained, telling gestures of Betterton and the best of his successors were matched by the action and stage directions of All for Love. Throughout All for Love, the characters are waiting, reviewing their lives, and changing their minds; as in Racine's Bérénice, the decision to act comes only in the fifth act. In All for Love, the actions and stage directions suggest moments of arrested movement: still pictures to be admired. By contrast, the public theatres of Shakespeare's time must have been too busy to stop for such a tableaux, except perhaps in rare "discoveries" or dumb shows.

One Restoration commentator, Richard Flecknoe, remarked that the London theatre after 1660 was "more for sight than hearing."[20] In the words of the Restoration playwright Thomas Shadwell: "There came Machines, brought from a Neighbour Nation; Oh, how we suffer'd under Decoration!"[21] Drury Lane, where All for Love played, was much less lavish in the use of scenes and machines than the rival Dorset Gardens, where Shadwell worked; All for Love did not call for startling spectacle or scene change—in fact, it all takes place in front of the Temple of Isis.[22] Yet, whether a play was spectacular and fantastic or austere and serious, the presence of changeable scenery helped to slow the pace. The dead-on perspective of the pictorial, and usually symmetrical, setting forced the spectator to consider the actors against the painted background. In Neo-Classical theatre, pose or attitude tends to be more significant than movement. This is true of the greatest Neo-Classical tragedies, those of Racine, and it is true of All for Love.

Dryden's stage directions for All for Love show the importance of the scenic background, the moments of silence and suspense, the effective pictures made by actors posed against the painted setting. At the beginning of All for Love, the Egyptian priests wait before the Temple of Isis, from which Antony must emerge. Entering for the first time, Antony "walks with a disturbed walk before he speaks." He only begins his big speech after he has "thrown himself down."[23] Such stage directions suggest a great contrast to the pre-Civil-War public theatre practice. (In fact, the most common Shakespearean entrance was in mid-speech.[24] On the old platform stage, the characters often came onstage saying lines that set the location for the spectators.) In Dryden's play, Octavia comes onstage "*leading Antony's two little daughters*" for a pathetic domestic confrontation. At the end of *All for Love*, Cleopatra applies the asp; as the stage direction notes, she "Turns aside, and then shows her arm bloody." This last direction is a reminder that *portebras*—the art of using the arms effectively and gracefully—belonged in Neo-Classical performance to acting as much as to dance. Dryden's Antony and Cleopatra die seated, stiffening into eternity like an Egyptian couple carved in basalt. With the two of them posed together—dead—Dryden's final stage picture is severely symmetrical, one of the great moments of Neo-Classical theatre.

Actors in English Neo-Classical tragedy were often described in terms of painting and sculpture. English writers of the early eighteenth century praised performers for statuesque beauty, marble countenances, just and measured actions, lovely height, and fine proportions; Nance Oldfield was praised for her "majestical dignity" as Dryden's Cleopatra.[25] Tall and graceful, Mrs. Oldfield was compared by Colley Cibber to a figure from a fine painting that "first seizes and longest delights the eye."[26] Mrs. Oldfield's Antony, Barton Booth, studied painting and statuary; as a result, Booth's "attitudes were all picturesque."[27] Mrs. Barry, who played with Betterton in *All for Love*, sometimes composed her face, Aston remembered, "as if sitting to have her picture drawn." In performance, Mrs. Barry's face "somewhat preceded her action, as the latter did her words." Mrs. Barry stressed the nobility of Cleopatra's love and excelled in the art of exciting pity.[28] (Neither Mrs. Barry nor Betterton could dance—a lack which may have kept them from succeeding in some of the more operatic Restoration tragedies but was not a hindrance in *All for Love*.)[29]

In place of the rapid movement and varied pitch of Shakespeare's time, the English Neo-Classical stage presented a slowly changing picture and sustained tone. In fact, after the Restoration, an "impulsive, spontaneous style" of acting was thought suitable only for the portrayal of madmen and savages.[30] While Neo-Classical ideals remained in force, English tragedy could not move quickly without causing laughter in the audience; from Dryden to Francis Gentleman (1770), critics complained that the old Elizabethan dramatists dispatched their characters with unseemly speed and that the spectators laughed at such precipitate action.[31] (There was no technical reason for keeping the pace slow: some Restoration comedies and adventure plays have very rapid sequences of scene changes.)[32] Dryden's rhetorical speeches and tableaux in *All for Love* kept the pace slowed to the correct Neo-Classical measure: *largo*.

After 1750, *All for Love* was rarely performed on the English stage, and by 1800 it was a play for the library.[33] The artistic and philosophical values of *All for Love* were antithetical to the new Romantic movement and to the new actors: a new English performance style appeared, based on

Charles Macklin's "broken tones of utterance" and on David Garrick's quick transitions.

Yet, theatrically, *All for Love* had a continuing existence far into the nineteenth century. Its slower pulse and pathetic pictures suited the acting style of the Kembles and the large Regency theatres (which required tableaux). When John Philip Kemble staged *Antony and Cleopatra* at Covent Garden in 1813, he took whole scenes and acts from Dryden's play.[34] In 1833 William Charles Macready acted Shakespeare's Antony at Drury Lane; but Macready was especially admired for a scene of stoic dignity entirely cribbed from Dryden's *All for Love*.[35] In theory, the "rules" ceased to matter in England; but in the practical world of changeable pictorial scenery and act curtains, producers sometimes used Dryden's longer scenes in place of Shakespeare's constantly changing locations.

Even today, two scenes in *Antony and Cleopatra* are usually staged according to Dryden. The triumphal return of Antony to Alexandria usually follows the full processional staging that Dryden gave the event. (In the First Folio, Shakespeare didn't even give Cleopatra a train.) And the most famous theatrical image associated with Shakespeare's Cleopatra comes from Dryden. On Shakespeare's placeless stage, the dead Cleopatra —a young boy—was whisked off on a daybed.[36] Yet almost all subsequent productions, from Garrick's to the Royal Shakespeare's in 1972, follow Dryden: that is, Cleopatra dies in the hieratic seated pose of Egyptian funerary sculpture. The Neo-Classical ideal did not remain dominant in the English theatre as it did in the French. *All for Love* remains a work of fine dramatic poetry, of powerful and lasting—although transplanted— theatrical images.

FORDHAM UNIVERSITY

Notes

[1]Charles Beecher Hogan, *Shakespeare in the Theatre 1701-1800*, I (1701-1750) (Oxford: 1952), p. 461.

[2]Preface, *All for Love, or The World Well Lost*, ed. David M. Vieth (Lincoln, Neb.: 1972), pp. 12-14. All citations of the play are from this edition.

[3]Preface to *Troilus and Cressida*, Dryden's *Essays*, ed. W. P. Ker (New York: 1961), pp. 201, 208, 215.

[4]*An Essay of Dramatic Poesy* (1668), in *Criticism: The Major Texts*, ed. Walter Jackson Bate (New York: 1952), pp. 129-60.

[5]William Van Lennep, *The London Stage 1660-1700* (Carbondale, Ill.: 1965). See calendar from 1660-1677.

[6]Actors after the Civil War were particularly eager to hear how lines had been spoken and particular bits of business performed in the old theatre. See, for example,

John Downes, *Roscius Anglicanus* (1708), quoted in B. L. Joseph, *The Tragic Actor* (London: 1959), p. 32; Thomas Davies, *Dramatic Miscellanies* (1784; rpt. New York: 1971), III, p. 161.

[7]Allardyce Nicoll, *History of Restoration Drama* (London: 1923), pp. 315-16.

[8]James M. Osborn, *John Dryden: Some Biographical Facts and Problems*, rev. ed. (Gainesville, Fla.: 1965), p. 204.

[9]Osborn, p. 205.

[10]Van Lennep, pp. 265, 328, 346, 435; Emmett L. Avery, *The London Stage 1700-1729* (Carbondale: 1960), II, pp. 517-21.

[11]Colley Cibber, *An Apology for the Life of Colley Cibber*, ed. B. R. S. Fone (1740; rpt. Ann Arbor: 1968), p. 63; Vieth, xxiii.

[12]William Dodd, *The Beauties of Shakespear* (1752; rpt. New York: 1971), I, p. 151n.

[13]See Arthur C. Sprague, *Shakespearean Players and Performance* (1953; rpt. New York, 1969), Chapter 1; Joseph, Chapter 2, especially pp. 28-31; John H. Wilson, "Rant, Cant and Tone on the Restoration Stage," *Studies in Philology* 52 (1955), pp. 592-98.

[14]Cibber, p. 63.

[15]Anthony Aston, *A Brief Supplement to Colley Cibber, Esq.* (1788), quoted in Sprague, p. 15.

[16]Joseph, pp. 12-15.

[17]Aston, quoted in Sprague, p. 15.

[18]Sprague, Chapter 1.

[19]Quoted in Bernard Harris, "The Dialect of Those Fanatic Times," in *Restoration Theatre*, ed. John Russell Brown and Bernard Harris (New York: 1967), p. 39.

[20]*Discourse of the English Stage* (1664), quoted in Robert Speaight, *William Poel and the Elizabethan Revival* (Cambridge, Mass.: 1954), p. 83.

[21]Quoted in W. M. Merchant, "Shakespeare 'Made Fit,' " in *Restoration Theatre*, p. 195.

[22]Dryden himself called the second Theatre Royal in Drury Lane "A Plain built House" with a "mean ungilded Stage." In A. M. Nagler, *A Source Book In Theatrical History* (New York: 1952), p. 206.

[23]Stage directions in Vieth ed.

[24]Bernard Beckerman, *Shakespeare at the Globe* (New York: 1962), p. 178.

[25]Joseph, pp. 33, 52, 60.

[26]Joseph, p. 52.

[27]Theophilus Cibber, quoted in Joseph, p. 60.

[28]Anthony Aston, Colley Cibber, quoted in Nagler, p. 227.

[29]Aston, quoted in Nagler, p. 215.

[30]Aston, quoted in Joseph, p. 40.

[31]Dryden, *Essay*, pp. 142-43; Gentleman, *The Dramatic Censor, or Critical Companion* (1770; facsimile rpt. New York: 1972), II, p. 177.

[32]Richard Southern, *Changeable Scenery* (London: 1952), pp. 126 ff.

[33]See *Drury Lane Calendar 1747-1776*, ed. Dougald MacMillan (Oxford: 1938).

[34]Shakespeare's *Tragedy of Antony and Cleopatra; with Alterations and with Additions from Dryden; as Now perform'd at the Theatre-Royal, Covent-Garden* (London: 1813); copy at Shakespeare Center Library.

[35]Prompt book, Folger Shakespeare Library, S.a.130. Both the *Atlas* of

November 24, 1833, and the *Morning Chronicle* of November 22 particularly praised Macready in a scene that the prompt book shows is all Dryden.

[36]The First Folio says "bed"; a daybed is suggested by Richard Hosley, "The Staging of Desdemona's Bed," *Shakespeare Quarterly*, 14 (Winter 1963), pp. 57-65.

FRANCISCO GINER

AND THE REDEMPTION OF SPAIN

Juan López-Morillas

I

Francisco Giner de los Ríos is, as a matter of course, assigned a position of unquestioned eminence in Spanish intellectual history. His life coincides with the formation of modern Spain, and his professional career is one of the forces which determined the intellectual and spiritual orientation of this formation. It would be hard to find elsewhere a similar example of one man's influence in fashioning his country's fate. That influence, it must be added, survived long after his passing and after the tragic events that have visited Spain since 1915. Even today, more than sixty years after his death, Giner's "spiritual presence" must be taken into account in any attempt to understand the history of contemporary Spanish thought.

Giner's professional career underscores the difficulties of a free, unsubmissive spirit forced to live in an environment dominated by authority, tradition, and dogma. In his youth he had embraced the philosophy of *Krausism*, introduced into Spain by Julián Sanz del Río (1814-1869), Giner's mentor and friend. In accordance with Krausist doctrine, Giner insists that philosophy is no mere speculation, but a profession of faith, a program of action, and that the philosopher's duty is to incarnate his ideas and prove their efficacy in every act of his public and private life. Thus, when Giner took over the chair of Philosophy of Law at the University of Madrid in 1866, he became what was then known as a "living textbook" and, as such, the object of vicious attacks by political and religious reactionaries inside and outside the university. Giner gave up his post voluntarily in 1868 when a few of his Krausist colleagues were expelled from theirs. He returned to the chair after the liberal revolution of September 1868 only to leave it again in 1875 when the restored Bourbon dynasty demanded that professors swear an oath of allegiance to the Church and the Monarchy. Giner was exiled for a short time to Cádiz and formally removed from his chair a few months later.

With this removal Giner's memorable professional and personal activity began. He was now convinced that the public universities, mere agencies of the Establishment, would be incapable of bringing about the intellectual and spiritual renewal that Spain so desperately needed. The only way to prevent stagnation was to create a "free center of study," and, as a result, the *Institución Libre de Enseñanza* opened its doors in Madrid in 1876. From the beginning, prestigious names in Spanish science, law, literary scholarship, and art joined him in his undertaking. Several generations of Spaniards, including many of those who achieved great distinction in all kinds of intellectual and artistic endeavors, were educated at the *Institución* during the period from 1876-1939. The *Institución* was abolished after Franco's victory in the Spanish Civil War.

II

I have often stressed Francisco Giner de los Ríos' tendency to criticize the sterility, ignorance, and complacency of the Spain of his time and, more specifically, the Spain of the Restoration.[1] His closest friends and colleagues allude more than once to this trait in the man whom they so greatly admired and to whom they so often resorted when in need of advice to help solve some problem of a personal nature. In the letters addressed to Don Francisco that are preserved in the Academy of History there are numerous examples of this "appeal to the master," often as a last resort, for there is evidence that most of the people who sought his advice accepted the opinions that he showered upon them with exceptional meekness. And, though unfortunately the letters in which Giner stated those opinions are not now available, we can guess from the replies they elicited that they were very frank and often scolding, and, perhaps because of this very fact, extremely effective for people doubtless accustomed to more conventional epistolary formulas. Don Francisco pulled no punches. He called a spade a spade, because it was his nature to do so: "Your admonishments do not trouble me," Joaquín Costa, whose candor was hardly less proverbial than Giner's, once wrote him, ". . .for I believe that if you were deprived of your individual right to grumble, what would become of you?"[2]

During the 1880's Giner's tendency to "grumble" became more noticeable, and his writings of this period display a level of irritability that was not to reappear until the mournful days of 1898. We do not know—and cannot know until Giner's own letters are collected and studied—what circumstances were responsible for this hypersensitiveness. There are hints that Don Francisco was undergoing a profound personal crisis at this time, and that his most assiduous correspondents had some idea of its causes and its intensity. To judge from some comments made by these correspondents Giner, a bachelor, had begun to feel lonely and, in a sense, incomplete. The man who had carefully sketched out the "ideal companion" for one of his students had no helpmate of his own, though it appears that on one occasion he thought he had found her. The man who had given so many spiritual children to the world was painfully aware that he had produced none of flesh and blood. It was useless to tell him, as one of his correspondents did, that "in this world one can be a father in many different ways, and I believe that you, who have so many pupils you think of as your own children, ought not to grieve because you do not have children in any other way."[3] But the fact is that Giner did grieve, that he was in the grip of a real anguish, and that this anguish, composed of frustration, yearning, and remorse, may well have spilled over into the nervous, impatient style evident in his writings of the period.

It would be a mistake, however, to attribute Don Francisco's restiveness to purely personal reasons. There are other, much more obvious reasons which have left their mark in Giner's publications during this time. Ever since the September Revolution the master had been paying particular attention to the problems of young people, in the despairing hope that the national redemption he so greatly desired might come, and must come, from that sector of Spanish life. He was mildly exhilarated by the young people's iconoclastic drives, their stubborn unwillingness to accept everything that had been established by tradition, dogma, sloth, or routine, their firm refusal to bolster, through their own participation, the perversions and chicaneries of "dishonorable Spain." Giner was pleased to observe that "the best [of them] glimpse the fact, though without wholly understanding it, that their job is not to consolidate and to exploit injustice, but to uproot it entirely."[4] In principle this was a praiseworthy ambition, but in the sentence I have quoted two notes of caution are apparent, one of them implicit: who are "the best of the young people" and how can they be distinguished from those who are not? The other is explicit: they do not understand but only glimpse what their mission is to be in overthrowing the established order. It is allowable to suppose that the superiority to which Giner refers is first of all moral. "The best of them" are the young people who have become aware of the vileness, falsehood, and cynicism of the society in which they live and refuse to form part of it. Moreover, they are the ones who keep a "holy anger" alive in their hearts, zealously fed by repeated examples of the general depravity. They are, in fact, as Giner says, the ones who "flee in shame from the wretched apathy they are invited to share and rush into the fray, an inescapable obligation for the good man in these cruel times, on whose ruined bulk they would like to heap the rage of Isaiah, of Juvenal, of Dante, and so bear the whole structure to the ground."[5] But—and let us repeat this—*the best of them do not understand*, and they do not understand simply because no one has ever taught them to understand, that is, to observe, analyze, and weigh the different ingredients in the social environment against which they are so spiritedly rebelling. In their radical negativism they hit out blindly, and as a result their noble intentions are weakened if not rendered wholly unproductive. "All grievances, even the most puerile; all curses, even the most outlandish; all Utopias, even the most absurd find a sympathetic echo in their souls."[6]

It must be noted, however, that the Giner who describes youth in this manner was writing in 1870, just after his thirtieth birthday, at a time when he was drawing up a tentative—and indeed quite negative—inventory of the results of the September Revolution. He feels the righteous anger of the young people of his own age, he shares the repugnance with which they view the corruption that surrounds them, he dreams of a healthy, virile, and honorable Spain. But, unlike most of the men of his age group, he tries to understand, to take in the meaning and scope of everything that he sees. His essay entitled "Youth and the Social Movement" (written in 1870) is the analysis of an "activist" generation by an intellectual who, in order to carry out such an analysis, must deliberately stand apart from that generation so as to view it in the proper perspective. It is not an easy task. Giner—how could it be otherwise?—feels closely linked to his generation; he wants to live in it and for it. Hence it is not strange that when he describes his generation he is ultimately speaking of himself, in terms that rarely achieve a super-ficial objectivity.

But "the new men"—Giner's term for them, in which there is a touch of malice—who had made or helped to make the September Revolution, and on whom so many hopes were pinned, failed completely. Zeal, rebelliousness, courage were no doubt desirable and necessary qualities in the task of bring-ing down of a hateful social and political system; but once the job of demolition was finished and the construction of a new order had begun, a very different set of qualities were needed: clearsightedness, honorable aims, creative intelligence, perseverance in action. The "new men," so apt at destruction, had showed themselves hopelessly inept when it came to building on what they had destroyed. Though he does not try to hide their mistakes in judgment, Giner nevertheless attempts to excuse them:

> In general, their conduct has been what might have been expected from previous experience as well as from all the individual and social circum-stances of their actions. . . .Isolated from the muted internal movement of classes; bereft of clear and well-defined principles, of convictions slowly formed in serious study. . . ; incapable of building, upon that shifting base of understanding and imagination, any solid and lasting construction. An irresistible force impelled them, with increasing violence, to devise and revive to their own advantage the same principles of government they had formerly despised. . .[7]

Or, in other words, the "new men" behaved just like the old ones, like the very men whose shameless maneuvers and corruption were responsible, according to the youth of 1870, for the country's prostration. On each of the levels through which they rose to power, the new men left fragments of the probity they had claimed to profess, scraps of the good intentions that had led them to take revolutionary action. When they had to choose between merit and reward, it was not hard to foresee that they would choose the latter, having learned their lesson in a society which acclaimed worldly success and prudently closed its eyes to the means employed to achieve its goal. Giner is right when he points out that the glorification of personal achievement is not an exclusive trait of Spanish society but is common to the entire Western world under the banner of the liberal bourgeoisie, with its exaltation of the individual and its view of society, not as an area of cooperation in the

248   THE REDEMPTION OF SPAIN

task of creating a more humane life, but as a battleground on which the strong would be separated from the weak, the victors from the vanquished. "And so it is," writes Giner, "that the young man, his spirit weakened, his moral consciousness clouded, his intellect unschooled, and his imagination erratic and untrammeled, sets out to seize his prey and everywhere finds the same universal conspiracy against duty."[8]

III

If I have dwelt at some length on Giner's attitude toward the youth of 1870, it is because I wish to point out something that has been rarely taken into account in presenting his work as an educator. It has been assumed that it was only after his exile in 1875 and subsequent removal from his university chair that he began to pay serious attention to pedagogical questions, separating them from the public schools and universities which, far from solving such questions, were precisely responsible for reducing teaching to "a purely external and mechanical job."[9] But the fact is that his decision to create the *Institución Libre de Enseñanza* was the last step—a step to which he was undoubtedly led by specific and somewhat fortuitous circumstances—in a long series of musings on the character and meaning of man's life and the best ways of helping it to be what it ought to be and not what society wants it to be. As early as 1870 Giner was advocating a "rigorous kind of teaching" whose aim would be to "offer to the world men who are sincere, natural, sober, magnanimous, original, manly, modest, healthy in mind and body, unconquerable friends of the good and implacable enemies of evil. . ."[10] A note of alarm can also be perceived in the feelings he expressed in 1879. Giner, who at that time still professed the Krausist philosophy of history, was convinced that humanity stood at the threshold of a new stage in its journey toward perfection, a stage foreshadowed by the general collapse of the Western world's institutions, usages, and objectives. It requires some effort to grasp this idea of a general and necessary crisis, amounting to a catharsis that will free the social body from all its evil humors, but it is an idea that forms the basis for Giner's thoughts, feelings, and actions during the decade preceding the Restoration. References to this crisis are frequent during the period in question,[11] and they are apt to strike us as abstract and unreal, arising as they do from a doctrinaire and aprioristic idea of history. With Krause's Ideal of Humanity as his guide, Giner commits to paper the plan he has inherited as a precious revelation from his master Sanz del Río, who in turn had received it from his mentor Krause. The view of the world that had been generally current since the Renaissance, with its exaltation of individualism and lack of concern for social objectives, was rapidly breaking down. Attempts to delay its collapse by specific remedies, or to accept it and compensate for it through revolutionary action, would be ineffectual in the long run, according to Sanz del Río, "until men and peoples. . .realize that they are, not creators, but collaborators in their own common destiny, and limit themselves to observing and obeying human laws in the transition from an imperfect history to one that is fuller and more positive."[12] The need to recognize what was, after all, an inevitable process, to willingly accept what was judged to be "human law," is precisely what aroused and justified Giner's simultaneous hope and despair. On the one hand, he firmly believed—at least during this period—in the inexorability of that law, and, on the other hand, he saw no clear indication among the youth of his time that, beyond a mere "presentiment," they had any idea of the magnitude of the crisis or were willing to face up to it either intellectually or spiritually. Hence Giner felt that it was indispensable to aim at a dual objective: a) to confirm by careful analysis that the sense of crisis which was disturbing the most intelligent of the young men did indeed have a historical and social foundation, and b) to begin the slow and difficult task of forming new generations capable of dealing with that crisis and hence of fulfilling the mission that history imposes on those of its protagonists who are abreast of their times. Both these objectives are combined in a formula that appears simple but extremely demanding in its implications: to educate for life, or, as Giner was to repeat so persistently, to *make men*, a very different matter from preparing them for a specific task or making them skilled in a trade. The raw material was there: "intelligent, active, energetic youth," with its anxieties, contrarieties, and presentiments—the youth which Giner himself, in a rare moment of despondency, judged "better suited to the Capitol than to Calvary." But, and let us emphasize this point, he felt like this only in his moments of discouragement, which he tried to overcome by an effort of will:

> There are those who believe that the moral unhealthiness of our youth is incurable, and that all the encouragements offered by men of good will are destined to bounce off the tough hide of our present-day emulators of Alcibiades. The man who says such things blasphemes against God and against the immortal tendencies of human nature![13]

The diagnosis, therefore, was perfectly clear. Spain's rehabilitation, if it were to be genuine, must begin by rescuing Spain's youth, already infected by the all-pervading corruption, but not without possibilities of cure if a timely attempt were made to keep the disease from spreading. No other social group offered any hope of redemption. Everyone else, especially those who had taken over the management of public affairs, had been perverted by all the age-old evils: backwardness, ignorance, shortsightedness, sophistry. And to these other contemporary evils had been added, born out of the cynical adulteration of representative democracy and, along with this, of political life in general. If "politics" were taken to mean the politics of the moment—that is, of the Restoration—nothing good could be expected of it, for, as Giner wrote in 1888, "among us politics always was, and continues to be, nothing but literature: a politics of orators, of writers, of poets, of journalists, of lawyers. . .sometimes of financiers as well, who usually serve only to further coarsen and deprave the political process."[14] Parliamentary garrulity and powerful business interests lived very cosily together under the cloak of systematic fraud imposed by the governments of the Restoration, a combination that was certainly not new in the political history of the Spanish nineteenth century (think of Mendizábal or the Marqués de Salamanca). But it was one which had acquired great importance, though divested of part of its picaresque character, in the last quarter of the century, under the aegis of the country's incipient industrial and commercial development. It was essential to rescue youth from both of these evils, not by preaching against the depravity of both modes of public action, but by encouraging young people to keep still for the time being, to change the flow of words into a wiser internal monologue. Perhaps this aspect of Giner's message has not been sufficiently emphasized; it first appeared in 1870, and in later years acquired by repetition the status of an article of faith. The formation of new generations would have to take place from inside out, from an "inside" enriched, of course, by reflection and presided over in its turn by the moral conscience. All knowledge, all experience, all doctrine, would have to be referred in the end to that internal judge, whose favorable or unfavorable opinion would determine the course of action to be followed. It should be stressed, however, that Giner does not advocate inaction. By putting the inner life first, he is seeking above all a basis for intelligent action, an antidote to the frivolity, cynicism, and routine that, according to him, beset most of his contemporaries and especially the best known public figures, precisely those who, in Unamuno's phrase, "make a noise in history." Nor should we forget, in this respect, that Giner, who was a good Krausist at bottom, professed a philosophy of action—responsible action, of course.

IV

When we read Giner's post-Restoration writings we must sooner or later ask ourselves about the efficacy which Don Francisco himself attributed to the redeeming task of the *Institución Libre*. The fact that this must necessarily be a matter of conjecture as long as we lack the pertinent documentation—that is, Don Francisco's correspondence, as yet unpublished—only whets our curiosity on this point. In view of the magnitude of the task that lay ahead of them and the meager resources to carry it out, we find it hard to believe that Giner and his collaborators did not temper their efforts with a good dose of skepticism. It is known that the plan to create an *Institución Libre* went through several phases. Apparently the first of these was the idea of opening a free university in Gibraltar. This plan came to nought almost as soon as it was put forward, but it opened the way to a new possibility, that of establishing in Madrid "a School of Law with six professors, and another of advanced studies in Philosophy and Science with four or five."[15] A more down-to-earth view of the budding organization's objectives extended this idea to secondary studies, and after 1878, when the primary school was established, the original plan of making the *Institución* a center for university-level studies was abandoned.

Each of these phases involved an increasingly balanced and realistic understanding of the pedagogical needs to be met. Perhaps it is an oversimplification to say that Giner and his colleagues gradually came to understand that it was necessary to deal with children and adolescents before they had time to "go bad" in the public and private institutions of the time. University instruction was already wholly professional and career-oriented, and as such it was confined to imparting a body of special techniques and information in which only a small fraction of the teacher's personality was engaged, together with an equally small fraction of the student's personality. Giner did not raise fundamental objections to such career-oriented teaching, though he did bewail the lack of interest displayed by many of the teachers and the indifference with which students received their instruction. He certainly deplored the specialization that reigned in the scientific disciplines, the ever-increasing fragmentation of the body of knowledge, but he was a man of his time and understood that this process was irreversible. Hence, rather than launching an effort to destroy it, which would be useless in any case, he thought it preferable to contrive a means to neutralize its unfavorable effects insofar as possible. If university teaching, owing to its intellectualistic nature, had the effect of lessening the individual's psychic unity and, because of its pragmatic nature, of destroying the essential unity of objective knowledge, then it would be necessary to base that unity and that knowledge, both elements being considered as an organic whole, on foundations solid enough to be capable of surviving the increasing tendency toward fragmentation.

Now, the idea and practice of teaching as the demonstration and exploration of an "organic whole" is above all the task of the genuine teacher, and in this respect Giner and his colleagues had every reason to be disappointed in view of a) the methods used to prepare would-be teachers at the time, b) the abysmal lack of materials provided for them, and c) the low social status of members of the profession. Most of the teachers responsible for the formation of future generations were condemned to a sordid and marginal existence, frequently in "the intellectual desert of a village,"[16] where the sense of vocation which presumably had led them to embrace a ministry so closely resembling spiritual suicide soon ebbed away. And so, as Giner points out, the teacher, out of pure frustration, "comes to terms with his position, which he thinks of as suited to his abilities and possibilities; he tries to deal with his problem with as little effort as possible, and teaches away as he pleases in the same spirit as the farmer mounding cabbages or guiding his plow."[17] Those high-sounding statements about the "greatness and dignity of the teaching profession," so often heard in the Normal School, were found to be nothing but empty and cynical phrase-making.

It was obvious that no single individual, no matter how strong his will, or any organization, no matter how vast its moral influence, was capable of changing this state of affairs in any essential way. And yet it is interesting to note that during the years of the Restoration and the Regency—doubtless largely through the influence of Giner and the *Institución*—the notion began to spread that the country's salvation depended on a far-reaching reform of instruction on all levels, especially the elementary and secondary levels. By

1881 the Taxpayers' League, with the Marqués de Riscal as its president, proposed that "the money spent today on non-productive services, such as the Army, should be applied to primary instruction, roads, canals, and other public works, and to the administration of justice."[18] But it was Joaquín Costa, an ardent follower of Giner's on this point, who elevated the notion to the rank of a presumptive government program when, in 1898, he included it in the manifesto of the Agricultural Council of Upper Aragon:

> Half of Spain's problem lies in the school. . . We must remake the Spaniard; perhaps it would be better to say that we must make him. And our present school system cannot cope even remotely with this need. . . What Spain needs, and must demand of the school system, is not merely men who can read and write; what she needs is men, and the formation of men requires educating the body as well as the spirit, and forming character as much, or more, than comprehension.

As was to be expected, the campaign of educational reform became especially vigorous after the Spanish-American War of 1898, when unhappy experience revealed to many troubled people that the national crisis had resulted not merely from a state of military inferiority but, rather, from a breakdown of the "national personality," the collapse of a whole mode of existence and of a way of understanding reality and dealing with it; or, if you like, a breakdown of the Spaniard himself, as well as the institutions he had created. Of these institutions, the one particularly inveighed against by Costa was precisely the university, "that factory of degree-seekers and frock coated proletarians," which, as he proclaimed with characteristic exaggeration, would have to be burned down, so that a modern institution could rise from its ashes.[19] Actually, almost all Costa's statements on matters of education reflect Giner's ideas of the *Institución*'s methods. Don Francisco rightly reminds his readers that "Don Joaquín Costa has been one of the earliest of our colleagues who have contributed toward forming the spirit of the *Institución*."[20]

V

"Toward national redemption through education," therefore, became the watchword that synthesized the concerns of Giner and his collaborators in the *Institución*. And I believe that "redemption" is preferable to other words such as "regeneration" or "reconstitution," so often used during the last decade of the nineteenth century, because this word implies the emergence of a *new man*, as in religious conversions, while the other terms indicate, rather—at least in the way they were used at the time—a desire to improve the material conditions of human life. I am well aware that the distinction is, perhaps, more verbalistic than real, since the effectiveness of teaching in the formation of youth depends very largely on the adequacy of the material means used to impart it. Joaquín Costa, for example, seemed to understand this when he preached his message of "school and pantry." On the other hand, it would be erroneous to suggest that the men of the *Institución* disdained the physical conditions and resources of the teaching process, for it is well known—and the *Bulletin* of the Institución constantly corroborates this—that they followed with great interest the proposals and practices of other countries with regard to teaching materials, nutrition, hygiene, sports, school trips, etc. But there is no doubt that, out of doctrinal conviction as well as natural inclination, Giner and some of his most important collaborators were first of all men of the spirit, inspired by a concept of man and society which they had inherited from German idealism through the philosophy of Krause. And it was precisely that concept which after all survived, despite the readjustments it suffered in confrontation with real life. The *new men* would have to be new men out of a sense of vocation, of willpower if you like, and not simply through alteration or improvement of the reality with which they had to deal.

And if redemption was what they were attempting, those who proclaimed it—the teachers—necessarily had to have a clear understanding of their role as redeemers. A large portion of Giner's writings on educational themes, especially during the 1880's, are focused chiefly on the character, sense of vocation, formation, and dedication of the individuals who are to be responsible for so demanding a mission. It is not strange, therefore, that, when Don Francisco sketches out his notion of the teaching profession, he should do so in terms appropriate to the selection of missionaries called to preach the Good Tidings *in partibus infidelium*:

> The teaching profession. . .like the priesthood, with which it has so many points of contact, especially in modern countries. . .demands, in the first place, well-balanced men of an ideal temperament, men who love all great things, whose intelligence is fully developed, whose tastes are both noble and simple, whose habits are pure, whose minds and bodies are healthy, who are worthy in thought, word, and deed, even in the ways in which they serve the sacred cause whose exercise is entrusted to their care.[21]

As we can see, the list of requirements for the ideal teacher is long and demanding, but it is in consonance with the "sacred cause" to which he is dedicated. Giner roundly declares that, in order to form a generation of *new men,* truly new men, the child and the adolescent must be rescued from the moral and physical decay to which they are doomed, not only by a society and a State whose opinions and actions have long been perverted, but by the family itself, the primary form of association, for the family is, in general, just as corrupt as other more complex associations and historical institutions. There is no reason to suppose that, taking into account the state of the Spanish family, parents can be effective agents of the hoped-for redemption:

> The father who sincerely believes that he adores his son because he is amused by the child's tricks—almost as he would do with a dog or a parrot—covers him with caresses and reduces his obligations to giving him bed and board and trying to set him up in life; that same father sees the careful education of his son as a troublesome burden, sees the teacher as a critic, and alternates between putting the whole unsupportable load on the teacher or resigning himself to carrying it as well, at least in appearence, thereby freeing himself from the guardianship which the school inevitably imposes on him.[22]

For the time being at least, school and family are hostile entities, participants in a struggle between "two ideals of what the child, the man, education, society, and life ought to be."[23] Nowadays, Giner says, the family—with notable exceptions, of course—is "perhaps the most serious obstacle which any attempt at educational reform will have to face," or, which comes to the same thing, the greatest obstacle in the path of national redemption. Out of indifference or ignorance, because it is inconceivable that they do so out of perversity, it is the parents who contribute most toward corrupting their children:

> When one sees so many indolent parents enjoying the present, condemning their children to the bleakest of futures; when one calculates what can be expected, for the redemption of the whole nation, from such conduct; when one witnesses the free development of all the evil germs deposited in the child by inheritance and his domestic and social surroundings. . .the observer can only exclaim with the profoundest bitterness, "If all parents were like this, how lucky are the orphans!"[24]

The difference in attitude between teachers and parents is fundamental and assumes the character of a struggle between a rational concept of life and a routine acceptance of it. Philosophy and history are placed in opposition, with the advantage clearly on the side of the latter. Giner knows this, but far from coming to terms with the knowledge, he rebels yet again—as he did so many times!—against the tyranny of history. As long as this tyranny holds sway, as long as what *ought to be* and what *is* do not become one, he tells us that "there will not be a real and true Spain, that is, a people worthy of inclusion in the civilized Humanity to come, a cultured people, in love with what is ideal, sincere, serene, balanced, at once gentle and energetic, honorable, patient, sensible, well fed and even clean, instead of this horde of epileptics that most of us are."[25]

BROWN UNIVERSITY

Notes

[1]Chiefly in my study "Francisco Giner: De la Setembrina al Desastre," read at the IV Congress of the International Association of Hispanists, Salamanca, 1971, to be published in the *Actas* of the Congress.

[2]Letter of Joaquín Costa to Francisco Giner; no date, but probably sometime in 1897. From Giner's archive in the Real Academia de la Historia, Madrid.

[3]Letter of Juana Lund de Achúcarro to Francisco Giner, dated April 8, 1888. From Giner's archive in the Real Academia de la Historia. The translations of this and other texts in Spanish quoted in this essay are my own.

[4]"La juventud y el movimiento social," in *Obras completas de D. Francisco Giner de los Ríos* (Madrid: La Lectura, 1916), VII, p. 120. All references to Giner in this essay are to volume and page of this edition of the *Obras completas* (*OC*).

⁵*Ibid.*, VII, p. 120.

⁶*Ibid.*

⁷*Ibid.*, VII, pp. 110-11.

⁸*Ibid.*, VII, pp. 128-29.

⁹*Ibid.*, VII, p. 129.

¹⁰*Ibid.*, VII, p. 130.

¹¹See my study "Las ideas literarias de Francisco Giner de los Ríos," in *Hacia el 98: Literatura, sociedad, ideología* (Esplugues de Llobregat [Barcelona]: Ariel, 1972), pp. 185-87.

¹²K. C. F. Krause, *Ideal de la Humanidad para la vida*. Con introducción y comentarios de D. Julián Sanz del Río. 2nd ed. (Madrid: Imprenta de F. Martínez García, 1871), pp. 26-27.

¹³*OC*, VII, p. 130.

¹⁴"Sobre el estado de los estudios jurídicos en nuestras universidades" (1888), *OC*, II, pp. 173-74.

¹⁵Letter to Gumersindo de Azcárate, dated July 23, 1875. In Francisco Giner de los Ríos, *Ensayos y cartas* (México: Fondo de Cultura Económica, 1965), p. 102.

¹⁶"Un peligro de toda enseñanza" (1884), *OC*, XII, p. 105.

¹⁷"Maestros y catedráticos" (1884), *OC*, XII, p. 90.

¹⁸Quoted by Giner in "El problema de la educación nacional y las clases 'productoras' " (1900), *OC*, XII, p. 239.

¹⁹Joaquín Costa, "La fórmula de nuestra revolución," in *El Pueblo* (Valencia) January 17, 1900.

²⁰"El problema. . . ," *OC*, XII, p. 238.

²¹"Lo que necesitan nuestros aspirantes al profesorado" (1887), *OC*, XII, p. 86.

²²"Enseñanza y educación" (1881), *OC*, VII, p. 105.

²³*Ibid.*

²⁴*Ibid.*, *OC*, VII, p. 106.

²⁵*Ibid.*

LA VORAGINE:
AUTOBIOGRAFIA DE UN INTELECTUAL

Randolph D. Pope

El autor de *La vorágine* nos invita a creer que su obra es la copia fiel de los manuscritos de Arturo Cova, remitidos al ministerio por el Cónsul de Colombia en Manaos. Aceptemos momentáneamente este supuesto: el texto es una narración autobiográfica compuesta de dos segmentos. El primero, el mayor, está escrito en cerca de seis semanas (hasta la página 342); el segundo se aproxima a la acción tomando la forma de un diario esporádico. El destinatario de esas páginas no es un ministerio anónimo, al cual casualmente llegan, sino un amigo filósofo: "No ambiciono otro fin que el de emocionar a Ramiro Estévanez" (342).[1]

Entre las obras que en la novela se atribuyen al supuesto escritor Cova se cuenta una tremenda requisitoria, escrita en compañía de Estévanez, que el experimentado rumbero Clemente Silva lleva al Cónsul de Manaos (cf. p. 339). Además ha dejado en la agencia de vapores de Santa Isabel una carta para el Cónsul (cf. p. 384). En esos escritos ha detallado sus observaciones sobre la suerte horrible que corren sus compatriotas esclavizados. Allí ha elaborado su protesta oficial. ¿Por qué escribe además una autobiografía?[2]

La autobiografía relata hechos del pasado, liberados ya de la inmediata urgencia del actuar, eslabonados a un futuro ahora conocido que les da una orientación definida.[3] "En breves minutos", escribe Cova, "volví a vivir mis años pretéritos, como espectador de mi propia vida. ¡Cuántos antecedentes indicadores de mi futuro!" (322). Sólo en la mirada retrospectiva, cuando el futuro es ya pasado, el presente es un signo resuelto, un antecedente. Lo que leemos, incluso en una autobiografía ficticia, es la interpretación que hace el autobiógrafo de su pasado. En sí mismas las experiencias carecen de sentido. Alfred Schutz, un sociólogo que dedicó gran parte de su obra a estudiar el fenómeno de la atribución de significados o codificación de la experiencia, concluyó que la significación no yace en la experiencia misma, sino que las experiencias se tornan significativas cuando se las observa en la reflexión.[4] Es el presente del escritor transformando el pasado, indicando significativamente hacia él. Los elementos que en esta estructuración aparecen como significativos no son los mismos si el escritor escribe apenas los ha vivido o diez años más tarde. Esta modificación del punto de vista, la divergencia entre el personaje de una autobiografía y el narrador, es lo que le da al género su tensión dramática. En general es una conversión, una vivencia trascendental, lo que obliga a reflexionar sobre lo vivido otorgándole de paso una nueva perspectiva. Cuando Cova hace el balance de su vida en el libro de Caja del Cayeno, estructura la narración de sus hechos a partir de las nuevas coordenadas que le proporcionan su experiencia de los llanos y la selva. ¿En qué difiere o se ha enriquecido el análisis de su propia historia? Esta es la pregunta que plantea la constatación de que el texto de Rivera se presenta como una autobiografía. La novela adquiere pleno sentido cuando se la lee no como una obra cuyo tema es la esclavitud o la selva, sino como la experiencia de un poeta que sobrevive aventuras que lo transforman parcialmente.[5]

La ciudad es el lugar al cual arriba la autobiografía: allí están el ministro, el editor y la gran mayoría de los lectores. Cova mismo es un hombre citadino. Pero la ciudad lo rechaza. En la metrópoli el original desaparece devorado por la multitud. Es reducido a un vagabundo, a un *flâneur*, a un espectador.[6] Dominada por el vértigo del comercio, la urbe devora al artista. En Cova persisten huellas del héroe romántico, como ya han sugerido Jean Franco y Luis B. Eyzaguirre.[7] Pero él pertenece a una generación posterior, a la de los decadentes, a los desengañados del ideal romántico.[8] Como en la literatura decadente francesa Cova se ha retirado en la ciudad a la astenia, a la voluptuosidad y a jugar con sus tentaciones de suicidio. Cova se identifica con quienes "atropellados por la desdicha, desde el anonimato de las ciudades, se lanzaron a los desiertos buscándole un fin cualquiera a su vida estéril" (288). De la ciudad Cova recuerda la violencia, el tedio, el hastío, el fingimiento: "Por todas partes fui buscando en qué distraer mi inconformidad, e iba de buena fe, anheloso de renovar mi vida y de rescatarme a la perversión. . . Logré conocer todas las pasiones y sufro su hastío" (75). Como el héroe de *Au Rebours* de Huysmans, Cova "venía de regreso de todas las voluptuosidades" (100).

Su concepto de la mujer no coincide con el pensamiento romántico, sino que es descrito perfectamente por la opinión que George Ross Ridge le atribuye a la novela decadente francesa: "Modern man is shown as a weak decadent consumed by modern woman, who is a vampire or a *femme fatale*."[9] La imagen que con mayor frecuencia se utiliza para caracterizar a la mujer en este contexto es la del vampiro, como en el caso de la destructora Mapiripana. Más de un sentido tiene la visión que Cova contempla en sueños cuando una voz le explica: "Yo soy tu Alicia y me he convertido en una parásita" (90). Esta concepción de la mujer reaparece en la fantasía de Cova cuando imagina la vida de Alicia en las plantaciones:

> Quizás no estaba de peona en los siringales, sino de reina en la entablada casa de algún empresario, vistiendo sedas costosas y finos encajes, humillando a sus siervos como Cleopatra, riéndose de la pobreza en que la tuve, sin poder procurarle otro goce que el de su cuerpo. Desde su mecedora de mimbres, en el corredor de olorosa sombra, suelta la cabellera, amplio el corpiño, vería desfilar a los cargadores con los bultos de caucho hacia las balandras, sudorosos y desgarrados, mientras que ella, ociosa y rica,

entre los abanicos de las "iracas", apagaría sus ojos en el bochorno, al son de una victrola de sedantes voces, satisfecha de ser hermosa, de ser deseada, de ser impura (205).

La madona Zoraida Ayram, que es una mujer varonil (319), destruye a Cova: "Mi decaimiento y mi escepticismo tienen por causa el cansancio lúbrico, la astenia del vigor físico, succionado por los besos de la madona" (354). Y Cova, imaginando lo que él cree que piensa la madona, vuelve otra vez a proyectar su negativa imagen de la mujer moderna:

> Quejosa de la suerte, agravaría su decepción al pensar en tantas mujeres nacidas en la abundancia, en el lujo, en la ociosidad, que juegan con su virtud por tener en qué distraerse, y que aunque la pierdan siguen con honra, porque el dinero es otra virtud (330).

No es un héroe romántico, por lo tanto, el que huye de Bogotá, sino un hombre que cree haber conocido los límites extremos de la decadencia, un poeta que no cree en la existencia de una mujer perfecta si no es en la fantasía de su propia creación.

Las fuerzas que lo persiguen representan los tres pilares de la sociedad: la familia, la religión y la ley; "sus parientes fraguaron la conspiración de su matrimonio patrocinados por el cura y resueltos a someterme por la fuerza" (57). En *Une Saison en Enfer*, Rimbaud escribía en semejante tono: "Je me suis armé contre la justice. Je me suis enfui". La huida no garantiza la liberación del sistema de interpretar la realidad que se ha adquirido con la vida urbana. Cova se define al comienzo en relación a la ciudad como "fugitivo" (59), teme que lo detengan "las autoridades (59) e intenta romper la línea del telégrafo. Todavía alientan en él esperanzas de regresar. Tiene el "deseo íntimo" de que alguien lo capture (59), y envía un peón a Bogotá a caza de noticias. Le pide a un amigo que intervenga, pero recibe tan sólo una carta en que se le recomienda la huida (60).

Esta acumulación de elementos que se refieren a la vida urbana, telégrafo, periódicos, dinero, cartas, no exigen de Cova esfuerzo alguno de adaptación. Puede resolver los problemas con la experiencia acumulada. Adivina que la estructura social que lo expulsa tiene poder en parte debido a que el individuo se lo concede. Pero no pasa de ser una vaga percepción intelectual: "—¿No crees, Alicia, que vamos huyendo de un fantasma cuyo poder se lo atribuimos nosotros mismos? ¿No sería mejor regresar?" (60). Todavía no ha adquirido una nueva perspectiva a partir de la experiencia.

En la segunda noche se ocultan cerca de un trapiche, que sienten gemir desde lejos como los batanes cervantinos.[10] Es la última actividad industrial que encontrarán, antes de entrar al mundo ganadero. Cuando necesitan un lápiz, ninguno de los arrieros que encuentran por el camino lleva ese instrumento, inútil en su esfera de comercio primitivo. Alicia será la primera en sentir el paso de la situación urbana a la ganadera, pues "no sabía montar a caballo" (59).

Están todavía en el aura de Bogotá.[11] En Villavicencio el General Jefe de la Gendarmería asegura haber conocido a Alicia cuanto era pequeña, y llama a Arturo por su único oficio conocido: "poeta". Tienen una figura tutelar, don Rafo, quien conoció al padre de Cova y los llama a ambos "niños". Sienten "un olór a pajonal fresco, a surco removido, a leños recién cortados", huellas de agricultura que ya no volverán a ver, y están "agradecidos de la vida y de la creación" (67). Lo que los personajes no sospechan, aunque sí lo sabe el narrador, es que están recién comenzando el camino de una experiencia que los llevará a otras épocas y regiones, obligándolos a confrontar sus recursos adquiridos, su educación, con aspectos del mundo no comprendidos en sus circunstancias sociales previas. Don Rafo relaciona todavía el presente al pasado (el padre al hijo) y a la ciudad con el campo: es "ganadero y mercader ambulante al por menor" (68). A Alicia la aflige todavía "el recuerdo del hogar" (71). En el horizonte los viajeros ven "ciudades fantásticas" (71). En un momento de descanso don Rafo da a Cova ciertos consejos, aparentemente sensatos:

> Y Alicia, ¿en qué desmerecía? ¿No era inteligente, bien educada, sencilla y de origen honesto? ¿En qué código, en qué escritura, en qué ciencia había aprendido yo que los prejuicios priman sobre las realidades? ¿Por qué era mejor que otros, sino por mis obras? El hombre de talento debe ser como la muerte, que no conoce categorías. ¿Por qué ciertas doncellas me parecían más encumbradas? (74).

El código social se impone a la realidad. También a la de don Rafo, que evalúa desde ciertos criterios que él comparte con otros miembros de la sociedad y que no coinciden del todo con los de Arturo, aunque no son radicalmente divergentes. ¿Qué significa aquí "bien educada"? Poco más adelante Arturo Çova dará su versión, ufanándose de que Alicia "en casa divide el tiempo entre la pintura, el piano, los bordados, los encajes. . ." (105), algo relativamente absurdo en los llanòs y ridículo en la selva. Si don Rafo esboza tendencias democráticas, siempre útiles al comerciante para alcanzar la aceptación social que desea, no oculta su interés medular con un consejo que no puede sino ser despreciado por Arturo: "Usted sólo tiene un problema sumo, a cuyo lado huelgan todos los otros: adquirir dinero para sustentar la modestia decorosamente. El resto viene .por añadidura" (74). La perversión del pasaje del Nuevo Testamento es completa: no vivir como los pájaros del campo, sino ahorrar. Cova contesta: "Yo miro las cosas por otro aspecto, pues las conclusiones de usted, aunque fundadas, no me preocupan ahora: están en mi horizonte, pero están lejos" (74).

El viaje altera el horizonte y cambia el aspecto de la realidad, al menos para Arturo Cova que, hay que adelantarlo, es además de poeta, un intelectual, lo cual le otorga una extraordinaria flexibilidad para absorber y elaborar experiencias nuevas.

En "La Maporita", la fundación de Franco en la cual Arturo y Alicia se hospedan, todavía se encuentran dentro de un círculo relativamente habitual. La manera de valorar que utilizan evidencia un mundo ordenado que pronto quedará atrás: "Complacidos observábamos el aseo del patio" (77). Por contraste, la casa de Zubieta era "desaseada como ninguna" (129). Ya empieza a ver Cova lo que antes nunca había visto. Para él orden y aseo eran conceptos asociados al hogar. Cuando deja "La Maporita" entra en una región en la cual la codicia y la avaricia crean situaciones caóticas: los vaqueros no trabajan o lo hacen tan mal que arriesgan inútilmente sus vidas, mientras que Zubieta entierra las monedas en que estanca su fortuna. Cova se mimetiza: "El pensamiento de la riqueza se convirtió en esos días en mi dominante obsesión, y llegó a sugestionarme con tal poder, que ya me creía ricacho fastuoso, venido a los llanos para dar impulso a la actividad financiera" (104). Pero las consecuencias de su borrachera, celos y tumultuosa reyerta lo conducen a la más absoluta ruina. Cova pierde por añadidura a Alicia, quien se escapa con Barrera, el enganchador. Todas estas pérdidas son lazos que se cortan y dejan huecos difíciles de llenar. Ya no es el fugitivo relativamente frívolo y con muchos recursos. Ha pasado a otra etapa: "Olvidada sea la época miserable en que vagamos por el desierto en cuadrilla prófuga, como salteadores. Sindicados de un crimen ajeno, desafiamos a la injusticia y erguimos la enseña de la rebelión" (175).

Poco antes Barrera lo saludaba todavía aplaudiendo su fama: "Alabada sea la diestra que ha esculpido tan bellas estrofas" (91). Ahora lo más aterrador para Cova es haber perdido contacto con el pasado y con la región donde sus habilidades eran cotizadas: "¡Nadie nos buscaba ni perseguía! ¡Nos habían olvidado todos!" (175).

Dos coordenadas determinan la vida que Cova recuerda: por una parte el cambio de la situación externa, y por otra su necesidad de adaptarse a las nuevas circunstancias. Esta actividad le revela la utilidad o inutilidad de su bagaje cultural. En la primera parte de la novela ha pasado de la urbe a la sociedad ganadera, perdiendo finalmente el dinero, la mujer y la fama. A este deslazamiento de las coordinadas sociales significativas corresponden los elementos de tránsito, el paso a una nueva manera de existir. La voluntad de cambiar es fuerte y clara en Cova: "Con la hora desvanecida se había hundido irremediablemente la mitad de mi ser, y ya debía iniciar una nueva vida, distinta de la anterior" (64). Explica que "iba de buena fe, anheloso de renovar [su] vida" (75). Más adelante encontrará un simbolismo adecuado: "En el sonambulismo de la congoja devoraba mis propias hieles, inepto, adormilado, como la serpiente que muda escama" (181). Pero la renovación a través de la destrucción y de la experiencia de la muerte va a ser muy diferente a lo que él esperaba, lo cual prueba que es auténticamente nueva.[12]

Al enfrentarse al llano lo hace con tipificaciones literarias: "Casanare no me aterraba con sus espeluznantes leyendas" (59). Pronto encontrará realidades, sin embargo, para las que no está preparado. La visita lo engaña, y aunque los venados parecen estar cerca, están a más de quinientos metros. Fenómenos de la región, explica don Rafo (70). En casa de Franco se le dirá claramente "Usté no manda aquí" (85). Discutiendo con Correa, un gran jinete, sobre la vida de los llanos, los interrumpe la madre de éste diciendo: "¡No contradigas, zambo alegatista! El blanco es más leído que vos" (109). Lo respetan, por lo tanto, pero no lo llevan a las faenas (110 y 145). Cova medita sin conceder del todo: "Quizás me aventajaban en destreza, pero nunca en audacia y en fogosidad" (110). Podrá ver más tarde que esto no basta cuando persiga a un toro tirando "el lazo una y otra vez, con mano inexperta" (160). Zubieta lo expresa muy bien al responder a la presentación que de Cova hace el empalagoso Barrera:

—El señor Cova es una de las glorias de nuestro país.
—Y gloria, ¿por qué?. . .¿Sabe montá? ¿Sabe enlazá? ¿Sabe toreá? (121).

Cova pretende substituir su ineptitud mediante gestos dramáticos, que revelan sin embargo la conciencia que él tiene de la vida ociosa que ha llevado hasta ahora: "Pensé exhibírmele [a Alicia] cual no me vio entonces: con cierto descuido en el traje, los cabellos revueltos, el rostro ensombrecido de barba, aparentando el porte de un macho almizcloso y trabajador" (147). El intelectual urbano ha sido lentamente demolido, reducido a la dimensión diversa que exige el llano. Cova advierte ahora que la leyenda era menos terrible que la realidad y considera que el remanso de la vorágine se encuentra en el mundo civilizado, la región más transparente para su modo de ver el mundo: "aquel ambiente de pesadilla me enflaquecía el corazón y era preciso volver a las tierras civilizadas, al remanso de la molicie, al ensueño y la quietud" (164). El incendio de "La Maporita" es la fulminación del pasado y de los sueños de riqueza que albergaba Cova. Pero constituye también una intuición del porvenir. No en vano hay en las llamas "claridades desmesuradas" (170). Entre los resplandores se advierte una serpiente que muerde su cola, y Cova goza el placer de la renovación: "Sentí deleite por todo lo que moría a la zaga de mi ilusión, por ese océano purpúreo que me arrojaba contra la selva, aislándome del mundo que conocí, por el incendio que extendía su ceniza sobre mis pasos!" (171).

El intelectual sometido a este proceso, despojado de la mayor parte de sus prerrogativas, empujado a la selva, está ahora dispuesto a escuchar, a entender, a compadecer. Todavía va a cometer múltiples errores: piensa todavía en el dinero (184), manifiesta indiscreta curiosidad (183) y casi mata al jefe de la familia de indígenas que los protege (189-90). Su aniquilación continúa físicamente, con la fatiga de la marcha, la alucinación y la experiencia de la muerte. Ha pasado de los ganaderos a los cazadores y recolectores y está ahora menos preparado que antes. Sólo el apoyo del rumbero Clemente Silva le permite sobrevivir: "Nuestro jefe en tales emergencias era, sin duda, el anciano Silva, y principié a sentir contra él una secreta rivalidad" (290). La destrucción del poeta ha sido concreta, evidenciada socialmente, y no es sólo simbólica. Esto le permite emerger de su obsesión privada y descubrir que Barrera no es solamente su enemigo sino el de todos los colombianos, que Funes no es un hombre, sino un sistema.[13] Sus pesares privados se integran a los colectivos. Pero esto no es todo: Rivera va a mostrar en las páginas que siguen otro aspecto de la "intelligentsia".

Karl Mannheim es el sociólogo que con mayor claridad ha mostrado el extraño papel que juegan los intelectuales en la sociedad.[14] Mientras que las diversas clases y grupos de poder se contentan con ver sus intereses revestidos por una ideología que los justifica, los intelectuales se ocupan en perfeccionarla, demolerla, entenderla o criticarla. Valoran opiniones diversas y escogen a sus miembros entre personas de todas las naciones, épocas y clases sociales. Están unidos por una educación común y el culto a la discusión y la crítica. Pero el intelectual, debido a su actitud y formación permanece siempre como incómodo aliado. Su crítica no tarda en renacer y está dispuesto al diálogo con los intelectuales que defienden al enemigo. Como lo definen Berger y Luckmann, los intelectuales son por definición marginados, expertos cuya habilidad no es apreciada por la mayoría de la sociedad.[15] Los intelectuales están siempre poniendo en duda las definiciones establecidas de la realidad. ¿Cómo es la relación de Cova con los grupos que él desea proteger?

Tres son las condiciones que se interponen para impedir una fusión de Cova, el intelectual, con el grupo que él pretende amparar: la pervivencia de coordenadas sociales significativas en el ambiente urbano, su condición de intelectual, y su sentido de la estética.

Cova se identifica con los hombres oprimidos que aprende a valorar: "Sepa usted, don Clemente Silva. . .que sus tribulaciones me han ganado para su causa" (280). Pero aunque incorpora su venganza privada a un plano social, no dejan de ocurrírsele dudas: "Qué debían importarme las desventuras ajenas, si con las propias iba de rastra" (282). Irónicamente todavía les atribuye un notable poder positivo a instituciones que la experiencia le ha enseñado a criticar. Enfrentado al caos, necesita tornar a ellas, como a un salvavidas que le impide hundirse en la marajada.[16] Se había alzado en armas contra los jueces injustos que se dejaban manipular en Bogotá para persequirlo. En los llanos había tenido ocasión de satirizar al Juez de Circuito de Casanare, que clama perdido:

—¡Favor a la justicia, que anda extraviada!
—Ora y siempre, respondió el mulato ingenuo (150).

Estévanez le ha contado a Cova cómo una justicia grotesca y entregada a los poderosos es en la selva lo "legal, correcto y humano" (346). Pero hablando con este mismo amigo, medita el rebelde Cova: "Amaba de la vida cuanto era noble: el hogar, la patria, la fe, el trabajo, todo lo digno y lo laudable" (329). Y para solucionar el problema de los caucheros intenta acudir al gobierno de su patria.

Conviene detenerse aquí en una historia intercalada, de la cual se supone que el autobiógrafo Cova ha extraído gran parte de la experiencia que ha afectado su personalidad. Es la narración de Clemente Silva, quien trata de ubicar a su hijo, Luciano. Este sensible niño huyó de su casa por no soportar la pérdida de honor que significaba para él el hecho de que su hermana hubiera huido con su amante. Por qué huyen sin casarse es un misterio, ya que habían intercambiado argollas y las familias estaban de acuerdo con el matrimonio. Don Clemente sufre: "Medio loco olvidé el hogar por persequir a la fugitiva. Acudí a las autoridades, imploré el apoyo de mis amigos, la protección de los influyentes" (237). Todo en vano. Su mujer muere de pesadumbre. Cova reacciona de acuerdo a la opinión que él tiene de sí mismo: "soy por idiosincracia el amigo de los débiles y de los tristes" (230), por lo cual ofrece patéticamente: "Sepa usted, don Clemente Silva. . .que sus tribulaciones nos han ganado para su causa. Su redención encabeza el programa de nuestra vida" (280). ¡Pero la causa inicial de la tragedia de don Clemente es precisamente un acto idéntico al realizado por Cova y Alicia! Y el paralelo no acaba allí. Clemente Silva ha conocido a un científico francés que llegó a la selva patrocinado por las compañías y que un día descubre, motivado por las cicatrices de la espalda de don Clemente, el significado de lo que ha presenciado sin comprender: "hasta entonces parecía no haberse enterado de la condición esclava de los caucheros" (250). El científico, poseído de su nueva misión, sin trequa ni disimulo sigue fotografiando mutilaciones y cicatrices. Opina que "estos crímenes, que avergüenzan a la especie humana. . .deben ser conocidos en todo el mundo para que los Gobiernos se apresuren a remediarlos" (252). Esta ingenua confianza en la justicia de los Gobiernos y en su inmunidad como extranjero tiene sólo dos consecuencias: sus informes crean "alarmas muy graves" (260) y "¡El infeliz francés no salió jamás!" (253). Su destino es semejante al de Cova y debiera de servirle de advertencia. Todavía otros aspectos de la historia de Clemente Silva podrían hacerlo recapacitar. A pesar de la recomendación de Balbino Jácome de que hablando nada se consigue (264), don Clemente considera que es su obligación hablar con el cónsul de su país: "¡Colombia necesita de mis secretos! ¡Aunque muriera inmediatamente! ¡Ahí le queda mi hijo para luchar!" (268). ¿Hasta qué punto el plan de Cova se basa en el de Silva? Este último, que para Arturo representa a su anciano padre (225), tiene los siguientes proyectos:

> Ir al Consulado de mi país, exigirle al Cónsul que me asesorara en la Prefectura o en el Juzgado, denunciar los crímenes de la selva, referir cuánto me constaba sobre la expedición del sabio francés, solicitar mi repatriación, la libertad de los caucheros esclavizados, la revisión de libros y cuentas en La Chorrera y en El Encanto, la redención de miles de indígenas, el amparo de los colonos, el libre comercio en caños y ríos (269).

Pero al desembarcar en el pueblo, don Clemente no se adapta. Sus costumbres "estaban hechas" y se sentía "extranjero" (271). El encuentro con el Cónsul es demitologizador. La ansiada fuente de poder y protección le comunica escuetamente: "Yo no soy de Colombia ni me pagan sueldo. Su país no repatria a nadie. El pasaporte vale cincuenta soles. . . . Ni soy abogado ni sé de leyes" (273). Finalmente le recomienda que hable con el señor Arana, "un hombre muy bueno" (274). ¿De dónde proviene, se podría preguntar el lector haciendo eco de las dudas de don Rafo, la confianza de Cova en que *su* apelación al Cónsul tendrá mejores resultados? ¿En qué código ha aprendido que los prejuicios, ideales y esperanzas priman sobre las realidades? Ciertamente en un sistema tan ceñido y fuerte que le hace olvidar completamente que él es un fugitivo de esa misma justicia que invoca.

Por el contrario, hay una veta de su carácter que encuentra relativo éxito: la violencia. Y en esto no está solo. Uno de los héroes de la novela es

Heli Mesa, quien ha asesinado (¿ajusticiado?) a un guardia que había arrojado un niño a los caimanes. Cova expresa su vehemente admiración: "Las manos de Heli Mesa me reconfortaron. Estrechélas ansioso, y me transmitían en sus pulsaciones la contracción con que le hincaron al capataz el temerario acero en su carne odiosa" (203). Mesa mismo opina que "Dios premió mi venganza y aquí estoy" (203). Cova cree en esta furia redentora y considera que los explotados deben rebelarse: "Yo no compadezco al que no protesta" (279). Luego amplifica:

> Siento que en mí se enciende un anhelo de inmolación; mas no me aúpa la piedad del mártir, sino el ansia de contender con esta fauna de hombres de presa, a quienes venceré con armas iguales, aniquilando el mal con el mal, ya que la voz de la paz y justicia sólo se pronuncia entre los rendidos. ¿Qué ha ganado usted con sentirse víctima? La mansedumbre le prepara el terreno a la tiranía y la pasividad de los explotados sirve de incentivo a la explotación. Su bondad y su timidez han sido cómplices inconscientes de sus victimarios. (280).

La muerte del Cayeno y de Barrera aparecen como actos de justicia que a Cova le parecen necesarios, por inquietantes que sean: "Definitivamente, desde ese momento me abandonó la paz de espíritu. Matar a un hombre. He aquí mi programa, mi obligación" (375). Volvamos ahora a la justificación que Cova da para escribir su autobiografía:

> Erraría quien imaginara que mi lápiz se mueve con deseos de notoriedad . . . No ambiciono otro fin que el de emocionar a Ramiro Estévanez con el breviario de mis aventuras, confesándole por escrito el curso de mis pasiones y defectos, a ver si aprende en mí lo que en él regateó el destino y logra estimularse para la acción (342).

"Los devoró la selva" es la cómoda opinión (quizás aliviada) de un funcionario del cuerpo consular, que mal hubiera entendido o apoyado el programa brutal y efectivo de Cova. La venganza en que se vincula lo privado con lo público se realiza efectivamente. Los apestados consideran a Cova como un redentor. El hijo nace. Con todo ello a la vista puede releerse ahora la línea con que Cova abre la autobiografía: "Antes de que me hubiera apasionado por mujer alguna, jugué mi corazón al azar y me lo ganó la Violencia" (57). Rivera, que no retrocedió en su propia vida ante la violencia y que gozaba extraordinariamente con la caza, está proponiendo un programa de acción que supere lo literario.[17] Esta enérgica proposición está dirigida a Estévanez, su compañero intelectual, que descansa literalmente con una venda sobre los ojos y entregado a la fatalidad.

El hecho de pertenecer a la clase intelectual crea para Cova un segundo problema. A pesar de que él desea ardientemente pertenecer a un grupo, es siempre un advenedizo, un afuerino. En el llano desea identificarse con los vaqueros, como ya hemos visto, pero su entusiasmo no basta para absolver su inexperiencia. Cuando están a punto de ser abandonados por los vaqueros, Cova los apostrofa:

> —¡Compañeros, yo les responderé de que nada pasa!
> —¿Y quién responde por usté, que es al que busca la autoridá? (157).

Rivera subrayó el deseo de identificarse que mueve a Cova, introduciendo la palabra "compañeros" que faltaba en la primera edición. El poeta elegante, urbano, es rechazado. Pero en él reside parte de la distancia Recuerda a sus "condiscípulos" (103) de Bogotá para ufanarse ante ellos en su imaginación. Tiene en la ciudad un "amigo" (60). En el llano, sin embargo, se asocia con Franco y don Rafo en una empresa comercial, e inmediatamente se siente superior. Conversando sobre el negocio con Franco, considera Cova que "el administrador de mis bienes estaba rindiéndome un informe" (104). Cova reserva siempre para los otros personajes las palabras "compañeros" y "camaradas" que repite a menudo, como si sintiera la necesidad de convencerse de algo. Una vez, enfermo y demolido, afirma "indagar en las miradas de mis amigos el estado de mi salud" (211). A Clemente Silva le propone, distanciándolo: "Ya seremos buenos amigos" (227). Y en el discurso en que asume el rol de los conquistadores dice confusamente: "Amigos míos. . . . Seremos solidarios por la amistad y el provecho común, pero cada cual afrontará por separado su destino. De otra manera no aceptaré vuestra compañía" (222). Los demás personajes no elevan esta barrera. Sólo el despreciable Pipa llama a Correa "socio" (206), mientras que los demás se consideran siempre "amigos" (296, 299). Franco increpa a Cova, cuando éste no se conmueve ante la muerte de dos indios que los ayudaban: "¿Nada te importan tus amigos?" (218). Es significativo notar que Rivera ha reemplazado "compañeros", que había escrito en la primera edición, por "amigos". Cova siente esta soledad, que él mismo en parte impone: "¿Por qué viviría siempre solo en el arte y en el amor?" (187). Cuando todos participan de un ritual indígena, él observa protector: "Miraba yo la singular fiesta, complacido de que mis compañeros giraran ebrios en la danza" (193). No colabora a crear un espíritu solidario cuando declara: "Aunque vosotros andáis conmigo, sé que voy solo" (290). Y, por último, se observa su extraña noción de compañerismo cuando inventa una excusa para sus amigos ausentes: "despaché a mis camaradas a trabajar en la cuadrilla que escogieran, por el pudor de verlos ociosos" (364). Su entorno presiente que Cova nunca se integra del todo. Cuando Arturo le pregunta a Franco, imitando a Cristo, qué dicen los otros de él, Fidel le contesta: "nadie quiere meterse en sublevaciones, desconfían de nuestros planes y de ti mismo" (337). El tránsito de Cova nunca es completo, pero hay que recordar que tampoco pertenecía plenamente a la sociedad bogotana. Es un intelectual, condenado a la marginación.

Finalmente, hay que destacar cómo el oficio de poeta se transforma también en arma de doble filo. Mediante la apreciación estética Cova es capaz de distanciarse de los acontecimientos. El caso más patente es su reacción ante el naufragio de los indios: "La visión frenética del naufragio me sacudió con una ráfaga de belleza. El espectáculo fue magnífico . . .cualquier maniobra que acometiéramos aplebeyería la imponente catástrofe" (217). La palabra "espectáculo" es una de sus favoritas. La mutilación horrible de un hombre se designa como "el espectáculo de

Millán" (197). Cova es un "espectador" de su propia vida (322) y la muerte de Barrera, devorado por los caribes, es "el espectáculo más terrible, más pavoroso, más detestable" (385). Su ingeniosidad ante lo horrible es inagotable: la fundación de Franco arde "con retumbos de pirotecnia"(170) y los brazos del Pipa, a quien le han cercenado las manos, "llovían sangre sobre el rastrojo, como surtidorcillos de algún jardín bárbaro"(380). Pero este sentido de la estética y de lo teatral es lo que le permite encontrar el tono exacto para conmover al Váquiro y para determinar cuándo acierta o yerra en sus discursos dedicados a Zoraida Ayram. En último término el lector se siente atraído precisamente por esta sensibilidad poética tamizando y revelando la vida y descubrimientos de Cova. Pero constituye una advertencia sobre la conveniencia y los límites del arte.

Arturo Cova se desplaza, por lo tanto, de un mundo urbano y moderno donde él ha formado su bagaje cultural, a uno primitivo de cazadores y recolectores, pasando por la etapa intermedia del mundo ganadero. Este tránsito destruye la adecuación que él tenía con su ambiente y lo obliga a observar la realidad circundante, descubriendo así niveles y experiencias sociales que hasta ahora él podía haber conocido sólo por las tipificaciones de su fantasía. Adopta la problemática de los hombres con quienes entra en contacto y pretende darles una solución mediante la violencia, aunque también por medio de la pluma, recurriendo con ella a las mismas autoridades que desprestigia en la narración. Cova es el intelectual, capaz de sobrevivir a un cambio tan radical y brusco, pero conserva en lo posible elementos del pasado y una actitud distante que le impide integrarse a los nuevos grupos que encuentra y con los cuales se siente solidario. Finalmente, su calidad de poeta le concede una visión estéticamente reflexiva que lo mantiene en una sensibilidad diversa a la de sus compañeros, pero que le permite escribir una obra de lectura atractiva para otros intelectuales y poetas que pueden observar en Cova una imagen instructiva.

DARTMOUTH COLLEGE

Notas

[1]En el supuesto "Prólogo" (p. 53) de la edición crítica a cargo de Luis Carlos Herrera Molina (Bogotá: Pax, 1974), que contiene las interesantes variantes que introdujo Rivera a la primera edición de 1924. Las citas en este trabajo se refieren siempre a esta edición.

[2]Naturalmente que nos referimos siempre aquí a una autobiografía ficticia escrita por un personaje de ficción, aunque no se adjetive así siempre para evitar la monotonía. Es sorprendente la opinión de Kessel Schwartz en *A New History of Spanish Fiction* (Florida: Univ. of Miami, 1972) referente a que "Arturo Cova is the author himself" (p. 254).

[3]Para una discusión más detallada ver mi libro sobre *La autobiografía española hasta Torres Villarroel* (Basil: Lang Verlag, 1974).

[4]Me refiero especialmente al libro de Alfred Schutz, *The Phenomenology of the Social World* (Evanston: Northwestern Univ. Press, 1967), en particular a la página 69.

[5]F. V. Kelin opina en su "Introducción de *La vorágine* al ruso", *Atenea*, 33 (1936), pp. 314-25, que "el tema principal del libro de Rivera es la esclavitud" (p. 321). Carlos García Prada, en su contribución sobre Rivera al *Diccionario de la literatura latinoamericana, Colombia* (Washington, D.C.: Unión Panamericana, 1959), p. 99, afirma que en *La vorágine* no hay "personaje humano de importancia" ya que el personaje "central" es la selva.

[6]Vid. el análisis de esta condición hecho por Walter Benjamin en *Charles Baudelaire: Ein Lyriker im Zeitalter des Hochkapitalismus*, que se encuentra en las páginas 509-748 del primer tomo de sus *Gesammelte Schriften* (Frankfurt am Main: Suhrkamp Verlag, 1974).

[7]Vid. Jean Franco, "Image and Experience in *La vorágine*", *BHS*, 41 (1964), pp. 101-110, y Luis B. Eyzaguirre, "Patología en *La vorágine* de José Eustasio Rivera", *Hispania*, 56 (1973), pp. 81-90.

[8]Vid. George Ross Ridge, *The Hero in French Decadent Literature* (Athens: Univ. of Georgia Press, 1961).

[9]*Op cit.*, p. 141.

[10]El trapiche/batán es otro elemento que puede añadirse a los ya señalados por Alfonso González en "Elementos del *Quijote* en la caracterización de *La Vorágine*", *RN*, 15 (1973-74), pp. 74-79.

[11]La ciudad no corresponde necesariamente al paraíso ni el llano al purgatorio. Difiero en varios puntos de la interpretación de Seymour Menton en "*La vorágine*: Circling the Triangle", *Hispania*, 59 (1976), pp. 418-34, quien ve en el viaje de Cova la caída del paraíso al infierno ocasionada por su orgullo, a pesar de que anota acertadamente: "Although the *sierra* may represent Paradise on the symbolic level, neither the narrator nor the author has any illusions about Bogotá or indeed about any city at all" (p. (419). El paradigma mítico que Leonidas Morales revela en "*La vorágine*: un viaje al país de los muertos", *AUCH*, 123, No. 134 (1965), pp. 148-70, no se inicia necesariamente en el paraíso.

[12]Richard J. Callan ha mostrado aspectos muy importantes de la evolución síquica de Cova que complementan la transición social a la que yo me refiero aquí. Vid. "The Archetype of Psychic Renewal in *La voragine*", *Hispania*, 54 (1971), pp. 470-76.

[13]El patriotismo exaltado es una característica de *La vorágine* que revela algo sobre Rivera y los límites de apertura de un intelectual.

[14]Vid. Karl Mannheim, *Ideology and Utopia* (New York: Harcourt, Brace and Co., 1936), en especial pp. 136-46.

[15]Peter L. Berger y Thomas Luckmann, *The Social Construction of Reality* (New York: Doubleday, 1966), especialmente pp. 116-18.

[16]Comparar con lo que escriben Berger y Luckmann: "All social reality is precarious. All societies are constructions in the face of chaos. The constant possibility of anomic terror is actualized whenever the legitimations that obscure the precariousness are threatened or collapse", *The Social Construction of Reality*, p. 96.

[17]Vid. la excelente biografía escrita por Eduardo Neale-Silva, *Horizonte humano: vida de José Eustasio Rivera* (México: FCE, 1960), en particular las pp. 127 y 152.

THE NOVEL AND THE
CONCEPT OF SOCIAL NETWORK

N. W. Visser

Literary criticism in recent years has been remarkable for the extent to which it has actively pursued a multidisciplinary perspective, opening itself to such diverse and potentially fruitful influences as philosophy, linguistics, semiotics, communications and information theory, psychological and psychoanalytic theory, sociology, structural anthropology—the list could be doubled and even trebled without coming anywhere near being exhaustive. For the most part these grafts and borrowings have been of the order of comprehensive analytic or theoretical systems: orientations or paradigms or approaches which attempt (or purport) to provide a ground for the entirety of literary studies. Without in any way wishing to constrain the search for such totalizing systems, a search which, after all, has revitalized our discipline, I should like to suggest that we entertain a different order of borrowing, of less comprehensive but no less fruitful scope and relevance. The particular borrowing I have in mind would provide us not with a general theory of literary art but with an analytical scheme that can be extremely useful in the study of a single aspect of literature, an aspect that is conventionally expressed in one of those standard pairings of critical discourse: individual and society.

Literary critics, especially critics of the novel, have long been interested in the relationship between the individual and society and have turned to it repeatedly, searching for ways of analyzing and expressing its salient features. For the most part their commentary has been devoted to the pressure of social norms on the individual, the career of the *parvenu* as he— or, as often in English novels, she—moves upward through the class structure, and the impact on the individual of the institutions of a society or broad political and social currents. In such studies society is conceived of largely in abstract structural terms: conventions, classes, institutions, historical trends. Far too often, as we try to match the individual's behavior with social considerations, these categories account for the actions undertaken by characters in a crudely reductionist manner, for while generalizations about the structure and norms of society can be apposite to the interpretation of patterns of behavior, they often fail to account in a convincing way for specific responses to particular circumstances. What we require is some way of examining the area intermediate between what Mark Schorer once called "the stream of social history and the stream of soul."[1]

Novelists, as Michel Zeraffa has pointed out, typically "make explicit the separateness of the abstract notion of society and the existential actuality of social relationships."[2] Shifting our critical focus from the abstract notion to the particularities of a character's set of social relationships is likely to give us a more precise analytical perspective; it will at the very least complement the more traditional undertaking. Unfortunately we have lacked a methodology that could shape such a mode of analysis. Critics have seized on the need for examining social relationships, but naming a need is not automatically to fulfill it. W. J. Harvey, for example, argues in *Character and the Novel* that by far the most important context for the examination of character "is the web of human relationships in which any single character must be enmeshed."[3] Apart from the additional statement that "the human context. . .is primarily a web of relationships; the characters do not develop along single and linear roads of destiny but are, so to speak, human crossroads,"[4] Harvey fails to develop this idea, devoting his chapter on the "human context" almost exclusively to a typology of characters: protagonists, background characters, and various intermediate types like the Jamesian ficelle. Lacking any methodology that would enable him to apply his insight, to explicate and operationalize it as the social scientist would say, Harvey is brought to a halt at the threshold of analysis.

It may come as a surprise to literary critics to learn that for a long time anthropologists were also frustrated in their efforts to examine social relationships systematically. Expert in describing social stratification and individual role, versed in structural-functional analysis of society in the manner of Radcliffe-Brown, against whose reductionist model they were reacting, British social anthropologists as early as the 1950s began to seek alternative methods of analyzing social action. The first intimation of a conceptual breakthrough came in a paper delivered to a research seminar by J. A. Barnes in 1954.[5] With the publication in the last three or four years of several books and numerous articles and monographs,[6] Barnes's method of "network analysis" has developed into a powerful analytical tool, one capable, *mutatis mutandis*, of greatly enhancing the study of the novel. Barnes and those who followed his lead did not invent the notion of social network; social scientists had long spoken of webs and networks of social relations, just as Harvey's reference to "a web of relationships" is entirely in keeping with a long tradition of invoking the notion in literary criticism. Barnes's contribution has been the transformation of what is in essence a metaphor into an analytical concept. The conventional use of the term evokes, as J. Clyde Mitchell has suggested, "an image of the interconnections of social relationships," but does not go on "to specify the properties of these interconnections which could be used to interpret social actions."[7] The analysis of social networks seeks to specify these properties and use them as an interpretative framework, thereby moving beyond insight to detailed examination, beyond suggestive metaphor to analytical concept.

Before going into more detail about the analysis of social networks, I should make clear what the method can legitimately claim to be and to offer us. It is not a substitute for the methods and models put forward by the sociology of literature in general or by Marxist criticism in particular, nor does it contradict or undercut or otherwise dispose of these more generalized methodologies. Neither for that matter does it necessarily or logically entail them. Without committing the analyst to any particular critical or ideological position, network analysis, by focusing attention squarely on concrete social relationships and by establishing a rich but by no means overly elaborate or jargon-ridden conceptual and terminological scheme, represents for the social scientist—or in the present case, the literary critic— a significant gain in analytical precision. An increase in precision may seem a modest claim, but we should not underestimate its magnitude. Network analysis, whether applied to the life-world or to literary texts, will rarely result in radical revisions of previous interpretative insights, nor will it automatically resolve hitherto recalcitrant interpretative cruxes. What it can do is enable the social or literary analyst to formulate and articulate insights with a degree of refinement and clarity not previously possible.

Transforming the notion of social network from a metaphor into a descriptive tool which makes the detailed analysis of social relations possible requires that we identify and explicate in a more or less systematic fashion the major morphological and interactional features of social networks. Although there is some disagreement among social scientists on such questions as which features in social networks should be singled out for study and how networks can best be analyzed (it would be too much to expect unanimity in a field so complex and relatively new), J. Clyde Mitchell has managed to isolate several characteristics which are germane to most studies.[8] Among the morphological characteristics, those pertaining to the shape or patterning of social links are *anchorage, density, reachability*, and *range*. Interactional characteristics, which involve the nature of the individual links themselves rather than the patterns they fall into, include *content, directedness, durability, intensity*, and *frequency*. To Mitchell's tabulation I should like to add the criterion of *proximity*.

Morphological Criteria

Anchorage. Usually a network is centered on a particular person whose actions the observer wishes to interpret; the person chosen is the point of anchorage, and his network is usually called a personal network.

Reachability. It is often important to know the extent to which a person can use someone with whom he has a direct relationship to contact people with whom he does not but who are for some reason important to him or, alternatively, the extent to which a person who is important to him can contact him through someone with whom he has a direct relationship. Reachability also specifies the number of intermediaries one person must go through to reach another.

Density. The extent to which the members of one person's network know each other is the density of the network. A person's network may be discontinuous; that is, he may have links with different groups of people.

Range. The number of actual social links a person has, relative to the total number of possible links within the specified set of people, is the range or size of his network.

Interactional Criteria

Content. The links between people can be of many kinds: employer-employee, shared religious affiliation, friendship, and so on. Usually content refers to these and other normative contexts in which two people interact. When a relationship is restricted to or dominated by a single normative context of a kind that rigidly defines roles (for example, a patron-client relationship), the relationship is called single-stranded or uniplex. A relationship which involves a greater number of role-relations is termed multi-stranded or multiplex. A further distinction can be made between ascribed relationships and relationships which a person builds through his own actions and choices.

Directedness. While many relationships are fully reciprocal, others are directed in one way only or have different contents moving in each direction. Put simply, unrequited love is a directed relationship, as is, in a different way, a patron-client relationship. The influence of one person on another will often depend on the direction of contents in their relationship.

Durability. Some kinds of links are typically more durable than others by their very nature (for example, kinship as opposed to employer-employee relationships). In most cases, and especially in urban societies, networks are dynamic in character, changing over time as new relationships are built and old ones fall into abeyance.

Intensity. Anthropologists measure the intensity of a relationship according to the extent to which individuals recognize and honor obligations or feel themselves able to ask others with whom they are linked to do the same. Intensity obviously involves as well one person's ability to exert influence over another.

Frequency. One of the more easily quantifiable features of a relationship is the frequency of contact between the parties. Frequency in itself is not a particularly important criterion, but it is important in relation to the opportunities for reinforcing existing ties or forging new ones. Without fairly frequent contact, new recruits to one's network are unlikely to move beyond specialized, uniplex relationships.

Proximity. To the criteria listed by Mitchell, I should like to add the criterion, implied in much of what he says, of proximity. Kinship ties can remain intense even if the parties are separated by great distance; however, proximity, which is closely related to frequency, is necessary for establishing new ties, and some relationships (neighbor relationships for instance) are largely functions of proximity.

Once identified, the criteria seem obvious and the analytical framework reasonably straightforward. Such are the virtues of most genuinely useful conceptual schemes. Network analysis, conducted according to the criteria identified here and to others that might emerge in the process of analysis, holds out greater promise for the literary critic. The method readily lends itself to any number of fascinating critical undertakings. The peculiarities of the social relationships in the early Hemingway, in which central characters try to form links that are at the same time both uniplex and intense, would be an interesting study, as would be the network of relations in E. M. Forster's *A Passage to India*; we may well find that network analysis could help to clarify a number of things in the novel, among them Miss Quested's inconsistent behavior, Mrs. Moore's decision to leave India, and the difficulties Fielding and Aziz have in establishing a close personal relationship. Indeed Forster's exhortation, "Only connect"--the inscription to his earlier novel, *Howard's End*, but one equally relevant to the central themes of *A Passage to India*—is an invitation to network analysis. To cite only one further example, critics have for some time noted the pervasive presence of the image of the network in *Middlemarch*, in which the narrator repeatedly makes such statements as, "I at least have so much to do in unravelling certain human lots, and seeing how they were woven and interwoven" (I.15).[9] The image points to a central feature of the novel's structure, and network analysis gives us the necessary analytical tool for pursuing the image through to its structural manifestations.

That network analysis is potentially a seminal contribution to the poetics of the novel seems to me unarguable. I would go even further. It is likely that the application of the method to the novel can in turn be of assistance to the social scientist. In examining social networks an anthropologist must perforce rely on observation, inferring the morphological and even interactional characteristics of a person's social network from his actions; at the same time he is forced to speculate on people's subjective perceptions of their relationships. It is difficult for him to determine exactly when a link between two people can be posited, to establish the point at which a link ceases to be uniplex and becomes multiplex, or to ascertain with any certainty the contents of a link, and it is even more difficult to assess the intensity of a relationship. The social scientist must try as far as possible to establish quantifiable criteria, yet so much that is important in relationships resists quantification. And however thorough his observation of social interaction, the social scientist is always aware that there is so much that he may miss. In these and other areas the literary critic has decided advantages. The world of the novel is different from the life-world in a number of ways that are of significance to someone interested in network analysis. For one thing, the fictional world, relative to the life-world, is finite and bounded; since all the characters are identified we have a complete set of interacting people and total network of relations among them, whereas one of the problems social scientists face is that in the life-world total networks are "general, ever-ramifying, ever-articulating."[10] Moreover, the fictional world is "pre-interpreted";[11] it is the product of selection and arrangement and it is part of a total structure of meanings. When we add to this special feature the access a novel typically provides to the private thoughts and inner states of one or more presented characters, we see immediately that in novels such things as the content and intensity of relationships, features about which the social scientist for the most part can only speculate, are often made considerably more explicit. Novels, whether through the rendering of a chracter's interiority or through a narrator's commentary, conventionally provide us with privileged glimpses into the motives and emotions underlying relationships and with a character's subjective perceptions of his relations with others. Furthermore, the novel is complete and fixed; the critic can go over it repeatedly, and what he goes over is the totality of the world he is examining, not the abstractions and selections of field work notes. Perhaps the greatest return the study of novels can make to the social scientist is that the action of a novel typically unfolds over a lengthy period of time. Anthropologists have insisted that the concept of social network, like the relationships it is designed to study, is dynamic; however, to date the exigencies of field work have prevented them from making detailed studies of the changes social networks undergo with the passing of time.[12] Novels can provide them with the continuous flux of social relationships, and should they turn their attention to novels they may well come across things not yet met with in field work situations that would enable them to refine the analytical model.

As is the case with all aspects of structure, some novels will foreground social relationships, some will very nearly dispense with them; consequently, some will reward network analysis while others will not. I can think of few better examples of the first type than Conrad's *Nostromo*,[13] a novel which is attractive both to critics interested in the broader social forces depicted in the novel and to those who prefer to focus on the portrayal of individual characters. For the former there is the interplay of groups and institutions: the cargadores, the miner, the Europeans and Blancos, the secret societies which spring up late in the novel, the "material interests" of the San Tomé mine and the railway, and so on. For these critics *Nostromo* is preeminently a political novel, inviting investigation of such things as the shift among the various groups of workers from something like a caste system based on job and national origin, before the Monterist revolution, to a perception of shared class interests implicit in the formation of the secret societies after Sulaco secedes from the republic, the cycle of revolutions, the impact of the "material interests" on the social order, and the weaknesses and contradictions inherent in the Ribierist government and other "reform" movements. For the second type of critic there is above all else the concern, common to so much of Conrad's work, with the destiny of the isolated individual, in this case characters like Decoud, Charles Gould, Dr. Monygham, and ultimately, Nostromo himself. Of course the distinction I am making is at best partial; neither kind of critic, whichever his emphasis, can examine the one aspect without some recourse to the other. And each will sooner or later come to talk about at least some of the relationships among the novel's character's, but, lacking a coherent and consistent method, they will do so for the most part in an informal, ad hoc, and largely impressionistic way. Network analysis can help to clarify the complex array of relationships and to reveal precisely in what ways they are critical in the unfolding action of the novel and in the fates of the various characters.

Certain features of social networks, as the very wording of the term implies, can be conveniently represented diagrammatically. The first diagram represents the nexus of relationships among the major characters in *Nostromo* at the point immediately before Nostromo and Decoud set off with the silver, when the array of social relationships is at its fullest. Social scientists have used various graphic devices to indicate particular features of relationships; for present purposes I have decided to represent only three important distinctions. The heavy lines indicate relationships that have the characteristics of multiplexity, high intensity, and strong personal content. The thinner lines refer to relationships that are multiplex but rather more specialized, impersonal, lower in intensity, and for the most instrumental. The broken lines represent relationships that are uniplex, sometimes merely conversational, and involve little more than some degree of frequency and proximity. Other important features, directedness and durability for example, will be brought out in comments following the figure.

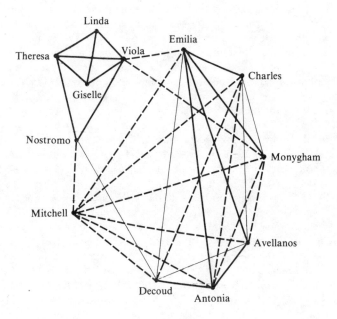

Figure 1

Since for the moment my interest is in the totality of relationships among the major characters, the network is not anchored, is not, at least in graphic terms, a personal network. Instead the characters, except for the members of the Viola family, who form a special cluster,[14] are evenly spaced round a circle. It is immediately clear from the diagram that Emilia Gould has the strongest, most extensive, and most effective network in the novel. She has direct relationships with all the other major characters except, oddly enough, Nostromo, with whom she comes into direct contact only in his dying moments. The only Englishwoman in the province, a woman dismayed "at the appearance of men and events so remote from her own racial conventions" (2.4.182), Emilia is "hostess to all the Europeans in Sulaco" (1.6.69) and is called by Avellanos "as true a patriot as though you had been born in our midst" (1.7.95). The number of multiplex and close personal relationships she has—more by far than any other character in the novel— gives Emilia a special centrality[15] in the social life of Sulaco; it is through her rather than her husband that the Casa Gould becomes the favorite meeting place of the Europeans and the local Spanish-speaking aristocracy. More importantly, she alone in the novel holds out the promise of community as opposed to isolation, even providing a means for the outcast Monygham's reintegration into the human continuity. Beyond her husband and Dr. Monygham, Emilia has close personal links with Avellanos and his daughter Antonia, as well as a multiplex but less intense and personal link with Decoud. Perhaps her most interesting secondary link is with Viola, the old Garibaldino, and through him to his family. Ostensibly a uniplex link dominated by a relation of "benefactress" to "protege," the bond is invested by Emilia with a characteristic warmth, which he in turn reciprocates. She sees to it that the railway will not threaten the existence of the Casa Viola, participates in the decision to have him granted the sinecure of the lighthouse after the death of his wife, and is in all ways "the providence of the Viola family" (3.11.573-74).

There are several noteworthy features of Charles Gould's network. It is by virtue of his control over the mine, the primary economic resource in the province, the "Imperium in Imperio," that he is the "Rey de Sulaco"; from the mine, and hence through Charles, flows effective power in the province. Gould sets out quite consciously to use the mine to effective radical restructuring of institutions and social relationships in Sulaco. He sees the San Tomé mine as a stabilizing force and is, at least temporarily, successful. The mine has a "steadying effect. . .upon the life of that remote province" (1.8.105) and becomes "a rallying point for everything in the province that needed order and stability to live" (1.8.122). Yet so preoccupied, ultimately even obsessed, is he with the mine that his social relationships, never very strong, grow progressively weaker. I have attributed multiplexity to his bond with Monygham, but it could well be argued that the link never moves beyond uniplexity. In either case it has little in the way of intensity or strong personal content. His relationship with Avellanos is even more peculiar. Avellanos is "the hereditary friend of the family" (1.6.76), and there is every reason for this largely ascribed relationship to grow into close friendship. All the necessary conditions exist. Their goals are compatible, even at times identical; the community is small and affords both proximity and frequency (the Avellanos home is across the road from the Casa Gould and Avellanos visits daily); moreover that part of the total network centered on the Goulds and the Avellanos family is particularly dense: all their acquaintances in Sulaco know one another. Yet, while the link is a durable one, Avellanos never becomes more to Charles than an intermediary, an access to other people and important groups in the community (as the next diagram shows). All of Gould's other links are uniplex, for the main merely conversational or narrowly instrumental, and nearly dormant. He relies on his wife to establish close ties in the community and tends to count on her network as if it were his own; what are for her links that have been carefully developed are merely ascribed links for him, existing becaue of his wife's links: "the best of my feelings," he says to her, "are in your keeping, my dear" (p. 79). Moreover, his obsession with "material interests," with the mine or at least with the "idea" it represents for him, eventually seriously weakens even his relationship with Emilia. The course of Charles's destiny is the process of progressively weakening social relationships, until he is left in isolation, a man for whom devotion to abstractions has replaced commitment to personal bonds.

There are two further characters I want to deal with before turning to the next diagram. Decoud and Antonia have a peculiar status in the community. In a society in which expatriate Europeans and the local Spanish-speaking aristocracy, the Blancos, occupy a shared niche at the very top of the social pyramid, Antonia and Decoud are neither clearly one nor the other. Decoud is godson to Avellanos and known to "everybody in Costaguana" as " 'the son Decoud' " (2.3.168), but from his long years as an expatriate in Paris he has become "the adopted child of western Europe" (2.3.173). Father Corbelàn says of him that his is "neither the son of his own country nor of any other (3.5.219). Antonia, "born in Europe and educated partly in England" (2.1.154), is in much the same position. She is recognized by the people of Sulaco, particularly by the other women of her age, as somehow an outsider: "it was generally believed that with her foreign upbringing and her foreign ideas the learned and proud Antonia would never marry—unless, indeed, she married a foreigner from Europe or North America." Yet, just as Decoud, though seen as not being altogether a Costaguanan, believes himself to be "a true *hijo del pays*, a true son of the country" (2.6.236), and is recognized as "the son Decoud," so Antonia's pride is accounted for on the grounds that "it is well known that all the Corbelàns were proud, and her mother was a Corbelàn" (2.1.155). Acculturated individuals, as the social scientist would say, deracinated, or at least déclassé, as the literary critic might put it, Decoud and Antonia are both of and not of the society of Costaguana, a circumstance which goes some way towards explaining how two people of such radically different temperaments and beliefs should be drawn to each other, though there are of course the close ties between their families: "My sister is only waiting to embrace you," Decoud says to Antonia. "My father is transported. . . . Our mothers were like sisters" (2.5.201).

Except for his largely ascribed relation with Avellanos and his close personal bond to Antonia, Decoud is virtually without personal ties in the community. His only other multiplex relationships are with Emilia Gould and Nostromo, and the latter is a curious one. It is a directed relationship; he is curious about Nostromo and makes a project of getting to know him shortly before the fighting breaks out. Although there is apparently some frequency involved in the relationship, it lacks any potential for durability, and when they are thrown into a situation of interdependence on the sinking lighter out in the Golfo Placido, "there was nothing in common between them. . . . [T]hey seemed to have become completely estranged. . . . This common danger brought their differences in aim, in view, in character, and in position into absolute prominence in the private vision of each. There was no bond of conviction, of common idea" (2.8.328).

In his isolation on the Great Isabel, Decoud turns in upon himself and dies, as the novel repeatedly emphasizes, of solitude. Even before the lighter sinks he feels that "his passionate devotion to Antonia, into which he had worked himself up out of the depths of his skepticism, had lost all appearance of reality" (2.7.296). Without the active, immediate support of some form of involvement with others, Decoud comes to "entertaining a doubt of his own individuality. It had merged with the world of cloud and water, of natural forces and forms of nature" (3.10.556).

Before commenting on the social relationships of any of the other major characters I should like to turn to the second diagram, which reproduces Figure 1 and adds to it the interrelations of the major characters with some of the more important secondary characters.

At first glance this array of lines and cross-hatchings might produce a slight sense of vertigo, but with a bit of patience it begins to come into focus. Like Figure 1, the diagram depicts the network of social relations at the peak of the Monterist revolt. I have introduced a slight departure from typical network theory by representing relations between individuals and groups (the miners, the Ribierist Party, etc.), but there are precedents for doing so in the work of social scientists.[16] One reason for introducing groups into the analysis is the light they shed on reachability in *Nostromo* by showing the intermediary functions of some of the major characters. We note for instance that Charles Gould has no direct access to groups which at one time or another are essential for his plan to use the mine as a means of stabilizing and restructuring the social order of the Occidental Provinces. When it becomes necessary to mobilize the miners, the railway workers, and the cargadores, he has to rely on others to intercede for him. The further point should be made that at this stage in the novel the groups of workers are quite separate from one another, a condition which alters after Sulacan independence when the workers come together in secret societies and themselves become an incipiently revolutionary force.

Figure 2 brings out the importance of Avellanos as an intermediary. He

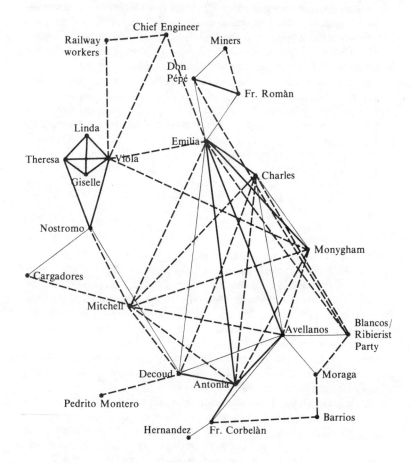

Figure 2

is Gould's access to the Blanco community and the Ribierist Party, and it is through him that Moraga, his nephew and the agent for the Gould concession in the capital, is recruited. His contact with the Blancos also leads to the recruitment of Don Pépé, whose close relationship with the miners enables him to lead them to the defense of the town, and it is in part through Moraga that General Barrios, who plays an important part in delivering Sulaco from Pedrito Montero, is first brought to Sulaco. If Avellanos is instrumental in recruiting Don Pépé, it is Emilia who builds a close relationship with him, so that here again Charles depends on his wife's network to augment his own. Whatever personal loyalty prompts Don Pépé to act, it is directed more towards Emilia than Charles, and the same might be said of the chief engineer.

The diagram also depicts the relationships which bring the cargadores and Hernandez, the bandit of the Campo who becomes Minister of War in the Occidental Republic, to the defense of Sulaco. Father Corbelàn, uncle to Antonia and, like Monygham, something of an outcast, uses his peculiar and unexplained relationship with Hernandez to bring him into the struggle for independence, and of course Mitchell, acting through Nostromo, brings in the cargadores.

One additional relationship depicted in figure 2 invites comment because of a characteristic of Costaguanan society which it reveals and because of a possible flaw in the orthodox model of network analysis which it points up. Decoud is compelled to leave Sulaco with Nostromo because when he was living in Paris he had publicly exposed Pedrito Montero, who was then passing himself off as a Secretary of the Costaguanan Legislation and is now invading Sulaco, as a fraud. The size of Costaguanan society above the levels of the peasantry and the workers is small enough that, even when people do not know each other, they know of each other. Furthermore, the cycle of revolutions has created a dense, tightly knit expatriate community in Paris —it was there that Antonia and Decoud first met—a community which follows events at "home" carfully and which in turn is the object of much curiosity for those who remain in Costaguana. Density is one of the chief interests in network analysis; however, attention has been focused on individuals knowing rather than knowing of one another. I have attributed to Decoud and Pedrito Montero a uniplex link, but there is no positive evidence that they have in fact been in direct contact, that Montero was even present when Decoud denounced him. A person's knowledge of others, as distinct from his direct and personal relations with others, has the potential for constraining or otherwise influencing his behavior and is therefore a factor which network analysis should ideally be able to take into account.

Since I want to conclude this examination of *Nostromo* with a look at the changes that Nostromo's social network goes through in the course of the novel, and since Mitchell is a pivotal figure in his network, it might be worthwhile saying something about Mitchell's social relationships before moving on. Mitchell, consular agent and superintendent of the shippng company in Sulaco, for all his lack of perception occupies an important position in the affairs of the province. As he says at one point, speaking more truly than he knows, "I am a public character, sir" (3.3.382). As a result largely of his position, he has one of the most extensive social networks in the novel, but as a man whose public role absorbs private personality, his links with others are, though cordial in most cases, (his relationship with Monygham is the exception), uniplex, functional, and lacking in strong personal content. He is for example, among the major characters, the only frequenter of the Casa Gould with whom Emilia does not form a multiplex bond, not because his link with her is bound up in a narrowly restricted role-relation so much as because he is incapable of relating to others in anything other than his role of "public character."

Crucial in the life of Sulaco and in the fates of the other major characters is Mitchell's link with Nostromo; just how crucial it is becomes clear as soon as we examine the novel from the viewpoint of Nostromo's personal network and the transformations it undergoes. The following three figures show Nostromo's personal network at various stages of the novel. The first (Figure 3) shows Nostromo's network of relations shortly after his arrival in Sulaco.

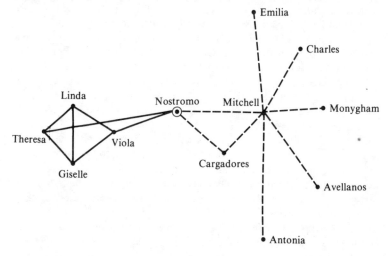

Figure 3

Nostromo, "with the weight of countless generations behind him and no parentage to speak of,"[17] enters Sulaco as bosun of an Italian ship. He is "admitted to live in the intimacy" (1.3.17) of the Viola family—a tie initially engendered by their common nationality—and he is persuaded by them to remain in Sulaco. From the outset, then, he has a close bond in Sulaco; however, as the previous diagrams have shown, the Violas form a distinct cluster with few ties to the community. Being taken on as foreman of the lightermen by Mitchell provides Nostromo with a position of potential influence in Sulaco, for, although the link is a uniplex one, he can use Mitchell's extensive network to enhance his own position. And indeed Mitchell's "mania for 'lending you my Capataz de Cargadores'. . .was to bring Nostromo into personal contact, sooner or later, with every European in Sulaco, as a sort of universal factotum" (1.6.48). So successful is Nostromo in the various tasks asked of him that before long it becomes customary to turn to him whenever something difficult needs doing. But while the community profits greatly from his various feats, it is more difficult to see exactly what Nostromo derives from being treated as a vital resource available to the community through the agency of Mitchell.

Bruce Kapferer has argued that network analysis provides us with an analytical model but lacks an explicit theory of social behavior which can give the model explanatory force.[18] Kapferer finds his theory in the idea of "social exchange" as developed by P. M. Blau,[19] a theory which, putting it somewhat crudely, posits that individuals undertake "voluntary actions. . . that are motivated by the return they are expected to bring and typically do in fact bring from others."[20] Such a theory, which views relationships as reciprocities of investments and returns, may appear to some to be narrowly reductionist, perhaps even cynical with regard to the contents of social relationships; it has the advantage, as Kapferer notes, of providing testable hypotheses about human behavior, and in the present context it raises the interesting question of what returns Nostromo seeks and in fact receives for his efforts on behalf of the people of Sulaco. Figure 4 represents Nostromo's network of social relations at the point in the novel immediately preceding his departure with the silver.

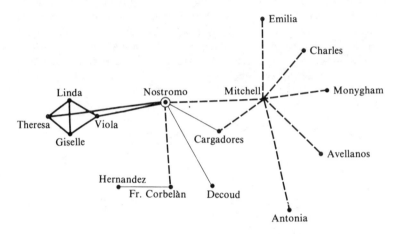

Figure 4

Taking into account the length of time he has spent in Sulaco and the services he has performed for the community, his network has changed surprisingly little. However much his efforts have brought him "into personal contact. . .with every European in Sulaco," such contacts have been fleeting; they have not grown into ongoing relationships, and he continues to be in contact with others chiefly indirectly, through the mediation of Mitchell. His investment has not led to expansion of his social network into the European-Blanco group; he is treated by them more as a resource than as a person, valued solely for his usefulness in practical situations and taken largely for granted. Neither, for that matter, has Nostromo received much even in the way of material reward for his services, and what he does get he spends lavishly, or gives or gambles away. What Nostromo does gain, of course, is prestige, which Decoud realizes is itself "a sort of investment"

(2.6.244). Even the prestige, which he has given so much to gain, is qualified in a special way. Of the three principal directions in which Nostromo's network radiates—towards the Violas, towards Mitchell and through him the Europeans and Blancos, and towards the cargadores and through them the people of the town—only the third genuinely enhances his sense of status and esteem. Viola's attitude toward him is purely personal, and Theresa scorns him more the more his reputation grows, while the Europeans do "not think of him humanely, as a fellow-creature," (3.8.483). Nostromo, who converts his material goods into prestige by acts of largess and converts his talents into prestige by acts of bravery, derives the sense of prestige almost exclusively through his now multiplex bond with the cargadores and the townspeople; he remains, in more ways than one, a "man of the people," *nostro uomo*. The very failure of the Europeans to recognize the meaning of the words they mistakenly take for his name is an index of how little he is their man, one of them. Those who value Nostromo are not those on whose behalf he strives. And if the link with Decoud seems to be an exception, it should be remembered that, as noted earlier in the discussion of Figure 1, the relation is a directed one; Decoud makes a point of getting to know Nostromo simply to satisfy his curiosity.

The final illustration (Figure 5) shows Nostromo's network at the end of the novel.

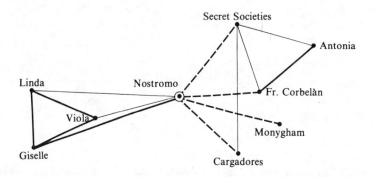

Figure 5

When Nostromo awakens the day after swimming to shore from the Great Isabel, in an important sense he is re-entering Sulaco anew, once more an orphan. His sleep "had been like a break of continuity in the chain of experience" (3.8.460).

> Nostromo woke up from a fourteen-hours' sleep and arose full length from his lair in the long grass. He stood knee-deep among the whispering undulations of the green blades, with the lost air of a man just born into the world. Handsome, robust, and supple, he threw back his head, flung his arms open,

and stretched himself with a slow twist of the waist and a leisurely growling yawn of white teeth; as natural and free from evil in the moment of waking as a magnificent and unconscious wild beast. Then, in the suddenly steadied glance fixed upon nothing from under a forced frown, appeared the man (3.7.458).

In the short time Nostromo had been absent—engaged in "the most desperate affair" of his life—the situation in Sulaco has changed so rapidly that the silver for which he was asked to risk so much is no longer of particular consequence. Having acted in secret, and returning to no expression of gratitude or esteem, he feels that "he had been betrayed!" (3.8.467). The entire foundation for his behavior is called into question: "Had I not done enough for them to be of some account, por Dios? Is it that the *hombres finos*—the gentlemen—need not think as long as there is a man of the people ready to risk his body and soul? Or, perhaps, we have no souls—like dogs" (3.8.487). In his belief that " 'I am nothing! Suddenly—' He swung his arm downward. 'Nothing to any one' " (3.9.509), he loses the impulse that had until now guided all his actions and decides to "grow rich very slowly" (3.10.562).

By the end of the novel, or at least by the time of the final climax on the Great Isabel, Nostromo's changed situation is mirrored in the substantial alterations his network has undergone. The death of Theresa has removed his most intense, if often antagonistic, link, and the departure of Mitchell has eliminated the tie through which he acted on behalf of the Europeans and Blancos. Of his remaining ties, his link with Viola has slackened, as has the one with the cargadores. Both are not directed links; Nostromo is looked to but barely looks back, and the same is largely the case with his connections with the newly formed secret societies. Father Corbelàn seeks to take the place of Mitchell, recruiting Nostromo to new and very different causes, but he remains indifferent. As for the link with Monygham, it is a negative one, although Nostromo is able to use it to contact Emilia for the final interview before his death.

His one remaining link that is personal, multiplex, and intense is the one with Giselle. But despite, or perhaps because of, its being based on "some profound similarities of nature" (3.12.585), the relationship, although intense, has a kind of emotional thinness, a lack of sustaining substance: "He could see it would be violent, exacting, suspicious, uncompromising—like her soul" (3.12.586). Like all of his relationships at the end of the novel, this one is colored by his obsession with the silver and its corrupting influence. His social network, based from the outset on faulty principles and perceptions, collapses in upon itself in the final part of the novel. His acts—collecting the silver, visiting Corbelàn, courting Giselle—have become secretive and often solitary: the society in which he moves has ceased to have any influence on his actions. He is alone, and his death is simply the symbolic form of closure, both of his peculiar destiny and of the novel, which signals the appropriate moment to begin bringing the curtain down. In the background, of course, a contrary set of signals operates; the cycle of revolutions is still as work.

Nostromo is so lavish and detailed in its depiction of social relationships that without expanding this commentary beyond reasonable bounds it is impossible to do justice to the topic. Before concluding this application of the analysis of social networks to the novel, however, I want to return to the question of the relation of the method to broader interpretive methodologies. Marxists and others concerned in one way or another with the sociology of literature will want some indication of how the systematic examination of personal bonds can be integrated into their larger perspectives. What can it reveal, for instance, about so-called power relations or forms of economic and political domination? If we remember that the control of resources and other forms of wealth does not in itself constitute power but rather becomes converted into power through the effort to influence other people directly or indirectly, the answers begin to emerge. In the case of *Nostromo*, network analysis gives us a way of precisely mapping the distribution and flow of economic and political power through the depicted society. We note, for example, that Charles Gould's control of the mine decreases in consequence in direct proportion to his progressively weakened social network. He has in a sense failed to grasp the principle that propels successful politicians in societies where office must be gained by popular election: get to know your constituents. It is its capacity for enabling us to see not merely that such things are the case but how and in exactly what ways they are so which constitutes the special contribution of network analysis. And even in works that lack the overtly political dimension of *Nostromo*, the analysis of social networks has the altogether salutary effect of focusing our attention on the tissue of human relationships that is so often of central concern.

UNIVERSITY OF WISCONSIN

Notes

[1]"Foreword: Self and Society," in *Society and Self in the Novel*, ed. Schorer, English Institute Essays, 1955 (New York: Columbia Univ. Press, 1956), p. ix.

[2]*Fictions: The Novel and Social Reality*, trans. Catherine Burns and Tom Burns (Harmondsworth: Penguin, 1976), p. 69.

[3]*Character and the Novel* (London: Chatto & Windus, 1970), p. 52.

[4]*Ibid.*, p. 69.

[5]Barnes's paper was published as "Class and Committees in a Norwegian Island Parish," *Human Relations*, 7 (1954), pp. 39-58.

[6]Much of the important material on network analysis is available in the following: J. Clyde Mitchell, ed., *Social Networks in Urban Situations* (Manchester: Manchester

Univ. Press, 1969); Jeremy Boissevain, *Friends of Friends: Networks, Manipulators and Coalitions* (Oxford: Basil Blackwell, 1974); and Jeremy Boissevain and J. Clyde Mitchell, eds., *Network Analysis: Studies in Human Interaction* (The Hague: Mouton, 1973). I should also mention Philip Mayer's *Townsmen or Tribesmen: Conservatism and the Process of Urbanization in a South African City* (Cape Town: Oxford Univ. Press, 1961), especially Ch. 18, "Network, Culture and Change," written in collaboration with Iona Mayer. Professor Mayer, who helped to pioneer the concept, encouraged my interest in applying network analysis to the novel. (Because of the repetition of authors and editors and the similarity of titles, subsequent footnotes will give more information than convention ordinarily dictates.)

⁷"The Concept and Use of Social Networks," in Mitchell, ed., *Social Networks in Urban Situations*, p. 2.

⁸"The Concept and Use of Social Networks," pp. 12-29. My tabulation of the characteristics of social networks follows Mitchell's more detailed and comprehensive account closely. the distinction between ascribed relationships and the ones built through personal choice is borrowed from Mayer, *Townsmen or Tribesmen*, p. 284.

⁹On the pervasiveness of images of webs and networks in *Middlemarch*, see J. Hillis Miller, *The Form of Victorian Fiction* (Notre Dame, Indiana: Univ. of Notre Dame Press, 1968), pp. 118-19. Miller's contention in his chapter on "Self and Community" that the novel "has a single pervasive theme: interpersonal relations" (p. 94) opens the way to network analysis.

¹⁰Mitchell, "The Concept and Use of Social Networks," p. 12.

¹¹The importance of the "pre-interpreted" nature of fictional worlds is pointed out by Maurice Natanson, "Phenomenology and the Theory of Literature," *Literature, Philosophy, and the Social Sciences* (The Hague: Martinus Nijhoff, 1962), pp. 91 ff. Natanson, however, comments only on the way in which the fictional world is in part interpreted for the reader by the characters. I have expanded the concept to include as well other factors which cause us to receive fictional worlds as pre-interpreted ones. Cf. Käte Hamburger, *The Logic of Literature*, trans. Marilynn J. Rose, 2nd ed., rev. (Bloomington: Indiana Univ. Press, 1973), pp. 228-29.

¹²On the problem of examining social networks over time, see Boissevain, preface to *Network Analysis*, ed. Boissevain and Mitchell, p. xi.

¹³I have used the Modern Library edition of *Nostromo* (New York: Random House, 1951) which contains an introduction by Robert Penn Warren and the prefatory note written by Conrad for the 1917 edition. Since several editions are in print, all citations give Part and Chapter numbers as well as page numbers.

¹⁴On the notion of "cluster," see Rudo Miemeijer, "Some Applications of the Notion of Density to Network Analysis," in Boissevain and Mitchell, eds., *Network Analysis*, pp. 53-57, and also Boissevain, *Friends of Friends*, pp. 43-45.

¹⁵Boissevain comments on the notion of centrality in *Friends of Friends*, pp. 40-42.

¹⁶See, for example, H. V. E. Thoden van Velzen, "Coalitions and Network Analysis," in Boissevain and Mitchell, eds., *Network Analysis*, pp. 219-50.

¹⁷Conrad, Note to *Nostromo*, pp. 6-7.

¹⁸Kapferer, "Social Network and Conjugal Role in Urban Zambia: Towards a Reformulation of the Bott Hypothesis," in Boissevain and Mitchell, eds., *Network Analysis*, pp. 83-110. See especially pp. 83-85.

¹⁹Kapferer refers specifically to Blau's *Exchange and Power in Social Life* (New York: Wiley, 1964).

²⁰Blau, quoted by Kapferer, p. 99.

XI. *Structuralism*

NEOFANTASTIC LITERATURE—
A STRUCTURALIST ANSWER

Jaime Alazraki

If some of Kafka's parables present, as it has been said "happenings that remain profoundly impenetrable and that are capable of so many interpretations that, in the final analysis, they defy any and all,"[1] one must conclude that an unequivocal interpretation of them is altogether impossible. This conclusion is inevitable and shouldn't surprise us since, as it has been observed, "Kafka was probably the first writer to pronounce the insoluble paradox of human existence by using this paradox as the message of his parables."[2] His message lies, therefore, not in the unlimited number of interpretations which the contents of his narratives invite, but in the principle Kafka uses for the configuration of his stories—a principle of indetermination founded on ambiguity that functions as the structuring norm of narration. Indetermination is but a warning regarding all forms of conceptualization and their implicit limits to our capacity to know, and ambiguity is the answer of literature, and art in general, to that human limitation. The result is a metaphor that escapes univocal interpretation in order to propose its terms as the only message the text is capable of eliciting. This message cannot be expressed but through this metaphor which, as in the case of the mystical that "expresses the inexpressible" for Wittgenstein, "is able to convey the mystery of existence but cannot be translated in the logic and grammar of coherent language."[3] Thus, all translation results in a mutilation or deformation: the coherence of language forcing these metaphors to lie in its procrustean bed.

A more sensible approach to the literature of the neofantastic[4] would then be the reconstruction or deconstruction of the functioning rules of its metaphors. In essence, what is sought is to design a *simulacrum* of the object, but a simulacrum, according to Barthes' definition, "directed, *biased*, since the imitated object shows something that remained invisible, or, if one wishes, unintelligible in the natural object."[5] Structuralism has extended this approach, we propose, for the neofantastic to the study of literature as a whole. Accordingly, it distinguishes between "criticism" and "politics." Criticism applies itself to the meanings of a text and it strives to interpret those meanings: poetics, on the other hand, seeks to reconstruct the structure according to which a text performs.

One can agree or disagree with this distinction. One can accept or reject the validity of the structuralist method as "a science of literature," but one cannot deny, as Robert Scholes has pointed out in one of the most comprehensive accounts of structuralism, "its already impressive achievements."[6] Basically, the structuralist approach is a relativism that aims at replacing old languages in order to speak in a new fashion, but it knows and admits

> that it will suffice that a new language rise out of history, a new language which *speaks* in its turn, for his task to be done: the history of the social sciences would thus be, in a sense, a diachrony of metalanguages, and each science, including of course semiology, would contain the seeds of its own death, in the shape of the language destined to speak it.[7]

What structuralism proposes then is a dialectics whose laws apply as well to its own theory. Even those who refuse to accept it as a closed system, as an onanism that rejects any bond with meaning, admit however that structuralism "is unreplaceable when meaning resists direct examination."[8] Mikel Dufrenne, for one, has explained that

> this is particularly true in the case of myths for which Lévi-Strauss elaborated the analytical instrumentation. These hermetic artifacts, the myths, only yield some of their secret if they can be confronted with each other, analyzed until the equivalent to a code can be discovered. The only road *to penetrate the impenetrable* requires the logic of combinations, and decoding consists in finding this logic. If one is to understand myth, one must first grasp it as a system of structure.[9]

Such would be the case of the metaphors of the neofantastic since they resist translation to a language of logical coherence, and because they represent an answer to the insufficiencies of causal language. Their translation is tantamount to asking irrational numbers to behave like rational numbers, or to attempt to reduce propositions that can by only formulated through non-Euclidean geometry to the terms of Euclidean geometry. What is intolerable at the level of rational numbers is expressed through irrational numbers; an operation impracticable in the first system is resolved in the second. Ernest Cassirer has observed:

> . . .for the great mathematicians of the seventeenth century imaginary numbers were not only instruments of mathematical knowledge but a special class of objects upon which knowledge had stumbled in the course of its development and which contained something that was not only mysterious but virtually impenetrable. . . . And yet, those same numbers that had been regarded originally as something impossible or as a sheer riddle upon which one gazed in astonishment without being able to understand it, developed into one of the most important tools of mathematics. . . . Like in the case of the various geometries which offer different planes of spatial order, imaginary numbers have lost the metaphysical mystery once sought in them since their discovery to become new operational symbols."[10]

If a criticism of translation is inapplicable to neofantastic literature, since such a translation reestablishes a logical order that the text seeks to transcend, the reconstruction and definition of its code is perhaps the only alternative of study and a possible road of access to its meaning. It is via their structure that these seemingly meaningless metaphors yield their meaning. It could be replied that for structuralism meaning is never indispensable since, according to Barthes' definition, "literature is but a language, that is a system of signs; its being does not lie in the message but in the system, and consequently the critic doesn't have to restitute the work's message but only its system."[11] Barthes refers here to meaning as translation, to the messages a text conveys through its natural language, and not through the system of linguistic signs with which literature creates its own code. What is sought, therefore, is not a paraphrase of the first language but the meaning connoted by the second language, or, what amounts to the same, by the system of signs coined by literature with language.

In his reflections on Vladimir Propps' book, *Morphology of the Folktale*, Lévi-Strauss distinguishes between the contents of language and the contents of form, between the signified in the linguistic signifiers and the signified conveyed by literature through its own signifiers.[12] There is a literal contents produced by the first system (languages), and there is a contents generated by the second system (literature). The meanings of the first belong to denotation; the meanings of the second, to connotation. In a myth, or in a litarary text, there coexist

> two systems of significations which are imbricated but are out of joint with each other; the first system (language) becomes the plane of expression of the second system (myth, literature); the first system is the plane of *denotation*, and the second system (wider than the first), the plane of *connotation*.[13]

The horizontal and vertical readings of the Oedipus myth done by Lévi-Strauss correspond respectively to the plane of denotation, the first, and to the plane of connotation, the second. The first is a literal reading of the myth; the second, a structural reading through which a system of relations is disclosed from which the myth's meaning surfaces. Towards the end of his essay "The Sorcerer and His Magic," Lévi-Strauss confronts us with the difficult problem of the intellectual condition of man:

> Only the history of symbolic function can allow us to understand the intellectual condition of man, in which the universe is never charged with sufficient meaning and in which the mind has always more meanings available than there are objects to which to relate them. Torn between these two systems of reference—the signifying and the signified—man asks magical thinking to provide him with a new system of reference, within which thus far contradictory elements can be integrated.[14]

In a similar way, the metaphors proposed by the neofantastic narrative seek to reconcile irreconcilable systems: to convey with a language that has conceptualized the world messages that escape concept. There are no objects that could correspond to the meanings conveyed by the language of those narratives (as there are no people who become insects or vomit rabbits);

natural languages lack the signs for translating the meanings of those signifiers. What neofantastic fiction proposes are those metaphors in which the terms of two contradictory systems have been integrated—its meaning rests in the structure of the discourse that has integrated them.

One example will illustrate to what degree interpretation, or rather over-interpretation, of these metaphors has lead to futile, and sometimes preposterous, results. The example is Cortázar's "House Taken Over." It has been translated as "an allegory of Peronism": the brother and the sister symbolize the parasite upper class, and the noises are the irruption of the working class into the course of history. Others have decided that the story "reveals the isolation of Latin American after World War II" or, perhaps, "the national solitude of Argentina during those same years." For some, this is the story of "an incestuous couple": decadent oligarchy killing time in a house that exceeds their needs. Furthermore, the story has been read as "a portrayal of conventual life: brother and sister are devout priests living under an imposed celibacy and they are suddenly expelled from their temple." It has also been suggested that the story is a recreation of the Minotaur myth: Isabel, unhappy Ariadne, holds the yarn, not in order to escape the house-labyrinth, but as a last effort to retain her lost paradise. Finally, "House Taken Over" has been interpreted as an X-ray of fetal life: the noises stand for labor pains; the explusion, for giving birth; and Isabel's yarn, for the torn umbilical cord.

The value of these interpretations lies, at best, like the Rorchach test, not in what they tell us about the story but in what they tell us about the interpreter. There would be, then, as many interpretations as readers, and although this is inevitably part of the act of reading, it cannot constitute the grounds a text requires to be studied. The structuralist approach offers a method of study which in the case of neofantastic metaphors permits us to deal with the signifier leaving out meaning as "a suspended signified." The criticism of translation has given us analogies of Cortázar's stories, translations of what is in the interpreter's mind but not in the text. In contrast, structuralism speaks more modestly of homologies—that is, of relations configured with natural language to become a second language through which literature emits new messages, signifieds which cannot be expressed through the first language.

The analogies of translation derive from the first language; the homologies that the structural method seeks originate in the second language, the language of literature. Gérard Genette has shown with an example of clasical rhetoric ("sail" as the metonymy for "ship") that a figure, although it must be *translatable*, cannot be *translated* without losing its very nature:

> Rhetoric knows that the word *sail* designates *ship*, but it also knows that it designates it in a different fashion from the word *ship*. The meaning is the same, but the process of signification, that is, the relationship between the sign and its meaning is different, and poetry depends on signification, not on meaning.[15]

In this example we know exactly to what "sail" alludes, and yet we cannot translate it without losing the figure and with it *its modality of outlook and of intention*. In the literature of the neofantastic we don't know what its metaphors name, and yet a story like "House Taken Over" has been paraphrased and glossed over with a freedom that cancels the text, effaces it to write a new one unrelated to the first. The creative imagination of the writer has been replaced by the reductionist endeavor of the interpreter. What we propose is a return to the text—which, it must be remembered, means *texture, textile, structure*—a return to a reading of the text which will prevent its loss and will permit its preservation by establishing the principles through which it is founded and upon which it rises as a signifying force.

HARVARD UNIVERSITY

Notes

[1]Heinz Politzer, *Franz Kafka; Parable and Paradox* (Cornell University Press, 1966), pp. 17, 22.

[2]*Ibid.*, p. 22.

[3]*Ibid.*, p. 15.

[4]The term *neofantastic* is used here to distinguish the fiction of writers such as Kafka, Blanchot, Borges, or Cortázar, with a clear fantastic imprint, from the fantastic genre as known and practiced by nineteenth-century writers. I have elaborated on the differences between the two genres in my article "The Fantastic As Surrealist Metaphor in Cortázar's Short Fiction," *Dada/Surrealism*, 5 (1975), pp. 28-33.

[5]Roland Barthes, *Critical Essays* (Evanston: Northwestern University Press, 1972), pp. 214-15.

[6]See Robert Scholes, *Structuralism in Literature; An Introduction* (New Haven: Yale University Press, 1974), p. IX.

[7]Roland Barthes, *op cit.*, p. 219.

[8]R. Barthes, M. Dufrenne, G. Genette, et al, *Estructuralismo y literatura* (Buenos Aires: Nueva Visión, 1972), p. 213.

[9]*Ibid.*, Mikel Dufrenne, "Estructura y sentido. La crítica literaria," pp. 207-23.

[10]Ernest Cassirer, *The Problem of Knowledge: Philosophy, Science, and History Since Hegel* (Yale University Press, 1974), pp. 71-73.

[11]Roland Barthes, *op cit.*, pp. 259-60.

[12]Claude Lévi-Strauss y Vladimir Propp, *Polémica* (Madrid: Fundamentos, 1972), pp. 30-31.

[13]Roland Barthes, *Elements of Semiology* (Boston: Beacon Press, 1967), p. 89.

[14]Claude Lévi-Strauss, *Structural Anthropology*. (New York: Doubleday, 1967, p. 178.

[15]Gérard Genette, *Figuras; retórica y estructuralismo*. (Cordoba, Argentina: Nagelkop, 1970), pp. 171-72.

ESTRUCTURA Y SIGNIFICACION
DE *ANNABELLA*
DE ANTONIO DI BENEDETTO

Malva E. Filer

Bien pudiera afirmarse que toda obra literaria es, en definitiva, lenguaje y que trama, escenario y personajes no existen como tales sino en cuanto palabras que han ido llenando el espacio literario. Esta afirmación, válida en principio para toda ficción de cualquier época adquiere, sin embargo, particular vigencia en la nuestra, ya que en la novela de las dos últimas décadas se ha intensificado la tendencia a que el lenguaje sea origen, medio y razón de ser del mundo que se presenta. Alain Robbe-Grillet, particularmente desde *Dans le Labyrinthe*, y Severy Sarduy, con *De dónde son los cantantes* y *Cobra*, por ejemplo, producen novelas en las que el relato no es un vehículo o instrumento que intente describir un mundo fuera del texto. La palabra juega allí con un universo que ella hace y deshace, compone y descompone como si fuera un *puzzle*. La escritura es la materia prima de esa realidad y en ella, en las obras de Sarduy, las palabras diseñan, estallan a veces en luz y color o movimientos.

Annabella (*Novela en forma de cuentos*),[1] de Antonio Di Benedetto, fue publicada en 1955 con el título de *El pentágono*.[2] A pesar de ser anterior a la difusión del "nouveau roman"[3] y, más aun, a las novelas creadas en la atmósfera estructuralista de los años 60, creo que *Annabella* pertenece al tipo de ficción que acabo de caracterizar. Aunque no representa el nivel más alto de producción del autor de *Zama*,[4] esta obra atrae la atención del crítico por las siguientes razones: se trata de un texto en el que la estructura funciona como un signo y esta estructura es creada por un lenguaje no denotativo, cuya intransitividad—opuesta al caracter transitivo del discurso referencial—pone en evidencia la literalidad del enunciado.[5]

En sus conversaciones con Günter Lorenz (*Diálogo con América Latina*), Di Benedetto ha declarado: "Escribo porque me gobierna una voluntad intensa de construcción por medio de la palabra. . . . Todo en mi literatura es ficción, podría decir algo así como realidades deseadas, quizás

como metáforas de la realidad."[6] *Annabella* podría describirse, efectivamente, como una construcción de signos, gráficos y lingüísticos, mediante los
cuales el texto dibuja una figura metafórica. Personajes y relaciones sólo
existen en ella como piezas y movimientos de un ajedrez de palabras, un
juego cuyo objetivo es extenuar, en la escritura, todas las posibilidades
concebibles del triángulo amoroso. Este triángulo se desdobla, a su vez, pero
conserva el vértice común de Santiago,[7] la voz narradora, quien es por
definición el amante traicionado. Los dos triángulos son transformados en
un pentágono, al establecer Santiago un puente entre sus rivales que sirve,
según él, para mediatizar su propia relación con ellos. Al mismo tiempo, la
estructura tripartita se reproduce en el esquema general del libro, que
presenta el juego de los triángulos desde tres puntos de vista: (1) la época
especulativa, (2) la época crítica y (3) la época de la realidad.

El desarrollo de la novela es representado gráficamente por el narrador
mediante una serie de diagramas que presento aquí, ligeramente modifi-
cados:

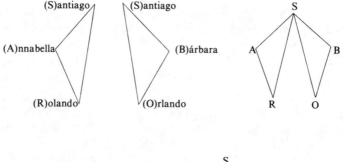

Para completar dicha representación sugiero la inscripción del pentágono
dentro del triángulo configurado por la estructura de la obra:

Sin rechazar la explicación dada por el narrador al diseño de su pentágono, podría también pensarse en el posible simbolismo de esta figura geométrica. El quinario, representado por el pentágono, la estrella de cinco puntas o el cuadrado con su punto central, tiene variadas significaciones según las distintas culturas. Tradicionalmente, el número cinco—según Cirlot[8]—simboliza al hombre después de la Caída, pero aplicado al orden de las cosas terrenas, significa salud y amor. Muchos amuletos y talismanes se basan en el número cinco, debido a las ya mencionadas connotaciones y, además, por estar el número asociado con la imagen de la figura humana. Sería arriesgado atribuir intenciones simbólicas a Di Benedetto, pero la elección de un grafismo, el pentágono, para representar el mundo de su novela, podría dar lugar a este tipo de interpretación.[9] Y, en verdad, Santiago es presentado, desde la Introducción, como el hombre después de la Caída, si no genéricamente, al menos como individuo.

"La época especulativa" ocupa el mayor número de páginas. En sus ocho secciones se encuentra el siguiente desarrollo: (1) creación del triángulo Santiago-Annabella-Rolando Fortuna, a partir del primero; (2) presentación sucesiva de las posibilidades de relación y eliminación de los vértices; (3) destrucción de la figura y regreso al punto inicial, por desaparición de Annabella y Rolando. Cabe señalar que las muertes se producen y se niegan sin la más mínima preocupación por la lógica, la verosimilitud o la sucesión temporal. Todas las posibilidades, aunque contradictorias, ocurren independientemente, como el la novela laberinto de Ts'ui Pên en "El jardín de senderos que se bifurcan".

Annabella es la mujer ideal, apenas vislumbrada en el entresueño de un hombre indiferenciado, que se siente desaparecer física y espiritualmente. Enlazando su cintura, Santiago realiza el despegue inicial en el vuelo que lo llevará a otro plano, el de un mundo que se agota en el texto, en el juego de la escritura que va proponiendo las distintas soluciones al dilema del narrador. Como afirmándose en esta empresa de creación por la palabra, el texto continúa hablándonos de la vida de Santiago y Annabella en el contrabajo, instrumento-casa de valor metafórico. La deserción de ella y su vínculo con Rolando completan el primer triángulo. Habiéndose formado esta figura clave de la novela, comienza el juego de posibilidades en que, alternativamente, desaparece uno de sus vértices. Primero muere Annabella, en "La suicida asesinada", título desde el que se introduce la ambigüedad que caracteriza el relato. Annabella muere de enfermedad, se suicida, es asesinada por su marido, es asesinada por el otro. El texto permite todas estas lecturas.

La sección siguiente funciona como un *intermezzo*, en el que el narrador, más humanizado, desahoga sus sentimientos de humillación diciéndonos que es "un poco más" que un conejito[10] pero, y en esta frase desiderativa expresa toda su frustración, "si fuera un poco más. . .". El juego de palabras y la ironía sirven para aligerar el tono auto-compasivo. Por ejemplo: "La señora, joven señora pintona, agradece al señor sedente que sea señor cedente" (pág. 55); o la expresión inventada "órbita necropolitana" (pág.

57). "El desesperado manso" nos habla de un Rolando a quien han matado y de Annabella, viva e infiel a Santiago. Inmediatamente se invierten los papeles en "El desalojado manso".[11] Ahora, Santiago y Rolando son, ambos, inmortales, lo cual produce, paradójicamente, un conflicto insoluble, ya que si Santiago no debe temer a la muerte, tampoco puede matar a su rival.

Habiéndose agotado las posibilidades de infidelidad realizada queda, por cierto, la infidelidad espiritual que, irónicamente, se materializa en las palabras "Te soy fiel" anotadas por Annabella al lado del nombre impreso de Rolando en la página de una novela recién abierta. Rolando, ¿hace falta decirlo?, está muerto ahora.[12] El último movimiento dentro del triángulo muestra la siguiente secuencia: (1) Santiago cree que Annabella ama a Rolando y éste no la ama aún. El futuro se ofrece indefinido. (2) Annabella y Rolando se han casado hace tres años y él está muriendo. Santiago es una araña que espía, a la espera de la muerte de su rival. Pero Rolando mata a Annabella antes de morir él mismo. Con ello desaparece el triángulo y queda sólo Santiago, origen y causa de esta figuración.

A través del texto analizado, las palabras se mueven libremente, dibujando y borrando triángulos, como si fuera cine de animación a través de sistemas luminosos. Pero esta técnica, de función aparentemente lúcida, produce aquí un efecto contrario, porque las transformaciones constantes del diseño parecen corporizar la angustia experimentada frente a lo inasible. Las experiencias tantálicas de Santiago en persecución de la elusiva Annabella encuentran expresión gráfica en este juego de vértices mediante el cual el texto se niega a sí mismo.

Me he detenido en el análisis de la primera parte del libro por ser ella más extensa y compleja que el resto de la novela. En marcado contraste con la "época especulativa", la "época crítica" se inicia con el deslinde de la realidad y el sueño. "Esta vez, por fortuna, no puedo dudar", dice la voz narradora. "Fue en sueños" (pág. 93). Annabella era "algo estatuario, aunque cálido y viviente. Yo desfallecía porque era algo remoto" (ibid.). La angustia se vierte en un canto que es un gemido en medio del sueño. Pero hay una realidad y una esposa, Bárbara, a las cuales volver. La afirmación rotunda de que Annabella es sólo un sueño está destinada a cancelar su eficacia como objeto de pasión. Pero para liberarse de la angustia, Santiago debe intentar la desmitificación de Annabella; transforma así a la amada inasible en "Anna cachorrera", decididamente inmersa en la prosa de la vida por una maternidad excesiva y animal. La imagen de Annabella, no muerta y pura como siempre la había soñado, sino viva y mancillada por la vida, es el último alto en el camino de regreso a la realidad.

La época de la realidad trae su propia serie de triángulos con los vértices Santiago-Bárbara-Orlando Sabino. Santiago no puede sobrevivir en una realidad donde, paradójicamente, tiene menos existencia que en la fantasía. "Mi marido es un loco que se cree mi marido", piensa—según él—su esposa. La adaptación de la frase de Cocteau que hace Santiago indica la ambigüedad de la relación entre realidad y locura, al mismo tiempo que establece su propia insuficiencia. Y la realidad aniquila la salida escapista a través de la cual él había procesado su relación con Annabella. Sólo le queda la abulia o la animalidad. Como no actuar y no reaccionar son sinónimos de no-existencia, a ella es condenado Santiago, luego de un juicio kafkiano que ocurre, como el resto de la novela, en el espacio mental constituido por la conciencia del protagonista.

¿Cuál es el crimen de Santiago? Bárbara ha matado a la esposa de su amante, para preservar el honor de éste. Pero Santiago ha cometido el delito de no vengarse de la traición de su mujer. Contra él se descarga la burla y el poder destructor de la humanidad. En esta parte del libro se intensifica la atmósfera de pesadilla, sin que sea atenuada por el humor o la ironía, como en las secciones precedentes. Así Santiago es "obligado a entrar en un cubo lleno de barro donde tenía que chapalear constantemente mientras durase el careo" (pág. 139) con Orlando. Como testigo aparece Rolando Fortuna, uno de sus demonios de la época especulativa. Pero no Annabella, porque, según las palabras del "Juez extraordinario", ella "no es. Annabella es aquello a lo cual se tiende" (pág. 143). Santiago es condenado a un viaje en auto, para el cual se le provee de un fantasmagórico Ford 29 de capota. Y en un alto del camino es eliminado por Bárbara, Orlando y Rolando, tres de los cinco vértices del pentágono.[13] Santiago va hacia el mundo de Annabella. Los dos vértices se confundirán y desaparecerán como una burbuja de aire.

¿Cómo explicar la estructura compleja y laboriosamente construida de *Annabella*? Ella no le era necesaria a Di Benedetto para describir un drama pasional, o para trasmitir la angustia existencial de su protagonista. Es evidente que el autor no se propone interesarnos con las peripecias que sufren los personajes, si así puede llamárseles, sino con la obsesión caleido-scópica a la que incesantemente se libra Santiago. Lo significativo no es lo que se narra, sino la narración misma, el dinamismo del lenguaje que va creando la realidad obsesiva y despiadada del texto. El dibujar y borrar de palabras que es la novela produce, sin duda, un efecto torturante, adecuado al motivo de la traición y los celos. Pero en ese juego de autodestrucción que se opera en el texto, sin embargo, reside al mismo tiempo la salvación de su narrador. En la Introducción a la obra, estaba ya sugerido el tema de la recuperación por la palabra escrita. El protagonista, leemos, "sacaba de su interior las desalentadas imaginaciones y las ponía por escrito, construía cuentos" (pág. 17). En este juego de la escritura es donde el narrador, bus-cándose a sí mismo, va creando su mundo. *Annabella* (obra) es la búsqueda de Annabella; y es, también, su negación. Por esta multiplicidad de respuestas que se cancelan, el personaje vencido triunfa sobre la inexistencia y encuentra reparación para su derrota. Se trata de una recuperación que es la metáfora de la vida.

BROOKLYN COLLEGE
OF THE CITY UNIVERSITY OF NEW YORK

Notas

[1]Buenos Aires: Ediciones Orión, 1974. Repárese en que el subtítulo indica una preocupación del autor por la relación formalista entre ambos géneros.

[2]Buenos Aires: Ediciones "Doble P", 1955.

[3]A ese respecto deben leerse las consideraciones que hace Di Benedetto sobre la posible simultaneidad en la experimentación con la técnica literaria por parte de escritores que producen en distintos idiomas y no se conocen en el momento de realizarla. Ver Günter W. Lorenz, *Diálogo con América Latina* (Chile: Ediciones Universitarias de Valparaíso/Pomaire, 1972).

[4]*Zama* (Barcelona: Planeta, 3a. ed., 1972); publicada por primera vez en 1956, es la obra fundamental de Di Benedetto. Ha sido traducida al alemán, francés e italiano.

[5]Ver, al respecto, la clasificación de los registros del habla hecha por Tzvetan Todorov en "El análisis del discurso literario", ¿*Qué es el estructuralismo?* (Buenos Aires: Ed. Losada, 1971).

[6]Lorenz, págs. 125-26. Roland Barthes, en *Essais critiques*, (Paris: Editions du Seuil, 1964), pág. 149, dice al respecto lo siguiente: "La parole n'est ni un instrument, ni un véhicule: c'est une structure, on s'en doute de plus en plus; mais l'écrivain est le seul, par définition, à perdre sa propre structure et celle du monde dans la structure de la parole. Or cette parole est une matière (infiniment) travaillée; elle est un peu comme une sur-parole, le réel ne lui est jamais qu'un prétexte (pour l'écrivain, *écrire* est un verbe intransitif).

[7]Llama la atención que en el sistema nominal escogido por Di Benedetto para su novela, los dos personajes femeninos (Annabella y Bárbara) llevan nombres sajones; que Orlando y Rolando sean las variantes romance y germánica de una misma raíz, y equivalentes en territorios lingüísticos distintos; que Santiago y Rolando-Orlando sean dos figuras contrapuestas de tan especial significación como lo fueron en el mundo medieval; que Santiago (Sanct-Yago) sea, en última instancia, el nombre del Yago shakespeareano; que Annabella traiga a la memoria al poeta Poe de tan infortunado destino; y finalmente también llaman la atención los apellidos Sabino (alusivo a una raza de hombres "traicionados" por sus mujeres) y Fortuna, con lo que el vocablo alude por sí mismo y por la asociación que establece con Juan de Mena y los geometrismos de su *Laberinto de Fortuna*. Asimismo, nótese que las figuras femeninas y Santiago no llevan apellido y sí, el grupo Rolando-Orlando.

[8]J. E. Cirlot, *A Dictionary of Symbols* (New York: Philosophical Library, 1962).

[9]*Annabelle* se presta a un análisis de símbolos y podría, tal vez, enfocarse desde un punto de vista arquetípico. El análisis estructural, elegido aquí, no excluye la posibilidad de distintas lecturas del texto. En ese sentido, pienso en la validez de lo afirmado por Tzvetan Todorov en *Literatura y significación* (Barcelona: Planeta, 1974), pág. 13: "Reconstituir el sistema de un texto individual no quiere decir aislarlo de todos los demás textos o buscar su originalidad irreductible. La unidad del texto es funcional, no 'etimológica'; las alusiones a otros textos, las aportaciones de todas clases forman parte integrante de él. Por el contrario, debemos negarnos a todo esfuerzo por reemplazar el texto presente por otro texto, que pretende ser más auténtico, cualquiera que sea el sistema de traducción (psicoanálisis, marxismo, ésta o aquella concepción filosófica) utilizado para pasar del uno al otro. El texto es múltiple, nunca es otro texto."

[10]La elección del conejito es aquí particularmente efectiva, porque la referencia a este animalito indefenso, objeto frecuente de experimentación y abuso, señala en el texto un paralelismo con la condición del protagonista.

[11]En esta complacencia por los juegos de palabras quizás haya una filiación

quevedesca o ramoniana, cuando no proveniente de algunos usos propios de la literatura francesa posterior a la Primera Guerra Mundial.

[12]Dentro del juego de posibilidades que es *Annabella*, el texto incluye no sólo aquéllas que en él se realizan, sino también, si usamos un lenguaje aristotélico, las que estén en potencia.

[13]Esta solución recuerda vivamente el estilo de escritura cinematográfica de la "Nouvelle Vague", particularmente Goddard, en años concordantes con la elaboración de *El pentágono* (1955). La coincidencia es significativa en tanto que en aquellos años la actividad de Di Benedetto era la de crítico cinematográfico.

A DESCRIPTIVE APPROACH TO
CLAUDE SIMON'S NOVEL
LEÇON DE CHOSES

Salvador Jiménez-Fajardo

In my analysis of *Leçon de choses*, Simon's latest novel, I take as a point of departure some remarks made by the author—at the now famous "Colloques" of Cerisy[1]—relative to his methods of composition. In his talk, significantly entitled "La fiction mot à mot," Simon refers to his then recent novel *Les Corps conducteurs* and to the function therein of words as "carrefours qui s'ouvrent au fur et à mesure que l'on écrit."[2] He rejects the notion that the traditional "logique du récit"—found wanting by critics in his own novel—based on fortuitous circumstance linked in a contingent chronology is either logical or continuous. The order he seeks is at another level:

> Est-ce qu'il n'est donc pas permis de se demander non seulement si, de même qu'indépendamment des choses representées (nature morte, paysage, nu) il existe une logique de la peinture en soi, il n'existerait pas aussi une certaine logique interne du texte, propre au texte, découlant à la fois de sa musique (rythme, assonances, cadence de la phrase) et de son matériau (vocabulaire, "figures", tropes—car notre langage ne s'est pas formé au hasard), mais encore si cette logique selon laquelle doivent s'articuler ou se combiner les éléments d'une fiction n'est pas, en même temps, fécondante et, par elle-même, engendrante de fiction.[3]

The key phrases here are "logique interne du texte" and "logique engendrante de fiction." Taking our cue from Simon, then, we may surmise that a proper reading of his work—and this obtains most remarkably for everything he has written since *La Bataille de Pharsale*, that is to say, *Les Corps conducteurs*, *Triptyque* and *Leçon de choses*—will require attention to the internal articulations of the prose. Among these we shall find the most suggestive to be repetition, synonymy, homophony, and broadly speaking, analogies of all kinds, including analogies of gesture and of situation; also special notice should be taken of the metaphorical potential of individual words for metaphor means "invention" since Simon finds in

metaphors the shape of the world: ". . .ce vaste ensemble de *figures* méta-
phoriques dans et par quoi se dit le monde."[4] This inner logic of prose is the
source of the two main activities of Simon's narrative: the invention of its
elements and their organization in a coherent structure. Even those concerns
which might at first sight appear constraints on the creative impetus find
their place also at this source: "Et le plus fascinant. . .c'est que ces nécessités
purement formelles. . .se révèlent être éminemment *productrices* et, en
elles-mêmes, *engendrantes*."[5]

Increasingly, these generative properties of prose have become the
central momentum of Simon's fiction. As we noted, such properties reveal
themselves in the field of resemblance (of sounds and words, of similes and
metaphors), and it is striking how Simon's reconstructive vision of the world
resembles that of the sixteenth century as it is recalled for us by Michel
Foucault early in the chapter "The Prose of the World" from *The Order
of Things:*

> Up to the end of the sixteenth century, resemblance played a constructive role
> in the knowledge of Western culture. It was resemblance that largely guided
> exegesis and the interpretation of texts; it was resemblance that organized
> the play of symbols, made possible knowledge of things visible and invisible,
> and controlled the art of representing them. The universe was folded upon
> itself: the earth echoing the sky, faces seeing themselves reflected in the stars,
> and plants holding within their stems the secrets that were of use to man.
> Painting imitated space. And representation—whether in the service of
> pleasure or of knowledge—was posited as a form of repetition.[6]

In this sense such fiction recaptures for us an all-encompassing cosmic vision
to which we have been blind since the Renaissance. Ideally, the reordering
activity of Simon's text should be echoed by a similarly generative interpretation on the reader's part with analysis as the first moment of construction.
One might wish our undertaking to be parallel to the author's in following the
rising structure from its foundation of single images, single words. However,
certain conjectures as to general lines of composition are necessary before an
adequate understanding of its details can be attempted. Here again we can
only hope that our intuition of form reflects in some small measure the
author's own esthetic aims.

Leçon de choses is divided into seven parts as follows: "Générique,"
"Expansion," "Divertissement I," "Leçon de choses," "Divertissement II,"
"La Charge de Reichshoffen," "Courts-Circuits." "Générique" and "Courts-
Circuits" are two and six pages long respectively, the latter constituting an
expanded echo of the former with partial verbatim repetitions. "Divertissement I and II" are monologs by the same character, long invectives in "argot"
that offer a narrow, frantic viewpoint on the narrative's war scenes.[7] The
novel *Leçon de choses* holds within itself in a counterpoint the elementary
textbook *Leçons de choses*,[8] and the exhaustive concerns customary to this
latter type of book, a window on the world of things, are not only echoed
but themselves contained in the fiction's own all-inclusive compass.[9]

Two central themes underpin the narration: the Janus-faced dyad of death and eroticism (or, in broader terms, creation/destruction) and the concept of composition itself, integrated in the fiction as an actively sought source of material. Three intertwined narrative sequences express, or rather establish, these themes: (1) Some women, a little girl and a man are strolling in the countryside. The man importunes the girl's mother for a rendezvous later in the day to which she agrees. The group stops on a cliff while the little girl has her "goûter." Later they watch fishermen bringing in their catch. At night the man and woman make love in a field. The man, heedless of the woman's warning, ejaculates within her. Having attempted to clean herself of his semen, the woman tries to embrace the man who asks her not to stain him. The woman outraged, runs away. (2) Four retreating cavalrymen are waiting inside a half-ruined farm. One of them, lying on a table by a window next to an automatic rifle, is watching the countryside. The other two are in charge of the ammunition. The sequence now bifurcates into two strands. The fourth soldier is lying on a cot, either dying or drunk, depending on the metaphorical pressure of the context. An officer enters and berates the soldiers for having shot out of turn or for keeping the lights on. The mattress from the cot is used to block a window. Night falls. (3) Two masons are remodeling this very building many years later. The older one is recalling some of the events from the war scenes, in which he participated, to his younger companion. They stop for lunch, move their staging, change, and leave at dusk. These sequences occur at different periods of time. The excursionists wear outmoded clothes, the military action takes place during the Second World War and the rebuilding of the house occurs in more recent times.

Each series expresses both terms of the duality construction/destruction as follows: (1) From the group of picknickers the child's mother and the man will eventually engage in clandestine lovemaking (conception); fearful of becoming pregnant the woman will try to rid herself of the man's ejaculation with a handkerchief (conception negated); as she seeks reassurance and affection from her lover, trying to embrace him, her soiled handkerchief in her hand, he cautions her not to stain him; furious and humiliated, she flees (final destruction of all positive elements in the episode). (2) The soldiers are plunged in the most blatantly destructive of situations, war, the house falling in ruins around them. One of them is idly reading the volume *Leçons de choses*, a schoolbook (instruction or elaboration of knowledge) describing, among other things, how to build a house, from forest and quarry to construction site. (3) The workers are remodeling a house, a process requiring the destruction of some parts and the building of others. Of comparable importance to this conjunction of contraries is the self-conscious character of the fiction's composition. There are numerous instances of interior duplication, elaborations of the concept of framing, of descriptive modes, and so on. Such attention restricts the import of events to expand that of their source, language. All this suggests to us that the very autotelic character of the literary text has become a basic support of its structure.

The concept of self-generating narration is underlined from the outset in the very title and organization of the novel's opening sequence, "Géné-rique."[10] In effect, it offers an introduction to, and an overview of, the central elements in the narrative (in embryonic form) as well as a trial run, so to speak, of its general movement and of its direction. It represents the initial penetration into both the linguistic and spatial source of the action. This source is a room in a tumbledown house. The room's description proceeds in three movements of increasing specificity. First is a panoramic presen-tation of the walls, floor, and source of light in the room. This description begins immediately in the metaphoric mode: "Les langues pendantes du papier décollé laissent apparaître le plâtre humide et gris qui s'effrite."[11] The paper covers, unsuccessfully, a disintegrating wall, an image that illustrates from the outset the idea of imperfectly contained dispersion (ultimately, the containment is undertaken by the esthetic cohesiveness of the entire work). A necessity to specify seems to threaten the description's advance as it offers, in parentheses, alternate renditions of objects, opening the text to further metaphorical development: "Immédiatement au-dessus de la plinthe court un galon (ou bandeau?) dans des tons ocre-vert et rougeâtres (ver-millon passé) ou se répète le même motif (frise?) de feuilles d'acanthe dessi-nant une succession de vagues involvées" (p. 9). The impetus toward speci-ficity discovers further items in need of completion, broken, corroded by time and use, or too numerous to mention (in this latter case it is the series that calls for completion). Finally, such all-inclusiveness must make room for the source of light and, by implication, the source of the description: "Du plafond pend une ampoule de faible puissance (on peut sans être aveuglé en fixer le filament) vissée sur une douille de cuivre terni" (p. 10). Attention to detail has lead the description from its object to its double origin: the light-bulb and the *on* who may look at it.

The second paragraph selects from this setting a number of items and emphasizes further the initial mode of description, pursuing thus the move-ment towards specificity. The items selected are pieces of plaster fallen off the wall. The descriptive form is a metaphor organizing these fragments as rocks and boulders broken off a cliff into the sea. The potential for this metaphor was present in the "vagues involvées" of the paper, and the paragraph actually begins with an elaboration of this image: "Au-dessous du minuscule et immobile déferlement de vagues végétales. . ." (p. 10). The sea is here an origin of metaphors and therefore of descriptive movement; consequently, the image introduces also the concept of arrested movement or of movement versus immobility ("immobile déferlement"), later to become an important element in the overall composition. Likewise, as it makes more evident the "human" or interpretive point of view (the presence of the observer is proportional to the metaphorical intensity of the description), the metaphor has acquired an impetus of its own and almost takes the text out of its spatial confines: "Sur leur face lisse adhère quelquefois encore un lambeau de feuillage jauni, une fleur" (p. 10). The sentence, though it remains itself objective, could almost refer to the debris from an actual cliff.

In the third paragraph the desire for total inclusion turns the origin and the form of the description into the matter described: "La description (la composition) peut se continuer (ou être complétée) à peu près indéfiniment selon la minutie apportée a son exécution, l'entraînement des métaphores proposées, l'addition d'autres objets. . ." (p. 10). This stress on organizing principles is based also on the contrast between completion (or containment) and dispersion. The "frame" is defined not only in terms of what it holds but also in terms of what it excludes. Among the latter items are suggested, as unrealized choices, the possible existence of another source of light outside the room, the presence of someone standing at the door (source of shadow or darkness) as well as sounds and odors prevailing in the room. All these elements are introduced by "Ainsi il n'a pas été dit. . ." (p. 11), that is to say, the description opens onto further possible areas of activity while negating their role in the present one. Furthermore, by hinting at what there is outside the room, the exit attempted by the last sentence of the preceding paragraph (quoted above) comes nearer realization.

An examination of the parentheses in "Générique" further confirms the double tendency towards containment and dispersion, while clarifying their status as funnel-like openings within the text that increases the latter's fiction-producing potential:

Paragraph No. 1

galon	(ou bandeau?)
rougeâtres	(vermillon passé)
motif	(frise)
carrelage hexagonal brisé en plusieurs endroits	(en d'autres comme corrodé)
divers objets ou fragments d'objets	(morceaux de bois, de briques, de vitres cassées, etc. . .)
une ampoule de faible puissance	(on peut sans être aveuglé en fixer le filament)

(pp. 9-10)

The direction of this group of interpolations is clearly towards inclusive specification. When the description is in danger of proliferating (as in the enumeration of objects in the penultimate instance), it is cut short by "etc." In this case previous offers of alternatives such as "un galon (ou bandeau?)" have become a decision to summarize—that is, a matter of artistic selection that brings closer to the surface the selecting mind, whose presence is more apparent yet in the very last item: "on peut. . ."

Paragraph No. 2

tables rocheuses soulevées en plans inclinés par la bosse	(équivalent en relief du creux— ou d'une partie du creux— laissé dans le revêtement du mur)

(p. 10)

Here the selecting activity expresses itself in the parenthesis by transforming a visual image into an abstraction; the shape of the pieces of plaster is *explained* (rather than merely described) in terms of its origin. Mere description gives proliferation, selectivity gives inclusion, design.

Paragraph No. 3

la description	(la composition)
. . .peut se continuer	(ou être complétée)
. . .d'autres objets visibles dans leur entier ou fragmentés par l'usure, le temps, un choc	(soit encore qu'ils n'apparaissent qu'en partie dans le cadre du tableau)
. . .il n'a pas été dit si. . .une seconde ampoule plus forte n'éclaire pas la scène	(peut-être par une porte ouverte sur un corridor ou une autre pièce)
. . .ombres portées très opaques	(presque noires)
. . .objets visibles	(décrits)
Il n'a pas non plus été fait mention des bruits ou du silence, ni des odeurs	(poudre, sang, rat crevé, ou simplement cette senteur subtile, moribonde et rance de la poussière)

(pp. 10-11)

All the parentheses in this series involve matters of artistic choice, composition, and containment. The description is referred to as "tableau" and manifestly seeing becomes the equivalent of ordering, assigning compositional values to the material, so that description is, in fact, invention. Again the human presence, is at the end of the first paragraph, makes itself felt with particular evidence in conjunction with a light source. In this case, the explanation of shadows on the walls and floor, including "celle, échassière et distendue, d'un personnage," is surmised as a lightbulb outside the room. It is interesting to note that lighting (or point of view) is at once a source of clarity and of shadow; man's shadow already stretches out over the room.

In sum, the desire for specificity leads to the fabulating activity itself and its origin. The containing power of the frame is used in its excluding capacity, as its contents are presented together with the selective decision that gave them body, by *mentioning* what has not been chosen. Thus, the arrangement also agglomerates around itself elements initially external to it. These elements are intimately linked to the human component in the scene, especially near the end where the more subjective sensations (hearing, smell) are mentioned. At the same time the description is seen once more straining at the enclosing walls of the room and searching a way out; the opening will be found later within the narrative, but always the room will remain the locus in terms of which everything else takes place. It is the fiction's topological core.[12]

The composition of "Générique" in three levels towards increasingly formal self-consciousness, to the point where mechanisms of framing, enumeration, and containment become the subject of its very development, clearly buttresses our second conjecture: autotelism is a source of the fiction and a central element in its pattern. Our first conjecture, namely, that the antinomial dyad construction/destruction represents likewise a controlling influence in this pattern also finds support at this early stage through the variations in "focusing" which characterize the description. This process becomes more evident at the crucial moments of the prose, the transitions from one level of narration to another (later it will be from one sequence to another), and its operation involves the passage between these levels. In "Générique" the first transition occurs following the sentence (quoted above) dealing with the lightbulb. From the abandoned profusion of objects on the floor, the describing consciousness (eyes only as yet) moves upward to the ceiling. There its attention focuses upon one detail, unintegrated in the preceding pattern: bulb and casing. The sentence (following upon "etc.") and the detail are free from integrating connections to the previous frame of description and may be seen as both its closure and a transition. In effect, the text resumes in the next paragraph as at the very beginning, with the papered wall, in a new "focusing," a slightly different framing. The second transition occurs as well through a "bridge" sentence (quoted above) that closes the preceding development: it refers equally to the room's debris and to a true cliff over the sea. Also, the sentence focuses on a detail of a magnitude unlike those common in the paragraph, thereby disengaging itself from its structure.

The temporary closure of "Générique"—and of the generated fiction itself—is accomplished by its counterpart, "Courts-Circuits," the last section of the work. "Courts-Circuits" reintroduces "Générique," substantially repeating it as well as some material from the body of the fiction in summarized form. That is to say, in "Court-Circuits" is found also the seed of the entire narration so that the impetus of this ending points backwards towards the origin. At the level of incident, two of the three sequences, that of the excursionists and that of the masons, cross one another in the house (the locale also of the war scene): a worker's hand is seen retrieving some belongings, immediately after the "promeneurs" arrive to examine the work in progress. This creates the temporal and spatial short-circuit in the section's title. The site of the narrative, the room, folds in upon itself to effect an endless circulating of text, a design that is suggested by the last sentences:

> Profitant de leurs allées et venues et des éclats de leurs voix, l'homme se penche vers la troisième et dit rapidement alors c'est promis ce soir ici? . . . Pour y voir plus clair l'une des femmes tourne le commutateur qu'elle referme précipitamment lorsqu'elle lit sur le panneau de la porte l'avertissement tracé par le contre-maître à l'aide d'un fragment de plâtre, mettant en garde contre les risques de court-circuit (p. 182).

The rendezvous is linked to some instances in which the erotic scene is situated within the room (as opposed to the greater part of this development occurring outside in a field). The feared short-circuit has already taken place, metaphorically; although the growing darkness allows for a possible conclusion (the light was on in "Générique"), it is only a temporary one since the light may be turned back on at the time of the assignation so that one sentence undermines the other (the last one), allowing thereby the continuing circularity.

The three levels of description present in "Générique"—objective (though not entirely), metaphorical, self-reflective—anticipate those inherent to the narrative proper. The three intertwined "stories," whose incidental matter constitutes the surface activity of the text, should be viewed relative to such connotative variations; these interrelationships ultimately erase the boundaries of all three sequences of events so that they become metaphorically interchangeable. Almost at once, in fact, events in each sequence are affected by those in the others, a necessary consequence of the "logique interne du récit."

The novel's second segment, "Expansion," begins with the depiction of a fixed image, an impressionist seascape later identified as Monet's "Effet du soir." In this representation to the second degree (a description of a picture of a scene), immediately and inseparably stressed are both the manner and the object of the painting: "Les flots verdâtres, les rochers violets, l'écume, le ciel bas, sont figurés indifféremment au moyen de petits coups de pinceau en forme de virgules ou de minuscules croissants" (p. 15). From this rapid initial sketch the description proceeds to its second form, a standing back (it begins with "De loin . . .") intended to offer a general impression and flowing into metaphor. These two approaches retain their coordinates to the entire scene as "vues d'ensemble." The third one, however, in its effort toward exhaustive detail focuses so closely on the style of individual strokes as to isolate them from their context: "De tout près on peut distinguer la matière de chacune des touches dirigées de droite à gauche, d'abord empatée, puis s'elargissant, dérapant en même temps qu'elle se relève comme une queue" (p. 15). The notation no longer even mentions color and is limited to the *shape* of the stroke. Such attention bypasses all representational significance in the picture, and the text (the description) must retreat once more: "L'image de l'immobile tempête est collée sur un papier pelucheux qui l'entoure d'une marge gris-vert" (p. 15). From this distance the wall itself (subject of "Générique") appears and a "generative" transition may be achieved to the next "picture," a window: "Elle est punaisée à côté de la fenêtre dont l'embrasure encadre un paysage champêtre. . ." (p. 15). Since the main concern so far has been for the text to find a proper focus, aspects of this concern will create the hinge between the frames:

l'image ⟶ paysage
l'entoure d'une marge ⟶ l'embrasure encadre

The "paysage" that follows is patterned in a similar series of changing distances until a comparable "transition" mechanism goes into action to introduce a new sequence:

(a) paysage champêtre . . .
(b) Trois femmes . . .
(c) L'une d'elles . . . agite un rameau feuillu pour chasser les taons
(d) Des feuilles de noyer . . . s'exhale un parfum . . .
(e) Les taons ont des ailes . . . piquetées de noir . . .
(b′) En avant des femmes marche une petite fille . . .

Gradually smaller elements of the scene are focused on, until the detail of the insects' wings—(a) to (e). The necessity to retreat becomes evident at this point (which taxes the capacity of even minute examination), and a wider field is framed at (b′), beginning now at a more manageable distance. At the end of the "cadrage" now attempted, attention has again been drawn to an area of isolated detail and new bearings are necessary: "La bande avançant à la queue leu leu laisse derrière elle au flanc du coteau un sillon irrégulier au fond duquel l'herbe ne se relève que lentement. Lorsque le tireur écarte la tête et cesse de fixer la mire à travers l'oeilleton de visée, . . ." (pp. 16-17). The scenery that follows is the same as before—"paysage champêtre"—but it is seen now through the soldier's "oeilleton de visée," ravaged by war. The frame has remained the same, the transition has taken place to another time. Apart from the focusing activity another element has contributed to the transition in this and the previous instance (painting to window, "paysage champêtre" to war scene): each time there has been a reference to immobility becoming movement. In the first instance it was "l'image de l'*immobile tempête*"; in the second, "l'herbe ne se relève que *lentement*. Lorsque le tireur écarte la tête. . . ."[13] Throughout the novel references to arrested movement or to some conjunction of movement and immobility play an important role in the elaboration of transitions. The very form of the descriptions we have seen so far is a species of pulsation, a metaphor also, in the focusing variations, for the constructive/destructive activity of language.

Other more strictly linguistic elements have collaborated in the growth of the text, initial approximations to the prose's progress through analogy, an aspect of the narration which is to gain in intensity as the fiction's momentum increases. Two main types of analogy are so far discernible:

(1) *Similarities of Sound:*

. . .sol couvert de longues herbes . . . et constellé de pastilles (*ombelles*, coquelicots)	Trois femmes . . . protègent du soleil par des *ombrelles* . . .
. . . chasser les *taons*	parfum *entêtant*

(2) *Similarities of Appearance:*

Elles portent des robes . . . *très serrées a la taille*, aux manches en *gigot*	L'une d'elles agite . . . un rameau pour chasser las *taons*

The shape of the insects resembles that of the dresses and their sleeves. Actually it is very difficult to find unalloyed analogies, as the comparisons by homophony (1) show: There are also similarities of design between the flowers and the parasols, while the insects' characteristic is their persistence ("entêtés").

If we have paid such close attention to the novel's beginning, it is because a vocabulary of design, gesture, connotation is being created at the same time as a proper distance of description and a proper frame of organization for the entire narrative are sought. As the text gains momentum these words, gestures, frames elicit segments of each anecdotal sequence as echoes of one another so that the entire fiction is soon suffused at once with eroticism and death while ironic self-reflection encloses the whole in a web of artifice, otherwise called art.

The linkages and interrelated patterns that characterize passages from one moment to another within the same anecdotal series illustrate with striking clarity how the metaphorical momentum of the text (which may be viewed as the counterpart, in purely descriptive prose, to expressed emotion in more explicitly dramatized fictions) manifests itself. This is especially true in erotic or death-related episodes when there are no inert elements left to the prose. Such is the case, for instance, in the following transition between two moments of the strollers' sequence from the fourth section, titled "Leçon de choses":

> La mer est calme. La bande de galets que recouvre et découvre chaque vague en se brisant puis en se retirant est d'une couleur brune, comme vernie, avec des ombres noires et des reflets bleu pale, argentés. La main qui joue avec le manche de l'ombrelle a une délicate texture de porcelaine. Le manche se termine par une poignée qui va s'évasant comme le pilon d'un mortier. Des oiseaux, des fleurs (chrysanthèmes?) sont finement ciselés dans l'ivoire jaunâtre, entourant le corps écailleux d'un dragon dont la gueule pourvue de dents recourbées ouverte sur une langue pendante constitue l'extrémité de la poignée. Il saisit son mince poignet qu'il abaisse et les doights délicats rencontrent le membre rigide (pp. 108-109).

The sea constituted, as we saw, the foundation of imagery on which the second paragraph of "Générique" rises; it was established from the outset as a key generative element in the novel and a manifestation of the love/death dyad. It remains in the background of the "promeneurs" sequence throughout; in fact, it is with the sea imagery of the painting ("immobile tempête") that the sequence is first introduced (see above). (The sea's role in the other sequences, though less explicit, is equally fundamental.) Its present reference manifests, in the first two sentences, the movement/immobility contrast while initiating the surge toward erotic imagery and ultimately sexual contact.

We note immediately that the opening sentence in the quotation could be read in two ways: (1) "La mer (sea) est calme"; (2) "La mèr(e) (mother) est calme." The woman in question, object of the man's advances, is viewed from the first as a mother; her daughter appears with her in almost every one of the series' moments and she starts out on the nighttime tryst only after mute expressions of love for the sleeping child. The woman's rendezvous represents a contradiction of her role as a mother, a role that she drastically negates at the culmination of the episode when she desperately tries to erase all traces of her lover's sperm. Elements of the entire quoted passage—and as much could be said, of course, of any other part of the fiction, especially in the proximity of transfer points—reverberate throughout the narrative. We select only one phrase to illustrate this mechanism, and we will follow its development merely up to its present instance.

(P. 108)   ". . . *bande de galets* que recouvre et découvre chaque *vague*":

The original forms of this phrase appear in "Générique" as: (a) *"un galon (ou bandeau?)"* and *"vagues involvées"*; (b) "immobile déferlement de *"vagues végétales* . . . sur le *galon* de papier fané."* Thereafter, various transformations of these words will join together apparently dissimilar contexts, one strand within a compact pattern of interrelationships.

(P. 16)   "La *bande* avançant . . . laisse . . . un sillon irrégulier": retrospectively, the grass is as the sea; *bande*, a band of hikers.

(P. 21)   "Sur la manche kaki sont cousus deux *galons* en forme de chevrons." The war scene is linked to the sea (*galons* ⟶ *galets*) and to the workers (*chevrons*) and also, of course, to "Générique."

(P. 22)   ". . . des mousses verdâtres qui s'inclinent alternativement . . . au passage lent des *vagues*." The appearance of *vagues* and *galons*, of a sea image and a war scene follow one another closely here. The movement of the water ("s'inclinent alternativement") anticipates "recouvre et découvre" (p. 108).

(P. 32)   ". . .couvercle décoré sur son pourtour d'un *galon* noir ou s'entrelacent deux lignes dorées et onduleuses comme une succession de vagues." The object described is the lid of a cigar box. The picture on it is of a peaceful, colorful setting, in sharp contrast to the war sequence wherein it appears. It is connected also to the apparently idyllic scene of the excursion and to the sea by the same complex of words. (Actually, other elements in the picture reinforce these bonds and establish others also to the workers' series.)

(P. 37)   ". . . un personnage . . . crie . . . quel est le con qui a tiré . . . *bande de* . . . le tireur . . . pointe vers la fenêtre." *Bande de* here means "bunch of" and recalls the "band" of excursionists (and the sea to which it is joined). Also, "con" is the more vulgar name of female genitals as well as an insulting appellative.[14] The sniper's pointing to the window makes clear the reference to the hikers who first appeared through a window and remain also bound to that frame. The soldiers are referred to as *bande de* several times hereafter.

Bander and *débander* also appear used in the "argot" sense of having and losing an erection, particularly in the feverish monologs of "Divertissement I and II." In fact, approximations of the generative group *galon (ou bandeau?)* —whose analysis we began in its form as *bande de galets*—are frequent in those two sections which represent a focusing of the text on the sea-like flux and reflux of words over the depths of an individual's unconscious. We mention only a few from "Divertissement I": *"chars à bancs,"* a slang name for Army vehicles, is often followed in the stream of "argot" by a reference reminiscent of the strollers' series, e.g., "où qu'ils allaient les gaziers dans leurs *chars à bancs* au goujon peut être ou tirer les moineaux à coups de grosse bite" (p. 61). Birds in general are part of the erotic scene (there are birds etched on the handle of the parasol which becomes the man's member —here *bite*). *"Goujon"* anticipates the fishermen's episode, part of the walk on the cliff. The next mention of *"chars à bancs"* (p. 65) is followed, after a few lines, by "Les femmes et les enfants d'abord," and so on. We selected the words *chars à bancs* because, although they are a more remote transformation of *bande*, or *bandeau*, they still illustrate the inner bonding of the text. The reminiscence would have been even clearêr had we used *bander*, for instance, an explicitly sexual referent.

(P. 75)   "La figure no. 120 porte comme légende *Bancs de galets* au pied d'une falaise." This sentence is from the textbook *Leçons de choses*. In the description of the figure that follows, the waves (*les vagues*) resemble rows of military tents (*galons*). A path follows the top of the cliff, dangerously close to the edge. A segment of the strollers' episode on the cliff follows.

(P. 77)   ". . . une mince *bande* d'un bleu plus foncé . . ."; "La *bande* bleue qui s'élargit . . .": Bands of color. The scene is now slowed down towards immobility and presented in terms of colored areas whose contained movement recalls the sea: "La vaste paix de l'ensemble entretient à sa surface une perpetuelle animation, comme s'il était doué à la fois des deux propriétés contraires du mouvement et de l'immobilité" (p. 78).

(P. 83)   ". . . un tapis de *galets* dont la couleur change. . . ."; "Les *galets* forment une *bande* blanche." Between these two mentions of *galets* within five lines we read: "par temps calme, comme ces jours," an anticipation of "La mer est calme." The strollers are on the cliff where ". . . ils contemplent l'immensité à la fois immobile et mouvante . . ."

. A comparison between these lines and a passage from "Divertissement I" will clarify the relationships at work and the manner in which they function in the highly figurative language of "Divertissement I and II."

Section: "Divertissement I"	Section: "Leçon de choses" ("Promeneurs")
. . . on se serait cru au balcon d'un sixième étage vue plongeante sur les *pavés* comme la bonniche qu'a des peines de coeur et hardi saute la dedans connard au grand *galop* pour changer sans *débander* et *valdas* comme si ça pleuvait toujours (p. 67).	Tout en bas, comme du haut d'une maison de plusieurs étages, on peut voir la grève d'où la mer s'est retirée laissant à découvert un tapis de *galets* . . . . Au pied de la falaisse les galets forment une *bande* blanche" (pp. 82-83).

The "pourvoyeur" (soldier in charge of ammunition) is the man whose monologs we read in "Divertissement I and II." He is here recalling his escape and his descent down a deep incline onto railroad tracks. (*Paves* ⟶ *galets*.) *Galop* retains slightly sexual overtones which always remain close to the surface in the "pourvoyeur's" figurative language. It is also another transformation: *galon* ⟶ *galets* ⟶ *galop; débander* ⟶ *bande; valdas* refers to "pastilles valdas," well-known cough drops, and is a slang term for blows, here explosions or projectiles. There is a reminiscence also of *galets* through the shape of *valdas*, which is reinforced by the water image ("pleuvait"). The thought of the "bonniche" (maid) throwing herself from a sixth floor pursues the connections to the women's series—They are on the cliff; also the little girl is scolded for going too near the edge. "Peines d'amours," or rather the furious disillusionment on the woman's part, will mark the conclusion of her lovemaking at the end of the series.

(P. 89)   ". . . la large *bande* bleu-vert qui l'entoure"; "la *bande* plus foncée

que déploie la mer." The marine scenery is again described as color patterns.
On the same page, between both instances of *bande*, we read (of a sailboat):
"Comme la mer sur laquelle il semble piqué, il paraît à la fois doué d'immo-
bilité et de mouvement" (p. 89).

(P. 96) "A l'intérieur de chaque *vague*, les *galets* qui forment le fond
semblent se soulever . . . comme un tapis . . ." Again as a "figure" in the
textbook, this instance of the words *galets* and *vagues* is a direct echo of the
quotation above (p. 83) to continue the network of interrelationships: sea—
women—representations. The monologs of "Divertissement I and II" can
be viewed as particular representations in themselves.

In summary, those few transformations we have followed are:

   galon [braid, decoration ——→ military stripe ——→ (chevrons)]——→
   galop ——→ galets (valdas), etc.

   bandeau (band, bandage) ——→ bande (band, bunch) ——→ bande (stripe,
   band of color) ——→ bander, débander [to have or lose an erection]
   ——→ chars à bancs (military vehicles, tanks), etc.

Next to these elements or their variations, regardless of the narrative sequence in which they appear, we find: (1) references of some sort to the
women's series; (2) references to the sea, its waves; (3) references to the
contrast movement/immobility; (4) quite often, also, though not invariably,
references to color contrasts, generally between light and dark hues (light
and dark areas of a woman's body).

Returning now to the extended quotation above which begins with "La
mer est calme" it is easy to see how the final transition is inevitable, since
almost all the terms in the passage are laden with multiple connotations. We
chose to trace the ancestry in the narrative of the first two sentences, farthest
away from the transfer point and also less obviously penetrated with erotic
suggestion, and yet the trajectory of those terms through the novel turned
them, too, into "carrefours de significations." The rest of the passage merely
needs to "funnel," as it were, some of these significations along a particular
path rendering the shift to explicit eroticism necessary. Progression begins
with color contrasts; the "bande de galets" is "d'une couleur brune . . . avec
des ombres noires," but surrounded by "reflets bleu pale, argentés": a central
element of darker color is encircled by more delicate tints. Gesture, action
become specific in the next sentence: "la *main* qui joue avec le *manche* de
l'ombrelle a une *délicate texture de porcelaine*." Parallel connotations are
becoming more precise. The final transfer is called forth by homophony and
focusing: "l'extrémité de la *poignée* ——→ Il saisit son mince *poignet* . . . et
les doigts *délicats* rencontrent la membre rigide" (p. 109).

Examined in this manner, the prose, as it reveals its inner articulations,
directs the reader's attention to the composition as such, along a path already
traced for him in "Générique." Other less specific facets of the novel intended
to emphasize its autotelic character are: (1) The use of fixed images, already
mentioned. They are reproductions of paintings, figures from the schoolbook *Leçons de choses*, the wallpaper flower design. Their descriptions

represent points of departure. When their generative impetus has been temporarily exhausted, their fixity remains available for the text to return to. In their role as beginnings—such as at the very outset of "Expansion" with the seascape (see above)—they also provide occasions for contrasting the movement of the description with the immobility of its object. (2) The prose of the textbook, whose didactic intent highlights, by contrast, the fiction's gratuitousness. Although of itself quiescent, the surrounding text's mobility penetrates it and transforms it too into a source of material. (As we indicate, it also represents the "constructive" side of the war episode.) (3) A series of incomplete words from newspapers, one in each sequence. Each newspaper is used in a manner stressing phallic, therefore generative, connotations.

(1) The sniper in the war scene uses a crumpled newspaper to clean his weapon; fragments of words are visible; the text offers its own completing interpretation: ...*iers* (ouvriers) *ivre*... (ivres) ...*ent* (périssent) *ecra*... (écrasés) ...*eux* (deux) ...*omb*... (tombés) ...*ement* (effondrement) *en*... (entraînés) ...*cor*... (encorbellement).

(2) The older workman uses a newspaper to wrap around his winebottle; on it one may read: ...*iers* (vacanciers) ...*ivre* (suivre) *ecras*...(écrasés) ...*eux* (affreux) *ac*...(accident) ...*ement* (effondrement) *en* (ensevelis)...*ut*...(chute) *roch*... (roches) *cor*... (corniche).

(3) The man in the hikers' sequence holds in his hand a rolled-up newspaper with the following: ...*iers* (cavaliers) ...*ivre*... (livrent) ...*ent* (courageusement *ecra*... (écrasants) ...*rieux* (furieux) ...*omb*... (combats) ...*ement* (de retardement) *en*... (ennemi) ...*roch*... (accroché) ...*cor*... (corps à corps).

(1) Appears in the war episode—about the workers.

(2) Appears in the workers' episode—about the strollers.

(3) Appears in the strollers' episode—about the war.

In each case the reconstructed words are a possible matrix for one of the sequences, but a matrix which was in fact not realized by the fiction, remaining as a possible construction available to it. There are also fragments from other extraneous texts which are sometimes easily recognizable ("sans fin, sans hâte, mais sans relâche"; a few lines elsewhere, recalling closely a Balbec scene from Proust's *A l'Ombre des jeunes filles en fleur*). All these elements are meant to underline the contingent character of the fiction as a text whose origins and coordinates are written words.

In conclusion, the basic dyad construction/destruction is manifested at all levels of the novel as the central component of its self-evaluating composition. The various transformations of the semantic group which we selected —*galon* (ou bandeau?), etc. up to the quotation ("La mer est calme", etc.) and beyond—reflected this through frequent references, for instance, to the movement/immobility couple, consequently to the sea and the erotic sequence. The various elaborations of the framing activity fall also into this category in that a frame creates esthetic relationships and also, by including certain areas of material it excludes, or negates, others, as a striking image of the concept of artistic selection. Likewise with the idea of focusing, whereby a composition is disintegrated through emphasis on a single detail, a new structure arising thereafter on a different plane. This technique is especially important in the early stages of the novel and throughout "Expansion," its first long section when the text is still seeking an adequate descriptive distance, but it retains a role until the end, particularly at transition points.

Following significant components (components *rendered* significant) of a landscape, a movement, an object, description moves from one compositional frame to another, from one sequence of events to another, in an objectivity that is merely apparent and actually manifests the complex metaphorical interplay of sex and death. Having situated the concept of generation at the source of his fiction, Simon, with the simplest elements, erects the spiraling structure of a self-reflective, self-elaborating text, wherein birth and death, that of his characters, of their history, and that of the prose that contains them, endlessly embrace to produce a renewed world of resemblance and analogy. The reader learns to see literary structure anew and to cast new eyes on a now more recent, more familiar world.

ILLINOIS WESLEYAN UNIVERSITY

Notes

[1] These were seminars at which gathered, in this instance (July 1971), French novelists usually included in the 'Nouveau Roman' group, as well as scholars and critics interested in their work. The proceedings of the 'Colloque' in the form of papers and discussions, were published in two volumes: *Nouveau Roman: hier; aujourd' hui.* 1. *Problèmes généraux.* 2. *Pratiques* (Paris: 10/18, 1972).

[2] Claude Simon, "La fiction mot à mot," *Nouveau Roman: hier; aujourd'hui. Pratiques*, p. 74.

[3] *Ibid.*, p. 78.

[4] *Ibid.*, p. 82. Italics in the text.

[5] *Ibid.*, p. 97. Italics in the text.

[6] Michel Foucault, *The Order of Things* (New York: Vintage Books, 1973), p. 17.

[7] These tirades are reminiscent of the opening passages in Céline's *Voyage au bout de la nuit.*

[8] In French education elementary science courses are called *Leçons de choses.*

[9] The blurb, enclosed by the editors and written by Simon, expresses in ironic hyperbole this thirst for completeness:

> Sensible aux reproches formulés à l'encontre des écrivains qui négligent les grands problèmes, l'auteur a essayé d'en aborder ici quelques-uns, tels ceux de l'habitat, du travail manuel, de la nourriture, du temps, de l'espace, de la nature, des loisirs, de l'instruction, du discours, de l'information, de l'adultère, de la destruction et de la reproduction des espèces humaines ou animales. Vaste programme que des milliers d'ouvrages emplissant des milliers de bibliothèques sont, apparemment, encore loin d'avoir épuisé.
>
> Sans prétendre apporter de justes réponses, ce petit travail n'a d'autre

ambition que de contribuer, pour sa faible part et dans les limites du genre, à l'effort général.

In a communication to the author of this essay, Simon mentions that, lacking a sense of humor, *L'Express* took the blurb literally and described the book as a work on sociology. This error was echoed on this side of the Atlantic by the *French Review* (Dec., 1976).

[10]The Larousse gives two principal definitions of this word—the first is from mathematics: "Se dit de l'élément d'un ensemble pris dans sa forme générale"; the second is from the cinema: "Partie d'un film ou sont indiqués les noms du producteur, du metteur en scène, des acteurs, etc." The first meaning contains the idea of potential development to be realized, of germ or embryo; the second draws our attention to the idea of representation and its techniques. Both emphasize aspects of structure. It is not unlikely that Simon had those meanings of the word "Générique" in mind—we recall his use, in Le Palace, of a dictionary definition of "revolution" as epigraph—and we can expect to find these definitions illustrated in the fiction's opening segment.

[11]Claude Simon, *Leçon de choses*, (Paris: Editions de Minuit, 1975), p. 9. Subsequent references are to this edition.

[12]We refer the reader interested in such problems of topology and fiction to Professor Bruce Morrissette's fascinating article, based chiefly on Robbe-Grillet's novels, entitled "Topology and the French Nouveau Roman," *Boundary*, 1 (1972), pp. 45-57.

[13]Hereafter, italics are mine unless otherwise indicated.

[14]*Leçon de choses* = Le con, les choses⟶ content of the fiction = the generation of a world.

ANOTHER BECKETT:
AN ANALYSIS OF *RESIDUA*

James Leigh

> Certain obstinate souls did not compre-
> hend, or pretended not to comprehend,
> that a new order had come, a necessary
> historical stage. . . .if the lottery is an
> intensification of chance, a periodic in-
> fusion of chaos into the cosmos, would it
> not be desirable for chance to intervene at
> all stages of the lottery and not merely
> in the drawing?
>
> Borges

To read Beckett today is at once absolutely superfluous and absolutely
essential—perhaps more to write about him. The eighty-odd books on his
work and the thousands of pages in scholarly journals have certainly said
all there is to say, given all the summaries that can be/need be given, all the
"selected bibliographies" necessary. Like others. Like Shakespeare. Like
Joyce. Like Borges.

There is in fact nothing to say. In a positive sense. For saying nothing is
not at all the same as not saying anything. The nothing that there is to say—
and that is said—is precisely that lowest point (*punctum*) in any standard
of comparison, that naught or 0—word or cipher—which, by marking the
place of absolute absence, makes a positional numeral system possible. It is
"what" makes it possible to say that for every arbitrary base *b*, every number
n can be written as a unique function.

Lowest point place of intersection between superfluousness and necessity. For saying nothing (here) is the only way that the text *itself* can be
approached—that is, if you want to approach it, the text is the primary
concern and not (the History of) Literature, Ideas, not the Message of
Samuel Beckett. Reader intersecting, you, me. In the pages. These (those)
pages present. . . .

Let us take three texts from 1965-66 (in French: 1966-67 in English).
Happily, they are already associated, already constitute a triad called

Residua,[1] so there is no need to extensively justify grouping them together. (The fact that the fourth member of *Têtes-Mortes*, "D'Un ouvrage abandonné," is omitted when the volume is translated as *Residua* permits the consideration to be limited to works written about the same time, leaving aside the one written in the 1950s.) We must also disagree with Ihab Hassan's assertion that the "trilogy that includes *Molloy*, *Malone Dies* and *The Unnamable* marks the highest achievement of Beckett in fiction."[2] For although it permits Hassan to move on to Beckett's theater and the conclusions he seeks to prove—"the pure and terrible art of Samuel Beckett finds its consummation in his plays" (p. 237)—it is a rather abrupt way of acquitting oneself of the necessity of reading the texts written after 1949 (or 1958, if *L'Innomable* is read in English). Rather than using a value judgment to attempt to justify narrowing the field, to justify the unjustifiable, we will simply and arbitrarily choose to consider these fifteen pages (seven and four and four): *Residua*.

There are certain obvious links between the parts of *Residua*. In "Enough," the narration is of the travels of two bodies, with moments of beginning ("I cannot have been more than six when he took me by the hand" [p. 154]), ending ("two steps and I was lost to him forever" [p. 155]), and interruption ("sometimes they [hands] let each other go" [p. 154]). There are also two bodies in "Imagination. . . ," but they are inscribed into specific locations, movement and interruption being functions of temperature and light. And a phrase in the final sentence of the second text casts it immediately into "Ping"; ". . .that white speck lost in whiteness. . ." (p. 164). In addition to whiteness, "Ping" also extends the preceding concern with bodies, ". . .all white bare white body. . ." (p. 165), and its non-sequential structure is in fact the very essence of interruption.

But while the connections are evident, so are the deviations. "Enough" is apparently the discourse of a narrator, an "I" recounting the time spent with a travelling companion, a stooped old man. In "Imagination Dead Imagine," however, there is no longer a narrator directly constituted as a participant within the scene, but rather in two ways there is an implication of narration. First, the scene is meticulously described, and considering the references to a closed space, to changes in light and temperature and to naked bodies in specified locations, the resonances with *The Lost Ones* are striking. Then there are appeals to an implied reader-listener who accompanies the description: "No trace anywhere of life, you say. . ."; "go in": "go back out"; "wait" (p. 161). Finally, in "Ping," although there is what might be called a description, it is absolutely disjuncted from that of "Imagination. . . ," both by the absence of an appeal to a reader and by the total lack of syntactic organization. The only kinship between the seventy "sentences" in the text and the ones that "express a complete thought" is that here they begin with capital letters and end in periods. In fact, the text is admirably described by a sentence in Claude Simon's *Les Corps conducteurs*: "La seule règle observée paraît être celle de l'accumulation et de la répétition, en hauteur ou en largeur."[3]

The net effect of this conjunction and disjunction, then, is to discourage consideration of the texts as simply being "about" something, as being the expression of communication of the author's meaning or intention. Rather than a static continuous mode of narration (or of discourse), the pervasive instability demands that the texts be read as a function of their *material existence as texts*, as an incessant theoretical elaboration of the practical application that they *are*. One cannot, for example, somnambulistically talk about narrator, description and referent, since these elements are constituted by the *difference* from text to text, and not at all by an identifiable stability in each one. It can be said, in fact, that this very difference, this tension between component parts, is *what* the texts are about. And as such, rather than merely questioning the generic divisions within "literature" or art," the texts challenge the traditional basis of both cultural and esthetic evaluation, the most basic relationships among reader, writer, and text.

Initially, it can be noted that "Enough" contains certain elements—narrator, character, memory—that are absent from the other texts. But while the presence of these conventions might tend to encourage its consideration within the limits of traditional narrative, the text incessantly undermines such an immobilization from the first paragraph on. Even before the beginning of "I" 's recounting of the travels with the old man, there is a pen. A pen that writes, notes: "When the pen stops I go on." The metronomic alternation between recounting and inscription might lead one to interpret it as the pen of a secretary or stenographer upon which/whom the narrator depends, the medium in which voice becomes writing. This passivity immediately vanishes however, and the pen (apparently) manifests a will of its own: "Sometimes it refuses." (Apparently, for we must assume that "it" refers to the pen.)

Another possibility arises from the location ascribed to "I" and the pen: "I don't see it but I hear it there behind me." It could be inferred that "I" is on a psychoanalyst's couch, unable to see the analyst, according to the precise instructions laid out by Freud for *his* art and craft. Even hypnosis can be read into it through the prescriptive first sentence: "All that goes before forget." But this interpretation is disrupted a first time by the strange final sentence of the first paragraph: "So much for the art and craft." Whose art? Whose craft? Those of the text we have before us? It is difficult to integrate this sentence into the elaboration of *any* external frame of reference, particularly one that would so radically predispose the reading. Then, throughout the text, the "voice" is that of "I." Even if the text is considered to be the notes of an analyst, it would necessarily be a literal, uninterpreted transcript, and, as such, the possibility becomes supremely uninteresting. For like discussing the text purely in terms of narration and description, such a reading is explicitly centered *outside the text*, within the very structures that the text tends to dislocate.

The alternating strokes—"I"=pen, voice=silence—of the first paragraph establish a general principle that can be seen to be at work in the continuing text: a tension between two poles is the most basic condition for the appearance of any single element. From the generality of the "I"="he" relationship, or the present (of narration: "I set the scene. . ." [p. 158]; "Now I'll wipe out . . ." [p. 159]) —past (of memory, of "fact": "I set the scene of my disgrace just short of a crest. On the contrary it was on the flat in a great calm") opposition, to the specificity of sexual references (I-lick-his-penis/he-touches-my-old-breasts), the one constant is that there is no instance of non-reflection, no factor that is not doubled.

(Since it is a non-rigid, plastic principle, however, the text cannot be reduced to a mechanical binarity that could be used to non-problematically "explain" it. For while this principle *determines* its conditions, its specificity is determined by those very conditions. Some pairs, for example, are complementary: the sexual partnership, or he-speaking and I-listening. But others are mutually exclusive, the affirmation of one demanding the negation of the other: "All I know comes from him. I won't repeat this a propos of all my bits of knowledge" (p. 154)/"For I don't remember having learnt anything in those [years] I remember" (p. 158). The principle must therefore embrace the two contradictory meanings of "dichotomy": a) a *simple* division of a whole into pairs, and b) the division of a class into two mutually exclusive sub-classes.

The complications of this principle begin in the first paragraph, in the first sentence, in the twin domains to which it appeals: "All that goes before forget"—memory and sequential time. Although "I" 's narration would apparently be a function of memory, memory comes to be not the entire time spent together, but rather of a certain period—ten years. The rest can only be surmised—"I cannot have been more than six. . ."—, for other than the "two events described," "life" is obscured: "It [our last decade] veils those that went before and *must have* resembled it like blades of grass" (p. 158).[4] But even narrated assertions are dependent on the powers of memory; as such, the possibility of misrepresentation is not excluded: "In the beginning he always spoke walking. So it *seems to me now*" (p. 158). And sequential time. The adverb "before" absolutely demands a point of reference in order for it to be intelligible. It demands a present as the separation between it and "after"; most of all, however, it is a purely intellectual construct. Having no material referent, it must *always* function within a narrative, descriptive, or discursive system, must always be used by a narrator or describer to put things in order for himself. As such, it need not be fixed into a represented framework of "what happens," but can (and must) be allowed to circulate as a function of "I" 's instability.

A more productive distinction between before and after, between present and past is the most obvious—the verb tenses. On one hand, "I" gives a recounting of events that occurred during the travels with the old man, narrated in the past tenses. But on the other hand, at least once on every page there is a present, now interjecting or "ejaculating" ("It's a mansion above" [p. 154], now reflecting on the veracity of the narration ("So it seems to me now"), now clarifying ("I am thinking of our hemisphere" [p. 158]), now interpreting ("It's then that I shall have lived or never" [p. 157]). It will be noted that this distinction of past and present corresponds to Benveniste's division of language into discourse and narration along the lines of tempo- rality.[5] For Benveniste, narration (*le récit*) is the positing of events as they appear on the "horizon of history": "Les événements semblent se raconter eux-mêmes" (p. 241). Discourse, however, is essentially the discourse of someone, rooted in a necessary I:you relationship, "someone" defined *only* as he that says "I": "je se refère à l'acte de discours individuel où il est pro- noncé, et il en désigne le locuteur" (p. 261).

Thus the final apparent negation by "I"—"now I'll wipe out everything but the flowers" (p. 159)—, the ultimate domination of the present discourse, is no more than a simulated resolution of the tension between narration and discourse, moreover an *affirmation* of the narration that necessarily passes through discourse, necessarily coexisting with it in order to exist. While the absolute domination of "I" by the old man would seem to be overthrown with the transfer into the present discourse, narration can also be found within that grammatical present: "I *can feel* him at night pressed against me with all his twisted length. It *was* less a matter of sleeping than of lying down" (p. 159). The present "freedom" is necessarily a function of the past "subjugation."

The relationship between narration and discourse is not that often found in the work of Robbe-Grillet (c.f. esp. *Instantanés*), where the text is inscribed between two, neither one nor the other, in a sense negating both, denying the distinction between the two. Here, however, the text is neces- sarily at once both discourse and narration, one effecting the other, the other affecting the one. While "Enough" *is* a present talking about a past, im- perfectly remembering that past, the present itself is determining as a future perfect—"It is then that I shall have lived or never"—, an "existence" yet to be realized in a contingent, *textual* present.

Textual. For lest this be read as simply the discourse of a transparent "subject" assimilating the demands of narration, it will be remembered that there is a moment when pure textuality asserts itself, a moment that cannot be subordinated to any partial description of the text. Namely:

> Other main examples suggest themselves to the mind. Immediate continu-
> ous communication with immediate redeparture. Same thing with delayed
> redeparture. Delayed continuous communication with immediate redeparture.
> Immediate discontinuous communication with immediate redeparture. Same
> thing with delayed redeparture. Delayed discontinuous communication with
> immediate redeparture. Same thing with delayed redeparture (pp. 156-7).

As the mathematical extension of the combinative possibilities of immediacy/delay and continuous/discontinuous, the paragraph cannot be directly assimilated into a past (real or remembered) or a present (of narration). Composed of examples that "suggest themselves to *the* mind," it can be combined neither with the old man-subject of the enunciation, master *in* the past, nor with "I"-narrator-enunciator, (apparent) master of the present. It immediately exceeds any master-slave dialectic, insinuating itself as a purely *disjunctive* (or de-combinative) energy: ". . .l'essentiel est l'établissement d'une surface enchantée d'inscription ou d'enregistrement. . ."[6] Neither expression nor description, it does not "take place"—that is, does not contribute to the elaboration of a represented experience, reproduced by/in the reader. Moreover it dissolves that elaboration. What it takes is space, space within the text, and as such, what it "expresses" and "describes" is the inextricability of language from thought, whether that thought is presently in the form of narration, description or memory.

Thus we have already begun to read "Imagination Dead Imagine," specifically, the end of "Imagination. . .": ". . .to see if they still lie in the stress of that storm, or of a worse storm, or in the black dark for good, or the great whiteness unchanging, and if not what are they doing" (p. 164). Not simply disjunction, but *disjunctive energy*, the "or" series is at once surface and means of inscription, the way the text is read as well as the way it is written: ". . .le 'soit' désigne le système de permutations possibles entre des différences qui reviennent toujours au même en se déplaçant, en glissant" (Deleuze/Guattari, *ibid.*).

The division of "Imagination. . ." into description of the physical properties of the enclosing space and of the two bodies enclosed reflects the metronomic dichotomy of "Enough" but expands it as well. For here the dominant mode is the imperative, precisely that of the absolute dependence upon its textual system: ". . .from this point of view, but there is no other" (p. 163); "Leave them there, . . .there is better elsewhere. No, life ends and no, there is nothing elsewhere. . ." (p. 164). From the "imagine" of the title through the various "go in," "go back out," and "but go in," the text is commanding and obeying, action and reaction, stimulus and response. Most of all, however, the "here" generated by this tension cannot be opposed or compared to an elsewhere; its presence as text is its own world, "the" world. The disjunction between inside and outside, the most fundamental condition of literature-as-representation, -as-expression is immediately denied as a function of the pervasive imperative: "Islands, waters, azure, verdure, one glimpse and vanished, endlessly, omit" (p. 161). And it is in this atmosphere that the text inscribes its own inside and outside.

Nevertheless, if the present text disrupts a traditional binary system (literature/reader, object/[for a] subject), it is clearly through the imposition of a similar apparatus. First in a general, mechanical way. The diameter of the enclosure is three feet, as is the distance from the ground to the summit of the vault. The circumambient wall thus reflects the division into two halves as well as enclosing it, since its height is half of the preceding measurement, or eighteen inches. Then inside the enclosure the transition is from black and cold to white and heat and vice versa. Linked to the same source

Ce dont nous avons besoin, c'est de déterminer *autrement*, selon un système différentiel, les *effets* d'idéalité, de signification, de sens et de référence. (Il faudrait aussi réserver une analyse systématique à ce mot "effet" dont l'usage est si fréquent aujourd'hui, ce qui n'est pas insignifiant, et au nouveau ("of which still no trace"), the variations of heat and light are interrupted from time to time by unpredictable, irregular pauses, and "the extremes alone are stable," the latter verifiable in the functioning itself, "stressed by the vibration to be observed when a pause occurs at some intermediate stage, no matter what its level and duration" (p. 162). Thus, although chance is inscribed as a function within the system, "the return sooner or later to a temporary calm seems assured." (Outside the enclosure, chance is the condition of the miraculous rediscovery of the enclosure, "the sighting of a little fabric quite as much a matter of chance, its whiteness merging in the surrounding whiteness" [p. 163].) And finally, although the text is a discourse in the

concept qu'il marque de façon indécise. L'occurence s'en multiplie en raison même de cette indétermination active. Un concept en train de se constituer produit d'abord une sorte d'effervescence localisable dans le travail de nomination. Ce "nouveau" concept d'*effet* emprunte ses traits à la fois à l'opposition cause/effet et à l'opposition essence/apparence (effet/reflet) *sans néanmoins s'y réduire.* C'est cette frange d'irréductibilité qu'il faudrait analyser.)

Derrida, *Positions*, 90

present tense, there is also an infusion of narration, the establishment of a duration opposed to description and to the measured duration of the alternating transitions within: "Never two gazes together *except once*, when the beginnng of one *overlapped* the end of the other, for about ten seconds" (p. 163). The "voice," the description that is discourse, is therefore also narration and must possess a kind of memory, an implication of the "real" existence of a referent, something incessantly denied by the text, and nonetheless affirmed once again by the statement-question of the final seven words: "and if not what are they doing."

The incipient binarism was already being undermined, however, and the text's final words are in fact an echo of others: "there may intervene, *experience shows*, . . .pauses of *varying length*"; ". . .may seem strange, *in the beginning*"; "But on the whole, *experience shows*, such uncertainty is not common" (all p. 162). At the beginnng, there is also the "no way in, go in, measure." "Existence" is posited, described, and immediately ignored as the primary condition of the continuing "description." The subsequent "meticulous" description is first of all based on the ("subjective") assumption of a possible truth, the positing of a working hypothesis: ". . .its minimum, *say* freezing point. . . ," "*say* twenty seconds." Thus what might have been called an almost scientific description ("like a physics text": Ruby Cohn, Back to Beckett[7]) is the function of a pervasive "subjectivity" (though it is a subjectivity irreducibly bound up with and functioning through a "you": "No trace anywhere of life, you say. . ."). Even more specifically, when at one extreme it is a question of temperature, although the gauge is subjectively posited, it is nevertheless an objective, scientifically measurable scale: "say freezing point": thirty-two degrees. At the other extreme, however, at white and heat, the evaluation is purely subjective, demanding even the corporal presence of the observer: "Strong heat, surfaces hot but not burning *to the touch*" (161), (It is indeed a physics text then, with a shift from Newtonian to Quantum Mechanics.)

With the consideration of the two bodies in the second half of the text, there is both a continuation of the preceding factors and an extension of them. In addition to the infusion of narration noted above, the body-description begins with an emphasis on a certain duration: ". . .the same source of which *still* no trace"; "*Still* on the ground, bent in three, . . .merging in the white ground. . .were it not for the long hair. . . , the body of a woman *finally*." Not at all a duration measurable in seconds or minutes as before: ". . .left eyes which at *incalculable intervals* suddenly open wide and gaze . . . ." Rather at once duration *within* the narration-description-discourse (". . .except once, when the beginning of one overlapped. . .") and *of* the discourse-description-narration ("still. . .still. . .").

Then there is life, the life implied on the first page: "bodies sweating." The life of the bodies can be verified by holding a mirror to their lips, but even this and the sweating do not suffice to guarantee their animation. Rather it is their eyes opening wide and gazing that ultimately permits their classification in the order of "living." But on the one hand, the intervals between the moments of this gazing are incalculable and, as such, cannot be described in the terms of the physical properties of the enclosure, not even as "say twenty seconds." And on the other hand, although the staring is what certifies them as living, it is an "unblinking exposure *long beyond what is humanly possible*" (p. 163). Both human and non- or super-human, observable but not analyzable, the "life" of the bodies moreover casts them out of simple description and into the textual subjectivity, either as perspective ("the effect is striking"; "the bodies seem whole"; "assuming two sides of a piece") or as temporal difference ("great white calm now so rare and brief"; "in the beginning"; "in the beginning, for one who still remembers").

The irreducible tension between the textual elements—narration/ description, continuity/discontinuity, and so on—culminates in a reversal that at once affirms and denies all that precedes it: "It is clear, however, from a thousand little signs too long to imagine, that they are not sleeping" (p. 164). The sentence marks the end of the concern with two bodies, not by saying the end, but by being the end. After, there is no description, no narration, only imperative: "Only murmur ah, no more. . . ," "Leave them there. . . ." It asserts the clarity, the presence of (the bodies') consciousness by appealing to another "presence," one twice removed. First as imagination, the mode of discourse-narration-description that the text *is* (—"from this point of view, but there is no other"). But then as merely potential imagination, the textual imagination being brought up short by a lack of time, the end of the duration that nonetheless is one of the essential properties of (the present) textuality. Moreover, with the extension into a multiple signifying system, the mechanics of the text become more explicit if not more understandable, more cohesive if not more comprehensible. Inasmuch as it is a question of becoming-clear-through-a-sign, the text's pervasive binarity is inscribed into the generalized principle through which it functions. And since the signs are not present, only potential, they "are" what they cannot logically be, the essential contradiction that makes the text more than the sum of its individual elements and oppositions. At once non-present presence and present non-presence, the text speaks its own language (while depending on its object to do so), designates its own object (while denying it) and imposes its own time (as a rapidly exhaustible duration). And as a transient inhabitant of our language, our time, and our world the text leaves as its residue a momentary disruption in the coexistence of thought and language.

The use of the above oppositions to read "Ping" is complicated most of all by its composition: one hundred and twenty different words combined into a total of one thousand and thirty-four; seventy separate groups of words each beginning with a capital letter and ending with a period; thirty-four pings.[8] For to begin by talking about a narrator-describer and an object described—even simulated—is to make assumptions that virtually eliminate the possibility of reading the text in/on its own terms. Certain words of course lend themselves to categorization under the aegis of "narrator" or "describer": on the first page, "all known," "like sewn," "almost white," "no meaning." Evaluation is certainly there. Others under "space": "white floor," "white ceiling," "white walls," "elsewhere," "within." And the body within. But comparing it to any other text—any other of Beckett's texts, for example—, it is immediately apparent that even if the standard lexicon of literary criticism and analysis is applicable there, which is hardly a self-evident truth, to use it here is to force upon the text the massive presuppositions of that lexicon. *How It Is* for example, perhaps a distant cousin of "Ping," at least begins "how it is I quote before Pim and with Pim after Pim how it is three parts I say it as I hear it." There is at least something—"I"—to hold onto for those who need to read it as an externally represented drama, who need an external consciousness to guarantee the unity and coherence of their own. For not all relish an excursion into chaos.

The word groups do not "express a complete thought" and are therefore not sentences, except perhaps the title, if it is considered to be an imperative. What is precisely lacking are verbs, predicates linked to subjects, predicating existence, actions, or occurrence. Rather the verbs present are all participles, some present, mostly past: "white body fixed," "legs joined," "hands hanging," "planes shining." As such they tend to be only locally descriptive, no longer expression or communication, no longer a continuum from point A to point B articulated by an external syntax.

Juxtaposed to "fixed" (the most prevalent past participle) is the continuous "presence" generated by the present participles (quotation marks marking its status as a purely lexical effect). On one hand, this simulated duration is opposed to the one repeated reference to time and duration found in the text: the "one second" found on every page. But on the other hand, there is another duration, neither designated nor indicated, a time inscribed into the text by the oscillation between "over" and "unover." The last few words of the text—"ping silence ping over"—manifest a dual function for "over": it both *is* and *says* the end. But since this is not the only occurrence of the word, its function cannot be limited to simply ending, to simply turning off the machine. For when "over" enters four times on page 167, the text does not end. As such, saying the end, saying what is (will be) the end does not suffice to bring about that end.

Nor is this purely textual duration established by a simple alternation between "over" and "unover." There is no dialogue between the two resulting in the finality of "over," no balance established. In the textual sequence there are three "unovers" (separated by other words and word groups), two "overs", one of the former, then five of the latter. But "over" and "unover" do not adequately describe the limits of the sequence, and it can, in fact, just as easily be associated to the interjected "pings" as to the order of their appearance. The last word group is indeed the only one in which there are three "pings" and one of only two cases where only one word—"silence"— separates two "pings." Moreover, just as it is impossible to justify a choice between these two possibilities, neither "over" nor "unover" can be qualified as positive or negative. Rather, like "ping," they both are fragments of the cycles of repetition and, as such, assimilate even the "end" into that repetition. In this sense then, the end is not the end, for like "wolf" cried too often, the unitary descriptive impact of "over" has all but dissipated in the repetition. And to end something must have begun.

And the body within.

The body is first of all and always not just "body" but "bare white body." Always. It appears as such only on the first two pages. Only. Its frequency diminishes rapidly as the text progresses, for it appears seven times on the first page, twice on the second and not at all after that. Subsequently, "it" enters twice as a fragment, as the words "bare white," "bare white one yard fixed. . ." and ". . .one yard invisible bare white all known. . ." (p. 167). It thus reflects what "bare white body" already was: fragments—"legs joined," "hands hanging," "eyes," "white feet toes," and so on. The body is not a character, not a "person" but rather is closer to what the text is, says: "traces blurs signs no meaning. . . ." Furthermore, in being always "bare *white* body," it too is absorbed into the cycles of repetition by "white," the most frequent word in the text, the "white" that is now "all white," now "almost white," now "white last color."

Considering the body as essentially fragmentary has certain benefits. First it flows immediately into a class of elements that, on the whole, do not participate directly in the cycles of repetition—namely, certain words that appear only once: flesh, nails, hair, torn, and scars, for example. While their appearance is singular and, as such, very striking, as corporal fragments they are necessarily also drawn into the general textual flow. But it cannot be overemphasized, they are drawn in *as fragments* and not *as body*: not as unit, character or person. Then, after the dissipation of "bare white body" and the instillation of "bare white"—two word groups after, to be precise—, fragmentation also assimilates the other eye, the "dim eye black and white half closed long lashes imploring" (p. 167). As has been frequently remarked by readers of "Ping," this is certainly not the "same" eye as the "eyes light blue almost white" (although the question itself presupposes reading in the mode of representation). But in as much as it is a fragment—not even a fragmented body, for it is only eye-black-white-imploring-lashes—, it draws on the textual conditions of the other at the very moment of its disjunction from it.

From another perspective, the class of elements-that-appear-only-once is complicated by the fact that it includes not only corporal references. "Torn," through its possible association with "scars," can be forced into this category. But what about the others? What about "afar flash of time" and "henceforth" and "unlustrous"? The precise effect of these apparently extraneous elements is the inhibition of the interpretation of the others in their class as implications of "humanity" (". . .we are drawn to the human resonance of 'flesh,' 'nails,' . . .": Cohn, *op. cit.*, pp. 253-5). Rather they certainly can be so interpreted, but such an interpretation must be cognizant of the fact that it is itself also immediately denied by the material mode of existence of those very elements—that is, as functions of the class of elements-that-appear-only-once.

The least human and apparently most extraneous element in the text is of course "ping." Compared to the others, it is difficult to even call it a word. In an interesting and ambitious reading of the text, David Lodge writes that he cannot satisfactorily explain it.[9] He does however, offer two possibilities: first, in a referential sense, "ping" might denote a noise external to the text: and second, as connotation, it "punctuates the text like striking a triangle in a complicated fugue." Later, he descriptively calls "ping" a noise external to the discourse which it punctuates at arbitrary intervals" (p. 88). Finally, it must be noted that for Lodge the pervasive question in his reading is whether or not "ping" is a part of the discourse.

We can begin with a comparison that Lodge suggests (although we will have to clarify his conclusions)—the relationship between "ping" and what precedes and follows it:

before "ping"	"ping"	after "ping"
body fixed	ping	fixed elsewhere
fixed one yard	ping	fixed elsewhere
body fixed	ping	fixed elsewhere
fixed front.	Ping	murmur
fixed front	ping	murmur
murmur	ping	silence
like sewn invisible.	Ping	murmur
planes meeting invisible.	Ping	murmur
silence within.	Ping	elsewhere
planes shining white	ping	murmur
fixed one yard	ping	fixed elsewhere
like sewn invisible.	Ping	murmurs
all known without within.	Ping	perhaps a nature
square yard never seen	ping	perhaps a way out
one second	ping	silence

always the same.	Ping	perhaps not alone
almost never	ping	silence
given rose only just	Ping	image
that not known.	Ping	a nature
almost white fixed front	ping	a meaning
only just almost never	ping	silence
one yard fixed	ping	fixed elsewhere
silence within.	Ping	elsewhere
that known not.	Ping	perhaps not alone
all of old	ping	flash
white last colour	ping	white over
over.	Ping	fixed last elsewhere
white ceiling never seen	ping	of old
white floor never seen	ping	of old
perhaps there.	Ping	of old
fixed front old	ping	last murmur
long lashes imploring	ping	silence
silence	ping	over

Something is immediately apparent in this construction. Namely, the words that follow "ping" tend to appeal more or less to an external space, either explicitly—"fixed elsewhere," "perhaps a way out"—or implicitly, minimally, as a deviation from the text's dominant physical concerns—"murmur"/"silence," five of each: an equilibrium, "a meaning." In order to accommodate all the terms that follow "ping," however, the principle of classification must be kept as vague as possible. "External space," for example, cannot be forced into the position of constituting a material referent. It must be defined as no more and no less than a mode of externality apart from the internality, the "presence" simulated by the text, and nevertheless owing its very "existence" to the latter. Rather than a represented, representable externality *appealed to*, it is moreover an *appealing-to-externality*, necessarily remaining within the potentiality of the present participle. As such, Lodge's evaluation seems a little too precise and carries in its wake too many consequences, for he describes the terms that follow "ping" as suggesting "the possibility of some other presence or place" (p. 89).

Equally as evident is that the terms preceding "ping" cannot be so classified. There are of course certain words that reflect and repeat those that follow. But there are more that relate to the physical "description," as well as to both the "body" and to the other eye. Finally, there are explicit references to some colors—"given rose" and "white"—, oblique references to other colors—blue and black?: "*almost* white," "white *last* color," and through the "long lashes imploring," to the black and white eye. In short, the words preceding "ping" relate to virtually all the textual forces at play, and not to the precise imprecision of appealing-to-externality.

From this it is possible to draw certain conclusions about "ping" itself and its function within the text. "Ping" can be seen to operate precisely as *punctuation*, as a point (*punctum*) which appears at random intervals and whose appearance is governed solely by chance. Moreover, "ping" is not *like* punctuation but literally *is* punctuation. There are no metaphors at work here. It is the arbitrary base that permits the articulation of the text into its various modes. And while its occurrence is purely a matter of chance, its other side, the other rule of its operation, is that what follows it relates to and generates an appealing-to-externality.

These two simple rules have an immediate impact on the reading of the text. First, we see again that the end is not the end: since "over" follows "ping," while it marks (the place of) the end, it necessarily inscribes as well its other function, its status as external appealing. Then, considering that title is "Ping," it can be said that the text is present (to the reader) first of all and irreducibly as a function of chance. What comes before the first "ping" is quite literally *everything*, in the broadest sense,—Proust, Shea Stadium, Genghis Kahn. . .—*that* "ping" appearing as the arbitrary inscription of a "beginning." And since what follows the first "ping" is the text as a whole, it can further be asserted that, as its primary "intention," the (a) text constitutes an appealing-to-externality, like literary texts have always done. But here, rather than elaborating a representation of "life," "the world" or "reality," the emphasis is on the appealing as act, as text. As such, it constitutes a simulacrum of fiction, reinscribing the latter's most elementary principles into an exploration not of the object of fiction, but of the conditions of those principles themselves.

But "ping" is not just punctuation. Phonetically, it is an explosive "puh" (+ ing) and thus is also directly related to breathing, necessarily demanding an intake of air before that explosion can take place. As such, it closely parallels the effect of its inscription—that is, its appealing-to-externality. It is half a breath present in the text, absolutely and irreducibly cut off from its other half, the other half that is nevertheless absolutely essential to its existence. As punctuation breathing or breathing punctuation, "ping" marks the necessity of the existence of an "outside" while it projects the very "outside" as a function of its own "existence." And the question "who breathes?" is rapidly being determined by what the text inscribes as "inside" —that is, the space of its textuality as disruption, displacement, and circulating fragments.

It is clear then, that Lodge has very precisely stated what "ping" is, even though he is dissatisfied with the result. His evaluation only needs to be clarified, "ping" only needs to be understood *literally* as punctuation and not metaphorically. His question whether or not "ping" is a part of the discourse is also answered, for it has the same status as punctuation in "normal" English, with a slight variation. Usually, punctuation is what makes a text possible on the most elementary level, present in its writing but absent from its reading: how does one pronounce a semicolon? The difference is that here, rather than simply indicating to the reader the necessary modification in emphasis and inflection, punctuation is a material presence in reading, articulating the text on the levels of signifier *and* signified *and* referent.

Finally, I would suggest that Lodge's dissatisfaction with his analysis is rooted primarily in his desire for the text to "mean" or "communicate" something, for it to be the discourse *of* someone.[10] In a sense, he reflects what Federman has called the "nostalgia of criticism [of Beckett's work] for the novel."[11] The text of course can be read as the discourse of someone and interpreted in numerous ways. But it has already inscribed the conditions of any such reading as the mode of its own functioning, and thus always has already recorded those interpretations within its circulating repetitions (and nonrepetitions). Most of all however, because the text materially *is* circulation and repetition, chance and necessity, it demands that any such interpretation recognize its necessarily fragmentary nature, recognize that it removes itself from the material functioning of the text by the very act of interpreting. For no matter what interpretation is elaborated, the text will always return to belie it (which in no way detracts from the validity and necessity of such interpretations). As such, the phenomenon "Ping" must be "understood" as the practical elaboration of a theory that it is *in the process of elaborating*, a theory that comprehends not only the present text, but others as well: fiction and criticism, language and its uses, in short, textual articulation, by, of, within.

("What is in question then. . .")

The punctuating of "Ping," "ping" as punctuation, makes the three texts a kind of progression, provides an element that can be turned back onto the other texts in question. Normally, the function of punctuation is to aid in comprehension. And in a sense, both of the other texts lack punctuation, that is, lack the specific articulation to be found in more traditional fiction. For a certain conception of writing, the determining modes of articulation are always external, they necessarily pre-exist any individual textual manifestation. But here, rather than appealing, implicitly or explicitly, referentially or allegorically, to the experience ("life" or "reality," individual or universal, with or without capitals) of the reader, the texts dwell in themselves. Within the parameters they inscribe. Themselves.

The narration-taking-place-in-discourse of "Enough" is disrupted once by the infusion of (its) textuality. ("Other main examples suggest themselves. . . .") But disruption is (was) in fact the dominant mode of the text from "beginning" to "end." Specifically, disruption appears as dichotomous oppositions in which there is no reduction of distance and difference. The "past" (the "life") remembered by "I," for example, is not simply a modification of presence, even of the specific presence (present) of the text. First physically in relation to the place of remembering and the place of "life." The latter is posited as a world, as a place with summits and valleys, days and nights, eternally mild weather and pelting downpours, and flowers. Of the former place little is said; there is only an implication that it is removed from the other place: "I don't know what the weather is now" (p. 158). But in place of remembering there is also the pen, the pen that needs time to note, that sometimes stops, sometimes refuses. Most of all, however, while "I" is subjected to "him," while "I" had only the desires he manifested" (p. 153) and "all I know comes from him" (p. 154), the past remembered is totally a function of the present (text). Thus the inextricability of flowers, present and past: "I see the flowers at my feet and it's the others I see. Those we trod with equal steps. It is true they are the same" (p. 156). And thus the dissolution of that past in this present: "Now I'll wipe out everything but the flowers" (p. 159).

But with the wiping out of the specificity of the past, the past that is always inscribed through the element of the present, the traces that remain —"Nothing but the two of us dragging through the flowers. Enough my old breasts feel his old hand"—reflect the mode of inscription of that past—that is, its inscription as traces, as fragments: penis, mucous membrane, Aquarius hands, Lyra, Cygnus, radishes. The appearance of the three disparate elements all along the text marks the limits of referentiality, for the references are to another world, "our" world, "reality," if you will. Moreover, the very paucity of the references define that world as a properly chaotic one, absolutely unable to provide the frame of reference necessary for "understanding."

Cut off from referential possibility (the external articulation of "literature," for example), "Enough" begins to elaborate its own space. But it is a space that still allows *its own* articulation, its own punctuation. It functions through a series of oppositions (I/he, present/past, day/night, hill/valley, memory/reality. . .), but they are oppositions that in one way or another, through form or content, are always exceeded. And it is precisely this excess that makes the dominant present (the only present) the *present tense*, the (as yet) unpunctuated filter through which everything passes, the everything still differentiated by the residue of the old opposition.

From this perspective, "Imagination Dead Imagine" can be seen as a kind of distillation. No narrator, no character, just the dichotomic alternation that becomes the dominant mode of the text: light/dark, hot/cold, inside/outside, movement/calm, life/death. One extreme is posited, assumed ("say freezing-point"), but the other demands the corporal presence of an observer ("not burning to the tough"). And it is precisely between two poles, as a function of *both* of them, that the textual space is elaborated, between the fortuitous imposition of a limit (within the limits of the text) and the necessary human presence (the writer that was there and the reader that will be: a presence none the less minimally designated as corpor(e)al).

The relationship between the measurements of the enclosure and the textual elaboration is significantly divergent from a similar process found in Robbe-Grillet's *Les Gommes*. There, the measurements (of both time and distance) on the first page correspond to the number of chapters and sections in the text.[12] The text therefore self-reflectively describes its disposition, prohibiting its consideration within the domain of "objective description." But in "Imagination. . ." the measurements reflect the most fundamental *principle* of the text's *operation*—that is, the incipient binarism both disrupted (as cause/effect, subject/object) and (re)produced (as description *and* discourse, existence *and* non-existence, possibility *and* impossibility). It was never a question of "objectivity" (from this point of view, but there is no other) or "realism" (no way in, go in), only the text is inscribing itself as the possibility of textuality in an irregular metronomic oscillation.

It is this possibiity of textuality that subsumes the specific "life" within the text. Life is literally inscribed within "what" the text posits both as its object and as the principle of its operation, within the two semicircles ABC and BDA and within its binary system. On one hand, life is verifiable by the implied reader-listener, the object of the text's imperative ("Hold a mirror to their lips": you must bring your own mirror, however). But on the other hand, on the other side, the bodies' life is related to *another* binary system, that of "a thousand little signs too long to imagine"—not "imagine" as the imperative of the title, not my (or your) imagination, but another imagination, at once present (because the text says so) and absent (because this is the only point of view), withholding its signifying system. And while these absent signifiers indicate the extratextual existence both of the bodies and of a governing consciousness, such a postulation in no way provides a solution to the text, does not make it suddenly understandable. The negation of extra-textual referentiality is one of the specific modes through which the text functions. The text pratically and theoretically inscribes its own limits, running the binary machine it constructs, and must therefore be considered to be a machine that produces its own contradiction as a by-product. (No critic need point out that it contradicts itself, for that is what the text says; that is what it is about.)

So "Imagination. . ." is also unpunctuated, but not in the same way as "Enough." In the latter, the general contours of indecision fall between past and present, subject and object, narration and description, discourse and textuality. That is, there is a lack of articulation at the juncture of domains punctuated by traditional literary values. In "Imagination. . . ," these oppositions are only present as traces, are assimilated into the category of "oppositions-in-general." And it is there, within *that* category, that punctuation is lacking. For once an opposition has been posited, it seems to run by itself. It runs by itself without consuming itself, for there is always a variation that generates another opposition that generates another variation. . . . In the oscillation between any two poles, there is no stable third term that can totally dominate the dichotomization. Between imperative and fortuitous assumption, there can be no ontological determination of reader and writer, both are functions of the text, both are there, on the surface, white on white. And given the nature of that surface, there can be no essential distinction made between reading and writing. Reading, like writing, must graft onto that surface its own articulation, its own punctuation, like "ping," for example.

What is in question then is textuality—the possibility of textuality. With what is a text written? Who writes, who reads, and how? What does it refer to? The question of literature, of fiction, asked not from without, but there (here), present, within. Most of all always a question, a questioning that by its inscription in, of, and on its own terms, its own term, is irreducible to the traditional categories of literature-to-be-understood, the categories it never-theless uses in its inscribing. There can be no passive reader here, no reader that only wants to know what "Samuel Beckett" has to say. That is the easiest question. Nothing.

If you want to write a text, you will need a theory. These fifteen pages are the theory. If you want to test the theory you will need a specific elaboration. These fifteen pages are the elaboration at the same time. And the "same time" is precisely that of its punctuation, punctual punctuation that imposes its transient, irregular temporality as a primary condition of its existence. Neither anti-fiction nor anti-literature, the textuality of these texts appears within the gaps between the oppositions they simulate—the oppositions you (will) use to read it.

MIAMI UNIVERSITY

Notes

[1] Page references are to *No's Knife*; London: Calder and Boyars, 1967. "Enough," pp. 153-59; "Imagination Dead Imagine," pp. 161-64; "Ping," pp. 165-68.

[2] Ihab Hassan, *The Dismemberment of Orpheus* (New York: Oxford University Press, 1971), p. 224.

[3] Paris: Editions de Minuit, 1971, p. 139.

[4] All underlinings in the texts quoted throughout this article are my own.

[5] Emile Benveniste, *Problèmes de linguistique générale* (Paris: Gallimard, 1966), pp. 237-50.

[6] Gilles Deleuze and Feliz Guattari, *L'anti-Oedipe* (Paris: Editions de Minuit, 1972), p. 18.

[7] Princeton: Princeton University Press, 1974, p. 248.

[8] Cohn, *op, cit.,* pp. 251-52.

[9] "SomePing Understood," *Encounter*, 30, 2 (February 1968), pp. 83-89.

[10] Vid. p. 86: "Beckett is telling us 'about' something. . ." "I suggest that 'Ping' is the rendering of the consciousness of someone. . ."

[11] Raymond Federman, "The Impossibility of Saying the Same Old Thing the Same Old Way," *Esprit Créateur*, 11, 3 (Fall 1971), p. 20.

[12] The chair is thirty centimeters from the table; leaving out the Prologue and Epilogue, the five chapters contain thirty sections. The counting of seconds (therefore) begins at thirty-one and continues to thirty-seven; the whole of the book contains thirty-seven sections. (When Richard Howard translates thirty centimeters as "eleven inches," the self-referentiality gives way to "objectivism.")